Advance Prais

Martyniuk has written a tantalizing tumultuous century ending with the fall of the Soviet Union. He writes with conviction and enjoys shattering stereotypes. In addition to a captivating account of family history and a vibrant travelogue, he provides unique insights on topics ranging from politics and history to art and economics. Drawing on experiences from his work in the private sector, the international arena and the government his argumentation is fascinating and persuasive. His elucidation of the fall of the USSR is original and credible.

Roman Serbyn, Professor of History at the University of Quebec, Montreal (retired)

During the Cold War, Radio Free Europe/Radio Liberty and Voice of America were America's most cost-effective means to inform and influence audiences in denied areas. Radio Liberty's Paris based audience research unit made a crucial but unsung contribution in this effort. By interviewing Soviet travelers outside the Iron Curtain, the SAAOR obtained substantial first-hand information on public opinion and life in the USSR. Preparations for every U.S.-Soviet summit during the 1980s took these insights into account and provided President Reagan with a better grip on Soviet reality when dealing with Soviet President Mikhail Gorbachev. Jaroslaw Martyniuk, an intrepid member of this unit, documents this chapter of Cold War history. He and his colleagues deserve the gratitude of our country for their dedication and sophistication in America's fight against communism.

William Courtney, former U.S. Ambassador to Kazakhstan, Georgia, and the U.S.-Soviet Bilateral Commission to implement the Threshold Test Ban Treaty.

When an opportunity arose to apply his oil industry expertise to a high-level position with the International Energy Agency in Paris, Jaroslaw Martyniuk embarked on a pivotal chapter in his life. Of particular significance was Martyniuk's transition a few years later to "undercover social science" work with the Soviet Area Audience and Opinion Research (SAAOR), a unit of Radio Liberty in Munich, during which he coordinated the work of interviewers across the European continent.

Monte Rosa presents a riveting and highly illuminating description of this largely unacknowledged project that provided vital information on the political attitudes of Soviet society prior to the USSR's collapse. Further enlivening the memoir are Martyniuk's many vivid accounts of urban and back road experiences throughout Western Europe. Filled with fascinating historical detail about cathedrals and hidden monasteries, mouth-watering recollections of gastronomical delights in the French countryside, heart-stopping mountain climbs and close calls with communist agents and police, tales of adventures and misadventures with a variety of friends who shared his lust for life and as well as intellectual curiosity – Monte Rosa never ceases to delight and uplift. *Lana Y. Babij, Educator and Holodomor Researcher*

Martyniuk takes the reader on his personal odyssey on the information battlefields of the Cold War. He oversees a stealth brigade of interviewers who gather information from Soviet tourists and émigrés and compiles them into sophisticated reports that target programming for the "freedom radios" that penetrated the information barrier of the Iron Curtain. While the West won the Cold War, the beauty of the memoir is in the journey rather than the destination. Martyniuk's interactions with a slew of fascinating characters, including Soviet dissidents and KGB operatives who "just wanted to be friends," are recalled in vivid detail. The reader accompanies him on his far-flung travels into the cultural heritage of European civilization as he imparts his insights. While reading you imagine yourself sharing a bottle of wine with the author in the Café Bonaparte as he recounts the extraordinary tale of an accidental spy.

Daniel Hryhorchuk, Professor of Medicine and Public Health at the University of Illinois at Chicago and author of two novels "Caught in the Current" and "Myth and Madness."

Jaroslaw Martyniuk's dynamic prose style excellently reflects the multitude of topics he deals with in this book: from his own assignment missions to his historical and architectural commentaries and breathtaking photos from his visits to many countries. *Monte Rosa* is a kaleidoscope of themes, images, and portrayals of places and personalities. It is also an enjoyable travel book and a real-life spy thriller from the Cold War era.

Larissa Zaleska Onyshkevych, author of "Borders, Bombs, and Two Right Shoes."

Monte Rosa

Memoir of an Accidental Spy

The untold story of undercover interviewing of Soviet
citizens in Western Europe during the Cold War

Jaroslaw Martyniuk

Library of Congress Control Number:		2017911588
ISBN:	Hardcover	978-1-5434-3908-3
	Softcover	978-1-5434-3907-6
	eBook	978-1-5434-3906-9

Print information available on the last page.

Cover photo, a view of Monte Rosa
from Liskamm, by Annina Reber – Bergführerin.

Rev. date: 08/31/2018

To order additional copies of this book, contact:
Xlibris
1-888-795-4274
www.Xlibris.com
Orders@Xlibris.com
722041

Contents

Introduction

THE POLITICAL SCIENTIST, novelist, and artist Alexander Motyl once wrote that memoirs and oral histories have a way of transmigrating into history. He and other friends encouraged me to write this book because it's a story that has never been told.

Another great novelist, Robert Graves, believed that all history begins with the memoir. His masterpiece *I, Claudius* contains a fascinating passage that brings out this point in a dialogue between Roman emperor Claudius and King Herod:

"I'm thinking of writing a book, the truth," said Claudius.

Herod asks, "Everything?"

"Everything. As a historian, you should write the plain facts, the kitchen details, even gossip."

"Why should you want to write such a book?" asks Herod.

"Because I owe it to the others, and to posterity to tell the truth, especially for dead friends. Because a man should keep faith with his friends dead or alive."

As I wrote this memoir, I realized that many of the friends in it are no longer alive. Some of them passed in the last few years. Like Claudius, I have written this memoir not only for friends who are still alive but also for those who have departed. They include Danylo Struk, Omelian Mazuryk, Aristid Virsta, Anton Solomoukha, Liuba Markewycz, Roman Kupchinsky, Leonid Plyushch, Zenon Babij, Yuri Kavka, Ivan Gula, Yuri Ozga and others. That is when it struck me like a pin through my heart: when people die, so much dies with them.

Finally, I have written it to honor the memory of my parents, Roman and Natalia Szut Martyniuk, and my aunts, uncles, and cousins no longer with us. The memoir is also a record for posterity not only for my children and my nieces but also for their children, grandchildren, and great-grandchildren. It is the greatest gift I can bestow to those future generations because in the profound words of the writer Terry Pratchett:

"If you don't know where you're coming from, you're not likely to know where you're going. And if you don't know where you're going, you'll never get there."

To be clear, this is not an autobiography. It is a memoir, how I remember my life, and the first obligation of the memoirist is to tell the truth. I've taken this route in the hope that I'm likely to get right what matters most. I wrote it from the perspective of a foot soldier in the twentieth century's titanic struggle between the forces of freedom and the Communist tyranny. In this respect, it is markedly different from the vast majority of memoirs people write today. It is the story of the first fifty years of my life, from the outbreak of WWII to the fall of the USSR, two seminal events that provide a convenient framework for this volume of my memoir.

I open with an episode that in retrospect turned out to be one of the high points that defined my life, the implosion of the Soviet Union. I call it my "Monte Rosa moment" because the week the USSR collapsed, I was scaling the highest mountain in Switzerland, Monte Rosa. The narrative ends with my first challenging climb, the scaling of Mont Blanc du Tacul. Between these rock-hard bookends I tell my story in straightforward linear time.

My father wrote a hundred-page manuscript in Ukrainian which spanned most of the twentieth century and provided vital input for the first years of my life, especially the early years of WW II in Ukraine. The present volume is, in a way, a continuation of his memoir.

In addition to memorable moments of my life, I include stories of other members of the Martyniuk clan, in particular, the fate of my grandmother in Vorkuta and my uncle Dozyk in Kolyma, both death camps in the Arctic wastes of Siberia. I also integrate an account of the ordeal of Father's sister, Aunt Anastasia during the dust bowl days in Oklahoma.

Six months after I graduated from the University of Illinois at Champaign/ Urbana (1963), I entered the US Army Intelligence School at Fort Holabird. A fluke in army scheduling placed me in a section where I was trained to analyze military intelligence gathered by U-2 spy airplanes, a skill I put to use during the next six years, and by sheer accident, I became a specialist in "spying" from the air.

The year 1979 was pivotal. Through a series of coincidences, I moved to Paris, France, to work as an administrator-diplomat at the International Energy Agency. In the mid-1980s, I morphed into a Cold War "warrior" working to bring down the "evil empire" as an undercover researcher, a story that has never been told by anyone anywhere. Radio Liberty's broadcasts undermined the Soviet Union from within, a process not unlike the slow, steady tunneling to bring down the walls of a seemingly impenetrable fortress. Not only had I observed the empire's dying years, but fate had placed me in a position to contribute to its demise.

No other organization or institution even contemplated doing what we managed in the Audience Research department of Radio Liberty: public opinion polling among Soviet visitors and tourists. I coordinated the work of fifty interviewers in a dozen locations collecting information on life in the Soviet Union. We gauged attitudes on important issues of the day, measured audiences to foreign radio listening, and provided essential feedback for the international broadcasters transmitting across the Iron Curtain. While our reports were widely available to the diplomatic and intelligence communities and other government agencies, the story of "how we did it" has never been told. It is the thrust of ten chapters of this memoir.

By the end of 1991, Communism expired under the weight of its internal contradictions and structural defects. Contrary to what many believe, the collapse did not happen in a vacuum. The United States and other actors played a crucial role in bringing down the "evil empire."

In addition to an autobiographical account and a travelogue, the memoir contains reflections on history, politics, economics, philosophy, art, and many descriptions of churches. Some readers will be surprised by my unconventional views of history. I also explore a number of leitmotifs that kept recurring throughout my life: survival, luck, freedom, and mountains, and the debilitating effect of political correctness on free speech and interpretation of history.

In retrospect, it is clear that my life was shaped by coincidences. Most people experience them occasionally. However, when seemingly random coincidences form a pattern over time, they become something else. Carl Jung referred to such coincidences as synchronicity. These incidents occurred throughout my life with astonishing regularity.

Turning points in my life have taken place in years ending in "9." I was conceived in 1939; in 1949, I immigrated to the United States. In 1969, I was discharged from military service, recovered from a debilitating disease, and got a new lease on life. Ten years later, in 1979, I ended up in Paris, and in 1989, the Berlin Wall came down, bringing in a new era.

My life has encompassed work in several areas: the private sector, government work, and the international arena, three distinctly different branches of civil society. These experiences have provided me with the ability to compare and judge the way these sectors function. Most of all, they enabled me to connect the dots, shreds, and fragments that shaped my worldview. Providentially, my life did not include the academic world, a path that might have deprived me of the ability to objectively judge the real one.

Like Einstein, I am a lover of freedom, and like Santayana, I am dedicated to the cause of truth, two guiding principles in my life. Getting at the truth is central to the study of history, and there is abundant history in this memoir. Nearly every chapter draws on lessons from history that can be applied to today's world, from the fall of ancient empires to twentieth-century wars, and from the impact of corrosive ideologies to the threat that Islam poses to Western civilization and way of life in the twenty-first century. Sadly, the only history taught in schools today is revisionist history infused with misleading postmodernist ideas, poststructuralist theories, insidious cultural relativism, and invidious political correctness.

Worse than inventing history is out-of-control political correctness, a pernicious notion threatening free speech. What is most unsettling is that the movement against "hurtful speech" has been spearheaded by supposedly liberal colleges and universities, institutions that should be promoting inquiry and free speech.

The precept of political correctness appears harmless, even admirable, but it is deadly to intellectual freedom and the productive and peaceful pursuit of knowledge. It leads to the doctrine that people should be punished for holding false and dangerous beliefs. In other words, it leads to inquisition and authoritarianism. As George Orwell warned almost seventy years ago, "Without the freedom to offend, freedom of speech ceases to exist," and, "If liberty means anything at all, it means the right to tell people what they do not want to hear."

I close this introduction with quotes from two American sages, the essayist George Santayana and the writer Mark Twain. Santayana, an immigrant like me, said, "Those who cannot remember the past are condemned to repeat it." Twain refined this aphorism by adding, "While history doesn't repeat itself, it sure does rhyme."

A word about dates, proper names, and units of measure. In this book, I sometimes sacrifice the pedantry of precise chronology and technical terminology to put across a point of great importance. I employ names and spelling most suitable in the context in which I am writing. Since most of the story takes place in Europe, I use the metric system—kilometers instead of miles, meters instead of feet, and so on.

Finally, travel has been an excellent teacher. During my life, I have been to over fifty countries, many of them on numerous occasions. Wherever I traveled, it was always with one foot in the present, the other in the past. I maintained a detailed log of places I visited from 1979 to 1991, destinations that appear in the appendix. I do not include travel after 1991, a subject for a follow-up volume.

1. A Curious Thing Happened on the Way to Monte Rosa . . .

I AM NOT SURE why I climbed Monte Rosa. Sensible men do not take up mountaineering in middle age. What I do know is that the week I was scaling Switzerland's highest peak, the Soviet Union fell apart. In a few days, the world was fundamentally transformed and a new era began. This was my "Monte Rosa moment," a confluence of events that changed the world and my life. That week, my body and spirit soared to new heights, literally and metaphorically.

Monte Rosa, a gargantuan mass of rock that includes several four-thousand-meter peaks, lies three thousand meters above Zermatt, a prestigious mountaineering and ski resort. The mountain has nothing to do with roses, as the name suggests. The appellation derives from an Aostian patois word *roëse*, meaning "glacier."

Its highest point is the Dufourspitze, 4,634 meters (15,204 feet) above sea level. Zermatt is to Monte Rosa what Chamonix is to Mont Blanc. The vast Rosa glacier plateau straddles the border between Italy and Switzerland and connects two formidable mountains—the indomitable Matterhorn and Monte Rosa. Although 260 meters higher than the Matterhorn, Monte Rosa is easier to scale. Both, however, are susceptible to unpredictable changes in weather and powerful winds, and climbers are advised to take precautions against cold temperatures even during the warmer months. The air pressure near the top is half of the pressure at sea level, and the wind chill factor may be as low as minus forty degrees Centigrade, which equals minus forty Fahrenheit.

I signed up for the Monte Rosa climb in May 1991. To get into shape, I did a lot of hiking in the Austrian Alps accessible from Munich. Our group of ten climbers met in Zermatt on Thursday, August 15. The goal was the highest peak in the Swiss Alps, ten kilometers due east and exactly three vertical kilometers above the picturesque village of Zermatt.

After a few days of acclimatization to the higher altitude, we were ready for the strenuous 1,600-vertical meter trial climb from Zermatt to the Hörnli Ridge (3,260 meters) roughly two-thirds of the way to the Matterhorn summit. The normal route to the pinnacle on the Swiss side, the Hörnligrat, begins here. On days with good weather in July and August, up to two hundred climbers and mountain guides scale the Matterhorn, but only 60 percent of these attempts are successful. Just above the Hörnli hut, I noticed numerous crosses and small monuments with names and photos of climbers who perished here, mostly young men who tried to climb the formidable pyramid without adequate preparation. Over the years, five hundred people have died on the Matterhorn. It appeared daunting and practically unclimbable, but with proper training, the guides assured us it was doable. In any event, that was not our destination. Our goal was the loftier Monte Rosa—ten kilometers to the east of the iconic pyramid, three vertical kilometers above the picturesque village of Zermatt.

WHILE PREPARING FOR the big climb, I was totally isolated from the outside world. I hadn't the slightest inkling that two thousand kilometers to the east of Zermatt, earth-shattering events had been unfolding on the Ukrainian peninsula of Crimea, where Mikhail Gorbachev was vacationing in his opulent dacha at the Crimean resort of Foros. Two heavy trucks had driven to the airport nearest the dacha and positioned themselves lengthwise across the airstrip. The approaches to the dacha from the sea were then quietly blocked by military ships, and KGB units sealed off the road to Gorbachev's residence and surrounded the compound isolating Gorbachev, his family, and thirty-two members of his personal guard inside.

At 6:00 a.m. on August 19, 1991, a TASS teletype informed the world that Gorbachev had been removed from his post as secretary of the Politburo for reasons of health. His responsibilities were being assumed by Gennady Yanayev, his vice president. Authority would be exercised on a temporary basis by a State Committee of the State of Emergency, led by Yanayev, Vladimir Kryuchkov, head of the KGB, and Dmitry Yazov, the defense minister.

Early that same morning, two kilometers above Zermatt, as the first rays of the sun were lighting up the seemingly unconquerable east face of the Matterhorn, our group of ten climbers lumbered out of a cable car next to the 3,883-meter Klein Matterhorn. The group split into two five-man teams, each led by an experienced guide, a rough-looking forty-five-year-old Swiss professional Peter, and a sprightly sixty-seven-year-old Manfred. I was in a group led by Manfred, a veteran climber who must have ascended Monte Rosa a dozen times. He seemed to know every hazardous crevice on the glacier. Though he was not as fast as Peter, I felt safer with Manfred.

As I was traversing the vast ice field between the Matterhorn and Monte Rosa, momentous events were taking place in Moscow. Russians were stunned at the news of the coup. By noon, Moscow time, Boris Yeltsin had taken charge of the Russian parliament's presidium and declared that he would resist the coup with all means available. At 1:00 p.m., a long column of tanks rolled down Kutuzovsky Prospekt, crossed the river, and split in two directions, surrounding the White House, the seat of the Russian Parliament. Flanked by guards, Yeltsin walked down the steps and approached the lead tank.

"Did you come to kill Yeltsin?" he asked the tank's officer.

"No, of course not," the officer answered.

Yeltsin's words reminded me of Napoleon's celebrated appeal to a regiment of infantry ordered to bar his way to Paris after he escaped from Elba and landed in France. Napoleon advanced alone to meet them and cried, "Soldiers, if there is one among you who wants to kill his general, his emperor, here I am." Suddenly, the soldiers began cheering wildly, "Long live the emperor! Long live the emperor!"

Yeltsin then climbed onto tank number 110 and told the crowd surrounding him, "We are dealing with a right-wing, reactionary unconstitutional *coup d'état* . . . I have no doubt that the army will go against the people . . . There will be no compromise with the plotters, and the criminals will be brought to justice." Yeltsin and his government had made a choice. That was the beginning of the end of the attempted putsch, though all was far from over.

AT ABOUT THE TIME Yeltsin was mounting tank number 110 in Moscow, I was scaling the west face of Monte Rosa. The gradient was getting steeper, and the four climbers I was tethered to by a resin rope trod slowly and carefully. It was just past noon, and the frozen snow was getting mushy and unstable. No matter how fit, we were at the mercy of the mountain. It was crucial to follow the footprints of the climber in front of me. As third in our group of five, I felt quite secure. If I should trip or slip into a crevasse, I would, in theory, be halted by two climbers above me or the two behind me. Manfred warned us that within sight of the summit, climbers tend to let their guard down, and this was where many accidents occurred.

With three hundred meters to the summit, I was gasping for air, not unusual in this thin atmosphere. Oxygen on the Monte Rosa is half the concentration at sea level. I glanced to the west and saw that we were at the level of the Matterhorn, which gave me my second or maybe third wind. After eight hours of climbing, Dufourspitze, the highest point of the Monte Rosa massif, was in sight. With another burst of adrenalin, I pressed on to the top of Switzerland.

Unlike my experience on Mont Blanc du Tacul, where static cloud severely limited visibility, the sweeping panorama from Monte Rosa was incomparable. The bright blue sky was marred by only a few thin vapor trails at ten thousand meters. We were above all of the surrounding peaks, just slightly higher than the tip of the Matterhorn.

Fifty kilometers due west, I spotted the rounded silhouette of Mont Blanc. An inner voice told me that this was a unique moment, perhaps even a historic moment. I experienced an extraordinary natural high that comes when summiting a challenging mountain, and I felt spiritually and physically renewed, half my age, and even fantasized about the next climb, the Everest or K2. I was Superman! Alas, the climax was intense but short. The jagged peak had hardly enough room for a tripod. The guides ushered us through one or two at a time, and that was it.

Exactly eighty meters below Dufourspitze, a refuge called the Regina Margherita Hutte offered Spartan overnight accommodations for climbers. The plan called for us to stay in the hut, get a hot meal, and do a little socializing before retiring to recuperate before the long descent to Zermatt the next morning.

As often happens in high mountains, the weather changed. Around midnight, a storm flared up from seemingly nowhere and continued for the next twenty-four hours, dumping a few feet of snow on the Monte Rosa massif. I developed a headache and was unable to sleep. I was in pain and nauseated, felt as if my eyes were about to pop out, and aspirin didn't help.

An experienced fellow climber told me it was the altitude. "What you're experiencing is not unusual. Your headache will vanish the moment you get below four thousand meters."

By morning, cold winds on Monte Rosa reduced the temperature to well below freezing. A thick cloud attached itself to the mountain like a magnet, reducing visibility to a few meters. No one in the refuge said anything, but it was evident that we were stranded. With the snow continuing the next day, it became apparent that we would not be returning to Zermatt that day as planned. I dreaded spending another night at this altitude but had no choice.

WHILE A SNOW STORM was whipping around Monte Rosa, in Moscow, General Victor Karpukhin, commander of the elite commando Alpha Group, was ordered to attack the White House on the morning of August 20. Soldiers in the group, however, said they did not want to fight the civilian population and, to the general surprise, unanimously refused to carry out the order. No elite military unit in the history of the USSR had ever refused to carry out such a direct order before. If not for this insubordination, history might have taken a different course.

There was a standoff, and a tense mood descended on Moscow. The rain was pouring down, but the crowd outside the White House got bigger and bigger. On Wednesday, August 21, the Russian Parliament began holding its session, the first sign that the crisis was over. At the end of the day, *Izvestia* announced that the last troops had left Moscow. The putsch to overthrow Gorbachev had collapsed, signaling the beginning of the death of the Union of Soviet Socialist Republics. The brutal political system built on falsehoods and maintained through terror had collapsed from the inside.

At 6:00 a.m. on Wednesday, the weather on Monte Rosa cleared. I fastened crampons on my thick leather *trappeur* hiking boots, preparing for the long-awaited descent. The air was crisp; not a cloud in the cobalt-blue sky. As the first rays of the sun burst on the eastern horizon, the tips of each of the "four-thousanders" to the west lit up like sparklers one by one. Soon, the mass of the majestic Matterhorn was bathed in the morning sun. The visibility was crystal clear, and I could make out the silhouette of the Mont Blanc massif fifty kilometers away.

The first part of the descent down the Grenzengletcher glacier was steep and dangerous. A fresh blanket of snow covered the smaller crevasses, so we moved slowly roped together in a tight formation. *Le piolet*—the ice ax— served as an important third leg to distribute body weight more evenly and an instrument with which to stop a slip. Right on schedule, as predicted, at four thousand meters, the headache causing me excruciating pain for two days evaporated. Eventually, the gradient became less steep. The expansive glacier got narrower and morphed into a brook and then a trail. Through the haze, I spotted a few dwarf pines and Zermatt and felt greatly exhilarated.

Zermatt is a large village that over the years has evolved into a world-class ski and mountain resort. The only way to access it is via a mountain cog railway. The town doesn't allow automobiles, but it has plenty of everything else—hotels, restaurants, pubs, and crowds of tourists that create a lively atmosphere year-round. I stopped at the first café bar I could find and ordered a pint of Klosterbräu. While I drank it, I sensed a palpable tension in the air. A group of people were gathered around a TV in the back of the bar. That is when I first learned of the putsch attempt and the aftermath of the failed coup. My first reaction was disbelief. Did that mean the Soviet Union was no more? It took a while to digest this information, but after a flurry of sensations, I became elated, uplifted, and ecstatic. It dawned on me that during the time I was on Monte Rosa, the Soviet Union had imploded; a tyrannical empire had begun to disintegrate. The nightmarish experiment in social engineering had utterly failed, and there was no turning back.

As I was reaching for new highs of personal freedom in the mountains, the Russian, Ukrainian, and other Soviet peoples were getting their freedom. They rid themselves of the Communist scourge, a vile and genocidal ideology that had enslaved them for three-quarters of a century. Even more astonishing was that five days after I summited Monte Rosa, another momentous event took place. On Saturday, August 24, three days after the coup to preserve the Soviet Union had come to an end, the Ukrainian Parliament, the Rada, voted for independence by 392 votes to 4, subject to a referendum on December 1, 1991. This historical verdict made a mockery of Pres. George H.W. Bush's stern admonition to the Ukrainian people not to break away from the Soviet Union.

The scene at the Rada marked the end of a process that had taken more than five years from the introduction of glasnost by Gorbachev and his colleagues. Ukrainians not only rid themselves of an inhumane system that had subjugated them for over seventy years but also shed Moscow's tyrannical yoke that oppressed them for three hundred years.

That night in a Zermatt hotel, pondering the dramatic turn of events, I was not able to sleep. Still bewildered the next morning, I took the mountain railway to the village of Täsch, where I had left my BMW, anxious to get back to my office in Munich to learn how these events would affect my Ukrainian and Russian research projects at Radio Liberty.

THE YEAR 1991 was a turning point in other ways. It was the year I left Paris for Munich, not without reluctance. After nearly twelve years, the City of Light had become home. It seemed I would spend the rest of my life in Paris and I had even purchased an apartment in the colorful neighborhood of Montmartre. Over the years, I made friends, learned the language, and got used to a comfortable life in a most remarkable place. French cuisine, wine, culture, and history were part of my life. During my dozen years in the French hexagon, I visited nearly every important region, city, or town, Romanesque and Gothic cathedrals and churches, Roman ruins and medieval and Renaissance châteaux, from the Alps to the Atlantic, from the English Channel to the Pyrenees. I point this out not to boast but to lay the groundwork for stories in later chapters.

I had no particular desire to move to Munich, but I had no choice. Radio Liberty was reorganizing, and the Soviet Area Audience and Opinion Research department (SAAOR) was being relocated to Radio headquarters in Munich. If I hadn't gone to Munich, I would have had to move back to the States, which I had no wish to do. However, once in Munich, it did not take me long to realize that it was not so bad. It turned out to be a fascinating city in the heart of Europe, within easy reach of many countries, especially the northern part of Italy. In four hours, I could hike in the Dolomites; in six, I could be in Verona; and in seven, Venice. Living in Bavaria had a special personal meaning, since my earliest memories are from a city on the Danube called Regensburg, about an hour's drive north of Munich. I had completed a full circle, from my childhood in Bavaria, via thirty years in Chicago and twelve in Paris, back to Bavaria again.

The management of RFE-RL had decided that the Paris-based SAAOR office should merge with its Eastern European counterpart, the Eastern European Audience and Opinion Research department, to form a unit called MOR. The new Media and Opinion Research department was part of the RFE-RL Research Institute. With Eastern Europe and the Soviet Union opening up, it seemed logical that research operations should be closer to Radio audiences in the east.

After the fall of the Berlin Wall, research in the Soviet Union became possible. In 1990, we approached two leading Soviet sociologists to see what kind of collaboration was possible. In Moscow, we contacted VTsIOM,[1] the organization headed by Yuri Levada, Russia's leading pollster. To test the waters in Ukraine, we got in touch with two sociologists at Kyiv's Shevchenko

---

[1]   All-Russian Center for the Study of Public Opinion (VTsIOM) (Russian: Всероссийский центр изучения общественного мнения - ВЦИОМ), established in 1987.

University—Valeriy Khmelko and Volodymyr Paniotto of the Sociological Association of Ukraine. The initial probes were promising, and by September 1991, MOR was ready to launch a full-fledged survey using standard Western methodology. Because this was the first survey of its kind, we were breaking new ground and we had to tread carefully. Before 1990, it was impossible to conduct in-country polling in the USSR. That is why for years, SAAOR carried out research using a methodology referred to in professional circles as "undercover social science," a unique way of picking the brains of Soviet citizens which is described in later chapters.

Energized by my conquest of Monte Rosa and morally uplifted by the disintegration of the Soviet Union, I started work on a Ukraine-wide survey scheduled to go into the field in late September. Most of it focused on media use, but there was a general public opinion section asking about political, social, and economic issues. One of the questions was:

> In the upcoming December 1 referendum, how will you vote on
> the issue of independence—for or against?

The period between August 24 and December 1 was one of heightened uncertainty. Would the Ukrainian people confirm or reject the Rada's August 24 vote for independence and sovereignty? Earlier surveys had suggested that they would not vote for independence. In a March 1991 All-Union referendum on the preservation of the Soviet Union, 76 percent of the participants voted to maintain the union. Then in July, a month before I set foot on Monte Rosa, Pres. George H. W. Bush showed up in Kyiv and lectured the Ukrainians about the perils of breaking away from the union.

President Bush's pronouncement was totally detached from reality and the wishes of the Ukrainian people. His discourse verged on the naïve, delivered by someone incapable of thinking outside the box. At the same time, it brought into question the competence of legions of Kremlin watchers, Sovietologists and Russia experts who believed the Soviet Union would not break up for the next fifty to a hundred years. Many still believed in the old "confluence" hypothesis—the West would become more like the Soviet Union, and the Soviet Union would gradually become more like the United States, a canard that has been around since the days of FDR.

The vast majority of these experts shared one fatal flaw: they saw everything through the prism of Moscow's official press. They studied the changes in the Kremlin's hierarchy and searched for subtleties in power shifts in the Politburo, but they ignored the elephant in the room—the nationalities question. Many specialists dismissed this issue as irrelevant, which made them blind to the fissures in the Soviet society. Only a few saw trouble brewing. In 1978, Hélène Carrère d'Encausse, a French academician, hypothesized that the USSR would break up because of the growing Muslim population.[2] She was right about the disintegration, but wrong about the cause. Another important visionary who spoke of an inevitable end of the USSR was Robert Conquest, the eminent historian and author of numerous books on the Soviet Union.[3]

In Munich, I had the good fortune to hear Robert Conquest address an audience of RFE-RL Research Institute analysts and journalists. Conquest was one of the few specialists who went against the grain, questioning the views of Establishment academics and experts. In particular, he criticized Western intellectuals for "blindness" regarding the Soviet Union and argued that Stalinism was a logical consequence of Marxism-Leninism rather than an aberration of "true" Communism. He sharply berated intellectuals such as Beatrice and Sidney Webb,[4] George Bernard Shaw, Jean-Paul Sartre, Walter Duranty, Theodore Dreiser, Bertolt Brecht, Romain Rolland, and others for being dupes of Stalin, and apologists for his regime. For his views, he was viciously vilified, especially by the progressive left. After the opening up of the Soviet archives in 1991, detailed information was released supporting Conquest's conclusions and view of history. He was one of the few historians who lived long enough to see his vision and life's work vindicated by history.

Conquest was also a poet known for witty limericks about Communism. One of my favorites was "A Compact History of the Soviet Union," which goes as follows:

---

[2]   Hélène Carrère d'Encausse, L'Empire éclaté, 1978.

[3]   Robert Conquest is an Anglo-American historian and poet notable for his influential works of Soviet history, which include *The Great Terror: Stalin's Purge of the Thirties,* its 1990 reassessment, and its 2008 fourth edition, *The Harvest of Sorrow: Soviet Collectivization and the Terror-Famine*, and *Kolyma: The Arctic Death Camps.*

[4]   The Webbs were supporters of the Soviet Union until their deaths. Their books *Soviet Communism: A New Civilization?* (1935) and *The Truth about Soviet Russia* (1942) gave a very positive assessment of Joseph Stalin's regime.

> There was a great Marxist called Lenin,
> Who did two or three million men in.
> That's a lot to have done in,
> But where he did one in,
> That great Marxist Stalin did ten in.

Conquest's lecture ended with the usual question-and-answer session where I was able to ask, "What would you like to tell people like Jerry Hough and his ilk who got the Soviet Union wrong?" His ready response: "I told you so, you fucking fools."[5]

WE LAUNCHED THE UKRAINE-WIDE survey in October and, by the end of the month, had the preliminary data. The results were startling. They showed that 88 percent of the thirty-two million Ukrainian citizens eligible to vote would say yes to independence in the referendum. Many knowledgeable individuals at the Radios found such findings incredible, and I was instructed to investigate what might have gone wrong with this survey. After all, it was the first one of its kind in Ukraine. Personally, I felt confident that the results were fairly accurate. I had been to Ukraine to supervise and observe the fieldwork, and make sure that the interviewers were properly trained and followed sampling procedures developed by the Sociological Association of Ukraine. I found little fault with the sampling or the conduct of the survey. The only thing left to do was to wait and see what the referendum results would reveal.

On December 5, the referendum results were released, and, to the astonishment of everyone at the Radio, 90.3 percent of Ukrainians cast their ballots for independence. Still, some thought that our survey results could be a fluke. The next step was to review the results by geographic region (*oblast*) and demographic category. Except for Crimea and some oblasts in Eastern Ukraine, the results of our survey corresponded closely with the results of the referendum. Crimea was an odd case because this was the only oblast

---

[5]   When Conquest's publisher asked him to expand and revise *The Great Terror*, Conquest is famously said to have suggested the new version of the book be titled *I Told You So, You Fucking Fools*. In fact, the mock title was jokingly proposed by Conquest's old friend Sir Kingsley Amis. The new version was published in 1990 as *The Great Terror: A Reassessment*.

with a majority Russian population, though even there 54 percent voted for independence.[6]

The Sociological Association of Ukraine demonstrated that they were competent pollsters, and this was the beginning of a fruitful and rewarding twenty-year relationship. Time and again, they proved to be trustworthy and reliable. Eventually, the association broke away from Shevchenko University and set itself up as the polling arm of the Kyiv-Mohyla Academy under the name of Kyiv International Institute of Sociology (KIIS), or KMIS in Ukrainian—*Kyyivskyj Mizhnarodnyj Instytut Sotsiolohiji*. To this day, some at KIIS refer to me as the godfather of the institute.

While our group of analysts in Paris in the 1980s did not predict the exact date of the collapse of the USSR (no one could do that), we were able to say with a high degree of certainty that something was not right with the Soviet Union. The data we collected during the second half of the '80s told us what the average Soviet citizen was thinking. This information provided a basis for reasonable assumptions and conclusions. Until 1990, the Soviet Union was a hermetically closed society. No organization or agency in the free world had attempted to systematically study public opinion there the way SAAOR did. We found a way to elicit information from Soviet citizens, which allowed us to paint a fairly accurate picture of Soviet public opinion.

---

[6]   See *Ukrainian Independence and Territorial Integrity*, Jaroslaw Martyniuk, RFE-RL Research Report, Volume 1, No. 13, 27 March 1992, page 64.

Training at the foot of the Matterhorn.

Preparing to ascend Monte Rosa. I'm on the right in light cap.

Approaching the foot of Monte Rosa.

Beginning the ascent.

The slope gets steeper.

The final push through fog; author on the right.

View from the summit of Monte Rosa toward
Liskamm and the Matterhorn on the right.

After being stranded on the summit for two days, the
group prepares to descend to Zermatt.

Descending toward the Gornerglestcher (glacier).

2. What Killed the Soviet Empire?

A FLURRY OF BOOKS have documented in great detail the events preceding the collapse, but hardly any of them have explained why the USSR imploded. Narratives by journalists and political scientists have offered little help in explaining what had happened in the Soviet Union during the decade and a half preceding the fall. On the surface, the pillars of the empire appeared to be solid, though, in fact, they were crumbling from within. Hardly any of the so-called experts[7] were able to see that they were made of inferior concrete, not unlike the bad concrete used in the housing complexes called *Khrushchovkas*.[8]

Norman Davies writes in his brilliant opus, *Vanishing Empires,* that "it is difficult to foresee events during a war or to explain various consequences. It is much easier to explain events with the benefit of hindsight." When he wrote this, he had hot wars in mind, but this applies equally to the struggle we call the Cold War.

I have no intention of replicating the work of these authors. They accomplished their goal of documenting the last days of the empire with a wealth of eyewitness accounts and testimonies of participants that make for fascinating reading. Most of these accounts, however, tend to be journalistic

---

[7]   Throughout this chapter, I use the term "experts" to refer to the array of Sovietologists, Kremlin watchers, sages in academia, the military, the media, politics, and diplomacy.

[8]   A low-cost five-story apartment building developed in the USSR during the time of Nikita Khrushchev. The mass-scale construction projects relied on flimsily-poured prefabricated concrete panels.

in nature and fail to take into account the long-term dynamics playing out in the Soviet Union—factors that directly or indirectly contributed to its fall.[9]

One of the most comprehensive attempts to answer the question "why" the Soviet empire collapsed was Victor Sebestyen's *Revolution 1989: The Fall of the Soviet Empire*, published in 2010. Sebestyen tells in great detail how the breakdown of the Iron Curtain became the catalyst for the disintegration of the entire Soviet-dominated realm. To show how it happened, he begins with the Soviet invasion of Afghanistan and concludes with the crumbling of the Berlin Wall a decade later.

One important factor that contributed to the disintegration of the Soviet Union was good timing. John O'Sullivan's masterful volume *The President, the Pope, and the Prime Minister*, notes that the appearance at the same time of three anti-Communist leaders—Ronald Reagan, Cardinal Wojtyła, and Margaret Thatcher—had a profound impact upon the destiny of Communism. Another important factor was the emergence of Solidarity, a massive underground movement in Poland, the most strategically important country in the Soviet outer empire.

IN OCTOBER 2014, I attended a book signing at the Woodrow Wilson Center's Kennan Institute, where Serhii Plokhy presented his book *The Last Empire: The Final Days of the Soviet Union*. Plokhy's opus has been hailed as the last word on why the Soviet Union expired. It had taken the academic community twenty-three years to talk about the central issue, the question of nationalities. Plokhy was the first to address this subject comprehensively, an issue that came closest to identifying the root cause of the collapse. He argues that the key to the demise was the inability of the two largest Soviet republics, Russia and Ukraine, to agree on a form for their continued existence as a unified state. In this respect, his book was a valuable contribution to understanding the final chapter of the USSR.

The nationalities question is an issue that many authors and historians have ignored, but not Plokhy. Drawing on newly declassified documents

---

[9]   Among the early narratives about the fall of the Soviet Empire that I've read were *The End of the Soviet Empire: The Triumph of Nations* by Hélène Carrère d'Encausse (1992), David Remnick's mesmerizing personal account of the final days of the Soviet Union, *Lenin's Tomb: The Last Days of the Soviet Empire* (1993), Jack F. Matlock Jr.'s meticulous account *Autopsy of an Empire: The American Ambassador's Account of the Collapse of the Soviet Union* (1995), and David Satter's *Age of Delirium: The Decline and Fall of the Soviet Union* (1996).

and original interviews with key participants, his narrative revolved around events, actions, and decisions of four key personalities: Mikhail Gorbachev, Boris Yeltsin, Pres. George W. H. Bush, and the future Ukrainian president Leonid Kravchuk, during the four months between August 24 and December 25, 1991. Plokhy shows that it was only after the Ukrainian referendum on December 1 that the fate of the Soviet Union was sealed.

Plokhy's book is a fascinating account of the final drama that sealed the union's fate and it is worth paraphrasing a section describing the tripartite summit held on December 8 in Viskuli, a hunting lodge in the Belavezha Forest, a nature preserve in Belarus near the Polish frontier. The summit was attended by Boris Yeltsin, Stanislau Shushkevich, and Leonid Kravchuk, leaders of Russia, Belarus, and Ukraine, respectively. Gorbachev was invited but declined to attend. There was bad blood between him and Yeltsin.

The leaders of the three countries met to discuss the framework of a new Slavic union. Yeltsin brought with him a copy of a treaty that he had drafted with Gorbachev a few weeks earlier. It only needed Kravchuk's signature. The treaty, however, offered nothing new for Ukraine, and Kravchuk would not sign it. Kravchuk then laid out his trump card: the results of the Ukrainian referendum, which overwhelmingly approved the independence of Ukraine. Yeltsin was impressed and made a last-ditch attempt to save what was left of the union, but Kravchuk refused to sign any document that contained the word "union." His argument was simple. He said that Ukraine had already determined its path in the referendum, and the path was independence. As far as he was concerned, the Soviet Union no longer existed, and the parliament would not allow him to create new unions of any kind. Moreover, Ukraine needed no such unions—the Ukrainians did not want to exchange one yoke for another. The Ukrainian population had voted for independence with astounding unanimity. Kravchuk presented Yeltsin with a fait accompli—Ukraine was leaving the Soviet Union.

Yeltsin then declared that without Ukraine, he would not sign either. It was then that they began looking for a new structure to replace the Soviet Union. They came up with a document titled "Agreement on the Proposed Creation of a Commonwealth of Democratic States." The term "union" was out. Commonwealth had a more positive connotation, and the Ukrainians approved with one caveat—that the term "democratic" should be changed to "independent" states. Everyone knew that full democracy was still a dream, but at the suggestion of Yeltsin's adviser Sergei Shakhrai, the three founding republics adopted a resolution to dissolve the Soviet Union altogether. He argued that Russia, Ukraine, and Belarus were not only leaving the union but also dissolving it. The final document contained the declaration:

> We the Republic of Belarus, the Russian Federation, and Ukraine, as founding states of the U.S.S.R. that signed the treaty of 1922 . . . hereby establish that the U.S.S.R. as a subject of international law and geopolitical reality ceases its existence.

When Gorbachev learned of this development, he screamed, threatened, and tried to overturn the accords to no avail. After two dramatic weeks, on Christmas Day, 1991, he officially resigned as the head of the USSR, and on December 31, 1991, the red hammer-and-sickle flag on the Kremlin tower was lowered for the last time. The Soviet Union was defunct.

Plokhy also concluded that the United States had little to do with the breakup of the Soviet Union, arguing that the United States never anticipated its breakup and, in fact, tried to use what influence it had over the situation to prevent it. It's true that there is no evidence that the United States engineered any of the events immediately leading up to the Kremlin's downfall. Messrs. Bush and Baker did try to keep the Soviet Union together in late 1991 but were doing so only to ensure that the end, when it came, would not be violent and destabilizing. That the end came with virtually no bloodshed was one of the great achievements of the twentieth century. Professor Plokhy himself credits the Bush administration with helping orchestrate its peaceful dissolution. It was no small accomplishment, especially if one considers the bloody ends of other empires.

I accept Plokhy's thesis that the most important factor that decided the future of the empire was the relationship between the two largest republics. The Soviet collapse in the final months resulted from the inability of Russia and Ukraine to agree on the terms of a unified state. He describes this as "the last nail in the coffin of the Soviet Union."

Plokhy's book, however, focuses entirely on events that transpired during the last five months of 1991, the final chapter in a drama that had been unfolding for a decade, if not longer. A gripping chapter to be sure, but the Soviet state was doomed long before that. Many signs suggested that the Soviet Union was in a slow terminal decline before August 1991, a decline that could only have ended in its downfall. I therefore take issue with Plokhy's view that "the collapse had nothing to do with the handiwork of the United States."

In reality, America had been involved in undermining the Soviet Union for decades. The effort had taken many forms and had the effect of tunneling under the walls of an impenetrable medieval fortress. The work required perseverance, patience, and systematic grinding down of the barriers enclosing the empire. Thus, to claim that America had nothing to do with the fall of the Soviet Union is misleading. The collapse did not happen in a vacuum. Copious evidence suggests that the West had, in fact, played a weighty role in bringing down the evil empire. To appreciate this chapter of history, it is necessary to examine events occurring during the ten-to-fifteen-year period before the collapse.

During the 1980s, I was able to observe the empire's last years. Working in Paris for the IEA/OECD and SAAOR provided unique insights often missing from the narratives cited above. Such insights allowed me to form a vision that differed from the mainstream versions, and filled in the gaps in conventional explanations. I've reduced them to three important causes: the role of nationalism in the USSR, the broadcasts of Radio Free Europe and Radio Liberty (RFE-RL), and gyrations in the world price of crude oil during the '70s and early '80s, factors largely overlooked by mainstream academics and journalists.

I never accepted the thesis that there was a single overarching event or reason for the fall. On the contrary, I believed that the empire was in such dire straits, the defects so grave, and internal contradictions so numerous that when they converged in the late '80s, the empire expired in what I would call a classic case of assisted suicide.

The reader should visualize the Soviet Union as a seventy-four-year-old impaired entity on protracted life support, appearing to be alive, but already prostrate in a coffin. The only thing left to do is hammer in the nails to keep it from resurrecting. The nails being the developments, big and small, that unfolded during the years prior to the final collapse and sealed the fate of the empire.

TO BEGIN WITH, THE SYSTEM had a built-in structural defect. It depended on an inherently dysfunctional model, tied to an unworkable utopian ideology. The years of Communist rule had choked the economy; stifling innovation, destroying initiative, and creating mind-boggling inefficiencies and corruption at all levels, but in particular among the ruling classes. The Soviet empire was dying under the weight of its statist economic yoke. Thus, no matter how many millions of parasites and enemies of the people were eliminated, murdered, starved, or imprisoned in the frigid wastes of Siberia, all efforts to reform the system were doomed to fail. Seventy years of Communism not only physically killed millions but also destroyed the spirit of its people. All efforts by citizens to help themselves in ways not sanctioned by the regime were severely punished.

Ironically, Socialism was defined as a commitment to equality, social justice, freedom, opportunities for the poor, respect for individual choice, and democracy. For a long time, the Soviet Union survived on such slogans, and the promise of a better day. Instead of a better day, though, the people got poverty, misery, tyranny, repression, concentration camps, and empty shelves. Corruption permeated the centralized economy from top to bottom, and the system became exhausted, bankrupt, and diseased. Realizing that the slogans were empty, the masses began questioning the system. Disillusionment set in and produced a crisis of confidence, deep cynicism, and lawlessness, not to mention alcoholism. The ossified state Socialism was collapsing from within, crumbling from its weaknesses and contradictions.

When Communist elites realized that the structure was failing, they vainly tried to reform a system that was intrinsically unreformable. Mikhail Gorbachev, the last Soviet leader, began looking to the West for solutions to his country's problems. To make the system more competitive, he introduced *glasnost, uskorenie,* and *perestroika,* policies that were doomed from the outset.[10] Gorbachev did the right things for the wrong reasons, for his overriding aim was to save Communism in the Soviet Union. That is why he was willing to let go of the Eastern European satellites, naively believing that the people there would choose to stay allied to a Socialist commonwealth. Gorbachev was also afraid that Soviet troops would not be reliable in enforcing domination over Eastern Europe, and he was probably aware that attempting another intervention on the lines of 1956 or 1968 would destroy his reputation.

He failed to realize that the loosening up of controls would lead only to further disintegration, and that any attempt to reform Stalin's centralized model of economic management would only accelerate the speed of its collapse. Gorbachev's staggering miscalculations eventually culminated in the death of the Soviet Union.

In addition to the structural weakness of the Communist ideology, several developments predating the Gorbachev period significantly contributed to

---

[10]　*Glasnost, uskorenie,* and *perestroika* translate to "openness," "acceleration," and "rebuilding," respectively.

the weakening of the empire. Every twelve years, the Communist world experienced some form of convulsion. One of the first was the 1956 Hungarian uprising. Twelve years later, in 1968, the Czechoslovaks introduced their "Socialism with a Human Face" revolution. Both were brutally put down by Soviet tanks. In the summer of 1980, the final crisis of Communism began with industrial unrest that engulfed Poland.[11] When strikes hit dozens of factories throughout the country, the Solidarity movement gained unstoppable momentum. The Kremlin was appalled, but the sclerotic leadership failed to intimidate the Poles.

About the same time, Karol Wojtyła was elected Pope and chose to be called John Paul II. When the KGB chief Yuri Andropov heard the news, he said, "The election of Wojtyła as the new Pope represents a danger to the Eastern bloc and a threat to the Soviet Union," a statement that turned out to be prophetic. In June 1979, when a rapturous reception greeted the Pope during his visit to Poland, everything changed. Solidarity got a boost the authorities were unable to counter. The Pope's prestige and his inspirational message to "be not afraid" lifted the spirits of not only the Polish people but also the entire Eastern bloc. The confluence of these events signaled the beginning of the end.

A second event that mortally wounded the empire was its invasion of Afghanistan in 1979. After two years, the Soviets realized that the war was unwinnable, but they did not know how to extricate themselves. If they admitted defeat, it would be a sign of weakness to their opponents everywhere, but as casualties mounted, the Soviet people began to question the wisdom of the war. I knew this from the feedback provided by our research with Soviet visitors. Afghanistan, the "cemetery of empires," eventually became the Soviet army's graveyard.

The decision by the United States to supply the Afghan fighters with shoulder-fired heat-seeking antiaircraft Stinger missiles was a game changer that turned the war in favor of the mujahideen and led to the Soviet retreat from Afghanistan. The Soviet pullout unleashed a chain of events with unintended consequences. Losing the war in Afghanistan forced the Soviets to abandon their "outer empire," though, at the time, they did not anticipate the effects of this. Their disastrous military campaign in Afghanistan made them reluctant to send troops into battle anywhere else, but without the implied

---

[11]   The protracted Soviet-Afghan War began on December 24, 1979, with the invasion of Afghanistan by Soviet troops. Twelve years later, almost to the day, the Soviet Union was no more.

threat of force, they were unable to hold on to their Eastern European empire. Today, it is eminently clear that the loss of these satellites led to the crumbling of the Wall and the lifting of the Iron Curtain, and that this development eventually provoked the disintegration of the Soviet Union.

The 1986 Chernobyl tragedy was yet another damaging blow to an already weakened system. After a reflexive denial minimizing the catastrophic nuclear accident that had taken place on April 26, the Ukrainian authorities staged a Mayday parade in Kyiv. When people discovered that the *verkhushka*, the leadership, were sending their children to Crimea away from the danger, they realized they were being lied to on a colossal scale and revolted. Unlike anything else in recent history, this event turned the people of Ukraine against the heinous system.

Finally, one cannot dismiss the impact of President Reagan's powerful words that gave the people imprisoned behind the Iron Curtain reason for hope. In his June 1982 speech before the British House of Commons, Reagan predicted that Marxism and Leninism would end up on the "ash heap of history." In a March 1983 speech in Orlando, Florida, he first used the controversial phrase "evil empire," referring to the Soviet Union. While these words caused an uproar in certain quarters, historians such as Yale University's John Lewis Gaddis have commended the use of the phrase. In his *The Cold War,* Gaddis argued that in their use of the phrase "evil empire," Reagan and his anti-Communist political allies effectively broke with the détente tradition, and laid the groundwork for the ultimate collapse of the Soviet Union. Later, Yuri Maltsev, an economist under Mikhail Gorbachev, supported Reagan's use of the phrase and labeled the USSR an "evil empire" in the introduction of the book *Requiem for Marx,* published in 1993. Even Andrey Kozyrev, the first head of the Russian Foreign Ministry, concurred that the Soviet Union had indeed been an "evil empire."

On June 12, 1987, with Gorbachev present, Ronald Reagan spoke the following memorable words at Berlin's Brandenburg Gate:

> General Secretary Gorbachev, if you seek peace, if you seek prosperity for the Soviet Union and Eastern Europe, if you seek liberalization, come here to this gate.

> Mr. Gorbachev, open this gate!

> Mr. Gorbachev, tear down this wall!

These simple but deeply penetrating words had a profound effect on lifting the morale of the people behind the Iron Curtain, encouraging them to intensify the struggle. Two years and four months later, the Wall came down.

Reagan's verbal attacks were backed up by a military strategy to confront the Soviet Union. Soon after his inauguration, he embarked on a massive buildup of US strategic offensive nuclear forces. In 1983, he unveiled an ambitious, futuristic proposal for strategic ballistic missile defenses, later called the Strategic Defense Initiative (SDI). An astute observer of Communism, he understood the Soviet mentality and weaknesses. Playing on their paranoia, President Reagan came up with a masterstroke, the "star wars," a bluff that intimidated the Soviet leaders into believing that they could not compete with the US military-industrial complex.

PLOKHY RIGHTFULLY RAISED the nationalities question, an issue that had been festering for a long time before the final collapse. The state that the Bolsheviks created was not monolithic, but they did their best to overcome national differences. For decades, nationalism was thought to be dead. Many progressives saw the Soviet Union as a model of a future society where malignant nationalism had been extinguished, or at least brought under control. Numerous intellectuals in the West considered nationalism to be a retrograde, negative force whose shelf life had expired with National Socialism, an ideology that had given legitimate liberal nationalism a bad name.[12] Whether it was a force for good or for evil is a question worthy of a separate discussion. The point to remember here is that by the 1980s, nationalism in the Soviet Union was gaining strength, and, eventually, national movements prevailed over the ideology of Communism. People lost faith in Socialism and turned to the only alternatives able to counter Communism: self-determination, national identity, and independence from Moscow.

Despite being from the Stavropol region, which hosts many Caucasian nationalities, Gorbachev did not appreciate the power of nationalities and their resentments under the Soviet yoke. He and his backers believed that the national question in the Soviet Union had been solved, but he was wrong.

---

[12] As argued by the leading spokesman for the philosophy of liberal nationalism Johann Gottfried von Herder. In the August 2014 issue of the *Nation,* Anne Applebaum also made a case that nationalism was a necessary step to arrive at a true democracy.

Discontent was widespread, especially in Ukraine after the Chernobyl disaster, and that was not the only place. Dissatisfaction had also been brewing in the Baltic States, the Caucasus region, and in the republics of Central Asia. The disintegration began on the peripheries in the non-Russian areas, with the Baltic region the first to produce mass organized dissent. In 1987, the government of Estonia demanded autonomy, followed by similar moves in Lithuania and Latvia, the other two Baltic republics. Once this Pandora's box was opened, nationalist movements emerged in Georgia, Ukraine, Moldova, Byelorussia, and the Central Asian republics.

Many embarrassed sages in academia and diplomacy boasted that they had seen the end coming. If they had, they offered no evidence of their foresight. A few in the intelligence community may have seen trouble brewing, but they failed to convey the seriousness of the situation to their masters in Washington. In any event, all were afraid to imagine what could happen when a society with nuclear weapons disintegrated. American leadership, therefore, dismissed such a scenario as so improbable as to be unthinkable.

In reality, hardly anyone saw the collapse coming. The expiration of the Soviet Union was a tortuous process involving a series of random and unforeseen events, complicated by sages looking at the wrong signals, scrutinizing *Pravda* and *Izvestia* and analyzing speeches of the Politburo for hints of things to come. Jack Matlock, the US ambassador, believed that those experts who depended on the Soviet press for news were wasting their time, even if they tried to discern messages between the lines. Soviet newspapers did not tell people anything they didn't already know, and most of what it told them was misleading and dull. Meanwhile, discontent was brewing in the republics. Other than sporadic anecdotal stories leaking out of the Soviet Union, no one had any insight into the minds of the average Soviet citizen, and for a good reason.

Most experts were not aware of the depth of nationalist resentment mainly because they did not have access to public opinion data on this crucial issue. Many believed that public opinion in the Soviet Union was nonexistent. Others thought it was possible to erase differences between nationalities and ethnic identities, and some even believed that this had been accomplished. The only organization that possessed such data was SAAOR, the audience research department of Radio Liberty. The information that we collected and analyzed pointed to growing discontent and discord among nationalities, and this allowed our analysts to draw conclusions that differed from conventional views. A more detailed presentation of these findings appears in chapter 33 of this memoir, "Unique Revelations and Insights."

One of the rare exceptions in academia was a study group established by Paul Goble at the University of Chicago in the 1970s that included Stephen Blank. They were among the first to recognize that a nationalities problem in the USSR existed. I cannot count the times I had to explain to supposedly learned people that there were fundamental differences between Russians and Ukrainians, Russians, and Lithuanians, Latvians and Estonians, Russians and Georgians, Armenians and Uzbeks or Tajiks, only to be mocked and branded as a hopelessly romantic nationalist. I argued that the Soviet Union was not a cohesive state but an artificial creation that, at the first opportunity, would fall apart. I was keenly aware that the dissimilarities among the Soviet people were not only linguistic but also historical and cultural. There were also vast differences in their psychological makeup. Indeed, the myth of "one happy family" led by "the elder brother" in Moscow was thought by many pundits in the West to be a given. Conventional wisdom, therefore, dictated that the question of national identity was a nonissue. If anyone raised it, such as diaspora communities of the captive nations in the United States and elsewhere, they were marginalized as irrelevant, dismissed as embittered nationalists with a grudge, or labeled as fascists or Nazi collaborators.

THE MAJOR FOREIGN BROADCASTERS transmitting to Eastern Europe and the Soviet Union were the BBC, Voice of America, Radio Free Europe (to Eastern European countries), and Radio Liberty (to the Soviet Union). The broadcaster the Soviet regime feared most was *Radio Svoboda*— Radio Liberty, because it covered topics of immediate concern to the Soviet people. The station broadcast in dozens of languages and addressed issues relevant to individual republics in their language.

Western broadcasts were particularly important in influencing attitudes and opinions to political crises such as the war in Afghanistan during the 1980s, or the Chernobyl nuclear plant disaster in 1986. When Soviet media was slow in reporting on relevant issues, or reported misinformation, Western radio filled in the gaps. SAAOR surveys of Soviets traveling in the West showed that a majority of respondents used Western broadcasters such as

RFE-RL and VOA as their primary source of information on the Chernobyl disaster.[13]

I always felt that Radio Free Europe and Radio Liberty played a crucial role in the fall of Communism in Eastern Europe and the Soviet Union. Radio Liberty, in particular, helped the Soviet listener to vet domestic media sources and discuss what was only talked about privately. RL's programming inspired Soviet citizens by letting them know that the people of the West cared about their plight. For decades, it kept the cinders of freedom and national identity smoldering. It gave the people in the Soviet republics hope. Without RFE-RL, the transformational events of 1989 and 1991 would not have been possible.

To appreciate the impact of RFE-RL on Communist society, it should be noted that the Cold War was, in essence, a war of ideas, and the winner would be the side that successfully implanted its vision in the opposing side's populace. It was a struggle to control the hearts and minds of the population. Soviet leaders recognized that RFE-RL was designed to challenge their control over both the population of the satellite regimes and the USSR, and the only way they could counter the broadcasts was through jamming. It was the Soviet Union's only defense against Western broadcasting. Disrupting Western shortwave broadcasts, however, required the construction of hundreds of jamming stations. The Soviets built some three thousand transmitters to block approximately 150 Western transmitter stations, but forty years of jamming came to an abrupt end in November 1988, when Gorbachev recognized the futility of these actions.[14]

The majority of the "experts" apparently missed the impact foreign broadcasters had on the Soviet public. I searched the myriad of books on the fall of the Soviet Union and found hardly a mention of the effect of Western

[13] *Cold War Broadcasting: Impact on the Soviet Union and Eastern Europe*, a compendium of studies and documents edited by A. Ross Johnson and R. Eugene Parta (Central European University Press, 2010). Of special relevance to this discussion is part 4, "Impact of Western Broadcasts in the USSR," and chapter 17, "Cold War International Broadcasting and the Road to Democracy."

[14] For a full treatment of Impact of the Broadcasts: Jamming and Audiences, see Cold War Broadcasting Impact, report on a conference organized by the Hoover Institution and the Cold War International History Project of the Woodrow Wilson International Center for Scholars at Stanford University, October 13–16, 2004, page 19. The same report contains a section (page 37) titled "Cold War International Broadcasting: Lessons Learned," by A. Ross Johnson and R. Eugene Parta.

broadcasters on forming public attitudes, promoting democratic values and undermining the monopoly of information on which the Communist regime relied. One of the few exceptions was Zbigniew Brzezinski, who noted that "RFE and RL were critically important weapons in the free world's competition with Soviet totalitarianism, and without them, the Soviet bloc might not even have disintegrated."

Freedom is a force of nature, like a river that can be dammed but not stopped. People all around the world have always craved to be free of despotic rule. Decades of persecution, repression and tyranny, the ruthless methods used to maintain an inhumane system by the Soviets, almost extinguished all hope of freedom. The subjects of the captive nations hated Communism and their rulers but, above all, despised their Soviet occupiers.

Western radios fought the tyrannical Communist regimes with truth, the best form of propaganda. Getting the message to people behind the Iron Curtain, however, was not simple. Listening to foreign radio on shortwave was forbidden and severely punished. The regime considered such broadcasts subversive and frantically tried to suppress them by jamming. Despite such efforts, a considerable amount of information filtered through to a substantial segment of the population, and these listeners, risking harassment and imprisonment, spread the word and kept hope alive.

Most Soviet citizens did not perceive Radio Liberty as a foreign station like the VOA or the BBC. Audience research showed that *Svoboda* was seen as an independent and objective source of news and information, a competitor the Kremlin feared and tried to silence. Radio Liberty provided information Soviet citizens were not getting from domestic sources. In other words, the station played a crucial role in exposing the Soviet system's "big lie." The effectiveness of the radios funded by the US Congress challenges the view that the United States had little or nothing to do with the fall of the Soviet Union. Thousands of testimonies by Soviet citizens, dissidents, and emigrants, people in a position to know, have vouched for the incalculable impact of the radios.[15]

THE UNITED STATES PLAYED a central role in the emergence of Ukraine as an independent state, and consequently in the breakup of the Soviet Union.

---

[15] For a comprehensive treatment of audiences to international radio in the Soviet Union, see *Discovering the Hidden Listener: An Empirical Assessment of Radio Liberty and Western Broadcasting to the USSR during the Cold War*, R. Eugene Parta (Hoover Press, 2007).

Until recently, the story of the so-called book program has never been told. Official US documents from the Cold War are only now being released, while eyewitnesses are either no longer with us or reluctant to talk.

The CIA funded the most successful publishing and book distribution operations in the Ukrainian and Polish diasporas throughout the Cold War: Prolog in New York and the Instytut Literackie in Paris were the organizations that published two influential intellectual magazines in the Polish and Ukrainian diasporas—*Kultura* and *Suchasnist,* respectively.

Prolog, like the Instytut Literackie, was financially independent of the diaspora and could publish books and articles from across the entire political spectrum focusing on nationalist literature. In the 1980s, the US government provided millions of dollars and technical resources for the emerging democratic movements in Ukraine and Poland. Prolog cooperated with the Czech opposition and Polish underground in the smuggling of books and journals to Ukraine, some of which were reprinted in Poland, and trained Ukrainians in underground printing techniques.

My involvement in smuggling books and video cassette players across the Iron Curtain was minor compared to the colossal work carried out by Prolog's director, the late Roman Kupchinsky, Stefan Welhash, and many others in New York. A few of my friends acted as intermittent couriers for Roman, among them Ivan Myhul, Taras Kuzio, and others who did not wish to be identified. Since parts of the operation were covert, it's difficult to say how many others were involved.[16]

CIA funding of these operations grew to its highest levels under Pres. Ronald Reagan in his crusade against the "evil empire." Liberalization in the USSR under Gorbachev also opened up opportunities for covert and overt operations in support of the democratic opposition. The American funding of Prolog was one of Washington's most successful covert operations in the Cold War; it played a central role in achieving Ukrainian independence and added another nail in the coffin of the empire.

In addition to Prolog, other organizations and institutions played key roles in the fall of the Soviet Union. The work of the Commission on Security and Cooperation in Europe (CSCE), also known as the US Helsinki Group, was instrumental in making Soviet citizens aware of their rights and duties. It was an independent US government agency created by Congress in 1976 to

---

[16]   A detailed account of an operation where I was involved appears in chapter 21, "A Covert Mission to Warsaw."

monitor compliance of commitments made under the Helsinki Final Act and the Organization for Security and Cooperation in Europe (OSCE). A friend, Orest Deychakivsky, was instrumental in organizing this effort. The group was particularly effective in Ukraine and Lithuania, and their work was vital in helping to seal the Soviet Union's fate.

A RARELY MENTIONED FACTOR that contributed to the fall of the Soviet Union was the drastic drop in the price of crude oil in the 1980s. Sovietologists and economic experts were aware that the Soviet economy was in trouble, but they attributed it to the inefficiency of a centrally planned economy. Otherwise, they believed that the Soviet Union functioned more or less like the Western economies and only needed some fixing, which is why they readily embraced and praised Gorbachev's reforms. The reality was different. The Soviet economy did not resemble anything in the West. It was so completely dysfunctional that it was unable to compete in world markets because it was incapable of producing anything that might be sold for hard currency.[17] As in Russia today, oil was the lifeblood of the economy. The Soviet Union depended almost entirely on oil revenue to subsidize wheat imports to feed its population. In the long run, such a condition was untenable.

During the '70s and '80s, the empire was on life support fed by a drip of liquid black gold. With the 1973 oil crisis, the price of crude oil quadrupled to twelve dollars per barrel, and after the second oil crisis, sparked by the Iranian Revolution in 1979, it tripled to nearly forty dollars per barrel. The ailing empire got a reprieve thanks to ever-greater injections of hard currency. This was a boon not only for OPEC but also for the Soviet Union, a country that had been producing nearly ten million barrels of oil per day. Only Saudi Arabia was capable of maintaining production at that level. The revenue from oil sales kept the "beast" alive until the 1980s, when the price of crude began to decline. By mid-decade, it had dropped to ten dollars per barrel. At the same time, Saudi Arabia flooded the crude market, and plummeting oil prices deprived the Soviet Union of oil revenue, its lifeblood. Few experts in the West were able to grasp the meaning of these developments, probably because they were unaware of the extent to which the Soviet economy relied on oil revenue for its survival. They assumed that because the USSR had muddled through

---

[17] Products the Soviet Union exported could be counted on the fingers of one hand, caviar and vodka being two.

for sixty years, it would survive for another sixty. There was a consensus that the Soviet Union was too big to fail and a collapse was therefore unimaginable!

Russophile sages such as Stephen Cohen of New York University argued that the Reagan administration's quest to pressure the Soviets into change would inevitably fail, since it was "predicated on wildly exaggerated conceptions of Soviet domestic problems. In reality, the Soviet Union is not in economic crisis; nor is it politically unstable."[18] Another academic of the "revisionist" school of Soviet history was Jerry Hough, a professor of political science at Duke University, hailed as one of America's most distinguished specialists on the Soviet Union. He made ludicrous statements such as "the level of terror in the Soviet Union has been much exaggerated," and placed high hopes on Gorbachev's perestroika to miraculously turn things around.

During the early '80s, I worked for the International Energy Agency, where my job was to track crude oil prices and production trends worldwide, including in the Soviet Union. Estimating oil output on a global basis was a complicated task. I developed a dossier of contacts in the oil industry and oil-producing countries to exchange production statistics on a country-by-country basis. Nearly everyone, however, lacked crude-oil production numbers for the Soviet Union, a major producer. The USSR was a closed entity, and oil production statistics were a state secret, which led to wildly diverging estimates. The only people who had an inkling of how much the Soviets were pumping were the folks at the CIA, who were reluctant to share such information with the oil industry through normal channels. Thus, whenever I happened to be in the United States, I paid a visit to petroleum industry analysts at Langley.

I vividly recall the first time I went through security at CIA's headquarters. Thanks to my position as principal administrator at IEA's Oil Industry Division, I was allowed to enter the inner sanctum of the world's premiere intelligence service. After being escorted by a minder through a maze of corridors, I arrived in the unassuming offices of the agency's oil industry division and was introduced to the agent responsible for keeping track of Soviet oil production. One wall of his modest office was covered by an oversized map of the USSR with colored pins designating oil fields, including a cluster around the Caspian Sea basin and Western Siberia. Next to the pins were production figures in million barrels per day. I was tempted to ask how they acquired such information but realized that it would have been

---

[18]   Stephen Cohen, *Rethinking the Soviet Experience: Politics and History since 1917* (1985).

inappropriate, so I just listened. I spent the next few hours getting a primer on the Soviet Union's oil production capabilities field by field, and was thoroughly impressed.

Upon leaving Langley, I was privy to classified information available to only a tiny group of insiders with a need to know. Back in Paris, I inserted this data into my worksheet estimating world oil production, information used in IEA's quarterly assessment of the global energy supply and demand. At the same time, an arrangement with my oil industry contacts allowed me to compile country-by-country output in the rest of the world. In exchange, without disclosing the source, I provided them with a range of the latest Soviet oil production.

Two trends were discernible during the 1980s: world oil prices were dropping, and the Soviet Union was experiencing difficulties in maintaining its high oil output. At twelve million barrels per day, the USSR was the world's largest producer. The CIA analysts told me that such a level of production was unsustainable, and that poor management, old technology, and lack of investment would eventually result in a decline. Time has shown that they were on the money.

The reason the Soviet Union attained such a high level of production was that it exploited easily accessible deposits to the maximum by drilling thousands of shallow wells. As new oil gushes out under natural pressure, the initial yield is high, but this so-called primary recovery extracts only a fraction of the oil in a reservoir. Improperly used, such exploitation damages a reservoir, sometimes permanently. With irresponsible primitive recovery methods, the Soviets undoubtedly ruined many viable reservoirs.

A drastic drop in the price of oil on the world market was probably one of the sharpest nails in the Soviet coffin. Lower prices meant less oil revenue to keep the Soviet economy functioning. The impact of lower oil prices was aggravated by a gradual decline in production resulting from inefficient extraction practices. The combination meant that the empire's life support system was in danger of malfunctioning. The Soviet Union was moving toward the edge of the abyss.

Except for a few knowledgeable analysts at the CIA, the potential consequences of the changing oil market environment were lost on Western Sovietologists, who failed to anticipate the impact lower-priced oil might have on the future of the Soviet Union and its Eastern European satellites. Cheap oil was the glue that held the empire together and paid for essential grain imports. When the oil dried up, they lost control of their Eastern European satellites, and at the same time wasted vast petroleum resources in the vain attempt to conquer Afghanistan.

To summarize this complex history, it is not unreasonable to conclude that the drop in crude oil prices followed by a decline in production created conditions that made the Soviet Union unable to subsidize cheap energy to Eastern Europe. This led to the loss of control of the satellites, and culminated in the fall of the Wall in 1989. The disappearance of the Iron Curtain led to the collapse of the entire Soviet Eastern European Empire and a prelude to the disintegration of the failing nuclear superpower. Suddenly, millions were released from the putrid cage Communism represented. No amount of *glasnost* and *perestroika* could have prevented its inevitable end.

3. Outbreak of World War II

ALMOST FIFTY-TWO YEARS to the day before my "Monte Rosa moment" and the collapse of the Soviet Union, a momentous event took place that would fundamentally change Europe. On September 1, 1939, the tranquility of western Poland was shattered by a deafening military thunderclap. Five German armies, a million and a half strong, swept across Polish borders from Pomerania and East Prussia. By September 17, the German advance, spearheaded by three thousand tanks, armored cars, and personnel carriers, reached the fortress of Brest on the Buh, a river that was to play a pivotal role in my life. World War II had broken out.

On the day the Germans ceremoniously handed Brest to the Russians, my father, Roman, was a prisoner in a Polish concentration camp called Bereza-Kartuzka, a town roughly halfway between Minsk and Brest-Litovsk. The war that erupted on the first of September 1939 would also determine the date of my birth.[19]

The Bereza-Kartuzka prison was formed by Pilsudski's regime in the mid-1930s, to incarcerate individuals who resisted Polish rule.[20] Enclosed by a five-meter barbed wire fence and guarded by several watch towers, it housed several thousand political prisoners, primarily Ukrainian nationalists—intellectuals,

---

[19]   The material in this chapter comes from my father's handwritten memoir.

[20]   Bereza-Kartuzka was a Polish concentration camp for those the regime considered subversive to the state. It was located in today's city of Bereza. "Kartuzka" refers to the Carthusian monastery grounds.

professionals, and students—and Jewish Communists. Roman wrote in his memoir that the inmates were unaware that war had erupted:

> We could hear the droning of bombers in the sky. We could see their German markings and instantly realized what that meant. The guards were bewildered and let up on the discipline. Soon two German prisoners of war were brought to the camp. They were interrogated and shot. On the 17th of September we heard artillery in the distance, and at the same time, the prison command announced that the Soviets had invaded Poland from the east. The writing was on the wall. On the morning of the 18th, all of the guards abandoned the prison. A few local inhabitants showed up, opened the prison gate and said: "they are gone, you can come out now."

As the Soviets and Germans were celebrating the partition of Poland in Brest, Roman continued,

> We knew that we had to get home quickly. We organized into groups according to destinations, distributed whatever food remained in the camp stores, and set out on foot to the regions where we lived. I joined a group of sixteen men from Kamianka County, and without further delay, we began our long trek home.

The flight from Bereza, my father noted, was dangerous and full of unexpected hazards. There was a war going on, but no one knew the extent of hostilities, where the front was, or if there was a front at all. With the situation in flux, the biggest problem for the former prisoners was determining who was a friend and who was a foe.

BEREZA-KARTUZKA was a concentration camp run by the Polish government between 1934 and 1939 to incarcerate individuals the Polish authorities considered a "threat to security, peace, and social order," in other words, people dangerous to the regime. To hide the harsh character of the camp, the Polish authorities referred to it as *Miejsce Odosobnienia*, a place of isolation or a detention camp.

The majority of scholars, including Timothy Snyder, Norman Davies, and Volodymyr Kubijovych, say it was unquestionably a concentration camp. Tiny by Nazi and Communist standards, the facility usually held one hundred to five hundred inmates at a time, but it was still a concentration camp. Apart from a small number of criminals, the vast majority of prisoners consisted of Ukrainian nationalists and Communists, individuals the regime believed posed a threat.

In 1938, the Polish government, fearing a rise in pro-German sentiment, arrested several thousand Ukrainians and sent them to Bereza without due process or right of appeal. Initially, each cell held fifteen inmates, but in 1938, the number of detainees in each cell increased to seventy. Immediately after the German invasion, another series of mass arrests took place, with thousands more detained and sent to the camp. According to Father, by the time the German tanks breached Poland's western border, the population of Bereza camp had swelled to fifteen thousand, and he was one of them, captured in the final wave of arrests.[21]

When my sister and I were growing up, he rarely spoke of Bereza, and when he did, it was only in snippets, so we only got the full story of his incarceration in 1986, when he wrote the first part of his memoir. Father wrote,

> On the day Hitler's army attacked Poland, the Polish police in Kamianka County rounded up sixteen men suspected of being Ukrainian nationalists. I was one of those arrested. Walking home from work at the grain storage depot in the village of Tadani, I stopped to chat with Deoniziy Kravec, a family friend, who warned me that "in unpredictable times such as these it is wise not to sleep in one's bed." I thought that Deoniziy had exaggerated the danger and ignored his advice. Later that evening, after everyone was sound asleep, the Polish police came to the village of Lany, outside of Kamianka Strumilova, and surrounded the house where I lived with my wife, Natalka. Two gendarmes entered and ordered me to pack my belongings and accompany them to the police station in Kamianka. When we got there, I discovered that a number of like-minded associates I knew were already there. The next morning, without any formalities, the group was escorted at gunpoint to the train station. The destination, we were told, was Bereza-Kartuzka.

---

[21]   Exact numbers are not available because in August 1939, after the last of the mass arrests had taken place, the camp's authorities stopped formally registering detainees.

At Bereza, the group was greeted with the customary welcoming ritual: running the gauntlet between two rows of guards swinging sticks and rubber truncheons. Father continued,

> I managed to get through with only a few bruises, but some of the older detainees who could not run fast were severely beaten and had to be carried away. Next, we were assigned bunks in barracks holding about 100 men each and immediately put on a will-breaking diet—no food for three days. Each day began at 4:00 in the morning with the toilet routine. Even this was regimented and meant to break the prisoners.
>
> Twenty men lined up along a concrete floor and were commanded: *rozpiąć się, załatwić sięi zapiąć się*—pants down, relieve yourself, pants up. We were allowed three minutes to defecate. Those not able to empty their bowels in the time allowed had to move around with distended bowels the entire day. For many, this condition was unendurable, particularly during physical calisthenics that lasted for hours on end.
>
> After washing with cold water, we got a meager breakfast of coffee and a piece of bread. The rest of the day was taken up by non-stop physical exercises. Those disobeying the routine were subjected to an even more severe physical punishment—*padnij, powstań, padnij, powstań*—fall down, on your feet, over and over. Anyone refusing to obey was beaten. The purpose for such calisthenics was, of course, to physically break our will to resist. After a week, the effects on the new inmates were beginning to show. Men became weak, emaciated and depressed.

Gnawing hunger was a constant companion. To this day, I recall Father describing how he noticed several men fighting over a dirty piece of pork belly skin that lay on the corridor floor. After sucking the remaining fat out of the skin, they passed it around so that a few inmates could chew on it to get a bit of the flavor to assuage their hunger. Other accounts confirmed that conditions in the prison were exceptionally harsh. There were constant harassment and beatings for anyone using the Ukrainian language. Any breach of discipline was punished by forced labor or solitary confinement.[22]

---

[22] Yurij Luhovy, a member of the Academy of Canadian Cinema and Television, produced and directed a documentary film about the Bereza prison, using

The entire compound was encircled by an electrified barbed wire fence. As a result, attempted escapes were rare. Although torture was not the order of the day, some Ukrainians were tortured to death during questioning, died from disease, or disappeared without a trace. The harshest treatment was reserved for OUN members.[23] By the time they were released from Bereza Kartuzka, they were broken men with health damaged by sadistic camp guards.

THE DISTANCE FROM Bereza-Kartuzka to Kamianka Strumilova, as the crow flies, was four hundred kilometers. In addition to the German and Russian armies, the countryside was teeming with remnants of the Polish regular army and an assortment of insurgent groups, fighting and maneuvering for control: the Polish underground, the Communist partisans, Belarusian insurgents, and recently formed bands of Ukrainian insurgents. The prisoners had to stay clear of these groups by detouring through back roads, fields, and forests, mostly at night.

Near the town of Kobryn, my father and his group came across a great number of Polish casualties; some wounded, others dead. It was his first exposure to the ravages of war.

> The stench of decomposing cadavers was unmistakable. Near Brest, our group of sixteen weak men encountered the first units of the German Wehrmacht. To our surprise, the Germans did not harrass us. On the contrary, since we hadn't eaten for days, they gave us macaroni and potatoes which we quickly ate half cooked. It relieved our hunger temporarily, but during the night I developed an excruciating abdominal pain, no doubt due to the undigested macaroni. The next day I was unable to keep up with the group and had to be left behind with a friend. With danger lurking around us, the group had to keep moving. Happily, after a few hours, my pains subsided, and both of us were able to catch up with the others. Our worst fear was being captured by the Bolsheviks. To stay clear of them we moved with great caution. Any contact with them meant capture with

authentic photographs, documents, archival footage, and eyewitness testimony from survivors. Roman Martyniuk's photograph appears there as one of the inmates. Other prominent inmates were OUN activists Roman Shukhevych, Dmytro Hrytsai, Volodymyr Yaniv, Mykola Lebed, and Stepan Bandera.

[23] OUN, Organization of Ukrainian Nationalists. More on this in later chapters.

unspeakable consequences, as some of the Polish army remnants were to discover. We knew that the Soviets would shoot anyone suspected of being a Ukrainian nationalist, though Communist underground formations were relatively safe from the Red Army.

In the forest around Vlodava, we came across the pitiful but brave remnants of Polish units hiding from the Germans and bypassed them. Marching at a breakneck speed of 40 kilometers a day we made it to the region of Kholm where the Ukrainian population provided us with food, shelter, and information on the whereabouts of the various military units and insurgent bands in the area. The fear of being discovered by the Soviets was unrelenting. We first spotted them around Hrubeshiv but kept our distance. Compared to the German troops we saw later, the Soviet soldiers were a pathetic sight.

We continued to Varyash where we were among our people. Everywhere the locals kept us informed about the location of the Soviet troops. We tried to avoid them by bypassing main roads and walking through wooded areas where our chances of being spotted were less. In Sokal, we split up into smaller groups. My group headed for Most and by the time I reached Velyki Mosty I was on home territory and knew that Kamianka Strumilova was not far.

Stepping out of the forest around Lany, Roman saw families toiling in the fields doing postharvest chores. Some, who saw him at a distance, said they recognized him and sent for Natalka, his wife. When she came out of the house, she did not believe it was him and went back inside. As he got closer, she recognized his thin, emaciated body and ran to meet him. He was alive, and he had returned. It was an extremely joyful reunion. They hugged, kissed, and stayed in each other's arms for a long time. Father noted that this was the most blissful, joyous, and moving moment of his life. Everyone dropped whatever they were doing in the fields and went home to celebrate Roman's return from Bereza.

SIXTY-THREE YEARS after the above events, while on a work assignment in Minsk, Belarus, I had the opportunity to visit Bereza Kartuzka. I was curious to see what remained of the Polish concentration camp. My friend and collaborator Andrei Vardamatski also had an interest in this chapter of history that took place in his country. He was vaguely aware that such a concentration camp existed, but Soviet sources he had access to only spoke of a place where Ukrainian and Belarusian Communists and revolutionaries were imprisoned. The Soviet version, of course, was incomplete. When I told him that it was primarily a prison for Ukrainian nationalists, he was very surprised.

Soon, we were on our way to Bereza-Kartuzka. To me, this trip was a pilgrimage of sorts to honor the memory of my father and other Ukrainian patriots that were incarcerated there. I was not quite sure where the camp was located, but with the help of a rough map and a sketch of the main camp building I copied from a Ukrainian book about Bereza Kartuzka, finding the camp turned out to be easy.

The three-story brick shell (see photo) was known as the "arrest block." In the past, the structure was a Carthusian monastery, hence Bereza-Kartuzka. Sometime after WWI, it became a prison, and after WWII, it served as a training casern for Soviet army officers. Eventually, the building was abandoned, and all that remained was a carcass. Its solid outer brick walls stood intact, but the roof and the interior floors had completely collapsed. Despite a "keep out" sign, I rummaged through the ruined interior of the casern taking photos. I must confess that inside the "block," I experienced an eerie feeling, as if the spirits of the tormented souls were still there, pleading, imploring, and moaning. Although I don't believe in spirits, there in the Bereza camp it felt as though that Father's was near me.

THE SOVIET ARMY arrived in Kamianka about the same time my father came home from Bereza and returned to his job as the manager of the grain storage depot of the local cooperative. The grain depot soon came to the attention of Soviet occupation authorities, and the commissar responsible for procurement of grain paid Father a visit. Their first meeting appeared to be cordial. The commissar tried to charm him by addressing Father with the familiar *ty*—you—instead of the formal *vy*. He said,

"Roman, before we came, your cooperative was collecting eighty to one hundred centnares of grain.[24] Now all you can come up with is eight to ten. What's happened? Why don't you organize your boys and raise the collection and you will be paid?"

---

[24] A centnar is a European measure that equals fifty kilograms, or approximately one hundred pounds.

"That will be very difficult," Roman responded, "because the people don't have any confidence in the new regime or the money you will pay them, but I will talk to them."

Two weeks passed, and the commissar came by to ask about the grain collection quotas. Roman responded that he did his best, but the people would not contribute. He realized that his blunt answer jeopardized not only his position but also his life. The real reason farmers in the region were unwilling to contribute more grain was that even though Western Ukraine had not directly suffered from the collectivization and there was no starvation, the memory of Stalin's collectivization and forcible requisition of grain in Eastern Ukraine was still fresh.

A day after Father's meeting with the commissar, without warning, a rash of arrests broke out, and for no apparent reason, people disappeared. This happened everywhere when the Communists first arrived, and was meant to instill general fear among the populace. Roman was spared from the first wave of arrests, but friends warned him that with his defiant background, he would be next. There was not much time to reflect. He faced two options: either go into hiding with the underground or cross the new German–Soviet demarcation line into the German protectorate called *Generalgouvernement*.[25] Roman felt that his chances of survival were better in German-occupied Polish territory than in Soviet-Western Ukraine, so he chose to flee.

Before daybreak on the last Sunday of October 1939, my father, Roman, with the help of the underground network, paddled across the Buh River near the town of Belz.[26] The underground on the German side was already well organized and steered Father to Hrubeshiv and from there to Modrynec, a small town nearby. There they examined his qualifications and instructed him to report to the local school board for a teaching assignment. At the end of November, he sent a message to Natalka, who was pregnant, to join him in the German-occupied territory. In early December, after the first snowfall, the underground smuggled Natalka across the Buh, and she joined Roman in Modrynec. Once again, they were joyfully reunited, and relieved to know they were safe from the Bolsheviks.

---

[25]   *Generalgouvernement* was that part of Poland delineated as a German administrative protectorate.

[26]   The Ukrainian underground was a loose network of likeminded patriots formed to resist foreign occupation. It had not yet taken the shape it would later as the UPA, *Ukrayinska Povstanska Armiya*—Ukrainian Insurgent Army.

Roman and Natalka settled in Modrynec. The teaching job paid little but was a way to establish themselves in the community, and the local people welcomed the new Ukrainian teacher and provided a small house, food, and sometimes money. Their existence was relatively tranquil, but during a war, things are by nature unstable. So far, they had been fortunate.

After three months of teaching, Roman was approached by an acquaintance named Soltys, who needed a translator to deal with the German authorities. He knew that Roman was fluent in German and made him an offer. As a translator, Roman would make 300 RM per month, the equivalent of 600 Zloty, a nice sum by prevailing standards. Work consisted of trilingual interpretation—Polish, Ukrainian, and German—for the large landowners in the region. There were twenty-four such estates (*filvarki* in Polish or *Gutbezitzer* in German) spread throughout the county of Hrubeshiv. This meant a great deal of travel, so to get around from estate to estate, Roman was provided with a carriage and two horses. Given Natalka's delicate state, this was an offer hard to refuse.

Although there was a war on, the situation in the spring of 1940 in Western Europe was inconclusive. The French and British faced Germans across the Maginot Line in a confrontation known as the "phony war." At the same time, Roman and Natalka, finding themselves in the German-occupied part of Poland, the *Generalgouvernement*, felt relatively safe and fortunate not to be on the Soviet side of the border.

As a grain procurement agent, first for the Soviet and later for the German regime, he was in a unique position to judge the way both authorities treated people. He found that compared to the Soviets, whose methods were always brutally coercive, the Germans generally treated Ukrainians decently and fairly. They were strict but correct. The Soviets had only one tactic: arrests, deportations, or vanishing into thin air. "No person, no problem" was the saying attributed to Stalin. If the Germans arrested you, you knew the reason. This was, of course, some time before Gestapo methods turned brutal.[27] At this time, except for the Jews who were rounded up *en masse* and deported, the Germans generally let the indigenous population alone. They did, however,

---

[27] Koch and Rosenberg, Hitler's advisors, each advocated a different approach in dealing with Ukrainians. Early in the war, Rosenberg regarded Ukrainians as natural allies in combating Communism. Koch disagreed and regarded Ukrainians as *Untermenschen*. Initially, Hitler sided with Rosenberg but, under pressure, decided in favor of Koch.

expect their subjects to comply with German orders for grain procurement and other foodstuffs for which the locals were paid with real money.

Father wrote that each of the estates employed around fifty people. The main crop was sugar beet. The estates also owned horses and cattle, and his job was to give the landowners instructions concerning planting and harvesting, and inform them how much of the crop would be purchased by the German authorities. These orders had to be precisely explained because the penalties for unfulfillment were severe. An estate owner could have his entire harvest confiscated, and property seized. Moreover, anyone challenging German orders was a candidate for the concentration camp.

Roman acted as liaison between the owners and the German authorities, the *Bezirkslandwirt,* who in turn reported to the *Kreislandwirt,* the regional German authority, located in Hrubeshiv. He had a good working relationship with the estate owners and earned their respect, and by and large, they cooperated, averting the need for harsh measures.

The winter of 1939–1940 was unusually cold. One of Father's tasks was to communicate to owners of estates the quotas to be fulfilled. Sugar beet is a cool-season vegetable that grows quickly, but its cultivation is tricky and labor intensive. The shallow roots can be easily disturbed, so constant thinning is necessary. From experience, Father knew that if things could go wrong, they would.

He described in some detail a disturbing event that took place one day outside his house.

> I heard the cries and screams of young women laborers. Some were being loaded on a truck by the gendarmes. I quickly intervened but was told that these women were being requisitioned as laborers for work in Germany. As soon as I saw this, I rushed to the German commandant and told him in strong language that if we lost any of these women, the estate owners would not be able to meet the beet harvest quota.

Roman's tactic worked. The same day, the commandant contacted the *Kreislandwirt,* the regional headquarters, and the requisition order was rescinded. Not one laborer was taken for work in Germany. His quick reaction saved about seventy young women from deportation to Germany. Needless to say, these field hands were very grateful, as were the landowners.

TWO WEEKS BEFORE I was born, German panzers entered Luxemburg and sliced through the Ardennes in Belgium and the Netherlands. On May 17, 1940, General Guderian's panzer divisions made a dash for the Channel, only to stop when their fuel was exhausted. After failed offensives by the British and French on May 22, the British decided to evacuate from the Channel ports.

As these events were unfolding, 1,500 kilometers to the east in Modrynec, Natalka Martyniuk went into labor. I arrived around 3:00 a.m. on May 25, 1940, precisely nine months after Father returned from Bereza-Kartuzka. I was thus conceived in Ukraine but born in German-occupied Poland. During the war, however, my birth certificate was lost, so to this day I, like President Obama, am unable to produce an original birth certificate showing when and where I was born.

A year later, on June 21, 1941, my mother, Natalia, gave birth to my sister, Ivanka, also in Modrynec. The next day, another earth-shattering event took place, probably one of the most fateful military engagements since Napoleon invaded Russia in 1812. Three million troops of the German Wehrmacht invaded the Soviet Union.

4. Hitler Invades the Soviet Union

A NIAGARA OF WORDS has been written about Operation Barbarossa, the German invasion of the Soviet Union on June 22, 1941. The Wehrmacht, under the command of Field Marshals Von Leeb in the north and Von Bock in the center, sliced through Soviet lines like a hot knife through butter. In the south, the German *Schwerpunkt* was led by Field Marshall Von Rundstedt, and on July 7, German panzers "blitzed" their way to Berdichiv, three hundred kilometers into the Soviet Ukraine. From then on, the Soviet position in Ukraine deteriorated rapidly.

To my father Roman Martyniuk, the invasion was no surprise. From his vantage point west of the Molotov-Ribbentrop demarcation line, the buildup of the German military was evident. Despite their efforts to camouflage deployment, only the blind and deaf could ignore what was coming. The German army rolled through Galicia with lightning speed, and when the panzers reached the Dnipro River, Roman felt it was safe to return home to Kamianka, now free of the dreaded Bolsheviks.

Back home in Kamianka, Father now faced the question of how to survive. By chance, his friend Alexander "Oleksa" Nakonechny learned that there was an opportunity to purchase a franchise to distribute leather in Kamianka and twenty-seven villages in the county. Father had a knack for business, but starting one required cash. He turned to the savings bank in Kamianka and, with the help of two close friends who cosigned for him, got a loan. Soon, the leather goods shop was up and running.

As this was wartime, scarce goods like leather were rationed. To obtain such products, German authorities issued ration cards called *Bezugsscheine*.

Farmers could get them when they brought in grain, potatoes, or meat. The cards often served as cash, and that was how a lot of trade was conducted. Unlike the Soviets, it was in the interests of the German administration to keep things as normal as possible, and this was their way of keeping *Ordnung*—order—and the system worked.

Demand for leather goods was high, and Father's business prospered. On most days before he opened the doors at 8:00 a.m., there was a long line of customers waiting. To help with the store, he engaged his brother Oleksa and other men. Our family moved into an apartment above the shop, and with a place to live and enough to eat, life was not only tolerable but comfortable. We even had a nanny, one of my mother's nieces, Emilia, who was fourteen at the time. We called her Mil'ka. My sister and I saw her as our second mother, until the fateful summer of 1944 when we had to leave Kamianka.

TIMES WERE TURBULENT, and the destinies of different people diverged. The fate of Roman's boyhood friend Oleksa Motyl was a riveting example.(Oleksa was the father of Alexander Motyl, the political scientist whom I mention in my introduction.) Both grew up in the village of Tadani, seven kilometers from Kamianka. Tadani was one of the villages that prided itself on having a library/reading room. This meant that the young inhabitants tended to be literate and politically informed. For a small village overlooking the beautiful river Buh, it produced a disproportionate number of historically aware, patriotic, religious, and dedicated young men who were subject to being rounded up for "dangerous" political activity and resistance to the Soviet agenda.[28]

In the mid-1920s, Roman and Oleksa had attended the gymnasium in Kamianka. During most of the school year, they stayed with relatives in the town, but often they walked the seven kilometers to and from the school. Kamianka and Tadani are connected by the river Buh, and during the winter months when the fast-flowing river froze solid, they were in the habit of covering this distance on ice skates. It was a fast and enjoyable jaunt. Father's memoir described a riveting episode that took place during the winter of

---

[28]   In 1992, *National Geographic* ran an article on the newly acquired independence of Ukraine and posted a map of Ukraine pointing out major cities such as Lviv, Kyiv, Chernihiv, and Odessa. Included on the map was an obscure name of a place no one ever heard about, Tadani. A *National Geographic* photographer, Tanya Mykhailyshyn-D'Avignon, whose father hailed from Tadani, put Tadani on the map of Ukraine.

1925 that is worth mentioning because it was an incident that cemented their friendship for the rest of their lives.

> After school we fastened our screw-on skates to our shoes and headed home. On one occasion, after I put my skates on I noticed that Oleksa had trouble with his. Suddenly I heard him shouting for help and as I looked back I realized that he had fallen through one of the spots where the ice was thin.
>
> Oleksa fell into an *osukha*, a spot where the river didn't freeze completely because the fast-flowing current kept the ice thin. Knowing that the edges of an *osukha* are dangerous, I had to think quickly. Very carefully I broke off some of the thin ice along the edge with one of my ice-skates and checked its thickness with my hand. Then I lay flat on the ice and extended my hand to Oleksa who was at risk of going under the ice. Worse, if the ice broke there was a real danger that both of us would be dragged into the hole. As I stretched out my hand to Oleksa I slowly pulled him out of the icy river. Safely on the bank, I made him take off his wet garments, gave him my warm jacket and told him to run home as fast as he could. In the meantime, I continued to skate to Tadani to warn his parents that Oleksa was on the way. I knew that Oleksa was exhausted and I feared that if he stopped along the way he might freeze. Luckily he arrived at the village at about the same time I did. His parents dressed him in dry clothes, gave him some hot tea and put him under warm covers. The next day he acted as if nothing had happened.

IN THE 1930s, Roman and Oleksa pursued different career paths. Roman split his time between his business and his involvement in the nationalist struggle against the Polish regime, while Oleksa decided to study law. In the fall of 1939, at the same time Roman crossed the Soviet-German frontier into German-occupied Poland, Oleksa returned to Lviv to complete his law studies. In his memoir, Oleksa wrote that this was a very tense period, and study of law was not on the students' minds. They believed that it was only a matter of time before a war erupted between Germany and the Soviet Union. In May 1940, they learned from the BBC that the German army had invaded France, and after France fell, most expected that Germany would turn eastward.

Soon, Oleksa interned in a Lviv criminal court and then was assigned to work as an auditor at the People's Commissariat of Justice in Ternopil. After one of his assignments in a district where the *Banderivtsi*—Banderites—were active, Oleksa discovered that his colleague Kostiv had been taken away by the NKVD. Soon, another friend, Slavko, disappeared, and since Oleksa was close to both of them, he was convinced that he would be next.

On Sunday morning, June 22, 1941, the German Wehrmacht attacked the Soviet Union along a three-thousand-kilometer front. Oleksa and a few friends, believing that the Germans had come to rescue Ukraine from Soviet tyranny, once out of earshot of the NKVD, welcomed such news with a resounding "hurrah." But the Germans were still far away, and to avoid suspicion, they were obliged to report to the law office the following day. The atmosphere was quiet and tense; no one knew what to say. Unexpectedly, Oleksa received an order to report to the local army barracks for induction into the Soviet Army. He got a short haircut and a uniform and, in a matter of a few hours, was transformed from a law clerk to an infantry soldier in the Red Army.

When Oleksa Motyl and his newly formed unit were crossing the river Seret, they heard the drone of German airplanes. This was the beginning of a chaotic retreat east, first on foot and then by train to Kyiv, where he was put to work picking vegetables on a collective farm. In August, the unit was sent to Myrhorod and then toward Poltava. As Oleksa's reserve unit maneuvered east of Dnipro, the men were unaware of the events that were playing out around them. Oleksa was one of the million men of the Red Army concentrated in the area around Kyiv, a city Stalin ordered Marshal Budenny to hold at all costs.

In August, the Wehrmacht encircled this huge pocket by a giant pincer movement from the south and north, tightening the noose around Kyiv. By mid-September, the ring closed, the largest encirclement achieved by either side during the entire campaign. Six hundred thousand Soviet troops were taken prisoners of war.

What appeared to be a resounding success, in retrospect, turned out to be one of Hitler's most egregious military blunders. Years later, having read a great deal about this crucial decision, I discovered that the encirclement of the Kyiv pocket delayed the offensive on Moscow by about a month. Eventually, the Wehrmacht reached Moscow where they were stopped by Stalin's ally, General Winter. The German army froze at the gates of Moscow, and for all practical purposes, the war was lost.

Motyl was among the six hundred thousand POWs caught in the pocket. The Germans were so surprised by their success, they did not know what to do with such a massive number of POWs. They put some on westbound trains to an unknown destination and uncertain future. On one of these trains, Motyl heard from a Ukrainian translator that the Germans would be releasing prisoners from Western Ukraine. When they reached Kirovohrad, this turned out to be true. They were fed one last meal, given papers saying that they were being released from German jurisdiction, and allowed to go home by whatever means they could find.

In his memoir, Motyl wrote,

> Overjoyed, we organized into groups, and began the long trek home. People were generous, feeding us and providing accommodation, and by the end of October, I made it to Lviv and then to Kamianka.

After four months of tortuous meandering through central Ukraine, Motyl returned home to Tadani at approximately the same time my father returned home from his twenty-month exile in *Kholmshchyna*, the Kholm region. Although neither Roman nor Oleksa mentioned this in their memoirs, it must have been a joyful reunion, the first of many to come in the coming years.

THE GERMANS WERE SPLIT on how to deal with the Ukrainians. The vast majority of the population was relieved to see the Soviets leave, but disoriented by the rapid turn of events. Most engaged in watchful waiting, a hiatus that lasted until September 1941, when the German campaign against Ukrainian national assertion began in earnest. The instrument used for the task was the *Einsatzgruppen*. They struck the cadres of the nascent Ukrainian national movement at the same time as they initiated the slaughter of the Jews.

Oleksa Motyl noted that German intentions became clear very quickly. The Germans viewed the occupied countries as a source of grain and foodstuffs for the Reich, and a labor pool for its military-industrial machine. At first, recruitment of laborers was voluntary, but, eventually, it became forced. Suspicion of the Germans was followed by distrust and, finally, opposition and outright resistance in the form of the UPA (Ukrainian Insurgent Army).

After the Germans lost the crucial tank battle at Kursk in July 1943, they were visibly demoralized. "Several things happened simultaneously," Motyl writes. "Deportation of young people for work in Germany increased, the activity of the underground movements, both UPA and Bolshevik, intensified, and the Ukrainian SS Galicia Division came into being. At the same time, the Gestapo began arresting suspect Ukrainians. For many, the choice was between joining the growing ranks of the UPA or certain death at the hands of the Gestapo or the bestial Bolshevik partisans."

Motyl continued,

> Worse off were the Jews. According to the regime's thinking, they were not humans and should be eliminated. From the outset, Jews were herded into ghettos, separated from the general population, where they were ordered to form so-called *Judenräte* with their own police.[29]

> The majority of the population was ambivalent concerning the fate of the Jews. They were neither overjoyed nor did they shed tears. By this time the nerves of the people were so shattered by the atrocities of both the occupiers that there was no strength left to act or react. In our village Tadani, there was never any question of informing on the Jews. On the contrary, we tried to help them by providing food.

In the fall of 1943, the Gestapo ordered the Ukrainian police to carry a pogrom of Jews in the Kamianka region. The police insisted that they were merely an auxiliary force and refused. A policeman who witnessed this told Oleksa that, on previous occasions when only five policemen with small sidearms and five rounds each escorted Jews in groups of one hundred, none of the Jews attempted to make a run for it.

Another eyewitness in Kamianka who confirmed these scenes was Daria Hasiuk-Markus, only nine at the time. Daria recounted how the helpless Jews were taken down to the river Buh to certain death, and none of them tried to

---

[29]   During World War II, the Germans established Jewish councils, called *Judenräte*. These Jewish municipal administrations were required to ensure that Nazi orders and regulations were implemented. Jewish council members also sought to provide basic community services for ghettoized Jewish populations. Forced to implement Nazi policy, the Jewish councils remain a controversial and delicate subject.

escape even though there were not many guards. Motyl explains that "these people were emotionally exhausted to the point that they passively accepted their fate. There was also the question of where does one escape to?"

My father's memoir noted that after he and my mother had returned home from exile in the *Generalgouvernement* with two infant children, "arrests were almost a daily occurrence. Ukrainian nationalists and Jews were rounded up, put on covered trucks, and taken to the forest where they were shot and buried." To add to the tension, Bolshevik partisan detachments began to infiltrate Western Ukraine, committing unspeakable acts of violence against Ukrainian civilians. One story that sticks in my mind was an incident recounted by my father's brother, my uncle Oleksa. Bolshevik partisans broke into a village near Kamianka and tortured a man who supported the Ukrainian partisans. To set an example, the NKVD tied him to a table and sawed off his leg with a regular wood saw. Later in DP camps and even in the United States, I heard of similar atrocities Bolshevik partisans perpetrated on local Ukrainians. Hearing such stories after the war provoked many nightmares and shaped my opinion about Bolsheviks.

During the winter of 1942–1943, the German army was stopped and trapped in Stalingrad, and in July 1943, the Wehrmacht was broken at the gargantuan tank battle of Kursk, a setback from which they never recovered. By March 1944, the front was only 150 kilometers away from Kamianka. Panic set in. Everyone knew what would happen if the Soviets came. They had had a taste of Soviet "liberation" during the twenty-one-month occupation between 1939 and 1941.[30]

---

[30]   The Soviet regime had been especially inhumane during the twenty-one-month occupation of Western Ukraine from September 17, 1939, to the end of June 1941. Mass arrests and deportations to Siberia and Central Asia first targeted Poles and Jews, and later Ukrainians. According to Polish sources, in 1940–41, one million people were deported of whom nearly half (40 percent) were Ukrainians. The violence and brutality culminated in a massacre of twenty-five thousand mostly Ukrainian political prisoners in Western Ukraine in eight days after the German invasion on June 22, 1941. Although this was one of the greatest single atrocities committed by the Soviet State, there is little mention of it in contemporary historiography. A sourcebook edited by Ksenya Kiebuzinski and Alexander Motyl, *The Great West Ukrainian Prison Massacre of 1941* (Amsterdam University Press, 2017), fills the gap and sheds considerable light on this tragic chapter of Ukrainian history.

For Roman and hundreds of thousands of Ukrainians, there was only one choice: flee west. In March, he relocated his family to the town of Turka in the Carpathian Mountains not far from the Polish and Slovak border. On July 12, he got news that his father, Petro Martyniuk, had died, and he decided to attend his funeral. He almost did not make it back. As the Germans were retreating, Soviet military planes were already strafing the roads and trains around Lviv. This is the way it would be until April 1945.

5. How I Survived the Eastern Front

DURING THE WINTER OF 1943-44, gloom and despair permeated the German army. Like the Huns who overwhelmed eastern Germanic Goths west of the Don nearly eighteen centuries before, the Bolshevik horde was forcing the German armies out of south-eastern Ukraine. By spring of 1944, signs of impending defeat were everywhere. The belief that Germany had lost the war led to a massive exodus of Ukrainians, who had a foretaste of Communist "liberation."

On June 21, 1944, the day my sister Ivanka turned three, the Red Army launched its summer offensive. The spearhead of the attack came at Brody, some two hundred kilometers east of Lviv, one of the most intense military actions fought by the Fourteenth Waffen SS Galicia Division, a division attached to the Thirteenth German Army Corps. The division, ordered to plug the hole in the front at Brody, had the task of defending Lviv. The division was hopelessly outmanned and outgunned but nevertheless fought bravely, even after its German commander, General Freitag, fled the battlefield. On July 18, the Fourteenth was surrounded, but part of it managed to break out of the encirclement. Of the twelve thousand men who fought at Brody, most were killed, wounded, or taken as prisoners. Only three thousand managed to return to German lines. Some joined the Ukrainian Insurgent Army; others escaped west. Forty years later, on the ski slopes of Switzerland, I met one of the men who broke out of the bloody encirclement, Orest "Gogo" Slupchynskyj, who would became a friend and ski partner.

Despite its defeat at Brody, the Fourteenth Division delayed the Red Army advance on Lviv by several days, allowing tens of thousands to escape the Soviet avalanche. My father, taking his wife and children, was among those who fled Lviv on one of the last trains for Turka near the Polish/Slovak border.

I CAN GIVE no real account of what transpired during the summer of 1944. My memory was only beginning to coalesce. Most of all, I recall the strong odor of the coal-burning engine puffing and pulling the overloaded train through the bucolic Slovak countryside of undulating hills, forest, fields, a village here, and a running stream there. It was warm, and the wheat and barley were ready for harvesting.

The train, packed with refugees, crawled on a route that was never direct. Sporadic bombardment of roads and railways disrupted the main arteries, causing trains to be rerouted, but we were moving west. After our train crossed southern Slovakia, it entered Hungary. In Miskolc, Father wrote, "We transferred to another train that took us to Budapest and still another to Bratislava." Roman believed that as long as we moved westward, we would eventually encounter the American army, but that was still some way off. We kept moving until we reached Trnava, fifty kilometers northeast of Bratislava. At Trnava, a walled town of many churches and a Jesuit university, our train came to a stop. It was mid-August, and the front had stabilized along the Vistula.

When the Russians halted on the Vistula, Father felt it was safe to remain in Trnava. Refugees like us were put up in the local schoolhouse, which provided a temporary shelter, but Roman had to find a way to sustain the family. Aware that most of the able-bodied men had been drafted into the German military, he looked for work. The local administration directed him to a nearby *Bauernhof*, a one-thousand-hectare estate with a manor, whose manager was a friendly Ukrainian named Vysochansky. Vysochansky needed someone to manage the grain depot and take care of the estate's sizeable beehive operation, and Father, qualified in both, was hired on the spot.

At the end of October, the Russians opened up Operation Budapest, and on November 1, they were already in Miskolc in the center of Hungary. As the front got nearer, the German authorities ordered all refugees to be moved to Germany. The German war machine needed laborers. Knowing that in such situations families were broken apart, Roman became extremely concerned. The Slovak police officer who ordered us to pack up for departure sensed that we were not eager to be shipped to Germany and quietly suggested that Father might wish to join the local Communist insurgency. Many Slovaks unfamiliar with Bolshevik ways were looking forward to Soviet "liberation." They could not understand why we were fleeing Communist liberators and doggedly asked, *"A cegosce ucikali?"* (Why did you leave?) Your country was liberated."

"You will soon discover what it means to be liberated by the Communists," Mother replied. She told the story so many times, it became etched in my memory.

For the time being, this sector of the front had stabilized, and we made it to our next destination, Breitensee, on the outskirts of Vienna. When we crossed the Slovak/Austrian border, the German authorities directed all refugees to the transit camp at Strasshof, a town twenty-five kilometers east of Vienna. In June 1944, it was a concentration camp for twenty thousand Jews from Hungary, the result of an agreement made to spare Hungarian Jews in an exchange called Blood for Goods. Jews sent to Strasshof were made to work as forced laborers in industry and agriculture in eastern Austria. Miraculously, almost all of them survived the war.

> Before entering Austria, we were ordered to undergo quarantine in Strasshof, which involved having all excess hair cut off and taking a shower, followed by delousing and disinfection with DDT. Understandably, the refugees did this with considerable trepidation. After all, it was a concentration camp for Jews. When we finished, to our great surprise, we were taken to clean quarters, given coffee and bread, and later a serving of thick soup.

Relieved to leave the Strasshof quarantine chambers alive, Roman wrote,

> We were put on a list of families to be shipped to Hamburg, which meant a journey to northern Germany under perilous conditions; trains were moving targets for allied fighters and bombers. To avoid deportation, I decided to move the family to different quarters. For the time being, we got a reprieve, but I knew that sooner or later we would be discovered, so in the hope of concealing our trail, I reported to the local *Arbeitsamt*— labor office—as a recent arrival trying to register for work. The *Arbeitsamt* directed me to the village of Grinzing, northwest of Vienna, where I was to report to work as a farmhand.

A wagon dropped us off in an empty barn at an estate where we slept on hay for the next few nights. As a child, I did not consider this a hardship and vaguely recall it being fun. Sleeping in a barn was better than a labor camp in bombed-out Hamburg.

Grinzing today is a charming town at the foot of the Kahlenberg wine country, but during the last years of the war, the fertile rolling hills were a bountiful vegetable garden. Father was assigned to a crew to unload wagons of fifty-kilogram (110 pounds) sacks of grain. The work in Grinzing, according to Father, was backbreaking, but compared to the fate that awaited us in northern Germany, our existence was peaceful and trouble-free.

After a week, the *Verwalter*, the administrator, insisted that my mother must go to work picking tomatoes. Roman protested that she could not leave two children without care and wrote a letter to the local authorities complaining about sleeping in the barn. Eventually, an inspector came and told us that we would be moved to proper living quarters, but Natalka, children or not, had to report for work. Thinking quickly, Roman took Natalka to the local doctor, telling him that Natalka was ill with asthma and unable to work. The doctor agreed and wrote a note to the *Verwalter* that Natalka was suffering from asthma and must be excused from work. When Father showed this note to the *Verwalter*, the man got even angrier and told us to pack up our belongings and report to the *Arbeitsamt*.

Roman was given several addresses where work was available, most involving grueling fieldwork on the large farmsteads. By chance, he chose a medium-sized farm near Breitensee, a district in the western part of Vienna.

Breitensee turned out to be a good choice. The owners of the estate, an elderly couple, the Hanaceks, had been living on the farmstead with their son, his wife, and child. When the son Albert was drafted into the army, the farm was shorthanded. The Hanaceks were Czech, and the old man spoke the language quite well. He employed two other workers who took care of a pair of oxen, three horses, six head of cattle and a few swine. My job was to plow the fields and prepare them for sowing. In late fall, Albert came home on furlough, and the two of us worked in the field. He brought with him horror stories from the Russian front of bloody fighting, intolerable cold, persistent hunger, and relentless pounding of Red Army artillery. He dreaded facing another winter on the Russian front.

Quite often two-engine American airplanes circled over and for no apparent reason strafed workers in the fields. These overflies became common, so we conditioned ourselves to listen to approaching airplanes. If we heard them in the distance, we dropped everything and ran away from the oxen team pulling the plow to find cover.

January and February 1945 were very cold, with temperatures as low as minus twenty-five degrees Centigrade (minus thirteen degrees Fahrenheit), and until the middle of March, temperatures at night fell below zero degree Centigrade (thirty-two degrees Fahrenheit). I had my first memory of playing in deep snow. One of the treasures we had acquired at that time was a hand-cranked Singer sewing machine that Mother used to make our warm coats, an instrument that served us for many years even after we emigrated to Chicago.

OUR FAMILY WAS LUCKY to be in a rural area. While people in besieged Vienna were cold and starving, our life at the Breitensee *Bauernhof* was safe and relatively comfortable. In the spring of 1945, after the Sixth Panzer Army counterattack in the direction of Lake Balaton got stuck in the sea of mud, the Germans began to pull back, and Russians launched yet another massive offensive. When the news reached us at Breitensee, Father prepared to relocate the family further west.

At the beginning of 1945, the United States Army Air Force (USAAF) began to attack the German lines by daylight. I recall the droning of hundreds of American bombers with their fighter escorts in the sky. Fortunately, we were far away from strategic targets. On Monday, March 12, 1945, that changed. Vienna underwent a massive raid, the biggest thus far. Eight hundred bombers and two hundred fighter planes of the US Air Force set out to hit the Floridsdorf refinery. The refinery received no severe hits, but the center of the city, only fifteen flight seconds away from Floridsdorf, was heavily damaged. In that raid, the Vienna State Opera House was burned, and the city was deprived of electricity, gas, and water. Thousands of civilians died in the attack, with hundreds buried in rubble and three hundred thousand left homeless. Father's friends told us that the air in the city was permeated with the nauseating stench of unburied corpses.

Father described this raid with great accuracy.

> Being ten kilometers from the Floridsdorf refinery on the Danube, and eight from the city center, we felt the earth trembling. Reverberations from explosions rattled the windows of our building and even the farmstead's iron gates jangled. The 12

March bombardment of Vienna was a clear signal that the time had come to move. With the benefit of hindsight, this was a good decision. Three weeks later to the day, the Soviets opened their offensive to capture Vienna.

On April 4, the Red Horde, like the Turks in 1683, was at the Gates of Vienna, poised to strike with the incongruously named Third Ukrainian Front. Among the city's population, ravaged by bombardment and starvation, panic was beginning to spread. Only this time, there was no hope of a Jan III Sobieski, king of Poland, appearing on the westerly horizon with his force of five thousand battle-worthy Ukrainian Cossacks, ready to rescue the capital of the Hapsburg Empire. By April 14, the garrison of Vienna had ceased to exist. The bombardment had reduced much of the city's beautiful center to rubble. Panic gripped the capital. Roads out of the capital were clogged with masses determined to save themselves from the Russians.

As soon as Father learned that the Soviet avalanche was rolling toward Vienna, he decided to move the family, yet again. Expecting the worst and aware that the trains were not reliable, Roman managed to acquire a horse and a wagon from a Greek Catholic priest, Father Solovij, who owned a spare wagon and two horses. It was truly the hand of God intervening at the most critical moment. Roman loaded the wagon with belongings and provisions we stocked up during our months at Breitensee and covered them with a tarpaulin. My sister and I, wrapped in a down comforter, sat in the back of the wagon. We thought it was jolly fun.

For a while, we traveled with the priest, a widower, with his daughter and son-in-law. The priest told Father that if he had remained in Ukraine, he would have been either deported to Siberia or shot, and that is why he decided to flee. Unfortunately, while on the road somewhere west of Vienna, he was killed by an American bomb. A little later, his son-in-law was killed in a similar manner, and the only person left from that family was his daughter, Maria.

The Soviet forces were literally like wolves at our heels. By mid-April, they completed the encirclement of Vienna, a pincer movement that closed at Tulln, a town on the Danube forty kilometers west of Vienna. Now they were in a position to push further west along both sides of the Danube. The only question was how far they would advance.

For our family, as well as for hundreds of thousands of refugees fleeing Russian "liberators," the last two months of the war were the most dangerous.

We were caught in a three-pronged vise: the Red Army advancing from the east, the remnants of the Wehrmacht troops moving from the west, and the American air force dropping their lethal loads from above. Ironically, the greatest danger came from the hundreds of American B-24 and B-17 bombers and P-38 Lightning fighters hitting German convoys on the road used by us and thousands of other refugees. I vaguely remember hearing the rumble of Russian artillery and, at night, the flashes and whining of Katyusha rockets. Their effect on the German troops was demoralizing. The roadside was clogged with wagons, hand-pulled carts, and dirty, exhausted refugees plodding along on foot, knowing what awaited them if they did not get away. The situation was chaotic. Random violence, carnage, and rape sanctioned by the Red Army were the order of the day.

ON APRIL 1, 1945, six hundred kilometers to the northwest, Allied forces had penetrated to the heart of Germany. American tanks reached Munster and Bielefeld, and soon the industrial Ruhr region was surrounded. While Soviet forces were besieging Vienna, the American Third Army under General George Patton thrust into Thuringia in central Germany. Nothing prevented American troops from making a dash for Berlin. But at this crucial point, Eisenhower chose not to head for Berlin. Instead, the Americans made a stand on the Elbe, sixty-five kilometers west of Berlin. At the same time, he ordered the American Seventh Army to thrust south toward the Danube Valley to break up the mythical southern redoubt.

On his own initiative, without consulting the military and political branches, Eisenhower sent a message to Stalin stating that US forces had no intention of advancing to Berlin. The Chief of Staff of the US Army, George Marshall, overrode remonstrations by the British and endorsed Eisenhower's decision. The dying Roosevelt, forever trying to placate his friend "Uncle Joe," did not intervene. This, of course, reflected the naïve desire of the US State Department to conciliate Moscow.

The action by Eisenhower, which caused Churchill to react with fury, proved controversial over the next sixty years. Many historians saw it as a strategic blunder that gave Russians a free hand to take Berlin, which they did in a vengeful and bloody battle for the capital. The Allies could have accomplished this with far fewer casualties, because the Germans did not resist the Western Allies with anything like the ferocity they displayed against the Red Army. At times, the vagaries of war play out in unpredictable ways. Curiously, Eisenhower's decision to order the American Seventh Army to thrust south toward the Danube was a stroke of luck for our family. It brought the American army into Bavaria, which was our destination.

MY FIRST CLEAR MEMORY is of the droning of American bombers, like the crescendo of a drum roll—first, distant and muffled and then louder and vibrating, shuddering, and, finally, dissipating in the distance, quiet again. I will never forget that unique droning sound.

It was the spring of 1945, several days after we left the vicinity of Vienna, and the USAAF was carrying out bombing raids on almost a daily basis. Some days, there were two or three waves of B-17s and B-24s flying at high altitude, heading for the front. The lower-flying P-38 fighter-bomber escorts often strafed targets of opportunity. The German convoys we were sharing the road with were such targets. People on the main road left their wagons and horses on the road and jumped into the nearest ditch or ran for the nearest woods for cover. After coming out from hiding, some would find their wagons overturned and their horses bloody, dead or dying from shrapnel wounds.

The operating environment of the B-24s was from eighteen thousand to twenty-eight thousand feet. The B-17s flew higher and were more difficult to see. I was able to distinguish between the bulky belly-shaped B-24s and the sleek silhouettes of the B-17s. One needed binoculars to see the B-17s, but the B-24s were clearly visible to the naked eye. Whenever we heard the distinctive drone of bombers approaching, we paused to count the airplanes. I remember this quite vividly because this was my first lesson in counting. I learned to count ten planes and then twenty, thirty, all the way to a hundred. The bombers came in groups of a hundred or so. A hundred would pass, and then another hundred would appear and so on, day after day.

Another picture implanted in my brain was that of aluminum foil strips falling from the sky like sparklers. I thought they looked pretty, but to question what they were never entered my mind. Some of them landed in nearby fields, and we were able to pick them up and use them to decorate items or toys. Many years later, I discovered that these shiny objects descending from the sky were chaff, radar countermeasures composed of small strips of aluminum to confuse or neutralize German antiaircraft defenses. I may not have been aware of the war, but I vividly recall the images of glistening chaff.

All the main roads were clogged by masses of refugees trying to put kilometers between themselves and the approaching Red Army. Allied bombers had completely disrupted railroad communications, and trains had stopped running. Refugees fled on foot, carrying suitcases or lugging hand-pulled carts or wagons. In this respect, we were lucky. We traveled on a horse-drawn wagon. The disadvantage was that whenever a German military column of lorries came in the opposite direction, we had to stop and move to the side of the road, which made for very slow progress. Worse, if the military column caught the eye of a P-38 fighter-bomber, we became part of the target. On rare occasions, heavy bombers dropped excess bombs on the convoys from higher altitudes. This, of course, could have a devastating effect on both the military and civilians. I remember my parents pulling my sister and me into a roadside ditch for shelter more than once, and distracting us with the counting game.

We traversed Austria from east to west following a rough trajectory from Vienna to Sankt Pölten and Melk, and we entered Germany at Passau. The rumbling of the Soviet artillery was no longer audible, though no one knew if the Russian avalanche had stopped or if they were pausing to regroup for another assault. Stalin was in the driver's seat, and with German resistance collapsing, Soviet tanks could be on top of us within hours.

During these last chaotic weeks of the Third Reich, the Germans took desperate measures. One was an attempt to strengthen the *Volkssturm*, the People's Defense Force. According to a directive issued by General Guderian in January 1945, all able-bodied men between the ages of sixteen and sixty were to be drafted into the *Volkssturm*. Recruits were given rudimentary training in the use of infantry weapons, but as a fighting force, they proved to be woefully ineffective. Most of the units were used for guard duty along strategic crossings and bridges, or for digging defensive trenches.

Somewhere near Passau, the road police stopped columns of refugees so that armed men could scrutinize the caravan for men able to carry a weapon. A patrol inspecting our column ordered a group of men to report for induction into the *Volkssturm*. Father was among those chosen. Resisting such an order would have had immediate and harsh consequences, so no one protested. He was forced to leave the family in the caravan of wagons and report at a rendezvous point where men of various nationalities gathered. The Germans were no longer fussy about who could or could not serve the Reich. We were no longer the loathed *Untermenschen*. At last, we got equal treatment under the Nazis.

But this was not the German army of 1941 or 1942. It was April 1945. Any remaining sense of discipline seemed to have evaporated along with any hope of winning the war, and no one wished to be among the last casualties. All of the regular troops were at the front, and those that were left were teenagers or old men. With discipline lax, orders confusing and contradictory, recruiting efforts were carried out haphazardly and half-heartedly, and when Father appeared at the appointed meeting place, only a few men in uniform showed up. He sized up the situation and decided to slip away at the first opportunity. That same afternoon, while the escorts were preoccupied, he quietly slithered away into the mass of refugees. All of this must have transpired over a period of a few hours because that same day, he managed to rejoin the family a little further down the road where he had left us. If he hadn't taken the risk, it is likely he would have been cannon fodder on the eastern front, or whatever remained of it.

On April 30, Hitler committed suicide, but the news did not get around, and Germany had not yet formally surrendered. With spring in the air, our wagon continued to roll toward Vilshofen an der Donau, near the Lower Bavarian-Upper Austrian Danube gorge. The stream of refugees, unaware that the war was nearly over, continued to move west like an unstoppable herd of wildebeest. Suddenly, a few kilometers east of Vilshofen, a town where the rivers Vils and Wolfach enter the Danube, the flow of refugees came to a halt. A rumor spread that the *Volkssturm* had mined the main bridge across the Vils. Others said that the Germans were looking for able-bodied men to induct into the *Volkssturm*. The fear of being trapped in a vise between the river and oncoming Russian troops was profoundly terrifying. People were alarmed, and some panicked.

Father did not wait to find out what caused the halt. He took a chance on a four-kilometer detour to a place called Grafenmühl, where there was a small bridge across the Vils. He broke off from the main road and guided our horse and wagon along a country road to bypass the blockaded bridge. Soon, other wagons followed. When we got to the bridge at Grafenmühl, he saw that it was guarded by a few Czech auxiliaries.

"Where are you going?" they asked.

"We are trying to get across the river to meet members of our family waiting on the main road with a military pass allowing us to proceed to Plattling," Roman improvised.

The guards accepted his story. By this time, they knew all was lost and there was no point in preventing people from crossing the river.

"You can cross the bridge, but I must warn you that it is mined. If you stick to the right side and move slowly, there is a good chance you will not detonate the charge."

This was probably one of the tensest moments Father faced during the entire war. Risk the crossing or turn back? No one knew what the military situation was like. We had not heard Russian artillery for several days, but that did not mean we were safe. Father had only one goal: advance west until we encountered Americans. He decided to take the risk, got off the wagon, and slowly led the horse across the bridge. The relief must have been overwhelming.

Encouraged by our example, other wagons followed. A few families got across, but when we were a safe distance beyond the bridge, we heard a massive explosion. When Father and Mother looked back, the bridge and the people on it were gone.

We continued to advance along the Danube in a westerly direction, and on May 5, 1945, we reached the town of Plattling, where we encountered the first units of the American Twelfth Army Group. On May 8, 1945, in Berlin, Nazi Germany officially surrendered. The war was over, and the Third Reich had ceased to exist.

The news of the war's end reached our cluster of four families, consisting of fifteen adults and children, near the town of Landau. The nightmare had finally ended, and we welcomed the news with an overwhelming sense of relief and joy.[31]

I can only speculate about the sensations my parents must have felt at that time. However, I can describe the sensations that registered in my memory with peculiar clarity. All of a sudden, the noise of war stopped. The rolling thunder of heavy artillery, the sirens followed by the droning of bombers, the rumble and clanging of panzers and motorized artillery, all ceased. The trees were in bloom, and the countryside had turned spring green, but for some odd reason, the odor of war remained in my head: the pungent exhaust of lorries, the odor of benzene and diesel, hay, horse manure, and, most unforgettably, the stench of rotting flesh.

Today, I realize how blessed we were to have escaped the Red Horde. A large segment of our extended family was not so lucky. They were condemned to the horrors of life in the Communist prison of nations for the rest of their lives. The most unfortunate ones lie buried in the wastes of the Siberian Gulag.

---

[31]   The four families included Evhen Aponiuk, his wife, and daughter, Iryna, who settled in Edmonton, Canada, and a relative, Tymko; the Longin Markov family (four members), the family of Mykhailo Daczkewycz—three members, including their son, Roman Daczkewycz, a childhood friend I grew up with in Chicago in the early 1950s—and us.

6. Family in the Gulag

MEMOIRS ARE THE ESSENCE of history. They are the building blocks you need to understand historical events. They have the power to bring the past to life. What follows is based on accounts given to me by my uncle Dozyk, my father's youngest brother, and other members of the family, on my visits to Ukraine following the collapse of the USSR.

At the end of WWII, my father, Roman Martyniuk, and his younger brother, Oleksa, ended up in Southern Germany, Roman in Regensburg and Oleksa in Neu-Ulm, while all the other members of the Martyniuk clan remained in Soviet-occupied Ukraine. If Roman and Oleksa lived through difficult times during the last year of the war, the fate of those who remained was a nightmare beyond words. I can convey only a small part of the hell they lived through for many years.

The photo taken in 1937 shows a large happy and relatively prosperous family. There were four brothers and two sisters. A third sister, Anastasia, not in the photo, emigrated to Canada in the 1920s, and at the time the photo was taken, she was living in the United States. A fifth brother, Mykhailo, had been tragically killed in a bomb explosion at the end of WWI.

The Martyniuk clan c. 1937. Standing—Uncle Oleksander
(Oleksa), Aunt Paraskevia, Uncle Petro.
Sitting: My father Roman, Grandfather Petro, Grandmother Maria (nee
Dudka), Aunt Kateryna and her husband, M. Khoma. Sitting on the stool
front center is Uncle Teodoziy (Dozyk), the Kolyma Gulag survivor.

Grandfather Petro Martyniuk, the family patriarch, although not
wealthy, was the proud owner of a fertile piece of land in Tadani, a small
village overlooking the scenic river Buh seven kilometers downstream from
Kamianka Strumilova (today Kamianka-Buzka), a medium-sized town forty
kilometers northeast of Lviv. There was something special about this place
that made some of its residents more active, resilient, hardworking, and
ambitious. A number had offspring who became successful and prominent
members of the Ukrainian diaspora in the United States.[32]

The breakthrough of the Red Army in mid-July 1944 at Brody sparked
a mass exodus. Hundreds of thousands fled west to escape the Communist
"liberators." By 1945, the eight-member Martyniuk family in the photo had
completely broken apart. After Grandfather Martyniuk was buried in July

---

[32]   The individuals include Alexander Motyl Jr., Tanya Mychailyshyn-
D'Avignon, Ivanna Martyniuk-Richardson, Daria Hasiuk-Markus, and Irena
Prytula-Petrina.

1944, only his sixty-four-year-old widow, Maria, remained in the village. Her daughters, Kasia and Paraska, were married and lived with their families near Kamianka. Maria's sons, Roman (my father) and Oleksa, fled west, and the other two, Petro and Dozyk, remained behind and soon found themselves in a quandary. They knew that sooner or later the NKVD would discover that their brothers had fled, which would have been sufficient reason for them to be deported to Siberia.[33] Dozyk, the youngest brother, having turned twenty, decided to join the Ukrainian Insurgent Army (UPA). Petro went into hiding but soon was discovered by the NKVD and taken to Lviv for interrogation. During the interrogation, he escaped by jumping out of a window when the guards were not looking. To avoid arrest and certain deportation, he changed his identity. As this was a time of enormous population movement and ensuing chaos, he managed to forge a German identity document. It displayed a painstakingly forged swastika stamp and included a new date and place of birth showing that he was one of the Ukrainians repatriated from Peremyshl' (Přemysl'), a city in the German-occupied part of Poland known as *Generalgouvernement*. After the war, Petro settled in Ivano-Frankivsk, married, and raised a family. For fear of being discovered, he did not return to his home village until 1992.

Eventually, the NKVD came to Tadani and began to ask questions. The only remaining Martyniuk in the village was the widowed grandmother Maria. Except for Dozyk, she had no idea where her sons were, and, even if she did, she probably would not have told them. Her response was unacceptable, so the NKVD arrested her, and confiscated the farmstead.

The prison in Kamianka was filled with other families from the vicinity, and the NKVD was relentless about punishing anyone supporting or even remotely associated with the UPA (which represented the majority of the people in the region). We now know that according to a March 31, 1944, order signed by Beria, the ruthless NKVD chief, all family members of soldiers in the OUN and UPA were to be arrested and deported.[34] In the fall

---

[33] NKVD, *Narodnyi Komitet Vnutreshnikh Del*, acronym for People's Commissariat of Internal Affairs, secret police during the 1930s and World War II.

[34] OUN stands for *Organizatsiya Ukrayins'kykh Natsionalistiv*, the Organization of Ukrainian Nationalists. UPA, *Ukrayinska Povstanska Armiya*, was its military wing.

of 1945, Maria Martyniuk was found guilty by a *troika*[35] and deported to the Gulag at Vorkuta in the Komi ASSR.[36] At the same time, they arrested members of at least six other families from the village, all deported to Komi with Grandmother Maria.

IN 1993, I VISITED TADANI, a picturesque village on the banks of the river Buh, for the first time since I was a child. I saw the house that belonged to my grandfather and visited the cemetery where several generations of my ancestors are buried. By yet another one of those uncanny coincidences that have peppered my life, I struck up a conversation with a couple of elderly women who still remembered the Martyniuk family. One of them was Marta Fliachyk, who, as a teenager, had been exiled to Komi along with my grandmother. After the 1953 amnesty, Marta was allowed to return home to Tadani. Although nearly fifty years had elapsed, she was able to tell me what had happened to my grandmother:

"The prisoners arrived near Vorkuta on a cattle train in the winter of 1945-46. We were dumped on a flat piece of taiga, told that this was our "new home" and given a shovel and an ax with which to build a shelter. At first, we slept on the frozen ground, and many froze to death."

Grandmother's ordeal, like that of other prisoners, was grueling, and she was less able to withstand the elements than younger people. She suffered from the cold and lack of nutrition but did not succumb immediately. She must have been a strong woman to have survived a place like Vorkuta for any length of time. Eventually, she was transferred to Ukhta and then to Lemyu, a settlement seven hundred kilometers west of Perm. Extreme cold, inadequate nutrition and exhaustion had taken their toll, and she died in Lemyu. Marta Fliachyk described her funeral as devoid of ceremony. "*Vykopaly yamu i pokhovaly.*" (We dug a hole and buried her.)

I wish I'd had more time to interview Marta, but it was a chance encounter, and I didn't anticipate writing about these events until years later.

---

[35]   A *troika* consisted of three Soviet officials who sentenced prisoners in lieu of courts during a period of mass arrests, starting in 1937.

[36]   Vorkuta and Kolyma had the distinction of being two of the harshest northern camps. Both lie near the Arctic Circle. Norilsk in the north-central part of Siberia was equally harsh, but this camp is not part of this story. Karlo Stajner's chilling memoir *7000 Days in Siberia* captures the brutal conditions of this remote Gulag.

Subsequently, I did some research and learned that the Vorkuta prison camp in the Komi Republic is known for its vast deposits of coal. At its height, the camp consisted of approximately 130 subcamps, mostly occupied by German POWs as well as prisoners from Soviet-occupied countries deemed enemies of the state. Most of them were Ukrainian nationalists or their families. Two million prisoners passed through the system there, and local historians estimate that there are two hundred thousand political prisoners buried in the permafrost in marked and unmarked graves. One of them is the grave of my grandmother, who was buried there in 1949.

THE FIRST AND ONLY TIME I met my father's youngest brother, Uncle Dozyk, was in Yevpatoria, on the Crimean peninsula, in spring 1997. I was aware that he had been sentenced to some Gulag in Siberia, but I had no knowledge of how he ended up there. Since the mid-'70s, when he was released from exile in Kazakhstan and allowed to settle in Crimea (but not in Ukraine proper), he had been living in a town called Dzankoi in the center of the peninsula.

Uncle Teodozij (Dozyk) Martyniuk, me and Dozyk's youngest
son Sashko. Photo taken in Crimea in 1997.

I made arrangements to meet with my uncle in Yevpatoria on the western shore of Crimea, where his youngest son, Alexander "Sashko" Martyniuk, was living with his wife and sons. Dozyk arrived from Dzankoi by train and was already waiting for my sister Ivanka and me in Yevpatoria. The meeting with a man whom I hardly remembered was extraordinarily moving. As a survivor of Kolyma, I expected to see a broken man, but Dozyk was a slim, sprightly, healthy-looking seventy-three-year-old with a subtle sense of humor. We began our conversation on a light note, exchanging the latest Brezhnev jokes. This was when I realized that Dozyk had a unique survival trait, a lightness of being. No matter how bad things got, he did not take it too seriously. His survivalist philosophy of life is captured by the Ukrainian saying, *"Yakos' to bude."* (Somehow we'll manage, or somehow things will turn out.) I had brought with me a small tape recorder, and during the next two days, I recorded Uncle Dozyk's narrative about his life, beginning with WWII, his incarceration in the Gulag, and his exile in Kazakhstan.

There are few things as emotionally moving as hearing a firsthand account from a Gulag survivor, let alone my Uncle Dozyk who survived the most brutal of the camps. No book or film about the Gulag can match the experience of looking into the eyes of an individual who has lived through the ghastly hell of Kolyma, especially if he happens to be a family member.

Uncle Dozyk described how for eight years, living on the verge of starvation, he was beset with a profound longing for his homeland in Galicia. *"Byly, byly, byly,"* he said. (They beat us endlessly, mercilessly, and senselessly). *"A mene vse tiahne na Ukrayinu. Tiahne povernutys' na ridnu zemliu."* (I yearned to return home, to my native land, Ukraine). I believe it was this longing, his sense of humor, and a measure of luck that helped him pull through the Gulag nightmare. Dozyk recalled his experiences calmly. It was as if he was telling the story about someone else. There was surprisingly little acrimony and bitterness in his voice. He considered himself lucky to be alive, unlike the millions whose lives had been snuffed out in the wastes of the taiga and the mines of Kolyma.

Dozyk was born in 1924 and at the age of nineteen became a courier for the UPA, when it was still in the process of forming into a cohesive fighting force. By 1944, a loose grouping of networks in Western Ukraine became part of the larger OUN organization, whose military force included some twenty thousand well-armed fighters. After the battle of Brody in July 1944, the Red Army broke through the front at Horokhiv with the objective of "liberating"

Lviv. The German retreat was so chaotic that they left behind an arsenal of ammunition and weapons, many of them new. Dozyk said this was added to the hoard of weapons they already had.

"It was time to act," Dozyk continued. "Our group of twelve young men from Tadani went underground. First, we tried to get our hands on as many weapons as possible—MG34 machineguns, MP40 submachine guns, and the new egg-shaped hand grenades. When the Germans retreated, we were 'liberated.'"

Dozyk quipped that "liberators" turned out to be "liquidators," because that is when people began to disappear. "Soon our detachment became part of a larger unit commanded by a German-trained officer with fighting experience, and all was quiet for a while. Although we continued to live in the village, our base of operations was in the forest across the marsh of the river Buh, where the NKVD rarely ventured. We had a reliable network of informers able to warn us when hostile forces were in the vicinity. On one occasion, as we were crossing the river Buh, we were spotted by a small NKVD detachment. We exchanged fire, and because they were few, we beat them off. However, it meant that we were discovered and it was only a matter of time before a larger, better-armed unit of the NKVD would show up in Tadani.

"That day came in mid-February 1945. Our informants sent a message that at 2:00 a.m. the next day, the NKVD planned to surround and raid the village. Forewarned, five of us with weapons in our hands, left the village earlier in the evening. As I stepped out of our house, I realized that it was already too late. The NKVD had taken positions along the road and surrounded the village. When they saw us, they opened fire from well-placed machine guns, and each of us ran in a different direction. The night was cold, but with bright moonlight reflecting against the white snow, visibility was good. I jumped over a fence and ran toward the cemetery. Unfortunately, the NKVD had placed a machine gun there and they started firing. Bullets whipped through the air. I returned the fire and lobbed two grenades in that direction. At the same time, one bullet hit my leather pistol belt which shattered. This one did not have my number, but the next one did. I was hit in the abdomen and fell to the ground unconscious.

"To this day I'm not sure what happened next except that the following morning I was in the Kamianka prison with an open abdominal wound and part of my intestine protruding. The officer in charge began to question me in Russian, and after a lengthy interrogation, I signed a paper and was put on a list of prisoners to be transferred to Lviv for medical treatment. Despite my wound, I was able to get around, shuffling sideways to prevent my intestines from spilling out.

"In Lviv, I ended up in the Jewish Hospital on Rappaport Street where a Polish surgeon examined my wound and asked, 'Are you a *Banderovets*, a Banderite?'"[37]

"Yes, I am," I answered.

"Hmmm," he reflected, "*nu ladno* (well, fine)," and left the examination room.

After a while, he returned. "You don't need an operation. It will heal by itself, though if you want, I can sew you up quickly but that's not going to change the outcome."

In other words, because Uncle Dozyk was a *Banderovets*, caught with a weapon in his hands, the doctor would not operate on him. He probably felt he couldn't take the risk, or perhaps in his mind, it was not worth the effort. In any event, the doctor hinted that whatever he did, Dozyk was likely to die.

But Dozyk did not die. The wound hurt terribly, but with time, the intestine adhered to the body, and the wound closed. After a long convalescence, he was strong enough to be moved.

Dozyk was sentenced to ten years of *katorha*, forced labor, with the stipulation that the Gulag administration could add ten more years at will, and if he survived that, ten more—in other words, forever. These extensions were given out routinely to those convicted of "agitation"—that is, someone who was either a member of OUN/UPA, or an old Communist suspected of Trotskyite sympathies.

Dozyk's first destination was Karaganda, a Gulag in Central Asia, followed by a year of work on the Baikal-Amur Mainline railway. From there he went to Magadan, and then to the gold mines of Kolyma, where chances of survival were extremely slim.

Karaganda consisted of ninety penal facilities where most of the prisoners were German, many of them descendants of Soviet Volga Germans who were collectively deported to Kazakhstan on Stalin's order in 1941. There were also Ukrainians and a large number of Balts, whose number swelled after the end of WWII. Dozyk was attached to a crew ordered to dig a foundation for a factory. Karaganda's soil, heavy clay, was difficult to excavate, and all digging

---

[37] *Banderovets or Banderivets* in Ukrainian, Banderite in English, a supporter of Ukrainian nationalist leader Bandera.

was done by pick and shovel. Prisoners removed the clay slice by slice, and the norm was three and a half cubic meters of clay a day. If the prisoner did 100 percent of the norm, he got five hundred grams of bread. If he did not, his ration was cut in half and then in half again. By then, he was a *dokhodyaga*, a goner—so weak he had little hope of recovery. Those who didn't work didn't receive any bread.

Karaganda was also a transit prison from where prisoners were sent to other destinations in Siberia. Dozyk's next destination was Tayshet, 225 kilometers west of Bratsk on Lake Baikal, to work on the BAM, the Baikal-Amur Mainline railway. The BAM, built as a strategic alternative route to the Trans-Siberian Railway, broke off from that railway at Tayshet and then proceeded around the northern tip of Lake Baikal, east to the Pacific Ocean. Its twenty-one tunnels and 4,200 bridges required constant maintenance. Dozyk worked among Japanese and German prisoners of war who formed a significant portion of the forced labor contingent, generally under a twenty-five-year sentence. Working on the railroad, he picked up a few words of Japanese and improved his German.

The *zeks*[38] were constantly moved from camp to camp along this railway. They were so numerous that they had no names, just numbers. A few kilometers after Camp 451 was Camp 452, and a few kilometers after that was Camp 453. During 1944–1946, most of the Far Eastern section was built by prisoners, and as many as 150,000 died of overwork and starvation. Of all the POWs who worked on the BAM, only 10 percent returned home. Virtually all construction work on the BAM stopped in 1953, after Stalin's death, and the line was abandoned to the elements for twenty-five years.

Uncle Dozyk used the term *po etapu*, in stages, to describe his movement from Karaganda to Kolyma, always in an easterly direction. From other accounts, we know that these journeys were brutally harsh, and many prisoners perished along the way. The authors Robert Conquest and Anne Applebaum have described at length the horrors encountered by prisoners crossing Siberia on prison trains, or voyaging between the Pacific ports of Vanino and Magadan.

The end point of the land transport for most prisoners was either Vanino or Bukha Nakhodka, ports on the Pacific Ocean. The inmates were kept there until they could be shipped by boat to Magadan, the capital of Kolyma.

---

[38] *Zek* is an abbreviation of *zakliuchonnyj*, a Russian slang term for a prisoner or a forced labor camp inmate.

This journey has often been described as "the journey into the abyss." The boats were old Dutch, Swedish, or English cargo steamers never designed for passenger use. The human cargo, short on food and water, was confined to below deck where conditions were unspeakably horrendous.

DURING OUR LAST MEETING in Odesa in 2011, Dozyk's youngest son, Sasha, recounted a rhyme that illustrated *zek* black humor about Kolyma.

> *Kolyma, Kolyma*
> *Chudnaya planeta*
> *Dvenatsiat mesatsov zyma*
> *Ostalnoye leto*

A rough translation,

> *Kolyma, Kolyma*
> *That miraculous planet*
> *Twelve months winter,*
> *The rest summer.*

In 1949, Dozyk learned that he would be sent to Kolyma. The news was devastating. The word was that no one ever returned from Kolyma. Even today, little is known about it because so few survived. Moreover, Stalin was still in power, and no one could have anticipated the changes to come after Stalin's death in 1953 under Khrushchev.

Kolyma was the most remote Gulag in the far northeast of Siberia near the Bering Strait that separates the Russian Far East from Alaska. The region gets its name from the river Kolyma, which is comparable to Alaska's Yukon, and the surrounding mountains. The area is rich in gold and other metals such as silver, tin, tungsten, lead, and copper, but "gold, gold, gold" was the driving force behind Kolyma, as Varlam Shalamov wrote in his memoir *Kolyma Tales*. This was the metal Stalin needed the most to purchase new technology and machinery from abroad. He demanded daily reports on gold production and sent out inspectors to examine the camps. Despite freezing temperatures and lack of accessibility, these resources were fully exploited, and there was no other way to accomplish this except by employing slave labor on a gargantuan scale.

Robert Conquest describes Kolyma's economy as "gold under ice." Most of it was in deposits, some of which were fifty meters deep. Work in these mines was a nightmare. No precautions were taken to protect the *zeks* against accidents, and in Kolyma, there were also lead mines, operated with minimum safety measures. Not surprisingly, all the prisoners eventually died of lead poisoning.[39]

To arrive in Kolyma, prisoners had to go through Magadan, a major staging center for inmates going to camps further north, where a vast and brutal forced-labor gold-mining operation was located. Dozyk's first assignment, however, was a logging operation in the Kolyma Valley in the winter of 1949. Logging was important because timber provided beam supports and bracing for the mines.

"They woke us up at five in the morning," Uncle Dozyk said. "Our work consisted mostly of cutting down trees and sawing wood. If the work did not kill you, the elements would. We were inadequately clothed for Kolyma temperatures. In the winter the thermometer would drop to −38°C. If it dropped below −40°C (at minus 40 Centigrade and Fahrenheit converge), we stopped working in the forest.

"Our garments consisted of a *fufayka* (a Soviet WWII winter uniform padded jacket and pants) with an over garment called *bushlag*. We had fur gloves that kept our hands warm if they did not get wet, but with our work they got wet all the time. To get to the logging site, we trod through knee-deep snow ten kilometers each way. By the time we arrived we were exhausted, with little strength left to cut trees." Dozyk smiled and interjected a bit of humor, saying, "There is no such a thing as a bad winter; only bad clothing."

Dozyk heard a rumor that there was a mass uprising somewhere in Kolyma in the winter of 1949-1950, but it didn't matter. "For us," he said, "things would not change. Food was a perpetual problem. We were constantly hungry. Every morning we got *balanda*, a low-quality prison gruel, some bread, and tea, but there was never enough. Logging is demanding work and consumes calories. No matter how much *balanda* we got in the morning, by noon we were hungry as wolves. In the evening, we got the same *balanda* or maybe some other kasha and beets. Going to bed, we were already thinking of the next day's ration."

After a year on the logging site, the camp administration discovered that Dozyk was skilled in metalwork, a trade that he had picked up at home in Tadani. He was transferred to a metal workshop at a mine called Spokoiny, a

---

[39] Conquest, *Kolyma: The Arctic Death Camps*, p. 107.

notoriously brutal camp according to Conquest, but this meant that he was released from grueling logging work.

By an incredible stroke of luck, Dozyk was assigned to the camp metal shop where he was put to work as a machinist and lathe operator. Most importantly, he would not have to descend into the mines, where many died within weeks. The one advantage to working in the mines was that there was no snow, no piercing wind, and the steam that thawed the frozen sand gave off some warmth. But, Dozyk explained, this was vastly offset by the lack of adequate ventilation and the poisonous fumes from regular blasting by ammonal, an explosive made of ammonium nitrate and aluminum powder.

Dozyk recounted that once he had to go down a shaft to examine a broken crane. He stayed in the mine for five hours and discovered the appalling conditions prisoners were exposed to on a daily basis. The fumes had a strong odor similar to eau de cologne, and after a while, it made him so sick that he had to step outside, while the poor *dogodiagi* (goners) had to breathe these fumes every day. A job that was even more deadly was carting thawed sand from the pits. Prisoners were expected to roll out wheelbarrows from the relatively warm mine directly into minus thirty degrees Centigrade temperature outside the pit. If they did not meet the norm, their ration was cut in half, and half again. These workers lasted about a month before they succumbed to pneumonia and meningitis.

As Robert Conquest noted, the whole world knows about the Holocaust, but very few are aware of the death camps in the Communist Gulag. Kolyma was only one such place, a system composed of hundreds of camps. Most people have heard of Dachau, Buchenwald, and Treblinka, but in the Soviet Union, there were hundreds of Dachaus, hundreds of Buchenwalds, and hundreds of Treblinkas spread across the wastes of Soviet Siberia.

"Just as Auschwitz has come to stand for the Nazi extermination camps as a whole," Conquest wrote, "Kolyma remains fixed in the imagination of the Soviet people as the greatest archetype of the sinister system under which Stalin ended, by hunger, cold and exhaustion, the lives of so many of his subjects. While Auschwitz and Maidanek are known the world over, Kolyma and Vorkuta are not. However, for Russians, Ukrainians, and Balts, Kolyma was a place of horror wholly comparable to Auschwitz and worse."

All camps near the Arctic Circle had high death rates, but Kolyma was the deadliest. Although the production of gold was important, the central aim was to kill off prisoners.[40] Cover-ups and destruction of records have made it difficult to estimate the aggregate numbers of victims. Unlike the Nazi concentration camps, reliable records were not kept. In Kolyma alone, estimates suggest that up to three million *zeks* may have perished.[41]

WHEN STALIN DIED on March 5, 1953, prisoners in the camp were overjoyed but did not dare show their delight. Almost immediately, the administrators and guards adjusted to the new situation, relaxed the rules, and dispensed less brutal punishment. Uncle Dozyk had a glimmer of hope that after he was freed, he would be able to return to Ukraine. Sadly, that was not to be. Although released, he was never rehabilitated. Instead, he got a *vovchyibilet*, a wolf's pass, which meant he was free but not allowed to move around or settle where he pleased. He applied for rehabilitation many times without success, and the reason was always the same. He was a member of the OUN/UPA, and these individuals were considered a threat to the regime long after most of the Gulags closed. In Uncle Dozyk's case, it was even worse because he had been caught with a weapon in his hands. After an amnesty was proclaimed, Dozyk's ordeal as a *zek* in Kolyma ended.

Dozyk's story awakened in me a new appreciation of "freedom," something he was deprived of for most of his life.

"I was freed in June 1953," he continued, "but I remained in Kolyma for a while. Agents were coming around to recruit workers for projects around Magadan, and one of them was looking for qualified people to work at a coal mine next to a new electric power plant in a settlement called Stekolny. They needed metalworkers, and I was offered a job there. The agent wanted me to come in such a hurry that, to my great surprise, they flew me from the Kolyma Valley to Magadan. It was my first airplane flight.

"When I arrived on the site, I discovered that the Russians had received a new power plant from the United States, made of stainless steel, an unheard-of luxury reserved only for military use in tanks and other armaments. The plant burned low-grade lignite, a brown coal used primarily for electric power generation. All of the surrounding mines were working to supply coal for this power plant.

"Even though I was 'free' I was not allowed to go where I really wanted to go, to my boyhood home in Ukraine. That road was closed to me no matter

---

[40]   Conquest, Robert, *Kolyma: The Arctic Death Camps*, UK, 1979, p. 17.

[41]   Ibid, pp. 13–15.

how much I pleaded my case. I did manage a *propyska*, permission, to go to Magadan, where I met many freed Ukrainians in the same situation.

"In Magadan, I met Tatiana Honchar, a prisoner who served a ten-year sentence for being a nurse with the UPA in Volyn Oblast. We fell in love, married and settled in Stekolny, 25 kilometers from Magadan.

"In Stekolny, we were assigned a small apartment, and I worked as a metal worker in the mines surrounding the electric power plant. Even though I was a 'free' man, I was expected to report to the authorities every two weeks. Life improved, if only slightly. My wife re-established contact with the outside world, but returning to Ukraine was still out of the question.

"It was then that Tatiana got news that her mother Maria was living in exile in Kazakhstan. When she learned this, we applied for a transfer to that Central Asian republic. I was aware that the authorities there were looking for people willing to settle on the virgin lands that Moscow central planners were trying to open up for agriculture. I applied, and got permission to relocate."

This is where my uncle Dozyk's Kolyma narrative ends, and his years of eking out a living in the virgin lands of Kazakhstan begin. After Magadan, Dozyk and his wife settled on a collective farm in Central Kazakhstan, not far from Tatiana's mother. In the '50s and '60s, they raised three sons, Petro, Ivan, and Alexander. Petro once told me that they were allowed to own a cow, an unusual luxury that provided milk and sustenance for the children. Without the cow, they probably would not have survived. In 1966, Tatiana died, and Dozyk remarried and was allowed to return to Ukraine—not to his native Galicia but to Crimea, nonetheless a welcome change after the nightmare of Kolyma and the inhospitable steppe of Kazakhstan.

Four years after I interviewed him, Uncle Dozyk passed away. His son Sashko told me he died peacefully at home after celebrating the tenth anniversary of the Ukrainian independence. His ordeal was not in vain. Ukraine was free at last.

ON A BUSINESS TRIP to Almaty in 2009, I met Uncle Dozyk's oldest son, Petro Martyniuk. Unlike his two younger brothers, he settled in Kostanai in Western Kazakhstan. With his help, I was able to piece together the story of his mother Tatiana's parents, Maria and Ivan Honchar. The story involved an escape from a Gulag near Krasnoyarsk, a saga that verges on the fantastic.

When Tatiana was sentenced to ten years for her activity in the UPA, the NKVD rounded up her parents and meted out the same punishment that

Maria Martyniuk, my grandmother, received in Tadani. Their crime: they were related to a member of the UPA.

In the fall of 1946, Tatiana's parents were sentenced by a *troika*, put on a cattle train, and dumped, along with hundreds of others, in a forest somewhere north of Krasnoyarsk. They were given an ax and a shovel and told to prepare for the winter. Krasnoyarsk is hot in the summer and extremely cold in the winter. They quickly realized that their chances of survival were slim and made a bold decision to escape. Aware that they were not too far from the Trans-Siberian Railway, they headed for a nearby junction to see if they could jump on one of the trains moving in a westerly direction. By luck, they stumbled on a military train carrying artillery and other weapons. The artillery pieces were covered with heavy tarpaulins to protect them from the elements, and Maria and Ivan slid under one. The train moved very slowly, seemingly in a circuitous route but, generally, in the westerly direction. After about three weeks, somewhere in central Russia, the train came to a stop.

Starved and emaciated—they had hardly eaten anything except what they managed to bring with them—Maria and Ivan walked away from the train to find some sustenance in the nearby forest. They ate some mushrooms that turned out to be poisonous, and Ivan got dreadfully sick. Fearing that he might die, Maria took him to a local clinic. It was a risky move, since they did not have identity papers, and that would be the first thing the hospital authorities would ask to see. Luck was with them. A Polish doctor realized their predicament and advised them to come up with a credible story for the local police. They made up a story about being on their way from the Far East, where they had visited their wounded son in a military hospital, and hooligans had robbed them of their belongings, including identity documents. Apparently, the ruse worked well enough to get them back to their village of Svytnytsi in Volyn', but that was not the end of their travails.

In the spring of 1947, Ivan died. Maria Kuzmivna was not able to give him a proper burial because she feared it would attract the attention of the NKVD, and that she would be found out in an interrogation. With the help of friends, she buried Ivan in the forest, but they did not dare to put a cross on the grave. Instead, they pounded in a wooden stake with two bent nails to mark Ivan's grave.

Maria Kuzmivna knew that if she remained in the village, sooner or later, she would be discovered; so with the help of trusted neighbors, she hid in the forest with the remnants of the UPA fighters for whom she acted as a courier. Unfortunately, in one of her forays to the village, she was discovered by the NKVD, interrogated, and sentenced to six years of exile in Kazakhstan. There, against incredible odds, she came across a woman from the group that had been dumped in the forest near Krasnoyarsk in 1946. Maria learned that all of the members of that group, except this woman, had perished from the exceptionally cold winter and starvation.

7. Bavaria after the War

BETWEEN JULY 1944 and May 1945, our family was caught between the Soviet Army advancing from the east, the Wehrmacht reinforcing the crumbling front from the west, and Allied bombers laying waste from the air. The constant movement and exposure to mortal danger took a toll on my parents. By the time we arrived in Bavaria, my father's hair had thinned and Mother had lost weight. Still, unlike many families, we survived with no one being killed, maimed, or raped, and thanks to Father and Mother's foresight and meticulous preparation, we did not succumb to severe malnutrition and starvation like thousands of others.

American bombers and the Wehrmacht presented a danger, but it was small compared to being captured by the Russians. The fear of that was overwhelming and dictated every decision and every move. Western Ukrainians had experienced the horror of Soviet occupation between 1939 and 1941—twenty-one months during which hundreds of thousands of the best and brightest were murdered, disappeared, or were sent to the Gulag.

For a few weeks after the end of the war, we lived like gypsies outside of Landau. Spring was in full bloom, and it was possible to survive outdoors. I had just turned five, and Ivanka was almost four. I distinctly recall how we enjoyed the gypsy life. Wrapped in blankets in the back of a wagon, moving from place to place, was great fun. Conventional wisdom has it that our existence as refugees during these years must have been so traumatic that it left lifelong psychological scars, but that's not true. The experience made us stronger, more adaptable, and able to face challenges. My sister and I are proof that such perceptions are poppycock, and that what counts above all else is parental love and protection.

The American soldiers we encountered in Landau seemed overwhelmed by the tide of humanity fleeing the Russians. Father wrote in his memoir that the provisional military authorities immediately undertook the colossal task of sorting millions of displaced persons and providing them with shelter— the opposite of what Soviets were bestowing on those they "liberated" in their zone. We ended up in a *Bauernhof,* a farmstead in the nearby village of Oberhöking, where the owner, Herr Grib, and Father worked out an arrangement whereby Father would help with farm chores in return for a roof and some food, including milk for my sister and me. Herr Grib also provided a stable and feed for our horse, Yurko, in exchange for Father allowing Yurko to help with the spring plowing. We got along well with *Bauer* Grib; he was satisfied with us, and we with him. When the time came to leave, he was sorry to see us go. Before we left, Father sold him Yurko, something that made him happy because there was an acute shortage of draft animals.

We left the Grib farm in the fall of 1945. The Americans proposed that all Ukrainian families in the area move to a military installation near the small town of Ganacker, barracks that used to house German military. The Ganacker camp, roughly fifty small residences lodging about three hundred residents, was an independent and self-organized entity where the UNRRA (United Nations Refugee Relief Administration) provided food, shelter, and essential medical services. In addition to accommodations, the camp had an administrative office and a communal kitchen. Residents were free to come and go and visit the nearby town or friends as they pleased. After nearly two years of constant displacement and the stress of war, my parents were greatly relieved to be settled in the company of their countrymen.

The first order of business was to elect a committee to run the camp, provide security, manage the central kitchen, and handle other chores. By unanimous vote, the committee selected Roman as *Kommandant*—commandant of the camp. My father was one of the few who spoke German and some English. Ganacker was one of several small refugee camps administered by the regional UNRRA administration in Dingolfing. The commandant was responsible for maintaining order, distributing food, and providing labor for things like road repair. The men were happy to take on such work because they got paid in cigarettes, a substitute currency that was more stable than the old German mark.

The camp had carpenter's and tailor's shops, and the refugees grew vegetables in low-lying fertile fields around the barracks. They dug trenches redirecting rain overflow, organized camp police, and set up a school for the children. Father initiated a course to teach the refugees basic German and English, and was also the paymaster. Every week, based on work performed, he paid workers by distributing packages of cigarettes.

According to an agreement concluded at the Potsdam Conference in 1945 after the war, the Allies, at the behest of Soviet authorities, were required to find and hand over any Soviet refugees located in the American, French, or British zones of occupied Germany. The British took this agreement seriously and handed over hundreds of thousands of Soviet refugees and former forced laborers to the Red Army. The French had more important issues to deal with than to seek out Soviet citizens for deportation, and the American occupation forces took the agreement with a grain of salt. They went through the motions of complying but rarely handed over refugees to the Russians on the scale that the British did. It is indeed a strange twist of fate how some families managed to escape deportation to the USSR, while others were forcibly handed over to the Russian authorities who condemned them to a ghastly fate in the Siberian Gulag.

Although we lived in the American zone, the policy of handing over Soviet citizens to the Russians touched our family. I vividly recall one calm day in the summer of 1946 when three two-and-a-half-ton trucks with American soldiers arrived at our camp. The officer in charge went directly to Father's office and gave him a list with names of individuals who were to be transported to Plattling.

The captain in charge told him, "We will come back tomorrow and expect these individuals and their families to be ready for evacuation."

Aware of rumors that US and British troops were rounding up Soviet citizens at gunpoint and taking them to Plattling, an embarkation point for repatriation to the USSR, Father immediately realized what was happening. He summoned the commander of the camp police and handed him the list of thirty names, allegedly Soviet citizens, with instructions to find them, followed by a wink. The commander needed no explanation to guess what the wink signaled. Forewarned, all of the men on the list mysteriously vanished into the night; some hid in the nearby forest, while others put as much distance between themselves and Ganacker as they could.

The next day, the trucks arrived to pick up the people on the list. Roman calmly explained to the captain that his police chief had done his best to find the individuals. The American officer realized that something odd was going on and showed Roman the list and instructions to carry out the order again. The police commander went looking for these men and, after an hour, came back to report that none of them were in their quarters. Roman once again explained that they had disappeared, and no one knew of their whereabouts. The officer, dumbfounded, shrugged. "I'll be back tomorrow at the same time and expect to see these individuals ready to board our trucks for Plattling."

By playing this dangerous game, Roman knew that he had taken a huge risk, perilous not only to himself but also to those involved in the cover-up. The next twenty-four hours were incredibly tense. He waited on pins and needles for the transport to show up the next day, but by late afternoon, it was evident that no one was coming. An overwhelming sense of relief followed. Perhaps the officer realized what had been going on and his conscience convinced him to disobey this inhumane order. Roman's quick thinking and good luck saved these people from certain enslavement or death. The thirty people on the list were undoubtedly grateful for Father's deft handling of this potentially critical situation.

This episode illustrated one of the most shameful chapters in post-WWII history. It amounted to forcible repatriation of refugees who had ended up on German soil at the end of the war. Known as Operation Keelhaul, it was a secret agreement between the Anglo-American Allies and the Soviets at Yalta to deport millions of men and women to the USSR against their will. The details of this disgraceful act were not fully discovered until 1971, by the historian Julius Epstein.[42] To this day, people still ask how such an ignominious act could have taken place and been hushed up for a generation. The answer lies in a secret codicil agreed to by Joseph Stalin, Winston Churchill, and Franklin D. Roosevelt at the Yalta Conference whereby the Western Allies agreed to return all Soviet citizens found in their zones to the Soviet Union.[43] Those most affected were Soviet prisoners of war, but the agreement extended to all Eastern European refugees. In exchange, the Soviet government agreed to hand over several thousand Western Allied prisoners of war whom they had liberated from German prisoner of war camps. This codicil was kept secret from the US and British people for fifty years.

---

[42]   Keelhaul was a form of torture and punishment in the British and Dutch navies where a man is tied up and thrown overboard under the keel of the ship.

[43]   The Soviets considered natives of the Baltic States and former Polish territories east of the Curzon line to be Soviet citizens.

At the end of World War II, there were six million refugees from the Soviet Union in Western Europe. Approximately three million of them were forced laborers (*Ostarbeiter*). On their return to the Soviet Union, they were treated as traitors, and most were transported to remote parts of the Soviet Union to work as slave laborers in the mines of Vorkuta and Kolyma. The British were ruthless in carrying out the letter of the agreement. The Americans carried it out half-heartedly. The Soviets never concluded their part of the deal.

The ultimate hypocrisy of the secret agreement at Yalta was that the United States, after signing an international convention opposing forced repatriation and verbally assuring the world they would never countenance such actions, agreed to insert fine print excepting from the ban all those who originated from nations given over to the Soviets at the close of WWII. While claiming to "make the world safe for Democracy," President Roosevelt and his cronies condemned millions to slave labor or slow death in the camps of the Gulag Archipelago.

Numerous survivors of both the German labor camps and the Soviet Gulag nearly all agreed that the Soviet camps were considerably more brutal and inhumane than any of the German concentration camps. Margarete Buber-Neumann, wife of Jewish Communist Rafael Buber, and later common-law wife of the notorious German Communist Heinz Neumann, testified to the horrors in her memoir. In 1937, Heinz was arrested by the NKVD and shot, and she was tortured and sentenced to five years of hard labor in Karaganda. In her memoir, she describes the horrors of the Gulag: "the cruelties, the filthy flea-infested lodging, the brutal cold, the forced prostitution, the killing labor, and searing hunger."

In 1940, without explanation, she was taken to Moscow, given an excellent meal, and put on a train with German Communists being returned to Germany in the cooperative spirit of the Hitler-Stalin accord. Five months later, she was incarcerated in Ravensbrück. Frau Buber-Neumann was in the unusual position of being asked, "Whose concentration camp was more horrible?" To her, it was manifestly clear: Stalin's camps held the edge on brutality and sadism. Her testimony was not unique. Many Ukrainians and Poles who experienced both German concentration camps and the Gulag agreed.

8. Childhood in Regensburg

IN EARLY 1947, we moved to Regensburg, a much larger camp for displaced persons, and one of several magnet camps set up for Ukrainian refugees. Others existed in Munich, Nuremberg, Neu-Ulm, Mittenwald, Landeck, and dozens of other places in Germany and Austria, but with about ten thousand Ukrainian refugees, the camp in Regensburg-Ganghofer was one of the largest. During the war, it had housed Luftwaffe personnel, and workers in the nearby Messerschmitt airplane factory. The Regensburg camp, administered by the United Nations Relief and Rehabilitation Administration (UNRRA) and later by the International Relief Organization (IRO), quickly became a self-reliant, culturally thriving community that reflected the life of a small town.

Given postwar conditions, its accomplishments were exemplary. There were schools at every level, including for mechanics and drivers; youth organizations; religious institutions; sports teams; theater groups; and chess clubs. Camp police provided security, and the refugees introduced a rudimentary monetary and banking system that involved printing camp currency and establishing sales outlets for commodities and consumer goods. It was a microcosm of a small city-state. With such incentives, everybody wanted to work; materials were secured, dormant skills and talents resurrected, and with great ingenuity, a number of small business enterprises established.

For our family, Regensburg offered advantages a smaller camp did not—schools, for one. My sister and I were of school age, and it was time to learn to read and write. Also, Father harbored a desire to complete his studies, and Regensburg offered the Ukrainian Technical and Husbandry

Institute (UTHI) also known as the Ukrainian Technical University. It had an enrollment of 1,300 students and offered five areas of study: agronomy and forestry, engineering, economics, veterinary medicine, and pharmacy. Father enrolled at the Faculty of Agronomy and Forestry from where he would earn a diploma before we departed for the United States.

Life was almost normal. A slice of Ukraine had been transplanted from Galicia to Bavaria, including religious and cultural institutions and political parties. Cultural and artistic life thrived, newspapers were printed, and a theater troupe under the direction of the famous actor Volodymyr Blavatsky gave performances. Mother, a theater enthusiast who had been an amateur actress in Ukraine, took us to see these plays. It was all there, a self-contained, self-ruled small city located on the grounds of the former Luftwaffe barracks. The barracks, however, were not made of wood. They were solid brick residences and homes.

Amazingly, Regensburg was spared from destruction by Allied bombers during the war. The city did not have industries the Allies considered to be of strategic value. Other than a damaged train station, the city remained practically intact. What Regensburg lacked in terms of industry, it more than made up for in architectural heritage and rich history.

IT IS OFTEN SAID that we are the sum of experiences we remember from childhood—things we saw, stories we heard, and interactions we experienced with different people. When family friends and visitors gathered in our small house, there were endless exchanges of war stories, accounts that I soaked up like a sponge. I began to comprehend what was taking place around me—stories that were shaping my worldview and forming my Ukrainian identity and my attitudes toward Communism, the Soviets, and Russia. The word most commonly used to describe them was *Bolshevyki*, the Bolsheviks, or the derogatory *Moskali*, Muscovites, both scornful terms. They were evil personified, vile, brutal, and cruel as a pestilence.

In the immediate aftermath of the war, I had not been able to attend school, but in Regensburg, I started first grade late but quickly adjusted. My sister and I walked to school, about a kilometer away, without the slightest concern that something bad might happen on the way. The teachers were strict, and problems with discipline were unheard of. They drilled us in proper orthography, something I had trouble with in the beginning, but eventually got the hang of and enjoyed. At near zero cost, we were taught to read, write legibly, and master math.

By third grade, I had already read a Ukrainian version of Robinson Crusoe called *Syn Ukrayiny* (Son of Ukraine) and was so engrossed with the plot that I read it again. We also memorized poems: I can still recite parts of Taras Shevchenko's poem *Ivan Pidkova*. All instruction was in Ukrainian, the only language I knew, except for a sprinkling of German I picked up on the streets of Regensburg from German children.

Once Father took me on a train ride to Munich to meet his friend Oleksa Motyl whom he hadn't seen since he left Ukraine. How they found each other is still a puzzle, although I know that a system of locating lost family members and friends functioned after the war. I recall people peering at public boards with names of people they hoped to find.

In his memoir, Motyl writes that at the end of June 1944, he vacillated between joining the UPA or fleeing west. The Red Army was so close he could hear the rattle of distant machine guns. Two close friends convinced him that resistance was futile, so he reluctantly joined them and thousands of others who fled the Soviet juggernaut. On July 20, Motyl headed for Lviv on foot. From there, he got transport for Sambir and, with a few friends, traversed Poland in two horse-drawn wagons, crossed Slovakia, and arrived in Vienna. In the spring of 1945, he reached Würzburg and, finally, Munich. Motyl's escape route was more circuitous than ours, but, eventually, we all ended up in Bavaria; our family in Regensburg, and Motyl in Munich.

I recall the train ride to Munich with uncanny clarity and can still name the cities we passed through—Traubing, Landshut, and Freising. The wagons were 1920s vintage four-wheeled, open passenger coaches that the Germans called *Donnerbüchse* (thunder box) because they made an inordinate amount of noise. An old high-stack coal-burning steam locomotive pulled the train, as most modern locomotives had been destroyed during the war. The engine huffed and puffed through the Bavarian countryside, producing clouds of steam and smoke from cheap coal, an odor that curiously I found pleasant. On bends, I stuck my head out of the window to get a glimpse of the locomotive and a whiff of that sweet-acrid odor until Father said it was dangerous. In the Landshut station, the train made a long stop to load coal and take on water for the locomotive. I was fascinated by the way the steam locomotive worked, a passion that stayed with me for many years.

Regensburg was spared the ravages of war, but Munich had been heavily bombed. There were roofless churches, wall-less houses open to the rain, and groups of despondent people moving about, foraging for God knows what. The center around the *Hauptbahnhof*, the main railway station where we pulled in, was in ruins. Everywhere I looked lay the detritus of war that my adolescent mind could not comprehend. The odor of broken masonry still permeated the air, overlaid by a sweet sickening smell of unburied bodies in the rubble. One of the first images at the station that struck me with the force of a branding iron was a hospital train marked with large red crosses. Even though the hostilities had ended, war casualties were being transported, transferred, or discharged. The sight of men with missing limbs, on crutches, with blood-soaked bandages disturbed me terribly.

There was great joy when Oleksa Motyl and my father met. They hadn't seen each other since the summer of 1944 and had a lot to tell each other about their adventures fleeing the advancing Bolshevik juggernaut.

THE PERCEPTION AMONG many Ukrainians in Regensburg and other DP camps was that their stay in Germany was going to be temporary. The Americans and Russians would clash, and there would be a war, which the Americans would win. After all, they had the atom bomb, and the Russian didn't. The war would be short, and we would return to our homeland. That was the hope. But as reality began to sink in, gradually refugees came to accept that they would not be returning to their homes, and they began to be more engaged in communal life and survival.

The camp at Regensburg was a microcosm that reflected the general political divisions of the time: 75 percent were supporters of OUN-B (Banderites), and formed the dominant group in the camp. Since 1940, the OUN had split into two factions, with the older, more moderate members supporting Andriy Melnyk (OUN-M), while the younger, more radical members backed Stepan Bandera (OUN-B). In local parlance, these factions were known as *Banderivsti* and *Melnykivsti*, the Banderites and Melnykites.

These two factions dominated political life in the camp, but there were also Ukrainian Socialists as well as monarchists or Hetmanites. Curiously, many of the elites, such as the professors at the UTHI, were Socialists whom the majority of camp residents considered arrogant and pretentious. The competition between the two factions OUN-B and OUN-M in the camp intensified, with the conflict manifesting itself in strange ways. Residents of the camp identified the faction they supported by displaying the colors of the Ukrainian flag in their windows or doors.[44] If their paper flags had the

---

[44]   The traditional Ukrainian flag consisted of equal-size blue and yellow horizontal stripes. The blue symbolized the sky, and the yellow the wheat fields of Ukraine.

yellow stripe on top and blue on the bottom, the resident was an OUN-M sympathizer. Blue on top implied he was an OUN-B supporter. Supporters of respective factions went around at night throwing stones at the windows of neighbors who displayed the "wrong" color choice. In addition to many broken windows, I heard stories of physical altercations. In retrospect, these fights seem silly. No matter which faction one supported, we had all lost the struggle for an independent Ukraine. It was not to be gained until 1991.

There were numerous reunions with family and old friends. The reunion with Oleksa Motyl was one, and the reunion with Father's younger brother, Oleksa Martyniuk, was another. Uncle Oleksa came to visit us from Neu-Ulm in 1947. The brothers had been separated since 1943 when Oleksa was drafted by the Wehrmacht as a "volunteer" worker, a *Freiwilliger*, and shipped off to the Leningrad front.

There was also a fun side to our existence in the camp. Since there was so much spare time, theater troupes sprouted, sports activities expanded, and scout groups grew. I joined the equivalent of a Cub Scout group, and I vividly recall the soccer games and displays of acrobatic horsemanship by the Kuban Cossacks. The first film I ever saw was in the school hall when I was seven. It was a war documentary depicting bombings of German cities, explosions, burning buildings collapsing, corpses in the streets, and lines of bandaged men and women with frightened children. It was a ghastly film that stayed implanted in my consciousness for many years. The reality of war caught up with me in the form of nightmares.

After we had settled in Chicago in the 1950s, I learned that many of my friends and their families actually lived in Regensburg at the same time that I did. Among them: Yaro Markewycz, Oleh Karavan, Slavko Boykowych, Yurko Myskiw, Ivan Myhul, and Roman Serbyn.

THE MEDIEVAL CENTER of Regensburg was accessible by tram. Also known by its Latin name Ratisbon, Regensburg was a remarkable city. In addition to its physical beauty, the city possessed a rich history and a unique cultural heritage dating from the Roman period. In AD 179, the Roman emperor Marcus Aurelius chose this site on the Danube to erect the large legionary camp of Castra Regina, whose 2.5-meter thick wall still surrounds the medieval city center.

One pleasant spring day in 1948, Father took me on the tram to the city center. We got off near Saint Peter's, Regensburg's Gothic Cathedral, and visited the Porta Praetoria, embedded in the facade of the *Bischofshof* (Bishop's

Palace), next to Saint Peter's. Father pointed to the formidable arch and explained how this simple invention made many Roman and later engineering feats possible. The largest surviving monument of its kind, the Porta Praetoria was regarded as the most significant Roman construction along the Danube. Its only equal in Germany was Trier's Roman city gate, the Porta Nigra. At eight, I was still enraptured by my first tramway ride, but in hindsight, it appears to have been the moment that sparked a lifelong fascination with arches, Romanesque architecture, Gothic churches, the history of Rome, and all that these subjects encompass.

The camp at Ganghofer was on a rise, offering panoramic views of the Danube valley. Apparently, Napoleon appreciated the importance of this site when, on his way to Vienna in 1809, he located his headquarters next to the church with two high Gothic steeples. On one of my trips to Regensburg, I revisited the church where the Greek Catholics held their services and where I received my First Holy Communion. Strolling through the church courtyard, my eye was drawn to a plaque on the wall of an adjacent building we called *dim varyativ*, house for the insane. It read: *Hier hat Napoleon I am 23 April 1809 Quartier genommen* (Here, on April 23, 1809, Napoleon I set up his headquarters). The adjacent church towers offered a bird's-eye view of Regensburg and the Danube Valley beyond. Napoleon chose this high ground to conduct his operations in the Regensburg area, opening the way for the *Grand Armée* to move toward Vienna and, eventually, to his last successful battle at Wagram in July 1809.

Finally, it should be noted that Pope Benedict XVI hailed from this region. It was at the University that he delivered his now famous Regensburg lecture in 2006. The address created a furor throughout the Islamic world because he cited a question posed by the Byzantine Emperor Manuel II: "Is it or is it not permitted and approved to use violence for religious rule and expansion?" The critics of the Pope claim that merely citing the old text is in itself a sign of intent to insult.

THE MAJORITY OF UKRAINIAN emigrants in the camps were educated, and most had a lot of spare time. They engaged in activities from continuing education to sports, and some pursued commercial ventures. My father was among the few who decided to start a business.

While food was generally available, there was a dearth of consumer goods. Children's shoes, in particular, were in short supply. In the summer, a lack of shoes was not a problem. From spring to fall, I recall, we ran around barefoot. In the winter, however, with snow on the ground, it was an issue.

In this scarcity, Roman saw an opportunity. He opened up a shoemaker's workshop specializing in shoes for kids. Using his Ukrainian experience and skills in the leather goods trade, he purchased essential tools and equipment and, with the help of a few assistants, began to make shoes for children. They sold like hot cakes, and Father enlarged the workshop and hired more helpers. The demand was so high that he expanded his operation to thirty shoemakers producing children's shoes in European sizes 20 to 30 by the hundreds, if not the thousands. I witnessed this operation, and Father taught me the technique of joining the top part of the shoe to the leather sole with a special glue and tiny wooden pegs. They worked better than nails because they expanded in the leather sole. Finally, the shoes were stitched together by hand, but soon Father invested in a shoe-stitching machine. Within a year, he became a successful capitalist entrepreneur.

The old German Reichsmarks kept coming in huge wads of hundreds and thousands. Often, Father entrusted me with counting the receipts, which is perhaps why I pursued a career in accounting. After learning how to count American bombers above Austria by the hundreds and Reichsmarks by the thousands, I developed a skill that became useful later in life.

JUST AS LIFE IN THE REGENSBURG camp began to settle into a routine, in February 1948, the Communists staged a coup d'état in Czechoslovakia. Prague's "third defenestration" left the democratically elected Czech president, Jan Masaryk, dead on the pavement below his office in the Ministry of Foreign Affairs. The ominous turn of events created near panic among refugees in Bavaria.

Four months after the assassination of Masaryk, on Sunday, June 20, 1948, the Deutsche Mark (DM) replaced the old Reichsmark (RM). I distinctly recall the appearance and the feel of the DM. The RMs were rumpled and smelly, while the DMs were crisp and shiny, almost unreal. The reform replaced the old money with the new Deutsche Mark at the rate of one new for ten old. Each person received a per capita allowance of DM 60, and all debts of the Reich were canceled. The introduction of the new currency was intended to protect Western Germany from a second wave of hyperinflation like the one after WWI, and to halt the rampant barter economy and black market trade where American cigarettes acted as currency. The move infuriated Stalin, who regarded it as a provocation. Anything the

West did, including introducing well-intentioned humanitarian acts like the Marshall Plan, was interpreted by the Soviets as an existential threat. Such paranoia spoke volumes about the Soviet mind-set and intentions. At last, the Americans and their allies were beginning to wake up to the looming menace the Soviets represented to Western Europe.

In retaliation, on June 24, the Soviets promptly cut off all road, rail, and canal links between the three western zones and West Berlin. Berlin was blockaded, which started a confrontation with the Soviets that turned into the first major international crisis of the Cold War. In response to the blockade, the United States and Britain launched an airlift of food and coal to the besieged city and distributed the new currency in West Berlin. This was the 1948 Berlin Blockade crisis.

By mid-July, the Soviet army of occupation in East Germany had increased to forty divisions, against eight in the Allied sectors. In response, at the end of July, three groups of US strategic bombers were sent as reinforcements. The Berlin blockade lasted from June 1948 to May 1949. Throughout that year, tensions remained high, but war did not break out. By the spring of 1949, the airlift was working efficiently, and its success brought embarrassment to the Soviets, who had refused to believe it could make a difference.

Father and other refugees in the DP camps saw this conflict as a prelude to a Soviet invasion. It was not an exaggerated fear. The Soviet armored divisions positioned on the Czech border were only one hundred kilometers away. This meant that Soviet tanks could be in Regensburg in three hours. Fearing the worst, Father organized a way to evacuate our family. With the money he had made from his shoe business, he purchased a used Ford truck and recruited a driver-mechanic. Gathering provisions and supplies was the collective effort of three families: the Myluses, who lived next door in a one-room apartment with their teenage son, Mykola; the Aponiuks, who lived nearby with one daughter, Irka; and us.[45] The Myluses were from Central Ukraine and survivors of the Holodomor, which had scarred them deeply. Mr. Mylus carried a few dry pieces of bread in his pocket wherever he went. Stories of the famine circulated in the camp, but few people knew of the extent of the tragedy because most refugees were from Western Ukraine, where there had been no famine.

---

[45] In 1949, the Mylus family emigrated to Brazil, and their only son, Mykola, became an Orthodox priest and continued to correspond with my parents. The Aponiuk family ended up in Edmonton, Alberta.

Even so, we stocked up on staples such as flour and sugar and other necessities for the escape. It included scavenging enough gasoline to take us as far as France. I distinctly recall the sweet smell of gasoline in the shed behind the house where we kept some pigs. All of this was done discreetly so as not to attract attention. Others undoubtedly would have wanted to join, but Father had calculated that there was room for only four families, twelve individuals including the driver-mechanic and his wife.

In the summer of 1948, Father took my sister and me on a test drive through the Bavarian countryside, my first trip in this kind of vehicle. With the cargo space uncovered, we sat on benches in the back of the truck holding on to the railing facing the wind. We were rolling at a leisurely pace along tree-lined motorways common in Europe, though to us it seemed as if we were flying like a rocket.

I doubt if anyone knew the group's destination. Would it be Switzerland? France? What we did know was that if the worst happened and the Soviets breached the Czech border, we wanted to be as far away from the Bolsheviks as possible. Fortunately, the Berlin crisis never developed into a hot war. Instead, the Cold War began. In April 1949, NATO was founded as an alliance between the United States and Canada and ten European countries, later joined by Turkey, Greece, and others.

A few months later, another totally unexpected event took place. On August 29, 1949, to the great shock of the Americans, the Soviet Union detonated its first atomic bomb. This came as a great surprise to the Americans, who had not expected the Soviet Union to possess a nuclear weapon capability so soon. In December 1949, Klaus Fuchs, a German-born physicist who had helped the United States to build its first atomic bombs, was arrested for passing nuclear secrets to the Soviets. The fact that the Soviet Union possessed the bomb turned the strategic calculation upside-down and caused the Americans to question their safety. Only three months after the end of the Berlin Blockade, the Cold War had escalated to an alarming level.

AS THE COLD WAR in Europe escalated, our family got a lucky break. In early 1949, Father's sister Anastasia, who had been living in the United States since the early '30s, sent us an official affidavit stating that she was willing to sponsor our family's immigration. It was an offer my parents could not refuse. Before getting our visas, the family had to appear in front of a consul who checked the documents, and made sure that no one in the family suffered from tuberculosis or another contagious disease. As soon as we got the consul's stamp of approval, we packed our suitcases. Father's business had been successful, and he had accumulated a considerable sum of money, but there was no point in taking Deutschmarks with us, and since buying a large amount of dollars was not an option, he purchased Omega watches, gold coins, and several late-model Leica cameras to sell when we reached America. Mother cleverly sewed the dozen or so gold watches into winter coats with fur collars, and Father put the cameras in leather cases, wrapped them in embroidered garments, put them in pots and pans, and tied a rope tightly around them.

The train to Bremerhaven, the port in northern Germany, was vastly more comfortable than the "thunder box" that took us to Munich. We boarded the USS *General W. M. Black*, a sturdy transport ship that plied the Atlantic and Pacific oceans during World War II.[46] After the war, it was used to ship immigrants to the United States, Australia, and South America. Women and children were packed like sardines in the vast hold and slept in bunks stacked four high. The men's bunks were only two beds high and vastly more comfortable. The rationale must have been that women and children needed less space.

During the tumultuous ten-day crossing, I felt nauseous only a few times, but Mother suffered from seasickness during the entire voyage, particularly on days when the sea was rough. Quite often, passengers in the hold in the hull vomited from their bunks, so there was a constant unpleasant odor. My sister and I often walked up several flights to the deck to breathe some fresh sea air.

When we got within sight of the New York City skyline, everyone rushed on deck to see the land of Washington and the Statue of Liberty. As passengers moved to the starboard side to get a glimpse of the monument, I experienced a curious sensation that the ship was not upright. I was too young to realize that it was listing. The joyful atmosphere was punctured by a sharp siren and a loud warning over the public address system to stop crowding the starboard side because there was a risk of capsizing. A few people moved to the port side, and that was enough for the ship to right itself as it headed for one of the Hudson River berths in New York's harbor. After experiencing the dangers of Russian artillery, American bombers, and mined bridges, we came close to calamity just a short distance from the Promised Land.

---

[46]   William Murray Black was a US Army general. A top West Point graduate (1877), he was chief of engineers during World War I.

Father's lifelong friend Oleksa Motyl, whom Father saved from drowning on the river Buh, and who had arrived in New York a few months before, came to greet us. We hadn't seen each other since our visit to Munich. It was a happy reunion. Motyl suggested that we stay in his place in the East Village, but Mother was ill and in pain and insisted that we continue onto Chicago. Months later, when a doctor finally examined her, we learned that she was suffering from gallbladder stones and had experienced an attack on board the ship.

Our train pulled into the LaSalle Station in Chicago on May 3, 1949. According to the Gregorian calendar, it was Easter Monday. It took most of the day for Aunt Anastasia to arrive from Lombard, Illinois, but I did not mind the long wait. I was intrigued by the plethora of new sights and the rumbling of the Loop Elevated train, which I could see from the cavernous waiting room of the LaSalle Station above Van Buren Street. Most of all, I was overwhelmed by the sight of the Board of Trade and the surrounding skyscrapers. It was hard for me to fathom that a building could be forty stories high when the highest structure I had seen, apart from church steeples, was five stories. When Aunt Anastasia and her husband, Tony Manek, arrived, they packed us into the backseat of their 1939 Chrysler. Even though the car was ten years old, to me it seemed like the epitome of luxury.

My parents, Roman and Natalia Martyniuk.

Wedding photo, 1938. Oleksa Motyl stands at top right.

The main block at the Bereza Kartuzka, the Polish
concentration camp as it appeared in 2005.

Father's leather goods shop Lederwaren (Shkira in Ukrainian) in Kamianka.
Mother on balcony looking down at my sister and me with our nanny Mil'ka.

Mother Natalia with my sister Ivanka, Grandmother Maria with arms around me and an unidentified girl, early 1944.

Photo from mother's official German identity card.

My Father Roman, Grandfather Petro Martyniuk and Uncle Oleksa Standing.

Family somewhere in Austria during the cold winter of 1944/45.

Regensburg looking at St Peter's (Dom) and the
medieval Steinbrücke spanning the Danube

First grade in Ukrainian school at Regensburg.
I'm standing top row, third from right.

UKRAINIAN ELEMENTARY SCHOOL at *Regensburg*
GERMANY — BAVARIA

Catalogue Number: *18/47*   School-year 1946/47

CERTIFICATION

It is to certify that *Martyniuk Jaroslaw*
born on *25th of May* 1940 at *Modrynec*
circle *Hrubeszów*, *Ukrainian* rationality, *greek-cath* religion has finished in the schol-year 1946/47, the *first "b"* class with general result *very good*

He(she) missed in the schol-year *47* hours, from them *—* not justified.

Regensburg the *June 30th* 1947

Headmaster   Class Master

My first report card

To Cub Scout troop in Regensburg: Ivan Myhul standing
front row at extreme right, I'm sixth from right just below the
scoutmaster; standing to my right is Rostyslaw Boykowych.

Porta Praetoria built during the reign of Emperor Marcus Aurelius in AD 179

The house where our family lived from 1946 to 1949 in Ganghofer, a suburb of Regensburg. My sister Ivanka stands at the top of the entry stairs.

The same house, formerly the Displaced Person's (DP) camp, fifty years later

9. The American Dream

WE ARRIVED IN CHICAGO with two suitcases. All our other possessions were scheduled to arrive a month later in two wooden trunks. My parents were extremely concerned about these trunks because they contained their life's possessions and valuables.

Aunt Anastasia "Nastia" and her husband, Anthony "Tony," and their two daughters, Anne "Jeannie" and Marie, lived in an unfinished two-story house that Tony was building on a three-acre lot in the Chicago suburb of Lombard. Having worked as a skilled carpenter, he was well qualified to build their family home. Located in the middle of a cornfield, near the intersection of North Avenue and Route 53, the house was a quarter of a mile away from the nearest neighbor. Although it was almost the end of the school year, my parents enrolled my sister and me in a little blue one-room schoolhouse in Addison, Illinois. The children were divided into two groups according to age and ability. Not knowing English, we were seated in the back of the classroom with the younger, less advanced students for the first few weeks, unable to understand a word the teacher said. Fortunately, she was patient, though the children teased us. We picked up English quickly via the "swim or sink" method: total immersion. Within a month, we were communicating with the other children.

My parents found seasonal work in a nearby greenhouse that specialized in cultivating fine flowers such as orchids and gardenias. They worked ten-hour days, six days a week, and Father was paid eighty-five cents per hour. Women, doing lighter work, got seventy-five cents. In the summer of 1949, Uncle Oleksa, Father's younger brother, arrived from Germany with his pregnant wife, Stefania. They were among the very few immigrants who crossed the ocean in an airplane. Soon, Oleksa began working in the greenhouse as well.

In the fall of 1949, my sister and I trudged across the cornfields to Route 53, where a school bus picked us up. I was thrilled with the ride because we passed sites that excited me: a small airport full of Piper Cubs and crop dusters, followed by a single-track rail line. I was mesmerized by the long freight trains pulled by a steam locomotive. At school, instead of paying attention to the teacher, I spent a lot of time drawing locomotives, airplanes, and tanks, and at home, I built Piper Cub model airplanes from scratch using strips of balsa wood.

The wooden one-room schoolhouse we first attended was too small to serve the postwar influx of children, and one day, I saw it being carted away to school heaven, which made me sad. The new school constructed on Lake Street in Addison was modern, but it seemed cold and impersonal. As my English was still not up to snuff, my homeroom teacher, a pleasant and patient lady, put me in the front row, in case I needed help. She had five dresses, and I could tell what day of the week it was by the one she was wearing.

During the summer of 1949, Uncle Tony put finishing touches on the house he had built from scratch. He taught me how to nail together two-by-fours, join floor planks, and lay cinder blocks. Every morning, he went to work in his old 1937 Ford Coupé—if he could start it. On the days he could not start his Ford, he drove to work in the 1939 Chrysler, a sturdier car that came with accessories like a radio and a defogging fan on the dashboard.

Uncle Tony made good money, $2.50 an hour, but carpentry was hard work, and on hot summer days, he had a habit of stopping for a few beers with his coworkers on his way home. When he arrived in good spirits and with another quart of Meister Bräu in a brown bag, Aunt Nastia, a religious and frugal woman, objected. She thought Tony was squandering money on drink, and this provoked endless arguments.

In the six months we lived in Lombard, my parents told and retold their war stories, and Nastia and Tony also recalled the hard times they experienced during the Depression in the 1930s when they lived in Oklahoma. At first, we were unable to relate to their hardships in Oklahoma, but with the passage of years and thanks to my reading, I was able to put their ordeal into context.

They experienced what Timothy Egan called "the worst of hard times," the dust bowl days in Oklahoma.[47]

My aunt and her family in America lived through one of the most difficult periods in the history of the United States: the Dust Bowl and the Great Depression of the 1930s. Aunt Nastia said, "For the first time in my life I experienced real hunger." Many years later, her words motivated me to memorialize this chapter of our family history. As she died in the mid-'60s, I turned to her two daughters, Marie Kukla and Anne (Jeannie) Corwyn, to piece together a story that had begun over a century earlier.

Uncle Tony's parents arrived from Ukraine as contract workers in the 1880s and had to work off their passage by picking cotton in Texas. In the early 1900s, when the US government, under the Enlarged Homestead Act, was selling dirt-cheap marginal lands in Oklahoma to anyone who planted a crop, Tony's father and his brother bought a 160-acre tract of land. Anthony Manek was born in 1906, soon after the family settled in Oklahoma. The family began planting a variety of crops but soon realized that the acreage could not be easily irrigated. A massive influx of new farmers, combined with inappropriate cultivation techniques and misunderstanding of the ecology, led to immense land erosion.

My aunt Anastasia, Roman's older sister, was born in 1907 in the village of Tadani in Galicia. In 1928, when she was twenty-one, she emigrated to Canada and worked as a maid for a wealthy Jewish family in Toronto. Grandmother Dudka, Maria Martyniuk's sister, my great-aunt Julie, who had emigrated to Oklahoma before WWI, sent Nastia a photo of an eligible young bachelor, Tony Manek. Tony traveled to Toronto to meet Anastasia, and the two found they had a lot in common and fell in love. Aunt Julie convinced Nastia to leave Canada and move to Oklahoma. After a brief courtship, Tony and Anastasia were married in 1930, in the Ukrainian Orthodox Church in Toronto, and then headed for Oklahoma and settled near the small town of Harrah.

Before 1890, this territory had been an Indian reservation, but what remained of the Potawatomi reservation was opened up to settlement in

---

[47] Many books have been written about the Great Depression. John Steinbeck gave voice to those who fled the dust bowl in his masterpiece *The Grapes of Wrath*. The story of those who stayed and survived is best told by Timothy Egan in his National Book Award Winning *The Worst Hard Times* (2006). His account corresponds closely with the ordeal the Manek family experienced during the great American dust bowl in the 1930s.

the land run of the 1890s. The soil around Harrah was so red that the local farmers, who spoke a mix of Ukrainian, Polish, and English referred to it as *chervinka*, suggesting a bloody red hue.[48] In 1930, despite a drought in much of the country, the high plains got enough moisture to produce a bumper crop. For the farmers, this meant that the price of wheat dropped to thirty cents a bushel, far below the cost to grow and harvest it. Worse, no one would buy the wheat because there was no place to store it; the elevators were full. Timothy Egan wrote:

> In mid-September 1930 a windstorm kicked up the dust of southwest Kansas and tumbled toward Oklahoma, a storm unlike anything seen before in the High Plains. The tractors had done what no hailstorm, no blizzard, no tornado, no drought, no prairie fire had ever done. They removed the native grass so thoroughly that by the end of 1931 it was a different land. A blast furnace descended on the Great Plains—hot winds hardened the land, rivers went dry and disappeared, no rain through the heat of July, August, and September. The rains deserted the Great Plains and would not come back for eight years. At the same time, the price of wheat hit an all-time low of twenty cents a bushel.

With unpredictable weather and negligible rain, raising any crop was hard work. Tony's first crop was cotton. It was backbreaking work. The cotton had to be handpicked, a task very hard on the hands, baled, and taken to the market. Very quickly Tony discovered that cotton did not pay. Cotton farming had crashed, and farmers were leaving the drought-crushed eastern half of Oklahoma. In the midst of this disaster, my cousin Marie was born on September 30, 1931.

The following year, the Maneks tried their hand at growing watermelons, but with everyone doing the same thing, there was a glut. Next, they tried raising tomatoes and then corn, but the prices for produce were so depressed it was impossible to make ends meet. Growing a bushel of tomatoes cost more than the twenty-five cents they got for it at the market.

With the native grass sod plowed under, land began to erode. Hot winds picked up the soil and sent it skyward. This was the beginning of the dust bowl years, and eking out a living in the dry red soil became extremely hard,

---

48   *Chervinka* in Ukrainian means dysentery, a disease characterized by bloody diarrhea.

if not impossible. In 1932, only twelve inches of rain fell—half of what was needed to produce a crop. Since the harvest of 1932 did not bring in the revenue needed to feed the family, in the winter of that year Uncle Tony took a job in a local dairy, milking cows by hand. It was demanding work that paid little. Moreover, the dairy owner was such a miser that he did not even allow Tony to take milk home for his infant daughter.

With farming a losing proposition, the Manek family decided to take their chances in Oklahoma City, where there was a small Ukrainian community and a church. They had heard through the grapevine that Wilson, the meat-packer, was looking for help because its unionized workers were on strike. The meat-packer was ready to offer work to scabs able to cross the picket line. The company needed experienced bricklayers, and Uncle Tony stepped forward. He knew what he was up against, but with a wife and a hungry child, he took the chance of crossing the picket line of men armed with bats and pipes. Although beaten and bruised, he made his way through the strikers and got the job. Now he had to show that he could lay bricks. Good with his hands, Tony observed how others were doing it and quickly became proficient. One thing led to another, and before long, Tony had a job as a maintenance man. The meatpacking facility had machinery that needed constant oiling and maintenance, so Tony acquired a new skill.

In the meantime, dust storms in the High Plains continued. March and April 1933 were the worst months. Steady winds flung fine-grained dirt on what used to be farmland. There had never been a drier summer. A region that had produced a surplus only two years before now gave only a few truckloads of grain. Farmers were leaving the drought-stricken eastern half of Oklahoma and heading for other parts of the country.[49] Egan notes:

> The worst was still to come. By 1934 the drought was in its third year. The whirlwinds made the sun turn orange, and a mass of

[49] Coincidentally, in Ukraine, 1933 was the worst year of the Holodomor—death by starvation—the Ukrainian genocide-famine where during 1932–33 four to six millions Ukrainians perished. The Holodomor was the centerpiece of the Soviet Union's ruthless campaign against nationally conscious Ukrainians opposed to Stalin's collectivization of agriculture. In addition to decimating Ukraine's political, intellectual, cultural, and religious elites, Joseph Stalin's Communist regime deliberately starved Ukrainian farmers. At the height of the famine during the spring of 1933, twenty-five thousand Ukrainians were dying each day.

dust filled clouds marched east. Cities from Chicago to Boston and New York slipped under partial darkness 1,800 miles wide. In April of 1935, the temperature reached 100 degrees Fahrenheit. Palm Sunday, April 14, started as a sunny day. Suddenly a mass of cold air from the north clashed with warm air in the south producing violent air currents. The sky turned black. The mother of all dusters hit, depositing a tremendous load of sand on a swath of land from Dodge City, Kansas to the Oklahoma panhandle. With the topsoil gone, the bare, sterile ground was weighted down with sand. The land had become a moonscape—empty and hideous.

In Oklahoma City, the Maneks rented a shack, which was all they could afford, while Uncle Tony worked hard at the meatpacking plant to save for a down payment on a lot to build a home. In this humble abode, my other cousin Jeannie was born in 1935, the worst year of the drought. At the same time, Aunt Nastia came down with double pneumonia and nearly died. A strong will, a desire to live, and good genes helped Nastia pull through the crisis.

Eventually, life became more tolerable. At least they were not starving like many who lived in the "Hooverville" shanty town across the North Canadian River. Cousin Mary recalled how thousands of folks there barely survived in shacks built of orange crates. Most were dust bowl survivors, farmers who couldn't make it but decided to stay in Oklahoma rather than migrate.

"HOW COULD SUCH a catastrophe have happened?" I asked myself when writing this story. Oklahoma lost most of its topsoil, and the land became barren. Soil expert Hugh Bennet, at the request of Roosevelt in August 1936, produced part of the answer in a report "The Future of the Great Plains." His conclusions were stark. First, it refuted the widespread belief that the climate had changed. In fact, the Great Plains drought was part of a prairie life cycle dating back eons. He concluded that there was simply not enough rain to raise crops.

Bennet blamed the government for the disaster by encouraging exploitative farming during the early 1920s. He also blamed the Department of Agriculture for misleading farmers. A mistaken homesteading policy led to overcropping and overgrazing, encouraging a system of agriculture that could not be sustainable. These were harsh conclusions that President Roosevelt found hard to take. His experts had been telling him that it was people, not weather and bad luck, that had caused the problem.

This would not be the first instance of catastrophic consequences caused by well-intentioned government initiatives. The next three-quarters of the century would see a number of financial and environmental crises provoked by the government. An obvious one that comes to mind today in agriculture is government-mandated support of ethanol.[50]

The Dust Bowl and the Great Depression were difficult times not only for my family but also for the United States. However, the notion of difficult times is relative. During the Depression, people suffered greatly from hunger. Times were hard, but nothing could compare to the traumatic events that took place in Ukraine at about the same time. A month after the American stock market crashed in October 1929, Stalin proclaimed that the Soviet Union had taken a "great leap forward," with forced industrialization and collectivization of agriculture. It began with an offensive against kulaks (*kurkul* in Ukrainian) and ended with mass famine in 1932 and 1933. Four to six million Ukrainians, representing about one-fifth of the peasant population, were deliberately starved to death. We will never know the full extent of the artificial famine because, on Stalin's orders, the 1937 census was suppressed, and statistics were continuously falsified or sanitized to minimize losses in population. The world did not discover the full extent of the genocide until 1991. My family was spared the ravages of collectivization and the Holodomor. They lived in Western Ukraine, which at that time was under Polish control. It was the inhabitants of Central and South-Eastern Ukraine that were the greatest victims of the deliberately caused famine.

The Manek family stayed in Oklahoma through 1943. In 1944, Uncle Tony moved his family to Chicago, where he got a job as a piano cabinet maker. Tony was a country boy at heart, a man who missed the open spaces of Oklahoma where he had spent his entire life. In Chicago, he felt closed in, so when a job opportunity in the suburbs came along, the Maneks decided to settle in Lombard, Illinois. In the late '40s, this suburb of Chicago was still sparsely populated and the land relatively cheap. Tony got a union job as a carpenter and, with the money they saved, the Maneks purchased several acres and began building a two-story house to which they welcomed us in the spring of 1949. But with the arrival of Oleksa, Father's younger brother

---

[50]   *Corn Ethanol: Who Pays, Who Benefits*, Ken Glozer (2013).

from Germany, conditions in the unfinished house became crowded and testy. That's when the two newly arrived families began talking about moving to Chicago proper, where there was a Ukrainian community, a Greek Catholic church, and a parochial school.

10. Life in Chicago in the 1950s

WE LEFT AUNT NASTIA'S house in the country in December 1949 and arrived in the City of the Big Shoulders in the dead of winter. Carl Sandburg's line, the "Hog Butcher for the World," captures one reason why Father traded Lombard for Chicago.[51]

Slaughterhouses in the city were always looking for able-bodied men. Roman and his brother Oleksa found work at the Swift meatpacking plant on the South Side. The starting wage was $1.10 an hour, higher than the seasonal work in the greenhouse. If you were a good worker, you could earn $1.30, and if the supervisor liked you, $1.50. Sixty dollars a week was a fair working wage. Father recounted, "On the meatpacking conveyor, I got a thick protective leather apron and an electric saw suspended from above for easier handling. My job was to cut a particular hog hindquarter bone every five seconds. Although tedious and boring, these jobs brought home the bread and offered immigrants a way to begin a new life without depending on government dole."

Although we lived on the near West Side of Chicago, some distance from the South Side stockyards, on days the wind blew from the south, I

---

[51] "Chicago," a poem by Carl Sandburg:

> *Hog Butcher for the World,*
> *Tool Maker, Stacker of Wheat,*
> *Player with Railroads and the Nation's Freight Handler;*
> *Stormy, husky, brawling,*
> *City of the Big Shoulders.*

could detect the foul smell emanating from that direction. As the saying goes, in pursuit of efficiency and profits, the meat-packers used every part of the animal's carcass but the squeal. Conditions and sanitary practices in meatpacking plants in the mid-twentieth century were better than those described in Upton Sinclair's novel *The Jungle,* but they were still dangerous places to work. Even today, the rate of injury in the meatpacking industry is three times that of the private industry.

There was an acute shortage of apartments in the city of four million. The population was growing, and no new housing had been built since the Depression. We found temporary quarters in a rundown one-story building on Evergreen Street near Damen Avenue, where we shared a ground-level apartment with three families—Father's brother Oleksa, his wife, and new baby daughter, Maria, and Mr. and Mrs. Mykola Lushniak.[52]

The unheated dwelling consisted of a kitchen and three rooms. The linoleum-covered cement floor was ice cold, and the only source of heat was a single coal-burning stove whose warmth hardly reached beyond one room. During the night, when the outside temperature hovered around zero (Fahrenheit), we lit the oven and all four burners of the stove for warmth.

Rats found a way into our apartment to escape freezing temperatures, and one night, Mr. Lushniak discovered one in his bed. He threw a blanket over the rodent and suffocated it. Knowing that the eccentric landlord considered the rodents his pets and even fed them, Mr. Lushniak did not bother to report the incident to him. If he had, he would no doubt have been threatened with eviction. In those days, there were few agencies where one could file a complaint.

At night, we slept near the small stove, trying to stay warm under layers of comforters and blankets. Father suffered the most. He worked the graveyard shift at Swift and would get home just as we were waking up. During the first winter, he labored in a refrigerated workplace and braved cutting icy Chicago wind to and from work. At home, it was never really warm. He rarely complained, but with constant exposure to the cold he developed rheumatism.

Every Sunday, we attended mass at Saint Nicholas' Church. It was always packed with immigrants like us, and through friends there, Father found a job cleaning offices at night at the twenty-five-story YMCA Building where

---

[52]   In 2013, the Lushniaks' son, Rear Admiral Boris D. Lushniak, MD, MPH, became the acting United States surgeon general with oversight of the operations of the US Public Health Service.

the pay was good. Most importantly, he escaped the frigid and foul working environment at the stockyards. Next, he became a foreman at the Palmolive skyscraper on Michigan Avenue near Lake Michigan and eventually worked his way up to become the managing superintendent of a building on Lake and Wabash. At the same time, Mother found day work as a seamstress in a tailor's shop. Our fortunes began to look up.

In the spring, we found a six-room apartment in a two-story vintage stone building on Artesian Street.[53] The building was old, but the apartment was spacious and felt like a palace after the previous home on Evergreen Street. Our rent doubled to sixty dollars per month, and although the second-floor apartment had no central heating, a coal-burning stove in the dining room and another one in the kitchen kept us relatively warm.

The landlords, Mr. and Mrs. Bobrowski, occupied the first floor. He was a kind and gentle man who gave us candy and chewing gum. His wife, however, was always complaining about the noise we made. She had a habit of pounding her ceiling with a broom to tell us to keep it down. With nine people on the second floor, she might have had a point, but we saw her as a witch.

In addition to Roman's and Oleksa's families, we rented out rooms to two single men, Mr. Alexander Nakonechny, Father's old friend from Ukraine, and Mr. Ivan Sakharewych, Oleksa's friend from Germany. The atmosphere in the apartment was always lively, with friends dropping by unexpectedly with news. The family gathered around the kitchen table to discuss current events, and there were endless war stories, news about the growing threat of Communism, American politics, and the possibility of war with the Soviet Union. This is also when I first heard about the grisly details of Stalin's famine of 1932–1933. Sometimes I listened to these conversations more attentively, but, just turning ten, my real interests were the newest automobile models, toy guns, and the price of cigarettes.

Nearly every male smoked. Father limited himself to three Pall Mall cigarettes a day—long filterless cigarettes he cut in two, so a pack might last him a week. Mr. Nakonechny and Uncle Oleksa smoked more and gave me two dimes to run to the candy store to pick up a pack, which cost eighteen

---

53   The solid turn-of-the-century two-flat with rounded bay windows was torn down during the 1980s when the neighborhood, overrun by Puerto Rican immigrants, had reached its lowest point. Today that stone façade building would be worth a small fortune.

cents. They let me keep the two cents change, which I put into a piggy bank. When I had my first dollar, I thought I was on my way to becoming a rich man.

Our tenant, Mr. Sakharewych, was a macho-type bachelor who bragged about this and that and flexed his muscles so we kids could feel how hard they were. He talked about cars and girls, and I listened with interest. Despite his boasting, he was a kind man.[54] On my birthday, he gave me a silver plated cap-shooting revolver. I was thrilled by the gift because every day after school, we played cowboys and Indians, or "good guys / bad guys." If you didn't have a toy gun, you had to do with a makeshift wooden one. My cap-shooting six-gun made me feel powerful, and everyone wanted me to be on their team. For hours, we ran around the alleys and gangways in the neighborhood, hiding, sneaking up on members of the rival gang, and shouting, "Bang, bang, bang." There were, of course, disputes about who shot first, but with a cap gun, the result was indisputable.

A few months after we moved to Artesian Street, on Monday afternoon, June 26, 1950, while on my way to the corner candy store to get cigarettes for the smokers, I heard newspapers boys shouting, "Extra, extra, read all about it." The oversize *Sun-Times* and *Chicago Tribune* headlines blared, "War in Korea: The Korean People's Army crosses the 38th parallel behind artillery fire at dawn on Sunday 25 June 1950." The Korean War had broken out. The news created alarm among Chicago's émigré community. Talk of WWIII was in the air. Sooner or later, many believed, it would come to a clash between the United States and the USSR—the war they had been expecting since 1948. What didn't happen during the Berlin blockade, they said, is happening in Korea.

After the Soviets had detonated their first nuclear bomb in September 1949, the world's strategic balance changed completely and utterly. The Soviets had been arming North Korea, calculating that the Americans would be even less willing to fight in Korea than they were in Europe, but they were wrong. The Americans responded with a protracted police action to push back the North Koreans to the Chinese border. Regrettably, they never finished the job, as General MacArthur advised, a blunder for which the world is still paying the price. The war ended after Stalin died in March 1953, and Korea

---

[54] Sakharewych eventually became the owner of Sak's bar and restaurant on Oakley at Chicago Avenue, a popular watering hole that in time was taken over by his son.

was divided along the 38th parallel. God knows what might have happened if Stalin had lived longer. The Korean War was the first of many confrontations with Communism during the coming decades, an on/off, cold/hot war that did not end until the "evil empire" imploded in August 1991—the week I climbed Monte Rosa.

THE WISE OLD REAL-ESTATE agent George W. Johnson once said, if you own good real estate, never sell it, and you will get rich. In mid-1952, my parents formed a partnership with Mr. and Mrs. Michael Daczkewycz, friends they had known from Germany, to come up with a down payment for a three-flat at 2023 Thomas Street near Damen Avenue, which they bought for $20,000. It was a solid 1930s light brick building with a ground-floor basement, three five-room centrally heated apartments, and a garage. Each apartment had solid oak floors, a fireplace, and bay windows. They occupied the first floor, we took the second, and the third was rented to Mr. and Mrs. Hryhorczuk, he an engineer and his wife a physician.[55] Today, the building would probably fetch fifty times the amount we paid in 1952.

The neighborhood I grew up in during this formative period in my life was a mosaic of ethnicities, mostly Eastern European. The Poles were the dominant demographic, followed by Ukrainians, Slovaks, and a mix of Germans and Anglo-Saxons. A little south, the neighborhood turned Italian. By the early 1950s, a lively Ukrainian community had established itself. Newly arriving immigrants converged here to be with their countrymen who spoke their language, to be near a school, youth organizations, Ukrainian shops, banks, and doctors offices. At the heart of the Ukrainian village stood the neo-Byzantine–style Ukrainian Greek Catholic Church of Saint Nicholas. Built in 1912, its copulas dominated the skyline as they do today. Next to the church was the grammar school run by the Basilian Sisters, and a little further on was Saint Mary's hospital.

At the turn of the century, this must have been a desirable place to live because the neighborhood had a few stately residences. Two short blocks north was the animated world of Division Street, a ten-mile east-west thoroughfare that began on the Gold Coast near Lake Shore Drive and continued to

---

[55] This building was home to two individuals who became prominent physicians. Hryhorczuk's son Dr. Danylo Hryhorczuk, born in 1950, became a physician and author of a fictional memoir *Caught by the Current* (2013) and *Myth and Madness: A Novel* (2016). Daczkewycz's son Roman Daczkewycz became an orthopedic surgeon.

Chicago's western city limits. The point at which Division Street met Milwaukee Avenue and Ashland was the Polonia Triangle, the gateway to the Wicker Park area also known as Bucktown.

By the time we moved to this part of Chicago, the original residents, Germans and Scandinavians who settled here in the nineteenth century, had gone further north, leaving behind many well-built homes. At the turn of the century, Jews from Galicia, Ukraine, and Hungary moved to Chicago and settled in the area. They formed the nucleus of a Jewish ghetto that expanded west along Division Street to Humboldt Park and beyond to Logan Square. Division Street with its wide sidewalks became an important commercial artery with clothing stores, kosher butcher shops, and theaters. At the same time, the first synagogues were built, and, eventually, about twenty of them served the Jewish community, which constituted about one-quarter of the district's population.[56]

The Jews were split among Socialists, secularists, Zionists, and Orthodox, but as the young became more Americanized, these differences faded. The ghetto produced a number of personalities and intellectuals, including Michael Todd, future husband of Elizabeth Taylor, writer Saul Bellow, and the Pritzker family, who became giants in the business world and one of the wealthiest families in the United States.

Between WWI and WWII, the near-northwest part of Chicago was overwhelmed with Polish immigrants. Polonia Triangle, surrounded by Polish Catholic churches, schools, newspapers, and even a museum, became the hub of Polish life. The Polish ghetto that spread into Wicker Park and Division Street became known as the "Polish Broadway."

We lived near Division and Damen, a lively intersection where two streetcar lines crossed. Four- and five-story buildings with ornate facades and cone towers exuded an aura of cosmopolitan urbanity, not unlike the cities in Europe. During the next forty years, the area would undergo a series of convulsions from good to bad, from bad to worse, and from worse to the pits as urban decay set in.

Many of my childhood friends, exclusively Ukrainian, lived within a few blocks of our house on Thomas Street: the Klymkowych brothers, the Ozga brothers, the Pihut brothers, and a little further, Yurko Kuzycz. Some bizarre incidents stand out—one of them the case of Ilarion "Liunko" Malyj

---

[56]   The bulk of Chicago's Jewish population lived in the Garfield Park area on the west side and neighboring Lawndale.

who lived nearby. I would stroll to Liunko's apartment to exchange baseball cards, play handball against a wall, or hand wrestle, and one day, to amuse ourselves, we shot beans through a straw at strangers across the street. Another time, Liunko challenged me to a finger wrestling contest. I hooked up my right-hand middle finger with his, we tussled for a minute, and then I heard a snap. When I let go, Liunko's middle finger was twisted at a forty-five-degree angle, sideways. I had broken his finger. I felt bad but not as bad as Liunko, who had to wear a brace on his middle finger for a month until it healed. We never tried finger wrestling again.

This incident could have ended badly for me too. I was taking piano lessons with Prof. Ihor Bilohrud, who was trained in the school of Stravinsky and other world-class pianists. He said I showed promise and began preparing me for a group recital downtown, which was a big deal. If I had broken my finger, my piano career would have been irreversibly interrupted. Instead, I continued to play the piano and study music theory until I entered college. I credit Professor Bilohrud with instilling in me a lifelong appreciation for music.

Other musically inclined friends in the "hood" included Myron Komarynski, a fellow aficionado of piano, and Rostyslaw "Kuksa" Klukowsky, a violinist and an occasional wrestling rival. All were members of *Plast*, a Ukrainian scouting organization that shaped our character and worldview. We were taught to think and behave like Spartans: to tolerate hardships, endure long marches, learn survival skills, sleep outdoors under an open sky, practice military-like night exercises, and get exposed to small firearms. We also immersed ourselves in the study of Ukrainian history, culture, and language. The culminating point of our training was a three-week summer camp in a wild forest, something I enjoyed immensely. The endurance tests we were subjected to in *Plast* made us tough, a quality that became handy, particularly during military service. My command of Ukrainian also made it easier to pick up Russian, and this would open up unexpected career opportunities throughout my professional life.

De Paul Academy, the all-male academy next to De Paul University, run mostly by Vincentian priests, taught me to be self-reliant and disciplined. Latin was obligatory the first two years. Later in life, I discovered that the study of Latin was extremely useful in picking up other languages. Through Latin, I improved my understanding of grammar, a subject I never mastered despite years of abstract diagramming of sentences that the sisters at Saint Nicholas insisted we do.

My first-year Latin teacher was a strict disciplinarian. Mr. McGrath, who was also the varsity basketball coach, never put up with nonsense from his students. Still, there were always a few wise guys who tried to test him. Mr. McGrath dealt with such troublemakers directly and resolutely. He would throw a soft blackboard eraser at those who slouched or did not pay attention. If that didn't work, he called the offender to the blackboard and instructed him to decline a noun or conjugate a verb. God forbid if a student was not prepared, or talked back. Mr. McGrath's face turned red, and the student usually got the message, but he had a way of dealing with those few who resisted. On one occasion, he grabbed a student by the shirt, pressed him against the blackboard, and slapped him across the cheek. From then on, everyone did their homework religiously, and, more importantly, the incident set an example for the rest of the class. The rumor spread around the school that Mr. McGrath was tough and you didn't mess with him. For the rest of the year, there were no disciplinary problems in any of his classes.

In those days, very few households could afford television sets. Films were the favorite form of entertainment, and our neighborhood had several movie houses. The Biltmore, an upscale movie theater designed in 1919 in Spanish Baroque style, showed films that had just finished their downtown run. The lobby had a red carpet, and usherettes escorted clients to comfortable velour-covered seats. The New Strand, across the street, did not have any of these amenities. Still, both theaters offered double features, but the New Strand's films were slightly older. For us, the main difference was the price. The Biltmore charged twenty-five cents compared to fifteen cents at the New Strand, and kids under twelve got in for nine cents. Children loved the New Strand because on Saturdays, they offered a bonus of three cartoons. Most of us, however, never got to indulge in such delights because on Saturday morning, we had to attend Ukrainian school, and the afternoon was taken up by *Plast* activities.

AT AGE FIFTEEN, I became interested in girls. I was easily distracted by them at school, during my music theory classes, and at *Plast*. On occasion, my infatuations got me into trouble. Dorothy was sixteen, and on first sight I was captivated by her enticing looks, luscious lips, and seductive figure. The problem was that dating non-Ukrainian girls in our closely knit community was not allowed. Our situation was similar to that of the Jews. We were expected to meet and marry some nice Ukrainian girl from a decent, God-fearing Catholic family, and Dorothy was neither Catholic nor Ukrainian.

The only way to spend a few hours with her was to ask her to meet me at the Biltmore Theatre. The summer was hot, and the theater was air conditioned. Meeting in the cool, dark theater where no one would see us seemed like a good idea at the time. Nervous but thrilled at the prospect of being with Dorothy, I told my parents that I was going to play tennis with my friends Siajko and Kuksa and then went to the Biltmore, where Dorothy was waiting for me. When we sat down, I slowly slipped my arm around her shoulder, and we began to kiss. Priests in high school told us that kissing a girl on the lips was not a sin, but open-mouth kissing was inviting temptation. I got excited, but that's as far as it went. In all, we spent more time necking than watching the movie.

When I arrived home that afternoon, I learned that while I was at the Biltmore, Siajko and Kuksa came to visit me and told my father they did not know where I was. Needless to say, he was angry and slapped me for not telling the truth. My friends found this amusing. I did not.

I recall another event associated with the Biltmore Theatre that was not amusing. In August 1955, Chicago police were searching for Richard Carpenter, a cop killer who happened to live a few streets away. Two or three days after the murder, another policeman by sheer chance spotted Carpenter inside the Biltmore and tried to arrest him. Carpenter resisted, a shoot-out followed and ended with Carpenter dead. The incident was eerily reminiscent of the shooting of another cop killer, John Herbert Dillinger, who, in July 1934, was killed by police outside the Biograph Theatre. The shooting created a commotion in the community, and for some time people hesitated to go to the Biltmore.

We lived near an invisible line that straddled the Wicker Park neighborhood and the Ukrainian Village. It ran along Division Street, a lively and vibrant street full of shops, people, automobiles, and colorful streetcars. The rumble and clanking of these streetcars added to the animated atmosphere of the entire area.

By the mid-'50s, the streetcars were gone, a marker that seemed to signal the beginning of the decline of this area. While the core of the Ukrainian Village held its own, the Wicker Park neighborhood embarked on a decline for the remainder of the twentieth century. The exodus of middle-class whites began in the 1960s. The Polish community, in particular, deserted *en masse* and moved to the suburbs. By 1980, Puerto Ricans became the largest ethnic group south of Humboldt Park. The Biltmore, renamed the San Juan, featured Spanish-language films, but that did not save the theater. In 1991, this venerable West Town landmark was torn down.

At its seemingly lowest point, the neighborhood's fortunes reversed. The revival started in the 1990s when a cluster of turn-of-the-century buildings around the small Wicker Park was restored. Soon, renovation and restoration expanded north and south of Division Street. Suddenly, the neighborhood got a second life, an unexpected resurrection from near death.

Observing the roller coaster from good times in the '50s to a thirty-year period of urban decline to newfound prosperity in the '90s begs the question why this part of Chicago, with all of its natural advantages and proximity to the Loop, declined in the first place. The answer is long and complicated and beyond the scope of this memoir. Still, I think it's worthwhile summarizing the main causes. It all began with the expansion of mortgage interest deduction in the 1940s, a move that subsidized home ownership but distorted allocation of capital and discriminated against renters. Construction of low-income housing around Chicago's Loop in the 1950s was followed by the building of freeways, which ripped up viable neighborhoods and made it easier for suburbanites to commute downtown while promoting the growth and proliferation of suburbs around Chicago. The last and most devastating blow came from a government-instigated policy of forced busing of black students into white neighborhoods, and vice versa. Four years after the Civil Rights Act of 1964, the Warren Court ordered that school districts must achieve racial balance even if it meant the use of busing as a tool. Forced integration of schools accelerated white flight to the suburbia. The ultimate irony is that forty years later, the courts admitted that busing did not work. Not only did it not improve academic performance among blacks, but race relations in forced-integrated schools were exacerbated by busing.

FIFTY YEARS AFTER the near demise of the Ukrainian Village, the neighborhoods around Division Street have undergone a complete transformation. The streetcars never came back, but the area is lively again, though the taverns of the 1950s have been replaced by trendy restaurants and bars. The once impressive corner at Division and Damen is blemished by a small ugly strip mall, and the only institution to have survived the upheaval is the Rainbo Club on Damen, where I once sold chances to raise money for my high school's fund-raiser. It is still there, with its 1940s sign intact, brimming with yuppies on weekends drawn by inexpensive beer. The Rainbo is no ordinary bar and deserves a momentary digression from the course of this memoir.

When I attended De Paul Academy in the mid-'50s, every year the school organized a raffle drive to raise funds for the upkeep of the school. Each student was required to sell twenty booklets with six chances. The price of each ticket was twenty-five cents, and as an incentive for every booklet sold, the student got to keep a quarter. Family and friends might buy a few, but for the most part, you had to find other ways of selling them. I came across the idea of peddling them to people in the twenty or so bars along Division Street. I worked my way one block at a time, toward Western Avenue. When I entered a tavern, I scanned for females and approached them first. They were a soft touch. Next, I approached the men at the bar, introduced myself as a student of De Paul Academy, and explained that "for a quarter, you can win $2,000 or a car." Because most of the customers in these bars were already tipsy and Catholic, the response was usually positive.

The experience instilled in me a sense of confidence in approaching strangers, helped me develop skills for a cold sell, and made me appreciate the value of money. After a few days of tramping through the neighborhood's taverns, I met my quota of twenty booklets and, in the process, earned five dollars. Most importantly, I came away with a sense of pride and accomplishment in helping De Paul Academy.

The Rainbo Club was one of the last bars where I dropped in to sell my raffle tickets. Situated on Damen Avenue, just off Division Street, it was one of Nelson Algren's favorite bars, and when Simone de Beauvoir visited Algren in Chicago, he took her to the club for a drink. Simone de Beauvoir was France's number-two existentialist (number one, of course, was Jean-Paul Sartre).

According to Deidre Bair, Simone believed that Nelson Algren knew America better than the snobs she met in New York. In February 1947 she spent two days with him, they became lovers almost at once, and she discovered "how truly passionate love could be between a man and a woman."[57] Algren at this time was writing his third novel, *The Man with the Golden Arm*. When Beauvoir returned to Paris at the end of May, she wrote Algren the first of 350 letters over the next few years. That's one reason why we know so much about their relationship. On her second visit to Chicago, Simone remarked

---

[57] An excellent and highly detailed background of the relationship appears in Deidre Bair's comprehensive biography of Simone de Beauvoir.

that the only time they went out was to go to the nearby YMCA to swim and take their daily bath. In the evenings, Nelson would take her out to some local dives. One of his favorites was the Rainbo Club, but, usually, they stayed in the apartment, content to read, write, and make love.

During Chicago's scorching summers, I often cooled off in the same YMCA swimming pool where the couple swam. I came close to intersecting with history at the Rainbo Club and the YMCA—close enough to link the French existentialist priestess and the American anti-intellectual snob with my days in the Ukrainian Village next to Wicker Park. I found it to be one of those synchronous coincidences that permeated my life, making me wonder if there is more to destiny than most like to admit.

It's hard to put into words all the stories of the '50s. What stands out most from those times are the activities associated with *Plast*, especially the summer camps and jamborees where we met and mingled with like-minded Ukrainian scouts from Detroit, Cleveland, Montreal, and Toronto. Lifetime bonds were formed, and we had unforgettable flirtations with young lady scouts, canoe excursions on lakes in northern Ontario, and hikes in the Adirondack Mountains, which culminated with the summiting of the two-thousand-meter Mount Marcy.

Back in Chicago, after Friday evening scout meetings, our group of sixteen- and seventeen-years-olds often headed for Moishe Pippic's hot dog stand on Western Avenue. Most of us ordered french fries and a Coke, since that's all we could afford. One pleasant early summer evening, we were munching on our fries when an attractive girl showed up. Naturally, we all gawked, and my friend Yarko Bilynsky tried flirting with her. Soon, she picked up her order and left. Less than ten minutes later, a bunch of local rowdies popped up out of nowhere ready to "rumble." Apparently, the hot dog stand was their turf, and no one was allowed to mess with their girls. The gang leader approached my friend Yarko and asked, "What did you say to that girl?" and before Yarko could respond, he punched him in the face, and all hell broke loose. Blows were exchanged in this unfair fight, with our side being outnumbered and theirs using brass knuckles. One guy hit me with something hard, so I put metal keys in my hand, threw a punch, and ended up cutting the inside of my hand. My buddy Siajko took on one of the big guys, exchanged punches, and got a bloody lip; while another friend, Yurko Baranowsky, ended up with a broken nose. It was a test of camaraderie and courage. Some stayed back, and one member of the group inexplicably disappeared, but we put up enough of a fight to send a message that we were no pushovers. The brawl lasted ten minutes; someone called the police, and the gang members vanished as fast as they appeared. For the next few weeks, that's all we talked about. The event became so deeply etched in my memory that after fifty years, I recall it as vividly as if it had been filmed.

This was when I learned to stand up to bullies, a lesson the forty-fourth president of the United States never had. It is little wonder he was totally disoriented when confronted with a bully like Putin. One does not deal with bullies through diplomacy because the only thing they respect, I discovered, is a fist in the face.

THE UNIVERSITY OF ILLINOIS, a state school, was obliged to accept most high school graduates with good grades. Remaining there for more than a year, however, was an accomplishment. In the '50s, the Chicago branch of the University of Illinois was located at the mile-long Navy Pier protruding into Lake Michigan. Warehouse storage had been converted to classrooms. The tuition was an incredible $135 per semester, and textbooks amounted to fifty dollars a semester. If you lived with your parents, and almost everybody did, you could get a first-rate education in almost any curriculum for around $200 per semester. The University of Illinois at Chicago's Navy Pier was known as a "flunk out" school. While many were accepted, only a few made it through the first year. The system was merciless but fair because it was based strictly on merit, and that is what gave the school its reputation for excellence.

At the university, Dr. Penisi, my advanced algebra professor, was an eccentric teacher with a sense of humor. On the first day of the semester, he told us, "Look to your right and then to your left. Only one of you will be here next semester." These words sent a powerful message to the students: either you studied or you were out. Those who failed to maintain a C average—and it was a sizable portion of the students—were put on scholastic probation for another semester, at which point approximately another half flunked out. By the end of the first year, between two-thirds to three-quarters of the students who had enrolled at the beginning of the first year were dropped. Those who survived the Navy Pier could continue working toward a degree at the University of Illinois campus in Champaign/Urbana, an experience that opened new vistas and possibilities.

11. From Champaign/Urbana to US Army Intelligence School

IN THE SPRING OF 1960, I completed the crucial first two years of study at the Navy Pier. It was an accomplishment. Many friends I knew didn't make it; they transferred to one of the less-prestigious colleges or technical schools in the Chicago area such as Wright Junior, Roosevelt University, or DeVry. Those who succeeded went downstate to the university's Champaign/Urbana campus to finish up their studies. Still others enlisted.

After ten years in America, my father finally bought a family car, a 1960 green four-door hardtop Chevrolet Impala. I was ecstatic. It meant a newfound freedom. I could take girls on dates in my car. 1960 was also the first year we went on a real vacation. We drove across the Great Plains from Chicago to Denver. I saw the Rocky Mountains for the first time, and was overwhelmed by the majesty of Estes National Park. This was probably the moment I became enchanted by high mountains, a passion that would grow throughout my life until it reached its culminating point on Monte Rosa.

At the University of Illinois, I studied accountancy and finance. The university's College of Commerce ranked among the most prestigious in the nation, and its Department of Accountancy among the finest in the country. Getting a degree in accounting in addition to finance turned out to be one of the most important decisions in my life because it launched me on a long and circuitous career path that eventually led to Paris.

That fall of 1960, John F. Kennedy was campaigning for the office of the president of the United States, and even though I was not old enough to vote I supported him, mainly because he would have been the first Catholic president in US history. When Kennedy spoke on the steps of the auditorium at the south end of the quadrangle, I was swept along by the hysteria of the moment. In fact, I got close enough to him to touch his shoulder. On November 8, Kennedy defeated Richard Nixon in one of the closest presidential elections of the twentieth century.

I spent the next three years in an exciting new world away from the constraints and inhibitions of my strict Ukrainian Catholic upbringing. I was exposed to a novel academic atmosphere, fresh ideas, and a libertine environment. During my first year at Champaign/Urbana, I lived in a men's dormitory. My roommate, Ivan Gula, and I were both business majors, but he tended to be serious, disciplined, and hardworking, while I was susceptible to dillydallying and having a good time. Ivan was also a man with a strong character and courage, as demonstrated by an episode that took place in 1962 in the dormitory.

The students in the room adjacent to ours were two hefty freshmen on a football scholarship. On occasion, they got rowdy, but no one dared say anything because they were six-and-a-half-foot, 250-pound brutes who did as they pleased. They were particularly disruptive late in the evening when most of us were studying. One evening, we heard a commotion in their room. Apparently, they were wrestling, and one of them was thrown against the wall separating our room from theirs with such force that the cinder block partition cracked.

Ivan had had enough. He knocked on their door and told them in no uncertain terms to knock it off. "We are trying to study and you're disrupting the peace." Other students gathered in the corridor to see what the commotion was about, expecting to see my roommate get pummeled. Nothing of the sort happened. The two rowdies apologized and sheepishly retreated to their room, and we finally got some peace. The reason I remember this incident so vividly is that one of the football players was Dick Butkus, a star player on the Fighting Illini team who later became the most feared and intimidating linebacker of his time while playing for the Chicago Bears.

THROUGH SOCIALIZING with the other Ukrainians on campus, I met interesting international students with a variety of backgrounds, persuasions, and convictions. Some of them were teaching assistants, pseudo-artists, aspiring musicians, and writers who congregated at the Capitol Bar on Green Street, a watering hole popular with the Bohemian crowd. At first, I was intimidated by the high intellectual level of the conversation, but eventually I was accepted because I was not seen as a typical American or a fraternity man that this group loathed. Here I received an education that was as valuable as the academic program I was pursuing.

To counterbalance the challenging accounting and finance courses during my junior year, I chose a few elective classes. Beginners' Russian was one. A course in Soviet economy another. The distinguished professor who taught the latter was a specialist on the Soviet economy, and through him, I discovered how the academic world viewed the Soviet Union. I learned about the five-year plans, how centrally planned economies worked, and about machine tractor stations and collective farms. My opinion of collective farming, however, was at odds with what the professor was teaching. His lectures mimicked what a student in the USSR might learn. In addition to being dry, his presentations avoided any criticism of how things in the Soviet Union really were. He maintained that collectivization had been necessary to improve the efficiency of Soviet agriculture, though he did admit that it had been a difficult time for the richer peasants who resisted collectivization. But there was no mention of the widespread famine in Ukraine, nor of the millions dead from starvation, nor of those deported to the wastes of Siberia. He repeated the Soviet canard that agricultural production declined because of bad weather.

I was aware of a different version of the history of collectivization and began to ask questions. The professor was irritated by my questions and comments, and dismissed them as unfounded rumors and Ukrainian nationalist propaganda. I was shocked. How was it possible that a professor of economics at the University of Illinois was not aware of the famine? In Saturday Ukrainian school in Chicago, I was taught that during 1932-33, five to six million Ukrainian peasants starved to death because they resisted Stalin's collectivization. The two versions did not match, but I had a lot of confidence in the diaspora version of history and decided to write a term paper to reveal the truth about the Ukrainian genocide famine.

The professor did not appreciate my paper. He questioned the sources I used because they were not published by known academics, and some were in Ukrainian. Instead of finding fault with the facts or refuting my conclusions, he nitpicked my English and questioned my use of Ukrainian phonetic spelling and punctuation. I earned a C+, the professor's way of doubting my interpretation of Soviet collectivization, the famine in Ukraine, and the nature of the Communist system.

His view of what happened in the Soviet Union during the 1930s represented the state of knowledge of that period. Mainstream historians simply did not know what had transpired in the Soviet Union because it was a hermetically sealed society. Foreign journalists and correspondents were forbidden to travel to Ukraine and the North Caucasus. The only information they got was propaganda approved by Stalin and the Politburo which was regurgitated by the *New York Times* correspondent Walter Duranty and others. Without access to firsthand sources of information, mainstream scholars had to rely almost exclusively on translated Soviet sources or glean information from those paradigms of truth and objectivity *Pravda* and *Izvestia*.

In later years, when I got involved in a project related to the Holodomor Memorial in Washington DC, I asked the question how it was possible that the whole world knew about the Holocaust, while the Holodomor lapsed into the memory hole of history. The short answer, I discovered, was that it had to do with false reporting during the 1930s by American journalists.

One of them was Eugene Lyons, a UP correspondent with impeccable leftist credentials who took up his duties in Moscow in 1928. He arrived with a preconceived notion of life in the USSR, and wrote dispatches that glorified the Soviet Union. Lyons remained UP's man in Moscow from 1928 until 1934, but the longer he stayed in the USSR, the more disillusioned he became with Soviet reality. Eventually, his reports began to expose the sham of Soviet propaganda, and Moscow demanded his recall. Upon returning to the United States in 1934, he wrote about his experiences and described how he and other correspondents had conspired with Soviet authorities to deny the existence of the world's only human-engineered famine. Unfortunately, only a few listened. The damage had been done.

The most diligent of the collaborators were Walter Duranty, head of the *NYT* Moscow bureau, and Louis Fischer, Moscow correspondent for the magazine *The Nation*.

"There is no actual starvation, but there is widespread mortality from diseases due to malnutrition," the *NYT* cynically reported on March 30, 1933. For his reporting on the Soviet Union, Duranty received the Pulitzer Prize for journalism. To this day, the *New York Times* still lists him among its Pulitzer winners.[58]

---

58   The book to read on this subject is S. J. Taylor's *Stalin's Apologist*, a biography of Walter Duranty, the *New York Time*'s man in Moscow, a man who did more

Duranty's dispatches were lies. Even as late as the spring of 1933, when the famine reached its peak, Duranty dismissed reports that people were starving. "Conditions in Ukraine are bad, but there is no famine," he wrote from Moscow. "But—to put it bluntly—you can't make an omelet without breaking eggs." Those "eggs" were the heads of men, women, and children, and those "few" were tens of millions. Even as late as the spring of 1933, when every day twenty-five thousand were dying of starvation in Ukraine, Duranty persisted: "Reports of famine are an exaggeration and malignant propaganda." Meanwhile, Louis Fischer reported in the March 1935 issue of *The Nation* that he had visited Ukraine in 1934 and had witnessed no famine.

A few journalists, however, managed to evade the censors. Among them were reporters such as Malcolm Muggeridge and the Welsh journalist Gareth Jones, who informed the Western world of the existence of famine, as did Harry Lang, the editor of the Jewish-Yiddish newspaper *Forward*, who was the first to mention that six million might have perished. Other sporadic reporting came from the *Christian Science Monitor* and the Hearst publications. The White House, however, remained indifferent because Pres. Franklin D. Roosevelt was getting ready to recognize the Soviet Union and the Bolshevik regime, which he did on November 16, 1933, a year after he was elected.

Contributing to the leftist chorus of solicitous praise for Stalin's new society were American diplomats such as US ambassador Joseph E. Davies, who argued that Stalin was a "clean-living, modest and retiring man . . . a stubborn democrat who insisted on a constitution which protected human rights." Davies never accepted the fact that Stalin's show trials were staged, and concluded that the execution of the accused, many of whom he knew personally, was justified because they represented Russia's "fifth column," who were conspiring to dismember the union.

May God have mercy on FDR for appointing such astute diplomats!

IN JUNE 1963, I graduated with a bachelor's degree (a double major) in accountancy and finance. Like many of my friends, I was on a student deferment program, but after graduating, like almost every healthy young man, I was subject to the draft. If I was drafted, I'd have little say in choosing

---

to influence early American attitudes toward Stalin's Russia than any other individual.

a branch of service or military specialty, and with things in Vietnam heating up, it was likely I would wind up in Vietnam as an infantryman.

To beat the draft, some opted for advanced degrees or got married, and others left the country, usually for Canada. I enlisted in an Army Reserve Intelligence unit where many of my Ukrainian acquaintances were already serving. To qualify, a candidate had to get a top-secret clearance and pass a language proficiency test in one of the major languages of the Soviet Union. I qualified in Ukrainian, Russian, and Polish and soon became a member of the 910th Military Intelligence Unit headed by Major Makin. The conditions of enlistment were six months of active duty, followed by a six-year reserve commitment. Some called us the weekend warriors because we met once a week and one weekend a month to train. Active-duty staff referred to us as the "six-month wonders."

I idled through the summer of 1963, waiting for an opening in the intelligence school, and finally got an order to report for an eight-week basic infantry training at Fort Leonard Wood, Missouri, followed by intelligence school at Fort Holabird in Baltimore, Maryland.

Going through basic training in winter was not a lucky draw. All recruits were subjected to harsh discipline and harassment by strict drill sergeants. It was a shock for a few, but most knew what awaited them and managed. No one wanted to be labeled a sissy. My induction into the US Army began with a GI haircut designed to humiliate. It was November 22, 1963, a cold rainy day. With our hair sheared off, we were issued uniforms and fatigues, given vaccinations, and then made to stand in formation. Later that day, when I was soaked to the bone and shivering, the public address system suddenly blared out the shocking news that President Kennedy had been assassinated. Stunned, we froze in disbelief, wondering if this was some bizarre drill or, worse, a joke. It finally registered; the announcement was real. The drill sergeant yelled, "Dismissed!" and we made our way to our barracks. That night, a painful strep throat kept me awake all night, and, in the morning, I reported to the infirmary and was given an aspirin and told to rest. After a night's sleep, I felt better, and joined the ranks of recruits. Harassment became a daily ritual, intended to toughen us up physically and mentally: calisthenics several times a day, long marches, inspections, "policing" the grounds (picking up stray refuse), and endless bayonet drills.

Woe to those who referred to their rifle as a "gun." The standard punishment for this offense was for the recruit to stand outdoors in inclement weather and point alternately at his M-14 and his crotch, repeating, "This is my rifle, this is my gun—this is for fighting, this is for fun." Most common was the "hurry up and wait" routine where recruits were instructed to march double time from the training grounds to the mess hall and wait half an hour for a hot meal.

The day we were issued the powerful new standard army infantry rifle, the M-14, we learned to disassemble it, clean it, and put it back together in under two minutes. It was forty-five inches long and weighed twelve pounds, and we had to carry it ten kilometers to the rifle range and back. The second half of the march was double time, so by the time we arrived at the range, our shirts were soaked in sweat. One day, a buddy, Dave Mattson, a big Swede from Minnesota, stood in freezing temperature in front of me in the formation, and I saw that the back of his shirt had turned into a thin sheet of ice. When I slapped him on his back in jest, the ice sheet broke like brittle glass.

The M-14 was a powerful and accurate weapon capable of taking down a man at a thousand yards but totally unsuitable for the guerilla warfare unfolding in Vietnam. Soldiers equipped with M-14s were outmaneuvered and outshot by opponents with AK-47s. Light (eight pounds), rugged, and fully automatic, the AK-47 was a formidable weapon. It used lighter ammunition, had few moving parts, and was easy to disassemble and clean. Most importantly, it never jammed like the totally new AR-15, designed to replace the M-14, tended to do.

THE DAY I CAME HOME for Christmas leave, my parents and sister hardly recognized me. I had lost weight, but felt fit and healthy. The most demanding part of basic training, however, was still to come: a five-day bivouac on frozen ground in a barren forest. Recruits referred to this piece of Missouri as the "state of misery." Sleeping outdoors was nothing new—as a member of the Ukrainian scout group *Plast,* I had done that dozens of times—but never in the winter. It was a cold January, with the ground hard as ice. Daytime temperatures might climb into the twenties (Fahrenheit), but at night, they dropped to zero or less. I was issued an air mattress and a sleeping bag; however, as soon as I crawled into the pup tent, I discovered that the air mattress had a hole in it and the sleeping bag zipper was broken. I spent an hour trying to blow up the air mattress and fumbling with the broken zipper, all to no avail. That night I hardly slept, but the next morning, though stiff and numb, I was able to function.

Years later, when I looked back at this episode in the "land of misery," I realized that it was nothing compared to Uncle Dozyk's ordeal in the wastes of Siberia, where winter temperatures dropped to the point on the thermometer where Fahrenheit and Centigrade converge (i.e., minus forty degrees).

ON THE LAST DAY of basic training, the newly qualified recruits got their marching orders. For the majority, it was AIT (advanced infantry training), which meant eventual duty in South Vietnam. These men did not cheer; fear gripped their faces. The war in Vietnam was still a low-level conflict that would not reach full intensity for a few years. Most of us with an identification number beginning with ER (enlisted reserve) were sent for specialized instruction in some other branch of the army. I still remember my serial number: ER 16 773 466. That came from the constant drilling of the code of conduct which emphasized that, in the case of being captured, the only information we were allowed to reveal was our name, rank, and serial number.

My original MOS (military occupational specialty) was supposed to be interrogator of prisoners of war. However, by a fluke in army scheduling, I was sent to the US Army Intelligence School at Fort Holabird in Baltimore, Maryland, to become an imagery interpreter (II), where I was taught to analyze military intelligence gathered by U-2 spy planes, a skill I put to use during the next six years.

Within weeks I was interpreting aerial photography and infrared imagery, a new technology that produced images from electromagnetic radiation reflected from a target in the infrared position of the electromagnetic spectrum. By sheer accident, I became a specialist in spying from the air.

All of this training came against the background of the Cuban missile crisis two years earlier. On one of its passes in early 1962, the U-2 spotted soccer fields along the coast. The analysts at Fort Holabird and Langley found this strange, since Cubans play baseball, not soccer. They deduced that there was a Russian contingent on the island, and further scrutiny revealed that the Soviets were building medium-range missile sites in Cuba.

In October 1962, the United States and the Soviet Union confronted each other in what was known as the Cuban Missile Crisis. As the crisis escalated to a breaking point, the world tottered on the brink of nuclear war. The crisis was defused when the Soviets backed down: the missile bases would be removed in exchange for a US pledge not to invade Cuba.

From that point, American intelligence services routinely monitored activity in Cuba. The Soviets armed Fidel Castro's Cuba to the teeth, and our unit of imagery interpreters was part of this exercise. Although they tried, the Cubans were not able to hide anything. Infrared photography picked up even minor differences in temperatures day or night. Tanks or mobile artillery pieces, in particular, were very easy to pinpoint because they emitted heat.

The U-2 was a remarkable high-altitude reconnaissance aircraft that flew up to seventy thousand feet and, in one or two sweeps of the elongated island, could pick up most of the military activity. A high-powered lens mounted on a swivel mechanism that rotated 180 degrees photographed everything from horizon to horizon.[59]

For the next six months at Fort Holabird, I spent countless hours peering through a stereoscope measuring the dimensions of buildings and obstacles, estimating troop strengths, and identifying an array of weapons and military vehicles. Soon, I was able to identify every type of armor, artillery, and APC in the Soviet arsenal. My enthusiasm for this work increased when we began to focus on Soviet bombers and fighters and the silhouettes of guided missiles from SAMs to SLBMs and ICBMs. We did this with the help of top-secret manuals containing photos and descriptions of Soviet weapons systems obtained from military parades on Red Square and aerial photography acquired by the already famous U-2 spy plane.

Scrutinizing the massive amount of negatives taken by the U-2s required thousands of man-hours. Every other day, huge rolls of negatives arrived at our installation. To speed up the operation, we worked directly with negatives, so I had to re-educate my eyes and brain to read everything in reverse. My task was to examine a particular area in Cuba for any changes in military installations, movements at ports, and airport traffic. If I spotted anything that looked suspicious, I asked the photo lab for enlarged hard copies so I could measure the dimensions of military equipment. We looked at everything that appeared suspicious, from self-propelled guns to artillery. Soviet tanks were the easiest to spot. Even when camouflaged with tropical vegetation, their engines emitted heat, providing the infrared sensors with clear silhouettes. Years later, when I joined the IEA, this experience proved useful in estimating Soviet crude oil production capacity.

---

[59]   Over the years, with digital cameras, its capabilities were enhanced. Today, sixty years after the U-2 was developed, fifty are still in service.

BALTIMORE HAD A UKRAINIAN community, and on one of my visits to the Greek Catholic Church, I met Olya, an irresistibly attractive young woman. Her Slavic face, penetrating dark eyes, and lips made of rose petals were a magnet for men's eyes. She hardly wore makeup, but she didn't need to. Her body was that of a fit nineteen-year-old athlete.

One Sunday, I gathered the courage to ask Olya if she would play tennis with me the following Saturday. To my surprise, she agreed. I went to the house where she was living with her mother and brother: a typical Baltimore row house not far from the Ukrainian church. When I arrived, I saw that the home was full of religious symbols, holy pictures, crosses, icons, and the like. They were obviously a religious family, but this was nothing unusual among Ukrainian households.

We continued our relationship for the duration of my stint at Fort Holabird; some tennis, coffee and cookies, and conversation. Once when her mother was out, I tried to kiss her. She gently turned away, and said that her mother might return. This happened several weekends in a row, and I was getting frustrated. I suspected something was not right, so I asked, "Do you have a boyfriend?"

"No, I do not," she answered, "but I have been promised."

I was perplexed. "Promised to whom?"

"I have been promised to Jesus Christ." She blushed.

That's when it dawned on me. Olya had set her mind on becoming a nun, and there was little I could do about it. Next, she apologized for leading me on.

"Why were you dating me?" I asked.

"I was testing my resolve, my commitment to Christ," she said. But she added, "You almost changed my mind. What I hope, for now, is that someday I may be able to teach your children in a Catholic school." With mixed feelings—I was becoming infatuated with Olya—I was discharged from active duty and returned to Chicago.

For the next few years, my life stayed on an even keel. My first full-time job, a junior accountant at Walgreen's headquarters on West Peterson Avenue in Chicago, was quickly followed by a position in the general accounting department at Amoco Chemicals in downtown Chicago. After five years, I left the company to become manager of general accounting at G. D. Searle in Skokie, Illinois.

During this period, I married and founded a family. My marriage to Areta produced two beautiful children: Darian, born in 1967, and Tamara in 1968. First, we lived in Evanston, Illinois, and eventually moved to Lincolnwood, where the children attended grade school. This routine suburban life ended in 1976 when we divorced.

Meanwhile, I had returned to Amoco Oil, and joined a small department that dealt with the newly enacted government price controls, a move that turned out to be one of the luckiest breaks in my life. The new job propelled me on a career that eventually took me to Paris.

Plast camp in Knox, Indiana, 1953. I'm standing
in top row, seventh from the right.

With friends at Plast Jamboree in Grafton Ontario 1957. From left: Jaroslaw "Sam"
Samycia, Rostyslaw "Kuksa" Klukowsky, me and Alexander "Siajko" Pleshkewych.

Me with "Vovkulaky" scout fraternity friend Vlodko Medwitsky 1960.

Basic training in Fort Leonard Wood, Missouri. 1964.

Summer training camp at Fort Carson, Colorado 1967. Top row, left to right: Yuri Kavka, Myron Kulas, Ivan Gula, Gene Andrus, Steve Dacio. Squatting, me and Yuri Ozga.

With nieces Lesia and Tanya Richardson in front of Amoco Building in
Chicago where I worked during the 1970s. Photo taken in 2005.

UNA Reception for Sen. Charles Percy in center.
Standing on his right Vera Kuropas and Ivanka Martyniuk on
his left. Marta (Gojewycz) Ozga standing on the far left.

Standard Oil Company (Amoco) ID card, 1972

IEA/OECD ID card, 1979

12. How the Oil Crisis of 1973 Got Me to Paris

WHEN PEOPLE ASK me how I wound up in Paris, the best answer I can come up with is that it was through an unusual series of synchronous moments that unfolded during the second half of the 1970s.

Amoco Oil was the successor to the Standard Oil Company of Indiana, an offshoot of the Rockefeller oil monopoly broken up in 1911. It had a reputation for being one of the best-managed oil companies in the world, with competitors in the industry characterizing the organization as "lean and mean."

A year after I returned to Amoco in the fall of 1972, Arab oil producers declared an oil embargo, banning shipments of crude oil to Western countries. Oil exports to the United States were cut off to protest American military support for Israel in its 1973 Yom Kippur War with Egypt and Syria, and the world experienced its first "oil shock," which brought soaring gas prices and long lines at filling stations, and contributed to a significant economic downturn in the United States.

The effects of the embargo were immediate. The price of crude oil quadrupled overnight to twelve dollars per barrel, and in one year, the retail price of gasoline increased by 50 percent.[60] There was a public outcry for the US government to take measures to protect the consumer from being gouged by the "greedy" oil companies who were seen as profiting from higher oil

---

[60] The price of gasoline on average rose from thirty-eight cents a gallon in May 1973 to fifty-five cents in June 1974.

prices. Public pressure was such that the Federal Energy Administration (FEA) brought out the equivalent of a nuclear option, mandating price controls on the oil industry. The objective of the regulations was to cushion the effect of higher crude oil costs on products the oil companies were marketing. Unfortunately, this was done without serious consideration for the potential consequences.

Gasoline prices in the United States went through the roof, and the US government aggravated the crisis by promulgating price controls on all oil products. Like other major oil companies, Amoco was obliged to create a special department to decipher and implement the complex regulations. The Price Controls section began interviewing individuals to deal with the complexities of these rules. I applied, and was hired as a senior accountant.

As is often the case, the government misdiagnosed the nature of the problem and underestimated the complexity of the oil industry. In March 1975, the United States imported about one-third of its crude oil from abroad to meet its refining needs. The balance, roughly two-thirds, was met by domestic production. There was not much the government could do about the price of imported oil, but they could mandate the price at which domestic oil was traded.

The FEA decreed that oil from wells produced before 1972 (old oil) could sell for no more than $5.25 per barrel. Domestic oil produced from new and old wells in excess of 1972 output would be sold for $11.50 per barrel and imported oil for $13.20. The effective domestic price paid by domestic refiners was simply the weighted sum of the three prices.[61]

The next step was to compute the so-called pass-through, the amount of increased costs a company was allowed to pass on to customers for its products. It was my job to take all of these factors into account and compute the allowable price increase or decrease for gasoline and other products. This exercise required an inordinate amount of record keeping and diligence, as well as knowledge of all aspects of the oil industry from exploration and production to refining, transportation, and marketing. It was a perfect opportunity for me to learn how a major oil company functioned, and because I was on the inside, I was able to appreciate the effort the company made to adhere to the price control regulations, some so complicated the government auditors examining our work did not understand.

---

[61] For the purpose of illustration, using 1975 data prices and proportions, the formula was (0.40) X $5.25 + (0.30) X $11.50 + (0.30) X 13.20 = $9.50/bbl.

Another part of my job was to act as the company's liaison with the FEA auditors, which meant field trips to refineries and Amoco's production facilities in Oklahoma, Texas, Colorado, and Louisiana. The objective was to verify crude oil production data, but in the process, I got to see a large chunk of the United States.

During these trips, I often combined work with pleasure. In Denver, I took in a weekend of spring skiing at Vail. In New Orleans, I heard a lot of Dixieland jazz, and in Houston, I experienced the seedy side of the city. In Oklahoma City, however, I witnessed how Evangelical Christians lived. In my opinion, the Oklahomans best represented the traditional American values of hard work, decency, and honesty. The thought of fudging statistics was inconceivable.

The folly of price controls soon made itself known. The unintended consequences of regulations began to surface: domestic oil production began to plummet, and imports increased, producing the exact opposite of what the oil price regulations aimed to achieve. Greater reliance on foreign sources, in turn, enhanced the unity of the oil cartel, and the Unites States became increasingly vulnerable to external pricing and production decisions. The price controls also led to a fuel rationing system, causing long lines at service stations.

Most seriously affected by oil price control, however, was the American automobile industry. The first oil crisis sent a signal to American automakers to begin manufacturing small cars. Until the 1973 oil embargo and ensuing energy crisis, large, heavy, and powerful cars were the standard. It is no surprise that with higher gasoline costs, buyers began to shift toward more-economical Japanese and European four-cylinder imports. As expected, Detroit reacted by introducing smaller, more fuel-efficient models. Then the government stepped in and unwittingly told the American consumer not to worry about the cost of gasoline; they would make sure it stayed low, and it was OK to keep buying gas guzzlers.

The message, of course, was not so direct, but the implications were clear. In the long run, the policy undermined America's ability to produce viable small vehicles, leaving that lucrative market to the Japanese and Europeans. Detroit lost the expertise to compete in the small and medium car market, and over the next forty years, American automakers struggled to stay profitable.

After a couple of years in the price control department, I got another fortuitous break. A Latvian colleague in the department grew tired of accounting and took up a new career as a ski instructor in Steamboat

Springs, Colorado. One of his responsibilities had been to file a form with the International Energy Agency (IEA) in Paris, reporting Amoco's crude oil costs. It was an easy report to prepare, and I inherited the task of filing it. This seemingly unimportant development was a vital stepping-stone to Paris.

The International Energy Agency was the international community's response to the oil crisis that was causing an upheaval in global politics and the world economy. Initially intended to respond to physical disruptions in the supply of oil, the IEA gathered a vast amount of data concerning the international oil market, particularly concerning crude oil supply and demand. When I realized that the organization was part of the prestigious Organisation for Economic Co-operation and Development (OECD) in Paris, my imagination began to stir. After my first visit to Paris, I told myself that if I ever had a chance to live in the city on the Seine, I would not let it pass.

DURING THE 1970S I got involved in politics in a tangential way. In 1976 my dear friend Borys Antonovych, a lawyer with a practice on Chicago Avenue, decided to run as the Republican candidate for a seat in the Illinois House of Representatives from the 19th district. In other words, he was running against Chicago's Democratic machine which did not wish to see him elected and campaigned against him. I, along with other friends that included Yurko Myskiw, joined Borys's campaign team led by Levko Kazanivsky. I recall this experience with fondness because the campaign allowed me to witness at first hand how the U.S. electoral process actually works. It also provided me with opportunities to mingle with a variety of public officials and journalists, who I met at salons organized by Mary Dunea on Lake Shore Drive next to Chicago's landmark Drake Hotel and other places.

Antonovych's campaign was a first for the ethnic Ukrainian community of Chicago. Prior to this, no American of Ukrainian descent in Chicago had run for a state office before. Being a novice to politics I learned by immersion and spent many hours knocking on doors, distributing leaflets, and soliciting votes for my candidate. The Ukrainian community, supported by other ethnic groups, displayed an unusual degree of solidarity. To the delight of everyone, in November 1976, Borys Antonovych was elected State Representative.

My sister Ivanka got involved in Chicago Republican politics some ten years before this. In 1964, Charles Percy, then president of Bell and Howell, left this prestigious position to enter politics in order to run for Governor of

Illinois. As a result, he sought the support of Chicago's ethnic communities. A friend of Ivanka's, an executive at Bell and Howell who was a "Percy for Governor" organizer, knowing she was Ukrainian, approached her about making inroads into the Ukrainian community. It so happened that a concert, sponsored by the UNA (Ukrainian National Association) was scheduled that weekend at Lane Tech (Chicago). Ivanka suggested to her friend that he bring Chuck Percy to the concert as a guest. They came together and she made sure that significant introductions were made— including one to Myron Kuropas, an educator who eventually served as Special Assistant on Ethnic Affairs to President Ford. Subsequently, Chuck Percy was invited as a guest of honor to a banquet of the Chicago Ukrainian community. My sister thinks of this occasion as one on which a seed was planted. It might have indirectly facilitated Myron's later incursions into Republican politics and leadership, as well as others in the Chicago Ukrainian community. Often this kind of coincidence, these behind the scenes moments, give rise to events that take on a life of their own.

I MOVED TO A HIGH-RISE apartment on Lake Shore Drive. Amoco was making money hand over fist. I increased my earning power, and my personal life improved when I met Zoe, a stunning Dalmatian woman. We were married in 1978. Zoe's father was a Croat, and her mother Italian, and when she was young, her parents moved to Nice, France, where Zoe learned to speak French. Through her, I became interested in learning French and signed up for a French language course at the Alliance Française in Chicago. Meanwhile, the idea of living in Paris continued to smolder in some deep recess of my mind.

Knowing that we would be vacationing in Paris in May 1979, I updated my resume and mailed it to the IEA with a letter asking if there were any openings in the agency's oil industry division. Two months passed with no reply, not even a courtesy acknowledgment of my inquiry. After a few days in Paris, an inner voice said that I should call the agency's personnel office to ask if they had received my resume. The personnel manager recalled seeing my CV but said the IEA did not have any openings. "I'm in Paris for a few more days," I persisted, "and I would appreciate an opportunity to come in and introduce myself." Ms. Burger must have sensed something different about me because she agreed to meet with me.

Knowing that first impression is everything, I was eager to show that I was not an average American cowboy. I wore a double-breasted Armani suit with an eye-catching Gucci cravat and a light-blue shirt with a pin-down collar. I told Ms. Burger that I had been employed by Amoco Oil for twelve years, that I spoke several languages, including some French, and added that I had lived in Germany when I was young. My words must have struck a chord with her because she admitted that there was an opening in the IEA's Oil Industry Division calling for exactly the kind of experience I described in my resume. That same day, she arranged for me to have an interview with the chief of the Emergency Oil Sharing Division, Joachim Koenig. The oil industry chief, Ian Torrens, was away on leave—another lucky break, since Koenig, seconded from the German oil firm Aral, appreciated my oil industry background, something Torrens, an academic, would not have done. Koenig complained that most of the IEA personnel were bureaucratic appointees from member governments who did not know much about the oil industry. He admitted that the agency had already chosen an Australian candidate to fill the vacant position, but the Australian abruptly had turned down the IEA's offer because his wife refused to relocate to Paris. His loss was my gain.

"The IEA," Koenig continued, "wants to fill the position as soon as possible," and he suggested that I return the next day to talk to the deputy director of the agency, Wallace Hopkins. Although Hopkins was a shrewd international lawyer, his knowledge of the oil business was limited. After the initial niceties, he said, "I am told that you are familiar with the US price regulations, so please tell me how Amoco calculates the pass-through for number 2 heating oil." Without hesitation, I cited the relevant regulation and explained the way the pricing formula worked. I had the answer at my fingertips, and Wally was impressed. He leaned forward, looked me in the eyes, and said, "The damn DOE regulations are such a can of worms that we can't make heads or tails out of them, and in five minutes, you explained a riddle we've been trying to figure out for the past six months." This was another synchronic moment of my life. In addition to being at the right place at the right time, I was asked the right question.

Before the interview with Hopkins ended, he told me that he had once had the occasion to work with people from Amoco Oil, and found that the firm was one of the best-managed oil companies in the United States. He was aware of its reputation for being "lean and mean." "I want you to come in tomorrow," Wally said, "to meet the director of the IEA, Dr. Ulf Lantzke."

I showed up promptly at nine o'clock and had a half-hour chat with Herr Dr. Lantzke. The conversation was not about my technical skills but about international politics, the Middle East, and the oil industry. Next, we switched to my Ukrainian background and my years in Germany after the war. The interview ended on a friendly note, and Ms. Burger said I would hear from them as soon as they reached a decision. Even though I had a good feeling about the way the interviews went, when I boarded the return flight to Chicago, I did not have an offer in hand and, short of a miracle, did not expect one.

A month later, a large envelope from the IEA/OECD arrived. To my amazement, it contained an offer of appointment to the position of principal administrator in the Oil Industry Division of the International Energy Agency. The terms of the offer were incredibly attractive: excellent salary, housing allowance, generous benefits, an annual thirty-day home leave and, to really sweeten the pot, a diplomatic—CD—status, a most extraordinary privilege. The status of a *fonctionnaire international* (international civil servant) commanded respect and admiration among the French. As if this was not enough, the whole package essentially was exempt from French taxes. As far as US income tax went, as an expatriate, I would benefit from the $70,000 foreign income tax exclusion, which would lighten my tax burden considerably.

It appeared as if all the stars were aligned in my favor until I read the small print. The three-year contract was nonrenewable. For personnel seconded from government agencies, this was not a problem because they had jobs to go back to, but for outsiders from the private sector, this carried a risk, especially since the job market in the United States was weak.

I wrote a letter to my superiors at Amoco asking for a three-year leave of absence. Amoco's personnel office replied that a one-year leave of absence might be possible, but three years was out of the question. I had to choose between a safe career at Amoco and a three-year stint with the IEA, at the end of which I might be unemployed. My heart wanted to go to Paris, but my brain questioned the wisdom of such a move. I discussed it with Zoe and my friends. She was willing to go along with any decision I made, but I had to make up my mind soon because the IEA wanted my answer within two weeks.

I finally turned to a decision-making tool that I had picked up at a management seminar years before. Using a decision-making tree that evaluated available alternatives for benefits and negative consequences, I found that the answer was clear: turn down the offer and stay with Amoco. Reluctantly, I wired the IEA informing them that for personal reasons I had to decline the offer.

I was unable to sleep. After a few days, I realized that I could not live with such a decision. The realization that this was a once-in-a-lifetime opportunity would not leave my mind. Consulting with friends Liuba and Yaro Markewycz changed my mind. I recall Liuba's prophetic words: "Slavko, take the job. Who knows what will happen in three years? The world might come to an end. *Carpe diem.* You can't predict what new opportunities such an experience might bring." That same day, I telephoned Ms. Burger asking if the offer still stood, and she said it did.

"I'll be in Paris in October," I replied.

13. Paris: The Early Years

I ARRIVED IN PARIS in the fall of 1979, on the eve of two earthshaking events. Iranian Islamic students stormed the US embassy in Teheran, taking sixty-six hostages, and at about the same time a Wahhabi-like extremist sect seized the Grand Mosque in Mecca.

Earlier that year, demonstrations in Iran had disrupted the Iranian oil sector, curtailing production and exports of crude oil. Falling oil output drove the price of crude up to nearly forty dollars per barrel, and long lines once again appeared at US gas stations as they had during the 1973 oil crisis. Then in 1980, following the outbreak of the Iran-Iraq War, oil production in Iran nearly stopped.

In Saudi Arabia, the Wahhabi extremists called for the overthrow of the House of Saud. The Saudi ruling family got very nervous, but the government, headed by King Khaled, did not crack down on the religious puritans. Instead, they made a Faustian bargain by giving the fundamentalists more power and say in the government. First, photographs of women in newspapers were banned, and then women on television. Cinemas and music shops were shut down. The school curriculum was changed to eliminate classes on subjects like non-Islamic history, and provide more hours of religious studies. The religious police became more assertive, and gender segregation extended to the humblest coffee shop. Saudi Arabia took an enormous step backward. This was the situation when I took the job as the principal administrator of the Oil Industry Division of the International Energy Agency in beautiful Paris.

I was lucky to find an apartment on the northern edge of the 16th arrondissement overlooking the Seine. By Parisian standards, the six-story hundred-year-old building on Rue Gaston de Saint-Paul was considered "new." A building was only "old" if it had been built before the Haussmanian reconstruction of Paris. Thus, most of the seventeenth- or eighteenth-century buildings in the Marais, Ile Saint-Louis, or Quartier Latin were classified as old, and the buildings in the upscale 16th and 17th arrondissements were deemed new.

The four-room residence on the third floor consisted of an imposing vestibule with a marble floor, a large living/dining room combination, a wood-paneled library with a fireplace, and a spacious modern kitchen. The bedroom and kitchen windows looked out onto the courtyard, while the living room and library faced the south. Three tall french windows let sunlight into the apartment, and gave a view of barges docked along the Seine, the quaint pedestrian bridge Passerelle Debilly, and an occasional *bâteau mouche,* one of the glass-covered sightseeing riverboats. Directly across the street was the Palais de Tokyo, accommodating the Musee d'Art Moderne, Museum of Modern Art. (In 2010, five works by Pablo Picasso, Henri Matisse, Amedeo Modigliani, Fernand Leger, and Georges Braque, valued at €100 million, were stolen from the Museum.) Most significantly, I had a striking view of the Eiffel Tower, the quintessential symbol of Paris. Half a kilometer away, across the Seine, it was as imposing as the Matterhorn, constantly changing its complexion. Some nights I'd open the windows to admire its silhouette, wondering, *Is this real, or am I dreaming?* I would be hard-pressed to describe a more ideal setting.

Life in Paris was everything I had imagined it to be and more. Around the corner was Place de L'Alma, with its many cafés, restaurants, cabarets, and movie houses. The Crazy Horse Saloon on Avenue Georges V, the Théâtre du Champs-Élysées on Avenue Montaigne, and the Lido on the Champs-Élysées were all within a five-to-ten-minute walk from Rue Gaston de Saint-Paul. I developed a keen attachment to Place de L'Alma. After my first espresso in the morning, I either hopped on the Line 9 metro or took the scenic bus number 63 to my office at the OECD. During the wet season, when the weather was miserable and depressing, all I had to do was to set foot on Place de l'Alma, and immediately my spirits lifted. Perhaps it was the subliminal pleasure I derived from knowing that my favorite square was named for the Battle of Alma, a Franco-British victory over the Russians in the Crimean War in 1854.

During the dark and gloomy days, social life intensified. Nonstop dinner parties, casual meetings with friends in cafés and restaurants, and outings to the countryside were all part of a frantic lifestyle. The invitations, of course, needed to be reciprocated, so after we had installed ourselves on Rue Gaston de Saint-Paul, we began entertaining. Catered cocktail parties or Zoe's epicurean dinners were served in full view of the Eiffel Tower. On one occasion, when friends from Chicago, Michael and Daria Kos, visited, Michael was so overcome by the sight of the illuminated tower that he kept repeating throughout the evening, "Can you imagine that we are dining in Marty's apartment with a full view of the Eiffel Tower? Can you believe it?" Later, whenever we met in Chicago, he recalled that moment in the spring of 1980.

Rue Gaston de Saint-Paul, a short dead-end private street, opened onto the busy Avenue de New-York. In 1997, this corner would witness the tragic death of Diana, Princess of Wales. The tunnel under Place de l'Alma, where the Mercedes-Benz driven by the intoxicated Henri Paul crashed, surfaces at the intersection of Rue Gaston de Saint-Paul and Avenue de New-York.

My jogging route along the Seine was arguably the most scenic jogging path in the world. Starting on the Right Bank at the Place de l'Alma, I headed east along the Seine to the ornate Pont Alexander III. The bridge connects the Grand Palais exhibition hall to the Esplanade des Invalides complex, which includes the Musée de l'Armée and the gold-laced Dôme des Invalides, containing Napoleon I's tomb. From the Invalides, I jogged to the tree-lined green space of Champ de Mars, whose gravel paths provided a perfect place for a sprint to the Eiffel Tower. Next, I crossed the Seine at the Passarelle Debilly, a pedestrian bridge facing my apartment on Rue Gaston de Saint-Paul. On weekends, when I had time, I ran along the Seine, through the Jardin des Tuileries, past the Louvre, to the Île de la Cité, and returned along the quays of the Left Bank. High on endorphins, every run through the heart of the city was a mind-blowing experience.

When I arrived in Paris, apart from a few colleagues at the IEA, I did not know a soul. Paris, however, was an international city where it was easy to meet all sorts of people. Within a few months, my circle of friends mushroomed to a network that included a mix of international acquaintances.

On my first visit to Saint Volodymyr's Ukrainian Catholic Church on boulevard Saint-Germain, I spotted a familiar face in the back of the church.

"Romko?" I said, hesitating.

"Slavko?" he responded. "What are you doing here?"

"I got a job at the OECD, and you?"
"I'm here on a sabbatical doing research."

It had been twenty years since I last saw Roman Serbyn. In our late teens we belonged to the same scout fraternity, the *Vovkulaky*. We continued our conversation in the nearby café where Roman introduced me to a Ukrainian-Canadian expatriate couple, Jurko and Daria Darewych. Jurij, a professor of physics at the University of York in Toronto, was also in Paris on a sabbatical. In time, the Darewychys, introduced me to the Mytrowych family, the Sztuls, Father Salevych, Prof. Aristide Virsta, and others. The circle kept expanding. Just before the Darewychys returned to Canada, they introduced me to yet another Canadian-Ukrainian couple who arrived from Toronto, Danylo and Oksana Struk. Danylo, a professor of Ukrainian literature at the University of Toronto, came to Paris to work on the English language *Encyclopedia of Ukraine*. Within a few months, I had a circle of friends and acquaintances that included not only the Ukrainian community but also colleagues at the IEA and a few Frenchmen. Eventually, Zoe and I met Chrystyna Roncin-Styranka and her husband, Jean-Claude, and Lisa and Yurko (Jorge) Alyshkewych. The latter introduced me to Omelian Mazuryk, an artist-icon-painter. Soon, I met two more artists who arrived from the Soviet Union, Anton Solomoukha and Volodymyr Makarenko.

Early in 1980, I received a letter from Ivan Myhul, a name that rang a bell. After Roman Serbyn had returned to Montreal, he passed on my coordinates to Ivan, who wrote me a letter:

Dear Mr. Martyniuk,

In March I will be in Paris on a sabbatical, and I wonder if you can recommend a place to stay.

Ivan later confessed that he did not immediately realize who I was. However, I recognized his name instantly and wrote back:

If you are the same Ivan with whom I went to school in the D.P. camp in Regensburg you are more than welcome to stay with me.

In 1948, Ivan and I were in the same third-grade classroom in a school run by Ukrainian emigrants in Ganghofer, a suburb of Regensburg. Since then, we had met only once, during a Ukrainian Scout Jamboree in Ontario in 1957. We lost touch again, until he showed up in my apartment on Rue Gaston de Saint-Paul in March 1980, with Marie, his attactive Belgian companion.

I became a full-fledged member of the Ukrainian diaspora in Paris. On Sundays, we met on Square Taras Shevchenko, next to Saint Volodymyr's Church, and a small group headed to Café Bonaparte on the Place Saint-Germain-des-Près, kitty-corner from the twelfth-century Abbey Church of Saint-Germain-des-Pres. To appreciate the significance of this location, a slight digression is warranted. Many Parisians considered Place Saint-Germain-des-Près to be the center not only of Paris but also of Europe and, by extension, the world. It had been the epicenter of intellectual life since the days when Jean-Paul Sartre, Simone de Beauvoir and Albert Camus frequented Les Deux Magots and Café Flore.

After two decades of patronizing the Café Bonaparte, I discovered a fascinating factoid. Jean-Paul Sartre lived with his mother in one of the apartments above Café Bonaparte, a small third-floor residence overlooking the square, until he died on April 15, 1980. Sartre's death was a momentous event. The mood in Paris was somber; Parisians were in deep mourning at the passing of their revered intellectual.

Why this French writer/philosopher/philanderer was so revered had always been a mystery to me. I made an effort to understand his writings and philosophy, but other than learning that the core of the existentialist philosophy was "action," I found nothing there except a lot of gibberish and apt titles of two of his works: *Words* and *Being and Nothingness.*

Sartre was a Communist sympathizer and once famously said that "every anti-Communist is a dog." He was a fraud who took a whole generation of French philosophy students, intellectuals, and snobs for a ride. In 1947, he learned that slave labor camps existed in the Soviet Union. He promptly declared that the Soviet government should not be condemned for this because the Soviet government in principle was against slave labor. This "fuzzy ball of fur," as historian Paul Johnson painted him, was responsible for giving credibility to one of the most sadistic systems in the history of mankind. He was living proof of the maxim that most true believers in Communism were intellectuals living in the West, while east of the Iron Curtain hardly anyone believed. And yet the French shed a sea of tears over the death of their "genius," evocative of masses mourning over Stalin in 1953.[62] Karl Marx claimed that "religion is the opium of the people," but in one of the great works of twentieth-century political reflection, another French philosopher, Raymond Aron, cleverly modified this aphorism by observing that "Marxism is the opium of the intellectuals."

ABOUT A YEAR AFTER we arrived in Paris, Zoe left me. To this day, I am not sure why. As the wife of a diplomat, she led a privileged existence, but she was restless and impulsive and wanted to pursue her studies in interior design, which she couldn't do in Paris. Nor was she allowed to work, which must have been very frustrating. After she had exhausted the possibilities available to diplomats' wives—she got a diploma from Le Cordon Bleu and did some volunteer work—she convinced herself that there was no future for her in Paris. Believing that I no longer cared for her, she decided to go back to the United States. I was temporarily distraught, but seeing that I could not change her mind, I resigned myself to a *fait accompli*.

My new friends came to the rescue, especially Anton Solomoukha. I distinctly recall the moment when I snapped out of my melancholy. It was after attending a performance of Beethoven's Seventh Symphony at the Salle Pleyel with Anton. Over a glass of wine on the Place de l'Alma, he joked, "It's not the end of the world. There will be others. There may even be many others." His attitude reminded me of words another good friend: "Never run after a woman. They are like metro trains—there will always be another one coming." I also took up running seriously. In the fall of that year, I participated in a demi-marathon, the twenty-kilometer race through the streets of Paris. I did not break any records, but out of five thousand runners, I came in 453rd.

In the years that followed, the word got around the diaspora that I was in Paris, and I could put them up or show them the sights of Paris. There seemed to be a never-ending stream of visitors, old friends and new, all drawn to Paris like a magnet. One evening in the fall of 1984, an old acquaintance from Chicago, Oleh Oleksyn, called and said that his employer, the Hong Kong Development Council, was transferring him from Hamburg to Paris and he was here on an exploratory trip to look for a place to live. I agreed to meet him for a nightcap at the Hotel Intercontinental near Place Vendôme on the Right Bank. We had a lot of catching up to do, so we talked until the

---

[62] One of the best exposes of this controversial man is presented in the biography of Simone de Beauvoir by Deidre Bair.

bar closed. Oleh had left Chicago in 1970, and by the time I met him, he had been living in Europe for nearly fifteen years. The talk in Chicago was that he had been recruited by the CIA, but I never found any substance to this rumor. Still, as rumors do when they are repeated, they take on a life of their own.

It was refreshing to reconnect with a friend whom I had known in the past. Oleh had seen a lot of the world, and his views on economic philosophy reflected mine. During our meeting, Oleh elaborated on the merits of free markets and unrestricted trade. He pointed to the clear success of Hong Kong, whose policy of no trade barriers or tariffs, minimal regulation, and low taxes made it one of the most prosperous places in the Southeast Asia.

14. The IEA/OECD: The Rich Country Club

THE DAY I STARTED work at the International Energy Agency (IEA), I set foot in the exalted world of the *fonctionnaire international*. The French had an absurdly high regard for international bureaucrats, seeing them as a closed circle of individuals who have reached a rung on the ladder where ordinary laws do not apply. It didn't take me long to figure out why.

The IEA was part of a bigger organization, the OECD (Organisation for Economic Co-operation and Development). Although affiliated, there was a vast difference in the way the two organizations functioned. The OECD had been around since 1961, and it operated in the impenetrable world of economic theory. The IEA, set up in 1974, dealt with the real world of oil. To carry out its mandate, the IEA had to be independent and free from interference by politicians. Unlike the OECD, nearly all IEA appointments were limited to three years. OECD's system of permanent contracts was scandalously corrupt and wasteful. By private sector standards, only a few of them were actually productive.

A permanent contract with the OECD was the equivalent of tenure at a university with unbelievably lavish perks. You had job security for life—short of murder, an OECD bureaucrat could not be fired. A *fonctionnaire international* enjoyed an incredible array of generous benefits, with the added bonus that their income was largely exempt from taxes. A permanent contract often meant that the individual stopped working efficiently. The International Energy Agency was different. Hardly any permanent contracts were awarded for the simple reason that the organization had a serious mission in which it could not fail: dealing with an oil crisis.

THE OECD'S OFFICES were located in two buildings on Rue André-Pascal in the prestigious 16th arrondissement. The Château de la Muette, the "old" building, housed the headquarters. The "new" building across the street from the château was where I worked. The buildings were connected by an underground tunnel. My office was on the third floor of the new building facing the château's main entrance. My working environment had gone from the thirty-fifth floor of Chicago's sleekest skyscraper, the splendid Carrara marble–clad eighty-story Amoco Building, to a modest office overlooking the Château de la Muette. Although the present château was built in the 1920's by Baron Henri de Rothschild, an older mansion on the site was used in the eighteenth century by King Louis XV to entertain his mistresses, including Madame Pompadour and Madame du Barry.

The current château was sold three years after the end of WWII to the Organisation for European Economic Co-operation (OEEC), which had been established to run the U.S.-financed Marshall Plan for reconstruction of a continent ravaged by war. In 1961, it became the Organisation for Economic Co-operation and Development (OECD), and by the time I joined in 1979, it consisted of the world's twenty wealthiest industrialized countries, known as the "Rich Countries' Club."

Monitoring the global crude oil supply was a challenging task. Every other month, I would attend an energy conference in London or The Hague, or visit tanker construction facilities in Rotterdam. I traveled to Brussels and Geneva to get a firsthand look at how international organizations like the European Commission (later the EU) and the United Nations dealt with the energy issues. These experiences expanded my understanding of the global oil industry. Most instructive, however, was collaborating with the energy experts at the CIA in Langley, Virginia. They shared with me insights that no one else was privy to, especially regarding the state of the oil industry in the Soviet Union, as I described in chapter 2.

The IEA's affiliate, the OECD, was an organization with the noble goals of "stimulating economic progress and world trade by identifying good practices and coordinating the domestic and international policies of its members." When my three-year contract with the IEA was up, I obtained an exceptional one-year extension, and then moved to the OECD for another two years. After six years collaborating with and working for the OECD, I determined that the organization was incompetent, and a colossal waste of resources. The majority of economists at these organizations were personable individuals, knowledgeable, refined, and accomplished in their fields. They had a talent for lofty words and grand declarations, but what they cared about most were their lavish salaries and perks. The international bureaucrats lived well, traveled a lot, and rarely worked long hours. Two-hour lunches were *de rigueur*. If you were at the level of an administrator, as I was, you were awarded CD automobile license plates, with the privileges such tags entailed.

Working for the IEA/OECD, I had access to amenities and privileges not available to ordinary people. Besides being able to park wherever I pleased (and in Paris, this is an inestimable convenience), the organization's cafeteria offered fine meals at a fraction of the street price, and I had access to the duty-free shop at the OECD and the US Embassy commissary.

One could argue that if the people working in these organizations were essential and productive, they might have deserved such compensation. Most of what they did, however, was not only non-essential but of questionable utility or even harmful. Over the years, I began viewing the entire OECD staff as a bunch of freeloaders and parasites. The OECD was moderately successful in collecting and disseminating economic statistics, but the job could have been done at a fraction of the cost by the private sector. I say this with considerable confidence because I have worked in the private and public sectors. Even worse, their record at predicting developments was abysmal: the overwhelming majority of their prognoses were off the mark, and no one—no economist, no analyst—has ever been held accountable.

The inability of economists at the OECD, or in other similar international fora to predict "big" events, is well known. They missed every one of the "Black Swan" moments of the last forty years.[63] For nearly two generations, the economists have been getting it wrong consistently and persistently, yet they keep doing the same thing over and over without realizing that their efforts are futile. I came up with three explanations why these economists have been mistaken for so long: excessive dependence on faulty econometric modeling, the arrogance and hubris of the economists working on these models, and the predilection of those in responsible positions for unwarranted optimism.

---

[63]   The Black Swan is a metaphor developed by Nassim Nicholas Taleb that describes an event that comes as a total surprise, has a major effect, and is often inappropriately rationalized after the fact.

This memoir is not the place for a primer on econometric modeling, but, briefly, the models used sophisticated multiple regression analysis with assumptions about variables such as wages, employment levels, changes in income, consumption spending, and others. Imperfect variables led to errors and faulty supply-and-demand hypotheses and produced inaccurate forecasts. I was asked to contribute assumptions about the price of oil. I knew that it was next to impossible to project such a price with any certainty and that my estimates were no better than intelligent guesses, yet the OECD economists treated them as a hard input. Quite often, the initial results appeared unrealistic, so it was back to the drawing board, reexamining the variables and massaging the numbers until a more or less reasonable scenario emerged.

I also noticed that the economists at the OECD tended to be very sure of themselves, and even though their econometric models were wrong again and again, they kept doing the same thing, hoping for a different outcome. The crux of the problem was that all models had a built-in supposition: the economists assumed that everyone was a rational actor. In reality, that is never the case. It is sometimes believed that economics is a hard science because economic models use vast amounts of statistical data. My suspicions that it is not a hard science were confirmed by some "locker room" revelations.

One of the conveniences of working at the OECD was that the organization provided locker rooms and shower facilities for joggers, and soccer and rugby players. Every other day, I was able to fit in a midday run in the nearby Bois de Boulogne and still have an hour for lunch. The locker room thus became a great source of inside information, insights, and admissions. There was a constant buzz about modeling inputs and assumptions. Conversations always focused on how to adjust this or that variable. The problem with changing one metric or assumption was that it impacted other parameters, leading to more adjustments, further complicating the model. The final prototype was an artificial creation with little resemblance to the original rationale of the model.

At some point, it occurred to me that the field of economics was no better than medieval medicine. It was a social science masquerading as a physical science. Economics has become the cousin of math, statistics, and finance, a social science corrupted into a predictive discipline that fails to correctly predict anything, a prescriptive discipline that prescribes the wrong policies, and an empirical discipline that collects data but misses the point.

The great Austrian school economist Ludwig von Mises saw this clearly. He observed that the conflation of economic science with business and politics was a grave mistake. Nevertheless, the Keynsian model prevailed, and economists have been stuck with its shortcomings and imperfections ever since.[64]

Proof that economics is a non-science materialized most conspicuously a quarter of a century later when nearly the entire profession was stunned by the extent of the 2008 economic crisis. With only a few exceptions such as Nassim Nicholas Taleb, Nouriel Roubini, and, perhaps, Niall Ferguson, mainstream economists failed to predict the economic crisis that rocked the world in 2008.

During my years with the OECD, I also noted an emphasis on presenting a positive outlook, even when the data did not warrant it. Pessimism was a career ender. Our modern society blindly believes that optimism is always a paradigm of good, while pessimism is a trait to be avoided like the plague.

In a 2013 article in *World Affairs,* Walter Laqueur, chairman of the Center for Strategic and International Studies (CSIS) in Washington DC, postulated that excessive optimism in the public domain often leads to errors of judgment and is, therefore, dangerous.[65] Once illusions are shattered, false optimism leads to dejection, disasters, and worse. As I write this memoir, this is precisely what is happening in many parts of the world.

Laqueur cited examples from recent history where optimistic mainstream consensus got it horribly wrong. In the case of reactions to the Arab Spring, Western political assumptions helped to produce diametrically opposite results. Politicians in the West proclaimed that fear of Islamism and the Muslim brotherhood was unreasonable, unfounded, and exaggerated. What happened was that, as soon as the Muslim brotherhood obtained the majority in Egypt, a new constitution based on the Islamic Sharia was imposed. The level of misjudgment by the buoyant Western establishment could not have been more egregious.

The same kind of misjudgments generated false optimism regarding the European Union. Borderless Europe would spur remarkable economic growth,

---

[64]   Ludwig von Mises was born to Jewish parents in the city of Lemberg, in Galicia, Austria-Hungary (now Lviv, Ukraine), which technically makes him Ukrainian. Mises emigrated from Austria to the United States in 1940 where he influenced the American libertarian movement.

[65]   Walter Laqueur, "Reality Check: The Hazards of Optimism," *World Affairs,* March/April 2013.

and the Euro would eventually replace the dollar as the world's exchange currency. This conviction was most pronounced at the very top: European politicians, bureaucrats, and the vast majority of elites were confident that the twenty-first century would be Europe's. In reality, we see today how Europe's open borders policy, one of the EU's central pillars, aggravated the catastrophic consequences of the migrant crisis of 2015-16.

15. Flirting with the KGB

DURING MY EARLY YEARS in Paris, I often attended receptions where Soviet diplomats were present. Most of these diplomats were, in fact, KGB agents, and soon I learned to distinguish the professional agents from the ordinary diplomats. The giveaway was the way they dressed and, more importantly, the money in their pockets. The KGB guys seemed to have more of it and were ready to spend it more generously than actual diplomats. Moreover, the intelligence operatives were eager to cultivate personal relationships with foreigners, while the real diplomats were more reserved and reticent.

The first KGB agent I met in Paris was Nikolai Kirilenko, who was with the Ukrainian delegation to UNESCO. My artist friend, the Parisian iconographer Omelian Mazuryk, introduced me to Nikolai during a *vernissage*, the opening of Mazuryk's paintings in an art gallery on Avenue Pierre 1er de Serbie in the 16th arrondissement.

Omelian was a Ukrainian painter from Poland who had already made a name for himself in the United States and Canada. Although only in his mid-forties, his thick head of hair was completely white. He was an affable individual, somewhat unconventional but unquestionably gifted. His interpretations of the classic icon in a contemporary style appealed to many in the Ukrainian diaspora.

In the spring of 1980, Omelian was preparing for an exhibit at a gallery that was close to my apartment on Rue Gaston de Saint-Paul. The gallery's owner, a black American woman by the name of Elmira Floyd, took a liking to Omelian's art, and I could see why. Omelian's icons had a hypnotic quality.

"It's all in the eyes," he once told me. "They have to penetrate your soul."

And they did. Many years later, on a visit to Poland, I learned that Omelian picked up the penetrating eyes trait from the famous Polish-Ukrainian primitive artist Nikofor.

Omelian lived in the distant eastern suburb of Vaujours, and I resided in the 16th district near the gallery. He asked if he could store his paintings in my apartment for a few days before the opening of the show on Thursday, May 29, 1980. I agreed, of course, and Omelian brought a couple of dozen paintings to my apartment before transferring them to the gallery for hanging, a day before the well-publicized vernissage.

By chance, Pope John Paul II was paying an official pastoral visit to France that weekend. The papal nuncio's residence where the Pope was staying was literally around the corner from my apartment, on Avenue du President Wilson. It was quite a coincidence that I lived close to the papal nuncio as well as to the gallery where Omelian had his exhibit, but then several other unusual things began to unfold.

Omelian's opening was a huge success, well attended by a mix of curious collectors, Ukrainian diaspora, dissidents, and a sprinkling of diplomats. That evening, he sold nearly half of the paintings he exhibited, an unusual achievement and a pleasant surprise for the gallery owner.

Before the vernissage, Omelian told me that he had invited some Ukrainian diplomats from UNESCO. Omelian was one of the few in the Parisian diaspora who had any contact with these "diplomats." Nearly all other Ukrainian diasporans avoided these diplomats because they believed that they were all KGB spies. Omelian, however, found a way to socialize with them, and they helped him organize an exhibit of his icons at UNESCO. Omelian returned the favor by inviting them to the vernissage.

During the evening, Omelian introduced me to Nikolai Kirilenko, the second secretary for cultural affairs for the Ukrainian SSR delegation to UNESCO. Nikolai, a short, stocky gruff-looking man roughly my age, had a crooked nose, which made me suspect that he was either a boxer or a street fighter or both. I doubt that he knew much about culture or art because his line of business was espionage. Being new to this game of deception, I was vaguely aware that he might be a Soviet agent with an agenda. Still, I was intrigued to find myself face-to-face with a genuine KGB spy. I made it a point not to show any surprise or bewilderment or ask any uncomfortable questions.

As we were exchanging pleasantries, I noticed that Nikolai became nervous. His eyes kept shifting right and left as if he was being watched, and he spoke in a low tone. People were looking at us, and it seemed he did not want it to be known that he was trying to befriend me.

Nikolai knew that I was a Ukrainian-American from Chicago who had recently been appointed to a relatively high post at the OECD. He was also aware that I was interested in art and played the guitar. Nikolai might have gotten some of this information from Omelian, but it's more likely that as a KGB agent, he did his homework. Moreover, there were moles in the Ukrainian community in Paris who kept the KGB operatives at UNESCO informed about the comings and goings of Americans and Canadians. Maybe he thought that my post at the IEA/OECD was a front, that I was a CIA mole brought to Paris on some undefined mission, and he wanted to find out what it was. This is also what the Ukrainian diaspora in Paris believed. Intrigue and espionage, real and imaginary, had been a staple of the Parisian diaspora since the end of World War I. The diaspora still had not stopped talking about the 1926 assassination of Symon Petlyura by Shalom Schwartzbard, an anarchist of Jewish descent and a likely NKVD operative.

On the face of it their suspicions were not unfounded. How does a modest oil accountant from Chicago turn up in a highly visible diplomatic post in Paris? Yes, I worked in the energy sector, but, surely, that was just a cover. Never mind that I was not a diplomat in the traditional sense. For every member of the diaspora I came into contact with, the only thing that mattered was that my BMW 520i carried CD plates. I also had unrestricted access to the US embassy commissary, which, in the eyes of the suspicious diasporans, was more than adequate proof that I was some sort of intelligence operative. All these facts percolated to the KGB agents at UNESCO, and whetted their appetites. The rumor was set in stone when it became known that I was acquainted with a State Department employee at the US embassy, Natalia Horodecka, a fellow American Ukrainian who, everyone was convinced, was working for the CIA.

And if the KGB had done their homework, they would have discovered that while in the US Army in the '60s, I served in an intelligence unit where I was trained to spy from the air, interpreting U-2 aerial photography and imagery, and interrogating POWs. I spoke several languages, and given my ethnic background—a refugee from Communism—I had a good reason to work for the cunning Americans. All these facts fitted nicely with their preconceived notion of who I was, and, I admit, I took a strange pleasure in being the focus of so much attention. For that reason, I neither confirmed nor denied any of these rumors, figuring that either way, no one would believe me.

Thus began my relationship with the KGB. For reasons still not entirely clear, I decided to play the game. Perhaps it was curiosity, the thrill of danger, or the belief that I could handle anything they might try. Most of all, it was a subconscious sense of duty to fight the evil of Communism that stemmed from my hatred of the genocidal Soviet regime that enslaved and ruthlessly exploited the country of my birth.

My new friends from UNESCO no doubt believed that I was a CIA asset and they wanted to know what I was up to. At the same time, they could have been looking for a way to ensnare me to work for them. That was, after all, the KGB's *modus operandi*: find out as much as possible about a target's personal life, habits, strengths, weaknesses, and vices, befriend the individual, and use that information to entrap him.

At Mazuryk's vernissage, everyone was talking about Pope John Paul's impending visit to Paris and what that meant for France, for the world, and for the future. On Saturday, May 31, he would meet with Pres. Valéry Giscard d'Estaing, and on Monday, June 2, he would conclude his visit with an address to the plenary session at UNESCO. Because this was a strictly official visit, His Holiness would not grant any private audiences—except one.

After the vernissage, Omelian and his wife, Natalia Horodecka, Zoe, and I went to a friend's apartment for a nightcap to celebrate a successful opening night. The atmosphere was cheerful, and after a few drinks, Omelian began to talk about the Pope. He told us that when he was a student in Krakow, the priest at the time, Wojtyła, was one of his professors. Omelian did not hold his liquor well, and I wondered how much of the story was true. An idea was floated that since the pontiff was in the neighborhood, this might be a good pretext for Omelian to get an audience with him. We kicked around the thought for a while, but it was late, and we broke up to get some sleep.

The next day, Omelian mentioned this story to Elmira, who immediately saw this as a great public relations opportunity.

"The Pope must visit the gallery," she declared.

Elmira may not have been an expert in iconography, but she understood the value of publicity. If there was a way to get the Pope to visit her little gallery, it would have been a fantastic publicity coup. The idea, of course, was preposterous: there was no chance that this or any other Pope on an official pastoral visit would agree to come to an icon exhibit, even if the artist was a former student. Nevertheless, a seed had been planted, and it kept germinating.

A Mazuryk family friend, Father Yaroslav Salevych, had mentioned that he knew Josyf, Cardinal Slipyj's secretary in Rome, who worked closely with John Paul's secretary, Monsignor Stanisław Dziwisz. Father Yaroslav joked, "If the Pope will not come to Elmira's gallery, he might at least accept a gift from his former student," meaning one of the icons that hung on the wall of the gallery down the street. What followed was a flurry of calls between Paris and Rome and a promise that we would have an answer on Sunday morning. On the morning of June 1, we all gathered in my apartment, anxiously waiting for the call from Rome. At noon, we got the news that Pope John Paul II had agreed to grant Omelian and his wife an audience and accept the gift, an icon of the Blessed Virgin.

It was a striking piece of art. The dark face of the Madonna stands out sharply against the background of bright red, yellow, and orange. Holding a thin cross in her right hand, the Virgin gazes directly at the onlooker. It is a stirring image that "touches the soul," as Omelian was fond of saying. In a technical sense, it was not a conventional icon. It was rather large, an eighteen-by-twenty-four-inch painting on canvas, and Omelian had used acrylic paint rather than traditional tempera on a wood panel. Still, its effect was hypnotic.

Since the gallery was closed on Sunday, we had agreed that Elmira would bring the icon to the nuncio in time for the audience with the pontiff. There were throngs surrounding the nuncio's residence, hoping to get a glimpse of the pontiff, and when Elmira finally showed up, she was empty-handed. She said she misunderstood the arrangement and thought that the Pope would come to the gallery, which, of course, was out of the question.

Minutes before the Mazuryks were to see the Pope, I turned to Elmira and shouted, "Give me the damn gallery keys!" Without a word, she handed me the keys. I sprinted up the Rue Freycinet, opened the gallery door, unhooked the icon, locked the door, and ran back down to the nuncio. I arrived just as the Pope's secretary opened the ornate iron gate of the nuncio's residence. The first question he asked was "Where is the gift?" I rammed my way through the crowd and handed Omelian the icon. For an instant, I thought I'd walk in with them but was told that only Omelian and his wife would be allowed to see the Pope. What was supposed to have been a brief audience turned out to be a thirty-minute chat with the Pope during which, according to Omelian, the Pope vividly recalled him as a student in Krakow in the '50s. Today, Omelian's "soul-penetrating" icon is found somewhere among the thousands of gifts in the storerooms of the Vatican, and an almost identical piece hangs on the wall of my apartment.

WITHIN A WEEK of the vernissage, Nikolai Kirilenko called to ask if I would meet him for coffee. He said he enjoyed talking to me, and had some gifts for me. I suggested meeting in Café de l'Alma, a charming café on the Seine that offered a view of the Eiffel Tower in the distance. This would be the first of a series of meetings with Kirilenko, who always brought some kind of gift. That day, he brought a finely-bound Soviet edition of the *Kobzar*, the sanitized collection of Taras Shevchenko's poems. All Ukrainians have a soft spot for Shevchenko, a poet of genius who single-handedly resurrected the Ukrainian language in the mid-nineteenth century.

Was he befriending me in order to recruit me? Curiosity is a drive as strong as sex or gravity, and, I admit, it overpowered me. What would a KGB agent say to try to engage me? This was an experiment that involved a calculated risk, but one I believed I could control. I was also motivated by a silly desire to give substance to the diaspora rumors that I was a CIA mole.

The conversation during this meeting consisted of mostly innocuous small talk. I put myself in listening mode and let him do the talking. Nikolai gave me a line about what a great job the Ukrainian delegation was doing to promote Ukrainian culture, how they were trying to promote peace through cultural exchanges, and so on, the usual propaganda he had been trained to spew out. For someone with no exposure to the Soviet system, this sounded persuasive. After all, who would be against peace and culture?

Over a cup of double espresso, I patiently listened to his well-rehearsed litany, but decided not to contradict him directly. Occasionally, I threw in a critical word about how dysfunctional the United States had become and how degenerate Europe was. He seemed to think I was sincere, and although I did this to make him feel at ease and to establish a rapport, I wanted to see what made him tick. Did he think I was a disgruntled naïve bureaucrat that he could manipulate? We spent nearly an hour talking about subjects of little importance, and then I sprang a question he did not expect.

"Nikolai, why did you ask to meet with me?"

He seemed momentarily baffled and then said, "I want to be your friend."

I remembered these words many years later when I had dealings with the FBI in Washington DC regarding the investigation of a possible Russian mole. One of the FBI agents told me that if they wanted a Russian target to cooperate, he would use the same words—"I want to be your friend."

Nikolai paid for the coffee, and on leaving the terrace, he pulled out a box of chocolates, saying, "This is for Zoe."

The gift of chocolates offered by a KGB agent suddenly made me nervous. In fact, it spooked me. I recalled that in 1938, an NKVD agent gave Yevhen Konovalets, the exiled leader of OUN in Rotterdam, a box of chocolates with a rigged bomb inside. When he opened the box, the bomb exploded and killed him. This booby trap was masked as a "present" from his "true friend" who turned out to be an NKVD agent, Pavlo Sudoplatov. Paranoia overcame me and I decided to take no chances. I threw away the chocolates into the nearest trash container. For all I knew, they could have been poisoned.

For our second meeting, I asked Nikolai to come to our apartment for dinner, but he declined rather brusquely. I suspect house calls were against KGB's operating protocol because it meant meeting in unfamiliar surroundings over which they had no control. Maybe in his conspiratorial mind, it was I who was trying to recruit him. So we met in a café again, this time on the beautiful place Trocadéro, also with a magnificent view of the Eiffel Tower. I gave him a photo book of Chicago's skyscrapers, and he brought me a bottle of Ukrainian *horilka*—vodka. His tactics changed. He began to play on my emotions, appealing to my sense of patriotism, love of country, or whatever nostalgia I might have felt for the motherland. The last mentioned was pointless, since I never had the opportunity to develop an attachment to my place of birth.

"In Ukraine, people lead good lives," he pontificated. "All their basic needs are met—education and medical care are free of charge." The usual prattle about the wonderful life in a Socialist utopia made me want to vomit.

Interrupting him, I said, "From what I've read and heard, except for the *nomenklatura*, the vast majority of Soviet people live in near poverty."

He was taken aback, and then suggested, "If you don't believe me, why don't you come to Ukraine and see for yourself? I can arrange a visit for you, and you may stay as long as you like."

His offer whetted my appetite, and I was curious about what might come next. I thanked him for the invitation and said I would think about it and give him an answer the next time we met. It seemed that Nikolai and his colleagues were serious about ensnaring me any way they could. A trip to Ukraine certainly sounded tempting. It would be a fabulous experience. However, my sixth sense told me that it could end very badly. In the USSR, the KGB would have had a great advantage, and their chances of entrapping me would have been high. I still had many relatives in Ukraine whom they could use to intimidate or blackmail me into doing their bidding.

For our third meeting, Nikolai invited me to dine at an excellent restaurant on Quai Branly near the Pont Alexander III. I don't recall what Nikolai ordered, but I had a Magret de Canard accompanied by a 1975 Pauillac. I thanked him for his invitation to visit Ukraine, but said that because of a heavy work schedule, I would have to turn down the offer. However, if things changed in the near future, I would be happy to reconsider.

Listening to Kirilenko's claptrap about Ukraine and the Soviet Union was getting tedious, so I abruptly switched gears. "Nikolai, can you explain to me why the Soviets invaded Afghanistan?"

As if expecting such a question, he responded, "Don't you know the Americans were about to invade Afghanistan? The Afghan government asked the Soviet Union to protect them from such an invasion."

The *kagabeshniki* (KGB agents) seemed to have set answers to provocative questions, no matter how absurd the responses sounded to Western ears.[66] When it became apparent that I did not buy his ridiculous explanation, the conversation cooled. Nikolai pulled out one final card to see if I would fall for it.

"*Jaroslawe Romanovych*," he said, "if you should ever be interested in an attractive woman who speaks fluent Ukrainian, I know someone you'd love to meet. Ukrainian women are the most beautiful in the world." He grinned.

The Beatles' words "And the Ukraine girls knock me out" suddenly flashed into my mind.

At this point, I realized I did not wish to pursue this ruse any longer and told him I was happily married, thanked him for the dinner, and said I did not wish to meet with him anymore. Nikolai's face turned red with anger. "*Ty shto, izpugalsa?*" he said in Russian—meaning, of course, to say *ty zliakavsia*, in Ukrainian—you got spooked. "*A pochemu?* (But why?)" Mixing the two languages showed the depth of Nikolai's annoyance at my change of heart. How dare I lead him on and then break off our relationship so abruptly!

The experience taught me much about the way the KGB operated. To recruit a target, everything was fair game. That night, I did not sleep well. What bothered me most was the awareness that the KGB had a long memory. They never forgot. The case of Konstantyn Warwariv would demonstrate that in the most distressing way.

---

[66] In 2014, Russia used the identical line to accuse the CIA of plotting the Maidan Revolution.

KONSTANTYN WARWARIV, a native of Ukraine, was an American diplomat who headed the US mission at UNESCO. For years, he had been a target of KGB attempts to recruit him. Warwariv emigrated during World War II and eventually settled in Washington DC. In the summer of 1977, he attended a conference in Tbilisi, the capital of Soviet Georgia. On the evening of the first day of the conference, a colonel of the Soviet KGB, Victor Cherkashin, knocked on the door of his hotel room. In his book *Spy Handler,* Cherkashin writes that he spent five hours talking to Warwariv, trying to recruit him—cajoling, threatening, and imploring Warwariv to work for the Soviet Union. Cherkashin sought to intimidate Warwariv by every means possible, even claiming that he had evidence of Warwariv's collaboration with the Germans during the Second World War. Warwariv protested, stating that he had diplomatic immunity, at which point Cherkashin said that diplomatic immunity would not do him much good if he "fell out of the window."

At 4:00 a.m., a weary Warwariv agreed to cooperate with the KGB. Next morning, he reported the recruitment attempt to the security officers at the American embassy. Diplomatic notes were exchanged between Washington and Moscow. Colonel Cherkashin got in trouble with the Communist Party hierarchy because this was the time of détente preparations, but he weathered it in time and was posted to Washington.[67]

Helpful in saving Cherkashin's career were two high-profile fellow Chekists: Vladimir Kryuchkov, later head of the KGB, and a conspirator in the August 1991 failed putsch, and Oleg Kalugin, a KGB general. Kalugin, in his memoir, describes several situations where the KGB went after defectors or people who misled them.[68] The KGB did indeed have a long memory.

As Warwariv was completing his tour in Paris, he returned to the State Department in Washington, fell ill, and died abruptly at age fifty-seven of mysterious causes. After Warwariv's death, through my contacts in the Ukrainian community, I met his daughter, Victoria, who was still living in the 7th arrondissement in Paris with her mother. Curious to learn more about her father's death, I invited her to dinner at the celebrated Brasserie La Coupole, and over a *steak-frites,* she said she was convinced that her father had been poisoned by the KGB in revenge for double-crossing them in 1977.

---

67   R. J. Chomiak, "A Breach That Was, and One That Wasn't," *Ukrainian Weekly,* March 25, 2007.

68   Oleg Kalugin, *Spymaster: My Thirty Two Years in Intelligence and Espionage against the West.* Philadelphia, 2009.

"He was in the prime of his life, in good health. Things like this don't happen without reason," said Victoria.

ALTHOUGH MANY SUSPECTED foul play, there was no hard proof that Warwariv had been killed by the KGB. Warwariv's death remained a mystery for nearly thirty years until I met Oleg Kalugin, the thirty-two-year veteran of the KGB and author of *Spymaster*.

On June 15, 2010, at a screening of the film *To Russia with Love: The Role of RFE-RL during the Cold War* at the Goethe Institut in Washington, I approached Oleg to tell him that I enjoyed reading his book. We exchanged cards and agreed to meet at the first opportunity. Despite some hesitations and misgivings, we finally got together on September 18, at Zola's, an elegant restaurant next to the Spy Museum in DC. Kalugin was on the board of the museum and also the director of a private counterintelligence school in Alexandria, Virginia. It was one of the most extraordinary meetings in my life.

Switching between English and Russian, I made an effort to charm Oleg as best I could, as we covered a lot of Cold War territory. I told him about my work for Radio Liberty out of Paris, and he recounted his efforts to recruit agents in the United States. He seemed relaxed and began to tell me details about his personal life. We finished off the two-hour lunch with a cognac *digestif* at the bar.

The exploit that interested me the most, and one that he covered in some detail in *Spymaster*, was the attempt to recruit Warwariv, the US ambassador to UNESCO, during a conference in Tbilisi, Georgia. As I mentioned, the attempt failed, and Warwariv reported the incident to the US Embassy in Moscow. However, what Kalugin did not say in his memoir is that, several years after the failed recruitment attempt, Konstantyn Warwariv, a healthy fifty-seven-year-old diplomat at the height of his career, suddenly and inexplicably died.

It was evident that Kalugin knew more about the circumstances of Warwariv's death than he let on in his book, so I pressed him on the subject. During the second round of cognacs, I asked him point-blank, "By the way, how did Warwariv die?"

Kalugin looked at me for a few seconds and then said, "Probably the same way Litvinenko did."

We ended on that note, and despite promises to continue our relationship, Oleg and I never met again.

16. Artists, Dissidents, and Writers

THE DAY I ARRIVED in Paris, I hardly knew anyone. Yet, within a few months, my network of acquaintances had grown like a mushroom patch after rain. Luba Markewycz was right when she said, "Slavko, don't hesitate. Go to Paris because you don't know what awaits you." In Paris, I met people I would never have been exposed to if I had stayed in Chicago, and they were all so different. The circle included an array of artists, art collectors, scholars, diplomats, academicians, dissidents, and writers.

Aristide Virsta, a professor of music at the Université de Paris–Sorbonne, was a connoisseur of art and a collector, a passion we shared. He was a friendly older man, elegant, slender, sporting a thin mustache. Virsta's position at the university gave him a cachet that other diasporans, I suspect, envied. It was not easy to penetrate the French academic clique.

There may have been some truth to the prattle that Aristide had an inflated ego. My relationship with him, however, was always cordial. Virsta lived in a cramped apartment in Bourg-la-Reine, just south of Paris, with his wife and two daughters. Every wall, nook, and cranny of his residence was filled with art by notable Ukrainian painters who lived and created in Paris before and after WWII: Alexander Archipenko, Alexis Grishchenko (Hryshchenko), Vasyl Khmeliuk, Michel Andreyenko, and others. While Virsta focused on old-established Ukrainian painters in Paris, I concentrated on collecting the new wave of artists such as Mazuryk, Makarenko and Solomukha in Paris, and Sazonov and Strelnikov in Munich.

Aristide's most prized possession was his villa on the Riviera, high above Saint-Raphael, with a view of the bay and Saint-Tropez in the distance.

During the summer, I often visited the professor with my children, Darian and Tamara, and sometimes friends. When I stayed at his villa on the Côte d'Azur, the professor never asked or accepted one franc for his hospitality, even when he was not there. I was amused by the diaspora's rumors and lack of understanding how he could afford a villa on the Côte.

Professor Virsta liked to impress. On being introduced, his first words were "I am a professor at the Sorbonne, I speak five languages, and I own a villa in Saint-Raphael." Still, he was a kind, intelligent, and courteous man. With him, you knew where you stood. At times, the professor operated on the margins of what the diaspora considered acceptable. He had Ukrainian friends at UNESCO with whom he often exchanged favors. They played on his vanity by giving him access to Soviet personalities that passed through Paris, while Aristide repaid them by making introductions to a select group of diaspora Ukrainians. After Gorbachev had proclaimed *glasnost*, it was easier to talk to Soviet citizens and Aristide wanted me to meet female members of the Ukrainian cultural delegation at UNESCO—ostensibly to discuss art. Although it was a few years since the Kirilenko business, I was still leery. My friends Ivan and Srjan were always warning me: "Slavko, be careful—they are very clever."

IN THE EARLY '80s, a few Soviet dissidents and artists arrived in Paris. Most were accepted by the émigré community, but a few were objects of suspicion among the paranoid Ukrainian diaspora. The community had a way of judging who was acceptable and who was to be avoided. When Volodymyr Makarenko turned up in Paris, the diaspora's antennae were put on alert. How could an artist who was not Jewish leave the Soviet Union? The community buzzed with rumors and speculations. The issue was quickly put to rest when the dissident Leonid Plyushch vouched for Makarenko.

The case of the artist Anton Solomoukha was different. He found a way to leave the Soviet Union by way of a *mariage blanc,* a marriage of convenience to a French Martinique-born student. To some, his story of marriage to a student sounded a bit fanciful, and the community was abuzz with rumors that Anton was a KGB mole placed in Paris to inform on the Ukrainian diaspora. There was speculation that his engaging personality and perfect Ukrainian provided an ideal cover. Moreover, there was no one like Plyushch to vouch for him.

Volodymyr Makarenko arrived in Paris from Vienna in the summer of 1981. My first meeting with Makar took place in their tenth-floor unfurnished apartment on Rue des Pyrénées in a working-class arrondissement. It was a very modest residence, but Makar and his wife, Victoria, were ecstatic to be free from the tyrannical regime and to breathe Parisian air. They radiated happiness. When I visited them with the Struks, we were entertained with anecdotes about life in the Soviet Union, Soviet humor, and impromptu sketches. Makar kept us in stitches long into the night. I realized that we in the West had forgotten the art of storytelling and joking.

As a young and talented artist in Dnipropetrovs'k, Makar wanted to go beyond the constraints of social realism and explore new paths in art, but such attempts were squashed and summarily reprimanded. Either you painted the way the party dictated, or you didn't paint at all. Harassed and threatened by the authorities, Makar knew that if he remained in culturally backward Dnipropetrovs'k, he would suffocate. He was desperate to leave the Soviet Union, but that was easier said than done.

When Makar was five, his parents separated. If it were not for his grandmother, who instilled in Makar his sense of Ukrainian identity, taught him to speak the language, and, in effect, raised him, he might have ended up as another *sovetsky chelovek*—a Soviet man. He always spoke of his grandmother fondly and was closer to her than to his biological mother.

In Paris, Makar started to paint and, within a few months, he was ready for his first exhibit. Those close to him often called him Makarchyk. He was a hit with the diaspora, who began to buy his paintings, and his fame spread to the United States and Canada, where he held exhibits in Toronto and Chicago.

Over the years, Makar told me stories he didn't tell anyone else, many revolving around his artistic accomplishments and sexual exploits. On one occasion, he surprised me with an astonishing revelation from life in the village as an adolescent.

"I heard rumors," he said, "that something terrible had happened in Ukraine during the 1930s, but no one would tell me what, so I went to my grandmother. '*Babstiu*, Granny, what happened here in the 1930s?'"

Makar told me she turned pale and got very nervous and then took him aside and covered his mouth with her hand. "Don't ever ask this question again," she said. "It will bring us nothing but trouble."

Makar obeyed and never asked.

His story illustrated the degree to which the Communist regime had managed to obliterate historical memory in Soviet Ukraine. For fear of arrest and deportation, no one talked about the mass starvation, the genocidal famine we today call the Holodomor. In fact, Makar admitted that he did not learn the whole story about Stalin's Ukrainian famine genocide until he was in the West. In the Soviet Union, the subject was anathema.

Makar was desperate to leave and applied for an exit visa at least ten times. Each request was denied without an explanation. Although he dreamed of Paris, he knew it was a fantasy. Moscow and Leningrad permitted a greater degree of artistic expression, but he couldn't get permission to move there. There was only one other alternative: Tallinn. In Estonia, artists were relatively free to paint as they wished, and Tallinn was the closest thing to a Western city in the Soviet Union. As soon as he got a *propyska*, permission to move, he went to Tallinn, where he continued to dream of Paris.

When the Helsinki Accords were signed in 1976, things began to change. However, you could only leave the Soviet Union if you were Jewish. While in Estonia, Makar met Kristian Feigelson, a French academic who helped him and his family leave the Soviet Union. Kristian arranged for his uncle in Israel to send the Makarenkos an invitation, claiming Makar's wife, Victoria, had Jewish ancestry. Vika's maiden name, Tall, sounded Jewish, and because the Soviet authorities did not verify such facts too closely and Makarenko was regarded a dissident artist, provocateur, and parasite, the family was permitted to leave Tallinn. First, they went to Vienna and, later, to Paris.

"This was the greatest moment of my life," Makar told me, "the fulfillment of a dream."

Until the last minute, he did not believe he would be allowed to leave the "Evil Empire," which, according to emigrants like Makarenko, was exactly what it was!

WITHIN A SHORT TIME, I learned that two other dissident artists, Volodymyr Strelnikov and Vitaly Sazonov, had recently arrived in Munich from Odesa. Together with the artists in Paris, they decided to hold a group exhibit in Metz, which had a Ukrainian community composed of descendants of post-WWII displaced persons. Most importantly, the city was located between Paris and Munich.

The show was dubbed immediately as the first group exhibit of *Ukryinskykh Nekonformistiv*—Ukrainian nonconformist artists—in the West. It was a historic moment in Ukrainian art history because it represented the continuation of a tradition of Ukrainian diaspora artists in France that had its roots in turn-of-the-century Paris.[69] Sazonov and Strelnikov were to take the train from Munich, and I would drive Makar and Anton from Paris. Each would bring a few paintings. We set out for Metz laden with paintings in my BMW 520i. The mood was buoyant and optimistic with Makar and Anton telling jokes and anecdotes. Cruising at 180 kilometers an hour, fifty kilometers over the 130 kilometers speed limit, I was unexpectedly pulled over by the national police at a random control point the local gendarmerie put up at whim. Two armed gendarmes approached me and asked me to follow them to their paddy wagon.

I'd never seen the inside of a French police wagon. It was like a miniature police station with all sorts of radios and sophisticated communications equipment. They examined my driver's license, checked my identification, and made several telephone calls. By the demeanor of the gendarmes, the infraction seemed to have the makings of a serious incident, something that might even jeopardize our trip. Finally, the officer in charge apologized for the trouble his subordinates had caused. "*Excusez nous, Monsieur Martinique, mais vous comprenez* . . . (We beg your pardon, Mr. Martyniuk, but you understand, we had to check you out). There are many stolen cars with diplomatic plates. You are free to go. *Bon voyage.*" No mention of speeding or any other matter. That was when I realized the magic power of CD plates. Even to the no-nonsense French national police, a *fonctionnaire international* was something sacred—one treated a member of the *corps diplomatique* with respect and discretion.

We were slightly ahead of schedule, so I decided to stop in Reims to show my friends two magnificent medieval gems—the High Gothic Cathedral of Notre-Dame de Reims where, through centuries, French kings had been crowned, and the lesser known but equally grand thousand-year-old Romanesque Basilica of Saint Remi.

After dropping off the artists to set up the exhibit, I immediately went to see Metz's jewel, the cathedral, one of France's many magnificent Gothic edifices. Emperor Charlemagne considered making Metz his imperial capital before he finally decided in favor of Aachen.

The group exhibit turned out to be a grand affair. I met Volodymyr Strelnikov and Vitaly Sazonov, both from the Russian-speaking city of Odesa, rare examples of Russians who, for one reason or another, chose to identify

---

[69]   Vita Sisyk documents this fascinating period in her superb catalog *Ukrainian Artists in Paris 1900–1939*, Rodovid Press, Kyiv, Ukraine, 2010.

themselves as Ukrainians. I got several copies of the exhibit poster signed by all four artists, one copy of which I donated to the Ukrainian Institute of Modern Art in Chicago.

ONE OF MY CLOSEST FRIENDS in Paris was Danylo Struk. I met him though Jurij and Daria Darewych in the fall of 1980. When the Darewychys returned to Toronto, their apartment on Rue Notre-Dame-des-Champs was taken over by Danylo and his wife, Oksana. A professor of Ukrainian language and literature at the University of Toronto, Danylo came to Paris to work on the English version of the *Encyclopedia of Ukraine* as an associate editor.

Danylo was at the center of my life in Paris. He and I were the same age, but he was a month older. Struk was not just a first-class intellectual, but also a mover and doer, a man of strong convictions, outspoken even when confronted with controversy. In pursuit of truth, he was never afraid to swim against the current. Danylo was also ambitious, decisive, and competent. In many ways, he reminded me of Ayn Rand's *Fountainhead* character Howard Roark, the embodiment of what she believed to be the ideal man who thought that individualism always trumped collectivism.

Having overseen the publication of the first volume in 1984 and the second in 1988, Struk became editor in chief of the encyclopedia in 1989. The first two volumes of the five-volume encyclopedia were edited by Volodymyr Kubijovych. However, when he passed away in 1985, Struk took over. The encyclopedia was the culmination of a process that began in 1948 in Munich when the Shevchenko Scientific Society embarked on the ten-volume Ukrainian language *Entsyklopedia Ukrayinoznavstva* on which the English version was based. With the publication of the last three volumes in 1993, Struk brought this monumental project to a close.

During the '80s, Danylo commuted between Toronto and Paris. Most of his time was spent at the Shevchenko Scientific Society headquarters in Sarcelles, north of Paris, but in Paris on weekends, he stayed in the apartment I had moved to on Rue Pelouze in the 17th arrondissement. Whenever he showed up, he had his itinerary planned to the hour, and if something didn't work out, he was ready with a Plan B. Danylo was a friendly individual with a sense of humor, and he was fun to be with. He was Canadian and I was American, but both of us were Ukrainian patriots and passionate Francophiles. Struk was also a gourmet and a wine connoisseur. Together we covered a lot of territory and visited some enchanting parts of *la France profonde* from Normandy to Burgundy, and points south.

I knew Danylo Struk for almost twenty years. A week before he passed away, we were supposed to meet in Paris to do one of our wine-tasting jaunts through France. His premature death in 1999 created a void in my life.

SOON AFTER I ARRIVED IN PARIS, Danylo introduced me to Leonid Plyushch, the Ukrainian dissident and mathematician, who had been allowed to leave the Soviet Union in 1976. Lyonia, as his friends called him, was part of the circle of Parisian-based Ukrainian professionals, intellectuals, and artists with whom I associated. He settled in Paris, and published the story of his ordeal in Ukraine in his book *History's Carnival*. Plyushch had been a *cause célèbre* of the Ukrainian diaspora in the mid-'70s.

Danylo and Lyonia shared a keen interest in Ukrainian literature, and I was privileged to be present at many of their discussions. Joining these meetings was the artist Volodymyr Makarenko and later Oleh Oleksyn. Lyonia and Makar developed a unique bond. Hounded by the repressive regime in Soviet Ukraine, both had been oppressed, albeit in different ways. To create freely, Makar was forced to abandon his native Dnipropetrovs'k for Tallinn. Lyonia's fate was much harsher. For his criticism of the totalitarian Soviet regime, Plyushch was incarcerated in a *psykhushka*, a psychiatric prison for severely psychotic patients. There he was given high doses of antipsychotic drugs, an experience that left an indelible mark on him, though it did not break his spirit.

On Sunday afternoons, it was customary to meet at Café Bonaparte, a short walk from the Ukrainian Catholic Church of Saint Volodymyr. Once Lyonia showed up, he was invariably the center of attention. He drank multiple espressos, smoked his *samokrutki* (rolled tobacco cigarettes), and expounded on his latest idea or discovery. In addition to being an erudite intellectual and a deep thinker, Lyonia was a courageous man—generous, tolerant, and large in spirit. A modest man of simple tastes bordering on the ascetic, he eschewed material things, especially when surrounded by fawning affluent diasporans who boasted about their wealth and lifestyles. Although Lyonia was fond of a good cognac or Armagnac, he was not a gourmet. What mattered to him most was what was in the heads and hearts of the people he met—their thoughts, viewpoints, and resolve to stand up for principles and truth.

Lyonia was fond of repeating Dostoyevsky's aphorism "Beauty will save the world." On one occasion, we got into a lengthy discussion, and I tried to pin him down on what he meant by "beauty." I maintained that truth is as important, if not more important than beauty, quoting from the Bible, "When you know the truth, it will set you free," and like Vaclav Havel, I argued that truth will prevail over ideology, lies, and hate. In the end, we found common ground in Keats's aphorism "Beauty is truth, and truth beauty—that is all."

IN THE SUMMER OF 1986, I enrolled in a six week immersion course to polish my Russian conversational skills. The first three weeks took place near Lambrecht, in West Germany, (That is where I met Eva, my future wife. She was studying to be a tri-lingual translator: German, Russian and Polish), and the last three in Madonna de Compiglio in Dolomies of northern Italy. Soviet émigrés, former dissidents, and human rights activists taught the six-week immersion course, and Lyonia was a member of this tightly knit group. In the lectures I attended on Russian literature and history, I sensed a patronizing and, at times, a condescending attitude toward Ukraine and Ukrainians, which I found strange. After all, the staff supposedly consisted of tolerant and open-minded individuals, defenders of human rights and dignity of man.

When we read passages from *Taras Bulba*, one of the instructors pointed out, "Look, even Gogol wrote in Russian." They seemed to regard Ukrainian as a substandard dialect of Russian, suitable for singing, but not high culture. Lyonia waited for the right moment to comment. Speaking calmly, he reprimanded his colleagues for not knowing anything about Ukraine, its real history and culture. He criticized them for their patronizing attitude toward Ukrainians and for viewing Ukraine's history through the prism of Moscow:

"How can you say anything about Ukrainian literature if you've never read it? Over the centuries, Russia has turned Ukraine into a colony, making fifty million Ukrainians their slaves. Despite years in the West, your views of Ukraine have not evolved since you left the Soviet Union: let them have their songs and their embroideries to keep them happy, but leave high culture to Russians."

There was utter silence, but Lyonia continued. "The moment we Ukrainians start to talk about our culture, our language, our history, and, most importantly, our independence, you call us nationalists, fascists, or 'Banderovtsy,' yet never a word about Russian nationalism, Russian imperialism. I see that nothing has changed, and that's a double standard I will not accept."

Besides being a profound and principled thinker, there was a more down-to-earth side to Lyonia. He loved good company, stimulating conversation, and humor. On more than one occasion, our circle of friends gathered to sing, drink, and tell stories. Such evenings lasted late into the night, occasionally until four in the morning, when the supply of wine, anecdotes, and jokes began to dwindle into pauses and, finally, silence.

Lyonia also had a strong attachment to nature. On weekends, he and his wife, Tanya, went mushroom picking in forests surrounding Paris. His favorite was the oak forest of Saint-Germain-en-Laye, northwest of Paris. Curiously, although he enjoyed this hobby, he did not eat mushrooms.

In addition to literature and philosophy, Lyonia had an interest in esoteric subjects such as Kabbalah, the ancient Jewish tradition of mysticism and structuralism in literature. He also had a passion for collecting *pysanky*, the richly-decorated Ukrainian Easter eggs. Lyonia was fascinated by their symbolism that dated to pagan times.

Leonid Plyushch, the Ukrainian intellectual, mathematician, philosopher, dissident, defender of human rights, passed away on the morning of June 4, 2015. I had lost a friend.

17. Life in Socialist France

ON MAY 10, 1981, I witnessed a tectonic shift in French politics. At around ten o'clock that evening, I was driving home from a dinner party and had to pass through the Place de la Bastille. The square was blocked by joyous crowds with red roses in their hands. I had to abandon my car and take the metro.

Earlier that evening, French television had announced that France had a new president. The Socialist Party candidate, François Mitterrand, had won 52 percent of the vote against 48 percent for Valéry Giscard d'Estaing of the Union for French Democracy. As soon as the news was announced, Parisians flocked into the streets for a mammoth street party. Corks popped, and champagne flowed. Twenty-three years of rule from the Right had come to an end. For the French, the *trente glorieuses,* thirty years of growth and prosperity, had not been enough. They wanted the Socialist utopia that Mitterrand promised—a good life through the massive intervention of the state. What they got instead was a Socialist dystopia.

It did not take long for Mitterrand's centerpiece projects—nationalization of key industries and big banks—to fail. A wealth tax was instituted. Businessmen and the rich packed suitcases full of cash and crossed into Switzerland. Growth crashed, unemployment jumped to two million, inflation increased to 18 percent, and, within a year, the franc was devalued twice. In March 1983, the franc was devalued for the third time. Still, the idea of a state that would provide a comfortable cocoon for the people of the Hexagon was not abandoned. The promise, however, proved impossible to deliver. Political promises and economic reality clashed.

Within a year, Mitterrand had to backpedal. The widespread 1981 nationalizations were rescinded, and by June 1982, policies of so-called *rigueur* were introduced. These amounted to contradictory actions, cuts in spending on the one hand, and a raise in the minimum wage on the other. The newly nationalized industries, which had been promised held up as guarantors of employment and prosperity, declared drastic job cuts. But the benefits, a fifth week of paid holiday leave, remained. The last illustrated how the so-called *droits acquis*, acquired rights, once granted, are impossible to retract.

Developments that took place across the channel in the UK at roughly the same time provide an interesting contrast. Two years before Mitterrand's election, Margaret Thatcher became the United Kingdom's first female prime minister. She embarked on an economic path diametrically opposed to that of Mitterrand's. During her tenure, she privatized certain industries, reduced the influence of trade unions, scaled back public benefits, and changed the terms of political discourse. Her free market policies were encapsulated in the memorable words "The problem with Socialism is that you eventually run out of other people's money."

Thatcher rejected the economic theories of John Maynard Keynes, who advocated deficit spending during periods of high unemployment, preferring instead the monetarist approach of the Chicago school economist Milton Friedman. These completely different approaches sent the two countries on opposing trajectories.

I often traveled to England on business, so I was in a position to observe the tenures of both Thatcher and Mitterrand during the 1980s. Working for the OECD provided an exceptional vantage point to compare the course the two countries had embarked on. What I witnessed firsthand was how the path of the two economies, roughly comparable in size and productivity, suddenly diverged at the beginning of the 1980s.

In the decade that followed, Margaret Thatcher put the UK on a solid fiscal footing and, despite loud squeals from the left, single-handedly reset the country's psychological mind-set. Mitterrand's Socialist policies, on the other hand, took the country down the tubes; economic malaise set in, and a decline in growth and productivity created a sclerotic and uncompetitive economy.

If there was one legacy that Mitterrand should be remembered for, it is chronic unemployment. A year before he took office, France's unemployment hovered at around 6 percent. When he left, it was stuck at 13 percent. When Margaret Thatcher took the helm, unemployment spiked to 12 percent, but by the end of the 1980s, it stabilized at 7 percent. For the next two decades, that two-to-one ratio remained fixed. After the failures had become apparent, I told my friends that after Mitterrand, Socialism in France would be finished for the next one hundred years. I was wrong. The French reelected Mitterrand in 1988 with an even greater margin of 5 percent.

Since I lived in the sheltered world of a *fonctionnaire international*, paid in US dollars, the series of devaluations gave me more purchasing power. The kind of system the French chose to have mattered little to me. The economic crisis in the early 1980s hardly affected my lifestyle, except in one respect.

Like many at the OECD, I had been banking with the venerable Banque Rothschild, the French branch of the Rothschild international banking family, which had had a long and bumpy history. In the 1930s, their holdings were nationalized, and in 1940, the Nazis seized their bank. It was restored to them at the end of the war, but in 1981 Rothschild Frères was nationalized by the French Socialist government of President Mitterrand.

Believing it was safe, I had invested a nice sum in one of the growth portfolios recommended by the bank. Within weeks of Mitterrand's election, however, the value of the portfolio began to slide. The Banque Rothschild was under attack—its stock plummeted, and the head of the French Rothschild branch went into exile in New York. For this, he was labeled a traitor.

Thirty other banks were also nationalized so the state could control sources of capital, but none were harassed as severely as the Banque Rothschild, because they catered to the wealthy. In any event, the shareholders in the nationalized banks received bonds from the National Banking Fund, the Banque Rothschild became L'Européenne de Banque and lost its illustrious name and distinguished cachet. In this respect, Mitterrand's election cost me dearly, and, eventually, I switched to the Société Générale.

Mitterrand's election was disastrous for France as well. He can best be defined as a pure cynic. A secretive and devious serial philanderer who maintained relations with some of Africa's worst dictators, he presided over a government that armed the genocide in Rwanda, and chose crooks as friends. Mitterrand was also a patron and protector of wartime collaborators and showed absolutely no remorse for his self-centered amorality before he died.

DURING MY FIRST THREE years in Paris, I lived with the expectation that my life there would soon come to an end. When my three-year nonrenewable contract with the IEA expired, I would have to return to the United States to an unclear future, a fact that gnawed at me continuously, but at the same time forced me to squeeze as much into my three years in the City of Light as possible.

In the spring of 1980, my old Regensburg friend Ivan Myhul came to Paris with his classy companion Marie Brébart, whom he was later to marry. We put them up on a foldout couch in the wood-paneled library which, with its ornate fireplace and superb view of the Eiffel Tower, was better than the most expensive hotel in Paris. Ivan and Marie stayed with us for several weeks, and it gave us an opportunity to get reacquainted and catch up on the missing years. Zoe had been attending a cooking course at the Cordon Bleu, so we enjoyed her gourmet cooking, and the conversation flowed as smoothly as the French wine I bought by the case at the US embassy commissary.

Although we had similar roots, our worldviews were distinctly different. While I spent my teenage years in Chicago, Ivan grew up in Minneapolis, where he lived with his mother. After I matriculated from the University of Illinois business school in Champaign/Urbana, I went to work in the private sector as an accountant, and fifteen years with Amoco Oil led to me to adopt conservative views on economics and politics. At the same time, I served with the US Army Reserve and perceived the war in Vietnam as an ongoing struggle with Communist expansionism.

Ivan's career followed a different path. He studied political science at the Université catholique de Louvain, Belgium's largest French-speaking university. After he had been awarded a PhD in Soviet studies by Columbia University, he accepted a teaching post at Bishop's University in Quebec, Canada. Ivan pursued the academic track and, as far as I know, never worked in the private sector or served in the army. That, in essence, explained our different views of the world.

Our conversations were long and spirited. Ivan thought that the state should play a central role in the economy, and that the government should own the means of production. He was a statist who believed, for example, that the state-owned auto manufacturer Renault was run more efficiently than a comparable privately-owned manufacturer of automobiles. I believed that government bureaucrats, no matter how well motivated and educated, were incapable of running anything efficiently. Based on my experience in both the private and public sectors, I subscribed to the view that big intrusive governments were more often the source of the problem than the solution.

Our conversation continued for the next quarter of a century until we began to sound like broken records and stopped quarreling. Still, no matter what topic we discussed, Ivan nearly always took the opposite side and rarely came to admit that he was wrong on anything. He seemed to be stuck in teaching mode, talking down to me and others as professor to student. By nature, Ivan was a contrarian, yet despite differences, we remain good friends to this day.

AS A MEMBER OF IEA'S oil industry division, I worked closely with my European Commission (EC) counterparts. The level of ignorance of these bureaucrats was at times astounding. Perhaps their greatest failing was how badly they understood the so-called spot market for oil. To them, the spot market represented predatory pricing practices and had to be regulated. During the group's working sessions, I explained that no such thing as a physical spot market existed. It was essentially a telephone network connecting small producers and marketers to cover temporary oil shortages. Large oil companies rarely, if ever, turned to the spot market. Every time I explained the spot market mechanism, the audience reacted with "Is that so? Why didn't someone tell me this before?" Even after such clarifications, some bureaucrats, as if tone-deaf, persisted, "Yes, but we must do something about the spot market."

One of my duties at the Oil Industry Division was to give presentations about the energy industry and oil markets to government officials, bureaucrats, professionals, and students pursuing advanced degrees. It was an IEA/OECD public relations effort, and often I was asked to address mixed groups of visitors on the topic of oil markets. My years with Amoco Oil had left me with a grasp of all of the aspects of the business—exploration, production, refining, and marketing. As the world was still reeling from the recent disruptions in the oil markets caused by the revolution in Iran and the shock of the hostage crisis, interest in the oil markets was intense.

Occasionally, someone in the audience would accuse the oil companies of engaging in predatory pricing or unfair competitive practices. I'd rebut such notions quite handily, since I knew how the oil industry functioned, and they did not.

On one occasion, I spoke to a group of graduate exchange students from the University of Amsterdam's international program. A young woman in the group, Zlatica from Montenegro (at that time one of the republics of Yugoslavia), expressed an interest in what I was saying, and informed me that she was a Communist and proud of it. I was unsure if this was an expression of youthful naïveté or a genuine conviction. I was curious to find out what made her tick, so we continued our conversation over coffee.

Although Yugoslavia was nominally a Communist country, it was more open to the West than the USSR, and I wanted to know how this hybrid model worked. It was the only country that managed to break with the Communist orthodoxy of Eastern Europe and the Soviet Union. Some Western academics and intellectuals sympathetic to Socialism viewed Yugoslavia as an example of Communism with a human face, a compromise between totalitarian Communism and capitalism. This was a model of convergence that some Sovietologists in the West regarded as inevitable.

"Ever since Tito broke with the Soviet Union," Zlatica claimed, "Yugoslavs have been trying to create a more humane Socialist model that combines the best management practices of free market capitalist economies with attributes of Communism. The Yugoslavs have found it in 'self-management.'"

The new approach differed from orthodox Communism in that it incorporated elements of capitalism. Allegedly, the workers had a stake in an enterprise and a voice in collective decisions, but to hear her speak, one would think that the Yugoslavs had discovered a new third way: common ownership combined with collective decision-making, a temptingly attractive idea, in theory.

History, of course, proved them wrong. Like any collective model, the Yugoslav system was subject to gross mismanagement, favoritism, nepotism, rampant corruption, and, of course, collective responsibility, which, in the final analysis, meant that no one was held accountable. The model favored certain groups, in this case mostly Serbs, at the expense of all the others, and it ended very badly in 1991.

IVAN MYHUL introduced me to other friends in Paris. Among them were Leni and Peter, a couple who lived in a penthouse apartment on the northern slope of Montmartre. Ivan knew Leni, a blonde German heiress to a family fortune, a Moselle vineyard, before she met Peter, a Hungarian Jew twenty years her senior. Peter was a short man with penetrating beady eyes. He was obviously intelligent, and his head was covered with an unruly white mane. Peter smoked a lot and drank. After the 1956 Hungarian Revolution, he ended up in Mexico, where he married and raised a family. He rarely talked about his past in Mexico, but from what I gathered, he was involved in some shady oil business and art dealings. Knowing that the oil industry in Mexico was notoriously corrupt, I was not surprised. On one occasion when he was drunk, Peter revealed that he had fled Mexico because fiscal authorities there were hounding him.

Leni and Peter were a friendly and hospitable couple who accepted me as a friend largely because I was Ivan's friend. I was not quite sure where Leni stood politically, but it would not be wrong to say that she tilted left, though not to the extent Peter did. He was a doctrinaire hard-line leftist and a Communist at heart, just not a card-carrying one. Ivan Myhul once described him as "ontologically closer to Engels' view of the world," whatever that meant. The couple pursued a lavish bourgeois lifestyle subsidized primarily by Leni's inheritance, and somehow I became part of their inner circle of friends. Leni also owned a spacious country home in Germany overlooking the Moselle near the town of Trittenheim. They spent their summers there, and I was often their guest.

Apart from their radical leftist leanings, Peter and Leni were very nice people—generous, nonjudgmental, well-read, and interested in art, film, and the theater. I was a regular at their dinner parties, which often included interesting people from Latin America, Asia, and Africa passing through Paris. Because I was of Ukrainian heritage from a mixed European/American background, they did not consider me a typical American, and the fact that I was a Reagan supporter didn't seem to bother them. Peter half-jokingly introduced me to his friends as "little Reagan," and I called him "little Trotsky," all in jest.

I was drawn to these gatherings because I wanted to find out what these people were thinking and what underpinned their radical beliefs. To them, I suppose, I was the token capitalist who made their evenings more exciting, especially as I worked for the OECD, an organization with a prestigious *cachet*.

Whenever Ivan attended these dinner parties, he and Peter tried to convince me that I was a Marxist but not aware of it. I argued that capitalism was by far the best system that satisfies mankind's materialistic needs, a statement they cleverly twisted, saying that is precisely what Marx had said: human beings are materialistic, and their basic drives are dictated by materialistic values, followed by a toast and laughter. Since Reagan had recently been elected president of the United States and Mitterrand had become the president of France, we spent countless hours debating the virtues and drawbacks of free market capitalism versus Socialism. The range of topics we covered included conditions in the Soviet Union, Yugoslavia, Cuba, and East Germany, and the level of unemployment in the United States. There was nothing original or new in these conversations, and, eventually, I found them tedious.

"Look at the Soviet Union," Peter would moralize, "everyone has a job, and you know that not having a job is extremely debilitating to the psyche. It robs a man of his dignity. There is no ethnic strife in the Soviet Union. Education is free, and you don't have to pay for medical care."

This was a verbatim regurgitation of Soviet propaganda. Such conversations usually dragged on late into the night, but the needle never moved to the right or left for any of us. He admired Fidel Castro with the same intensity that he detested Ronald Reagan.

"Castro stood up to American imperialism and capitalist exploitation of the country," he ranted, "and thanks to Soviet support, Cuba now has a just and equitable society."

I argued the obvious: "Castro's revolution was brutally repressive, with tens of thousands of political prisoners and thousands of executions. In an attempt to eliminate 'parasitism' and 'exploitation,' all private property has been confiscated, including all food retailing, bars, restaurants, dry cleaners, carpentry workshops, automobile mechanic shops, and even shoeshine stands. The masses live in dire poverty."

His response was the mantra: "The revolution had to get rid of the parasites. All Cubans now have access to free education and health services." The fact that health services were the equivalent of one aspirin a day did not matter.

Peter believed in a Socialist utopia the same way Jews believe in the coming of the Messiah, and Christians in the resurrection of Christ. It was no longer ideology; it was religion. I don't know why I even bothered to argue. Maybe I harbored the hope that I might make him come around to my way of thinking. But if anything came out of these discussions it was the realization that even intelligent people, once they've accepted the Socialist faith, are unlikely to change their views.

In the early '80s, Peter used to arrange a small party to attend the *Fête de l'Humanité*, a festival the French Communist Party had been organizing since 1930. It was held on the grounds of the Le Bourget airport north of Paris. To satisfy my curiosity, I went to these events on several occasions. I was surprised at the number of people that turned up—some years up to half a million—to hear top names in music such as Stevie Wonder, Pink Floyd, Juliette Gréco, Johnny Hallyday, and, later, Cesaria Evora. In addition to music, the festival included numerous ethnic food stands with regional specialties. It was a lot of fun, but I wondered how many knew that the affair was primarily funded by Moscow.

Through my work at the OECD, I had met Jaime Ruiz, the head of the Spanish delegation to the organization. Jaime had the bearing of a tall Spanish aristocrat with a trimmed *royale* beard. He was married to an attractive German woman, and they made a distinguished couple. Jaime and I shared a passion for flamenco, and one spring evening in 1983 he invited me to a performance of a flamenco troupe at the Spanish embassy, and gave me a couple of extra tickets in case I wanted to bring friends. I knew that Peter liked flamenco, so I invited him and Leni to join me. It was a fabulous evening of flamenco *toque* and *baile*, guitar and dancing, in the majestic setting of the embassy. After the performance, I introduced Peter and Leni to Jaime and his wife. It appeared that they had a lot in common—both men were Spanish speakers with German wives. Peter, always anxious to develop relationships with diplomats, invited us all to a dinner party in their penthouse. That first dinner party seemed like a success, mainly because politics were largely avoided. But a few months later, when I met Jaime at one of the industry working group meetings at the OECD, I asked how they were doing. He said the couples had stopped getting together. "Peter's views were too extreme for me."

At that point, I realized that my relationship with Peter and Leni would not last much longer. Despite outward niceties of comradeship, our political views diverged too much to sustain a relationship based on shared values and interests. It all came to a head during one of our last conversations that focused on the current division of Germany into Western Germany (BRD) and Eastern Germany (DDR). The symbol of this divide was the Berlin Wall that split the German nation into two countries. To me, locking up people behind a barbed wire fence was one of Communism's most odious sins.

I stated that "if the Berlin Wall should ever come down, it would be the end of East Germany and the two Germanys would reunite."

Peter, visibly agitated, said, "That's absurd, they are two different countries now. Any thought of German reunification is ridiculous." Five years later, of course, the Wall did come down.

After that exchange, I began to see Peter and Leni less and less, and when it became likely that I would leave the field of energy economics to work for Radio Liberty, I put our relationship on ice. I never fully trusted Peter, with his murky life in Mexico and his connections to Communists in Europe. More important, I simply did not want him to know what my new job would entail. As a result, I hardly saw Peter for the next few years. We met once or twice by chance, but our encounters were cool, for which I felt a twinge of guilt. Life at times is strange and awkward, but when I got a new job with RFE-RL, I had no choice. I had to be careful with whom I associated. I had one regret about not seeing them again socially. I never had the satisfaction of hearing Peter's reaction to the fall of the Berlin Wall, the reunification of Germany, and the implosion of the Soviet Union in 1991. Peter, a heavy smoker, died of a heart attack in 1992 at the age of sixty-five. Perhaps the disintegration of the Soviet Union had been too much.

IN 1984, I ATTENDED a United Nations international conference on chemical control management in Geneva. When two members of the Ukrainian delegation saw my name tag, they approached me. They were surprised to find someone of Ukrainian origin at a conference such as this, and after introductions, we agreed to meet. It seemed like an unusual opportunity to have contact with professionals in my field from Ukraine at no apparent risk. Oleh was a chemical engineer and head of the delegation, a Galician from Western Ukraine who spoke Ukrainian fluently. His colleague Victor did not.

Early the next day, I ran into Oleh in the corridor and said, "*Dobryi den* (Good day)."

"*Dobryi ranok* (Good morning)," he responded hesitatingly.

Immediately, I sensed that he was uncomfortable speaking to me, nervous and evasive. He explained apologetically, "*Vy rozumiyete moye stanovyshche, mij kolega* (You understand my position, my colleague)," without finishing the sentence. It took me only a second to realize that his partner was the proverbial KGB "escort" assigned to keep an eye on the delegation from Ukraine to ensure he didn't make any illicit contacts with foreigners or, worse, defect. On the last day of the conference, when the KGB watchdog was not around, Oleh told me openly that he'd been thinking about defecting, but because his wife and children in Ukraine were *de facto* hostages, he had not yet found a way. Would I help? At this point, Victor spotted us talking and quickly approached, and that was the end of the conversation.

This encounter left a powerful impression on me. It confirmed what I already knew, but being so close physically to someone pleading for help was upsetting and painful and confirmed my belief that, forty years after WWII, the Russians still did not trust the Ukrainian elites. It demonstrated that the USSR was not only a prison of nations but also a prison of people. Even though we exchanged cards, I never heard from poor Oleh again.

ANOTHER SOCIALIST OF UKRAINIAN origin in Paris I wanted to meet was François Mitterrand's chief of staff, Pierre Bérégovoy, who eventually became the minister of Finance and, later, prime minister of the French Republic. Unfortunately, I never met him because he was literally unapproachable.[70]

Bérégovoy, the son of a Ukrainian café owner from Normandy, left school and went to work in a textile factory at the age of sixteen. A self-made man from the working classes, he eventually wound up as one of France's ruling elite during the 1980s. And yet the elites never accepted him as one of their own. He did not fit and was ridiculed by the inner circle as *"le petit Russe,"* becoming the butt of many jokes. The worst insult to Bérégovoy was that he was never invited to personal gatherings such as New Year celebrations because he was not a Frenchman *de souche,* of root, as the saying goes.

That's why even as prime minister, Bérégovoy showed signs of insecurity and was always going out of his way to impress those around him. He was genuinely struck by what he achieved and found it hard to suppress his delight. "Who would have thought," he once told journalists in his lavish dining room in the north wing of the Louvre, "that an immigrant's son would one day be sitting in the splendor of the Louvre, eating from the finest antique Limoges plates?"

In the spring of 1993, after being disparaged one last time by Mitterrand, he told his chauffeur to drive to the canal outside Nevers, where he was mayor. He stepped out of the car and shot himself in the temple.

---

[70]   The Ukrainian equivalent of *Beregovoy* was *Berehovyj*, meaning someone living near a riverbank.

18. Exploring Picardie

THE FRENCH HEXAGON is rich in history, natural beauty, architecture, gastronomy, and wines. From the English Channel in the north to the Pyrenees and the Mediterranean in the south, from the Atlantic in the west to the Rhine and Alps in the east, every region offers something interesting to see. During my twelve years in France, I managed to explore every corner of the hexagon worth visiting. In this chapter, I focus on a region north of Paris called Picardie.

As soon as my contract at the IEA/OECD was extended, I bought a new BMW 320i at what seemed to be a bargain 64,000 FF, which translated to $8,000. Inadvertently, I was the beneficiary of Mitterrand's Socialist policies, which resulted in a doubled devaluation of the franc. By 1985, the FF would be worth ten cents on the dollar. The BMW was the ultimate ticket to freedom, a machine that for the next twelve years would propel me on Western Europe's superb network of *autoroutes, autostradas, autobahns,* and *autopistas* to nearly every corner of Europe.

At about the same time, I moved from a small courtyard apartment in the 8th arrondissement to a more spacious one in the 17th. This area of Paris was very French, very bourgeois, and next door to a small but fabulous island of greenery, the Parc Monceau. I could jog in the park, shop in the lovely Rue de Levis market, and walk to the Champs-Élysées and Étoile, the Grands Boulevards, and the Opera district. The area had a special *cachet* because many of the Impressionist painters used to live and work here a century ago. The nearby Gare Saint-Lazare, for example, was immortalized by artists such as Claude Monet, Edouard Manet, and Gustave Caillebotte.

I began to travel further, faster, and more frequently than before. I wanted to see as much of France and Europe as I could before my inevitable return to the United States. The attractions around Paris were endless—medieval cathedrals, castles, and royal residences near Paris or along the Loire Valley. When people in Canada and the United States got word that there was a Ukrainian-American diplomat living in Paris, I became very popular. People I hadn't seen in ages called and asked if I could suggest an inexpensive hotel in Paris. More often than not, this was code for "Can you put us up for a few nights?" I lost track of the number of people who came calling, and soon had to begin saying no.

In June 1984, my sister Ivanna Richardson and her husband, Ted, visited me with their three daughters, Tatyana, Alexandra, and the baby Adrianna, who was only a year old at the time. I wanted them to see a few of my favorite places north of Paris—the Château of Chantilly, the medieval town of Senlis, the Romanesque church at Morienval, and the picturesque castle of Pierrefonds, fancifully restored by Viollet-le-Duc in the nineteenth century. I had done this tour so many times with friends, I was able to do it blindfolded. Our first stop, Chantilly, roughly fifty kilometers north of Paris, was one of the most impressive of French châteaux. The castle and its grounds, part of the Forêt de Chantilly, were dazzling.

Our last stop was Senlis, a charming medieval town that happened to be a place of pilgrimage for Ukrainians. This is where Anna Yaroslavna, daughter of Prince Yaroslav the Wise of Kyiv, and wife of the French king Henry I, lived and ruled France in the eleventh century. On one of my visits to Senlis in the early '80s, I met Father Roger Hallu, SM, author of a rare monograph about Anna by a non-Ukrainian scholar, *Anne de Kiev: Reine de France.* The aging priest gave me a copy.

The book tells us that Senlis, the ancient Gallo-Roman town of *Civitas Silvanectium*, became part of the French royal domain under Hugh Capet, founder of the Capetian dynasty, who was proclaimed king there in 987. In 1027, Henry, the grandson of Hugh Capet and son of Robert the Pious, was crowned King of France. After a bloody five-year struggle for power with his three brothers, Henry prevailed, and peace returned. Soon, Henry became engaged to Matilda, daughter of the German king Conrad III. Unfortunately, she died before the marriage was consummated, and Henry waited ten years before he married another Matilda, the niece of the German emperor Henry III. Within a year, and without issue, she died as well. Poor Henry, it seemed, did not have much luck with wives, and this naturally raised concerns over the dynastic succession.

Marrying someone from one of the powerful neighboring duchies surrounding the Île-de-France could have serious consequences, and taking a wife from one of the weak city-states in Italy or from Spain was not sufficiently prestigious. Henry had good relations with Edward, the king of England, but Edward did not have any daughters to spare. Henry heard stories of a great kingdom in the east whose capital was adorned with "one hundred churches and four hundred towers"—surely a medieval exaggeration. Feeding on news that ambassadors and merchants brought back from Kyiv, the courts of Europe were abuzz with the splendor of the "pearl of the Orient," a city second only to Constantinople. In addition, a defrocked Cluniac monk brought back news of the splendid marriage of the sister of Yaroslav the Wise to Casimir, king of Poland in Krakow. This confirmed the existence of a strong sovereign in distant Kyiv that did not pose a threat to France.

The twice-widowed King Henry sent a delegation to Kyiv to investigate the possibility of marriage to Anna, the daughter of Yaroslav the Wise.[71] The mission to this faraway land, a two-month 1,800-mile (3,000 kilometers) journey, consisted of the bishops of Châlons and Meaux, and the king's trusted nobleman Gasselin de Chauny. The undertaking was a success—the engagement took place amid festivities and religious services in the thirteen-domed Cathedral of Saint Sophia. Anna's two sisters had already married—Elizabeth to Harald Sigurdsson, king of Norway, and Anastasia to André, king of Hungary.

Anna arrived in Senlis, then the capital of France, and on May 19, 1051, in a ceremony in Reims, married Henry I and, at the same time, was crowned queen of France. Shortly afterward, in 1052, she gave birth to a son, Philippe, followed by Robert, Hugh, and a daughter. It is in this way that Anna became the great-great-grandmother to thirty French kings and noblemen. She ruled France while Philippe was a child, becoming the first queen of France to serve as regent. When Anna came to France, she brought with her a Glagolitic (Old Church Slavonic) copy of what became known as the Reims Gospel, used during the enthronement of all French kings from 1059 to 1793.

---

[71]   Jaroslaw, Iaroslav, and Yaroslav are interchangeable; spellings vary with country. In this memoir, I use the Polish spelling Jaroslaw when referring to myself, because that is how my first name had been recorded on my birth certificate. When talking about the Grand Prince of Kyiv, I use Yaroslav.

There are two sculptures of Anna in Senlis: a recent bronze statue in the courtyard of Saint Vincent's Monastery, and an older one at the entrance to the monastery. For many years, the inscription at the foot of Anna's statue at the monastery read *Anne de Russie*, an inscription that was a constant irritant to the Ukrainian diaspora. For years, Ukrainians in Paris were talking about rectifying this misnomer to *Anne de Kiev*, but the name was literally cut in stone. Success finally came after Ukraine became independent when the Russophiles in France were no longer able to conflate Russia and Ukraine.

ON OCCASION, I TOOK friends who shared my passion for Gothic architecture on a tour of five cathedrals: Noyon, Laon, and Soissons in Eastern Picardie, and Amiens and Beauvais in Western Picardie, where High Gothic reached its apex. These jewels of French medieval architecture have remained intact for eight hundred years.

The Gothic Renaissance that brought Europe out of the so-called Dark Ages began in the 1130s with Abbot Suger's half-Romanesque, half-Gothic experiment at Saint Denis, north of Paris. The style quickly spread north to Noyon, Laon, and Soissons. This initial burst of innovation known as Early Gothic ended with the construction of Notre-Dame de Paris in 1163. After a thirty-year hiatus during which the lessons of Early Gothic were absorbed, the second wave of creative building was launched and reached its zenith in the form of High Gothic edifices at Amiens (1220) and Beauvais (1225). There were, of course, dozens of other great Gothic churches erected between these two periods (Chartres, Reims, Bourges), but the ones above form convenient bookends that encompass seventy-five years of intensive progress in building and innovation.

My tour of Picardie usually began with Noyon's Cathedral of Notre-Dame, an impressive transitional cathedral whose construction was begun in 1150. Charlemagne was crowned King of the Franks in Noyon in 768, as was Hugh Capet in 987. Not too far away was Laon, whose imposing towers were visible from a distance, an outstanding example of mid-twelfth-century Gothic architecture, built at roughly the same time as Notre-Dame de Paris, though it never achieved the fame of the Paris cathedral. Only twenty-five kilometers further along the ruler-straight N-2 is Soissons, whose cathedral is another superb achievement in stylistic refinement.

If there was time, I would show my guests the ruined castle of Coucy-le-Château-Auffrique, halfway between Soissons and Laon. Constructed in the 1220s by Enguerrand III de Coucy, the castle rivaled in size both Richard the Lionheart's Château Gaillard on the bluffs overlooking the Seine, and the residence of the kings of France, the Louvre. One of its lords, Enguerrand VII de Coucy (1340–1397), has been immortalized in Barbara Tuchman's *The Distant Mirror*.

The central narrative of the Gothic evolution in northern France was a continuous quest for taller, airier and brighter, and more ornate construction. Structural engineering advances allowed for greater height and took the weight off the walls, allowing for the installation of large windows. One way to illustrate this trend is to look at the growing height of the cathedral naves. While the nave at Saint Denis was relatively modest at twenty meters, Noyon, the next cathedral to be built, had a nave of twenty-three meters. The one at Laon increased to twenty-four meters and, ten years later, those at Soissons and Notre-Dame de Paris reached an impressive thirty-three meters.

The height of naves stabilized until around 1195 when the race resumed. Notre-Dame Cathedral at Chartres attained a commanding thirty-seven meters, only to be surpassed in a generation by Amiens (1220), whose nave soared to a dizzying forty-three meters. The race to reach heaven stopped in 1225 with Beauvais at forty-eight meters (157 feet). The Beauvais builders saw they could not build any higher when their attempt to reach fifty meters failed, resulting in the choir nave collapsing. When construction resumed, the cathedral was only half completed and remains that way to this day. The era of High Gothic came to an end. Rayonnant and Flamboyant Gothic, which followed, focused on ornamentation rather than height.

Today, Europe is turning away from Christianity. Church attendance is down not only in France but throughout Europe, and with limited resources, fiscal pressures, and drastic demographic changes, I fear that these cathedrals might go the way of churches in the Levant, in Syria, in Egypt, in Turkey, and in Kosovo, wherever Islam has become the dominant religion. A few showpieces such as Hagia Sophia in Istanbul might remain museums, but most churches risk being subjected to willful destruction, comparable to the obliteration of old churches and monasteries in Mosul in 2014, and the demolition of ancient shrines, temples, and monuments at Palmyra in 2015, including the exquisite 1,800-year-old Arch of Triumph, which framed the approach to the city.[72]

---

[72] At the time of the writing of this memoir, the author learned that the Hagia Sophia in Istanbul has been reestablished as a mosque, and that the monuments of Palmyra have been destroyed for the second time.

19. La France Profonde

THE MORE I TRAVELED in France, the more I realized that the republic was not one country but a score of provinces and regions, each retaining its laws, customs, and architecture. The boundaries might be invisible, but the difference between the regions was pronounced. It was the provinces that made France rich, and during my twelve years in the hexagon, I saw more of these provinces than the average Frenchman was likely to see in his lifetime.

On a flight from Washington to Chicago, I met a French diplomat, Minh-Hà Pham, and her husband, who were going to Chicago to explore the city's architecture. I overheard them speaking French, so I struck up a conversation. Minh was a science counselor with the French embassy in Washington DC, and her husband was an architect.

"We have an apartment in Paris," Minh said, "and recently purchased an old farmstead in Burgundy. We're trying to turn it into our country home."

"Where in Burgundy?" I asked.

"Near Avallon," she responded.

"I often used to pass through Avallon on my way to abbey church at Vézélay. Your farmhouse must be somewhere north of the Parc naturel du Morvan," I remarked.

They were astounded. "How do you know France so well?"

That was the beginning of a two-hour conversation that began in Burgundy, veered off to the Loire and then Normandy, the Massif Central, Dordogne, Quercy, and the Bordelais. We finished the verbal Tour de France in Languedoc-Roussillon, the broad swath of the Midi that stretches down from Provence to the eastern Pyrenees.

On approaching O'Hare, we discovered yet another shared interest—the saga of the Cathars, the mediaeval heretics that Frenchmen from the north brutally expunged from history in the thirteenth century. We exchanged cards and said we'd continue the conversation back in Washington.

Although Paris is home to one-fifth of the population of France, it is no more representative of France than New York of America. The best way to experience it is to break out of the Île de France. I enjoyed traveling with friends and my children, Tamara and Darian, and often alone. In the spring, my favorite pastime was to roam the forests surrounding Paris. A hiking club I belonged to organized some splendid day trips. Rain or shine, the groups met at a designated train station and headed for one of the hiking trails, usually north of Paris. Summers meant drifting south to the Midi, the Côte d'Azur, Provence, Languedoc and Roussillon. The best time to visit south-central and southwestern France was the autumn. During the winter, when Paris was under a perpetual cloud cover, I would escape for a week or two of skiing in the French Alps or Switzerland.

ONE OF THE UNMATCHED pleasures of living in France was the wine. One sunny weekend in May 1984, I joined my friends Jurij Darewych, Volodymyr Makarenko, and Danylo Struk on a wine-tasting outing to the Côte d'Or in the heart of Burgundy. The literal translation of Côte d'Or is "the Golden Slope," but the name is actually an abbreviation for Côte d'Orient, or "east slope." The "slope" stretches along a narrow forty-kilometer band, one to two kilometers wide, split into the northerly Côte de Nuits and the southerly Nuits-Saint-Georges. South of the Côte d'Or is the Côte de Beaune, which connects to the Côte Chalonnaise, and eventually transforms into the vast wine-growing regions along the Rhone.

Darewych, who was familiar with the area, directed us to the village of Fixin, just south of Dijon. The owner of the Clos du Chapitre, Luc, a gruff-looking middle-aged man in blue work clothes, led us down to his cellar containing two rows of stacked oak-barrel reds. But, first, there was a lecture about the property and a bit about the region's colorful history, to which we listened patiently. Luc told us that the wine in Fixin is identical to its famous neighbor Gevrey-Chambertin but costs half the price. He then asked if we wanted to begin with last year's harvest, which was still "green," or go directly for the more mature vintages. We soon realized that last year's vintage was undrinkable. He grinned and moved to the older barrels. After Luc tapped loose the bung, a wooden stopper wrapped in burlap, he took a tapered glass pipette, drew a small quantity, and drained it into our tasting glasses. We examined the wine for color, sniffed it, and took a sip.

The correct procedure, Luc said, is to hold the wine in your mouth, suck in the air, make a gargling sound that tumbles the wine on the tip of your tongue, and then spit it out onto the earthen floor. Spitting out good wine seemed sacrilegious, but after a dozen tastings, I realized why. The urge to swallow was strong, and we did. Jurko, who had some experience in these matters, had brought *baguettes*. The idea, of course, was to neutralize the alcohol and clean one's palate between tastings. After our stop in Fixin, we each carried our *baguette* under our arms.

Gevrey is where it all began in the seventh century, when monks found that this *terroir* produced an extraordinary wine. After tasting the district's wine, I discovered why Gevrey-Chambertin was Napoleon's favorite. Its deep red color, strong bouquet, and high alcohol content made it unforgettable. Further down the Route des Grands Crus, we stopped at the Clos de Vougeot, one of the most famous vineyards in the world. Barely a kilometer down the road, the community of Vosne-Romanée produced the greatest variety of high-priced wines. Its prized property, the Romanée-Conti, in spite of its small size of just five acres, is one of the greatest and most expensive of Burgundies. When we knocked on the manor's door, we were unceremoniously snubbed with the words *"On ne fait pas la degustation* (We don't do tastings)."

Our next stop was the capital of Côte de Nuits, wines that distinguish themselves by their firmness and full texture, with so much body you could, so to speak, bite into it. I took a liking to this type of wine, which reminded me of similar heavy, full-bodied reds such as Pommard and Pomerol. At the medieval town of Beaune, we had a "grand finale" tasting of wines from all of the neighboring regions in a *cave* next to Beaune's signature landmark Hôtel-Dieu.

On way back to Paris, we couldn't resist one last detour to the appellation of Chablis, a thousand-hectare (2,300 acres) area that produced a wine "distinctive in character, strength, and hardness, with an elegant fruitiness from the marriage of the Pinot Chardonnay grape and the chalky soil." It was the perfect finish to an unforgettable weekend of wine tasting with friends. Many more would come in the vast region from the Côtes du Rhone to the Medoc peninsula, west of Bordeaux.

IN NOVEMBER of the same year, 1984, I had the opportunity to drive my friends Odarka and Omelian Mazuryk to Périgord in the south-central

France. Omelian's reputation as an icon painter had spread far and wide, and he was getting invitations from the most unexpected places. One was from a church group in the town of Périgueux.

We left gloomy Paris and headed for the sunny south. During the winter months, northern France was stuck in a cycle of fog, rain, and perpetual drizzle, while lands south of the Loire seemed to enjoy mild weather and sunny days for most of the year. We set aside a few days to explore a part of France overflowing with Romanesque churches, old castles, and history. Aquitania, or Aquitaine, is "God's country"—fertile, rich in the variety of the products it grows, and home to the great wines of southwestern France.

It did not take much to persuade Odarka and Omelian to detour to Fontevraud, an abbey southeast of Saumur that served as the necropolis of Plantagenet royalty. Henry II, king of England, his wife, Eleanor of Aquitaine, and their son, King Richard the Lionheart, were buried there at the end of the twelfth century, along with other members of the royal family. A tour guide explained that the abbey, founded in 1101, was unique in the Middle Ages for housing both monks and nuns. After the French Revolution, many churches closed as abbeys and became quarries, sources of cut stone. Fontevraud was saved from destruction by Napoleon's edict to turn the abbey into a prison.

Our next stop was a Benedictine monastery of Notre-Dame de Fontgombault (pronounced "Fongobo"), where we caught the afternoon guided tour, followed by vespers in the cavernous Romanesque church where the monks intoned a harmonious Gregorian chant. I was mesmerized by their free-flowing rhythms sung in unison. While different from the chanting of Tibetan monks, the Gregorian chant I heard in the abbey church that day had a calming effect.

Founded in 1091 by hermits who lived in a grotto on the banks of the Creuse River, the abbey got its name from the spring or "fount" of Gombaud. The monastery, sacked and laid waste by Calvinists in 1569, was restored at the end of the seventeenth century and went into decline after the French Revolution. In 1905, the remaining Trappist monks were expelled and moved to the United States to form the Monastery of Our Lady of Jordan in Oregon, and after WWII, the abbey became a Benedictine community.

On the way to Périgueux, we stopped at Brantôme and Bourdeilles. Brantôme's abbey was an important stop on the old pilgrimage route to Santiago de Compostela, and Bourdeilles was a lovely village on the edge of the river Dronne boasting a medieval castle with a thirty-five-meter donjon. The panorama of the surrounding countryside extended over a vast region where much of the Hundred Years' War between the English and the French had taken place.

There was a funny moment when we got to the top of the donjon. Omelian couldn't resist commenting that we were looking at France from its highest *bordel*, a play on a Ukrainian word for a bordello. As corny as this *double entendre* was, back in Paris, it provided copious material for stories about our trip.

Périgord had always been known for its gastronomic delights—foie gras, truffles, ceps, chestnuts, walnuts, strawberries, fine cheese, wines, confit of duck, and other preserves. We arrived at Périgueux on a Thursday afternoon, a day before Omelian's icon exhibit was scheduled to open in a gallery near the Cathedral of Saint-Front. A family helping with the exhibit asked us to stay in their home on the outskirts of the town, a manor that reflected their respectable standing in the community. The invitation included dinner that evening, which was a gastronomic feast that opened with pâté de Périgueux, composed of foie gras with truffles. For the main course, we were served beef fillet in the classic sauce Périgueux, made almost exclusively from truffles and flavored with Madeira, and we finished with the region's traditional dessert, crème brûlée.

The next day, a Friday, I helped Omelian with the finishing touches for the vernissage that evening. At the same time, I was anxious to visit the Cathedral of Saint-Front, whose bell tower dominated Périgueux's skyline. For Southern France, a cathedral in the Byzantine style was a drastic departure from the Romanesque ones dominating the region. The curious style of the cathedral, built after 1120, has given rise to a discussion about whether Saint Front's was a copy of Saint Mark's Basilica in Venice or the church of the Holy Apostles in Constantinople. I've seen both, and I'm certain that the architect copied Saint Mark's.

We remained in Périgueux for another day, so while Omelian and Odarka were busy with the exhibit, I hopped in my car and took a whirlwind tour of the region south of Périgueux. I first drove to the wine country around Bergerac and Monbazillac and then went east along the Dordogne River that wound through dozens of harmonious towns and villages, bastides, prehistoric caves, and cliff-top castles, to Château de Beynac and back to Périgueux.

FORTY THOUSAND KILOMETERS of marked trails called the Chemins de Grande Randonnée (GR) cover every corner of the Hexagon. Choosing a destination was challenging. In July 1988, my companions, Omelian Mazuryk and Jurko Darewych, expressed a desire to go somewhere off the beaten path in the heartland of France. The town of Saint-Flour in southern Auvergne, a sparsely populated mountainous region in central France, seemed like a good base. Covered with vast forests and dormant volcanoes, its rugged highlands stretched as far as the eye could see, and one could walk all day without seeing another human being. Its volcanic hills were endowed with hot springs and thermal stations such as La Bourboule and Vichy, also known for their mineral waters. The region was also home to some of the loveliest Romanesque churches in Christendom, including Saint-Nectaire, Orcival, Issoire, and Brioude.

After a long drive from Paris, we checked in at one of Saint-Flour's hotels in the old town. Its restaurant offered local fare at what seemed like reasonable prices. Auvergne's cuisine is hearty, consisting largely of pork and lentil dishes. The savory dish I ordered, pork stuffed with cabbage, was served with potatoes and covered in rich bouillon with stale bread on the side. The hearty meal, washed down with a dark, muscular tannic wine from nearby Cahors, prepared us for our next day's adventures.

A commotion from the town's central square woke us up. It was Saturday, market day, and farmers from the surrounding countryside were setting up stalls to sell sausages, cheese, and other local produce. After a quick *café au lait* and croissants, we checked out the market to stock up on a few basic provisions for our three-day hike that would eventually take us to the Parc naturel regional des Volcans d'Auvergne. It was a mild November day, and the weather looked promising, so we did not even check the forecast. With rations in our backpacks, we took a branch of the GR 6 in the direction of Chaudes-Aigues, a spa town famous for its hot springs.

The twenty-five-kilometer stretch offered a combination of forest, quaint villages, and two special historical attractions. The autumn air was invigorating, and the trees had already turned golden yellow, with shades of orange and rust. Marching at a good pace, up and down hillocks, crossing brooks and streams, we aimed to reach the ruins of the Château d'Alleuze on the river Truyère by noon. We only had to ford a small rocky stream called Ruisseau de Villedieu.

Hopping along a few boulders, I made it to the other side and waited for Omelian and Jurko to follow. Midway across the stream, Omelian lost his balance and fell into the shallow stream—backward. Our first reaction was to break out in laughter. Omelian, however, lay in the cool stream, looking dazed. Fearing that he might have hit his head on a rock, we jumped into the water to help him. Luckily, he was only stunned. He had a hard time getting on his feet because his back was weighed down by his backpack, so Jurko and I helped him up, but in the process, our hiking boots got soaked.

With a kilometer or so to reach our first destination, we sloshed in our soggy footwear until we came to a bend in the river and saw in the distance the impressive ruin of the thirteenth-century castle built on a square plan, with round towers in each corner. There are numerous castles like this one in the region, many vestiges of the Hundred Years' War, but few match the splendid site of Château d'Alleuze.

It was sunny, so the first order of business was to dry our shoes, socks, and clothes. As the gear was drying, we snacked on bread, cheese, and sausage we'd bought that morning at the Saint-Flour street market and took photos of the fortress. As soon as our shoes and socks were more or less dry, we continued toward Chaudes-Aigues, still about fifteen kilometers away. While crossing the Truyère at the Barrage, I noticed thick clouds rolling in, accompanied by ominous lightning, and then came thunder and a drizzle. The shower turned into a downpour, and we ran for the nearest tree cover. The rain did not let up, and we decided to make a dash for the village of Fridefont. We got off the path onto the road and slogged along for the next hour, soaked to the bone, our hiking boots still soggy from the stream crossing. We continued walking in the rain for the next three kilometers. As we approached Fridefont, a hamlet of one hundred, the rain stopped, and a rainbow appeared on the horizon.

The air was fresh and sweet when I noticed the aroma of recently baked bread, which took me back to a childhood memory of standing in line for our ration of bread in DP camps in postwar Germany. This time, the scent came from the communal oven in Fridefont, where they had just finished baking *pain de campagne*—country bread. Small rural communities bake bread once or twice a week. We were lucky to arrive on a day when they had just finished baking.

"I just took the bread out of the oven," the baker said. "It needs to cool for another hour before I sell it." Then after noticing our wet garments, he continued, "If you are hikers looking for a place to stay overnight, there is a *chambre d'hôte* in the farmhouse down the street. Tell Madame I sent you."

Madame, *la concierge*, showed us a simple four-bed room and gave us some towels. We hung our wet clothes up to dry, and I stepped out to get the bread. I also picked up some butter and tomatoes in a small *épicerie* and two bottles of red wine. In the meantime, my friends set up the table with our remaining sausage and cheese, and we sat down to enjoy the aromatic, still-warm *pain de campagne* and go over the day's adventures.

The Massif Central, the great land mass stretching from the Limousin to the Cévennes, encompasses the volcanic peaks of the Auvergne and Cantal. We had one day left to hike along the extinct volcano craters in the Parc naturel regional des Volcans d'Auvergne, west of Saint-Flour. A thousand words could not adequately describe the unique character and beauty of this primal landscape.

ONE OF THE MOST ALLURING aspects of the French hexagon was the countryside, *la France profonde,* which you saw as soon as you got off the main thoroughfares. In the north, the landscape was characterized by large fields of golden wheat, barley, and oats. There was plenty of corn, along with bright yellow patches of sunflowers and rapeseed. In the south, there were more fruit orchards, apples, pears, peaches, cherries, and the ubiquitous vineyards that produce Frances's most coveted liquid export.

On my most recent tour through the French countryside some twenty years later, I noticed that fewer people occupied the land, and there were more nearly-empty villages. The quaint farmers' markets that had thrived in the '80s had shrunk or been replaced by *magasins à grande surface*, supermarkets.

The reason the French countryside I once knew had become depopulated, I suspect, had to do with French farmers being subsidized. The French had lobbied Brussels for subsidies to help the small French farmer remain viable and stay on the land they had occupied for centuries. But in practice, the subsidies went to large industrial farms, and this had the effect of killing off small farmers. The biggest recipients of subsidies turned out to be sugar and banana growers in France's overseas territories, a long way from the poor upland farmers. The French countryside is dying, and soon it will resemble the vast farmlands of Kansas, Illinois, and Iowa: productive but peopleless.

20. Cruising with Anton

THE PARISIAN ART AFICIONADOS, Lisa and Jorge Alyshkewych, introduced me to Anton Solomukha in mid-1980.[73] In the summer of that year, I visited him in the sparsely furnished two-room fifth-floor walk-up he shared with his wife, Nadine. My wife Zöe and Oksana and Danylo Struk were with me. It was a bright apartment with a northern exposure looking out onto Avenue Daumesnil near the Gare de Lyon. In Paris, there are advantages to living on the upper floors—less street noise and more light, the latter a commodity in short supply in the densely populated capital.

Anton was thirty-five, five years my junior, and still high on the narcotic called freedom. He arrived in Paris a year before I did, and his joy at being free and in Paris was palpable. That day, I bought three of his paintings, Botticelli-like canvases of imaginary Renaissance figures exuding warmth and serenity that reflected Anton's newly-found inner peace in Paris. Anton was primarily a figurative painter, but soon he began to experiment with other forms of expression. He loved to play with images, and amused himself by rearranging the world around him with surrealistic fantasy. He told me once that illusion was necessary to survive in the world we live in, a trick he invented to cope with censorship and the dreary life in Soviet Ukraine.

Anton said that his father was an inspector of schools for Soviet Ukraine and a close acquaintance of Nikita Khrushchev, the General Secretary of the Communist Party of the Soviet Union. Khrushchev spent many years in

---

[73]   Anton used the French spelling of his last name—Solomoukha. In this memoir, I use the English transliteration Solomukha.

188

Ukraine and was fond of Ukrainians, or at least that was the myth. Anton said that when he was a boy, Khrushchev visited the Solomukha household. Although an evil despot and a ruthless butcher in real life, Nikita liked children. Once, he picked up little Anton, put him on his lap, and said, "What a good-looking boy. One day you'll make a fine Communist."

Anton never became a Communist. In fact, he detested the inhumane system that robbed men of dignity and creativity. He rejected social realism and wanted to paint and experiment like artists in the West. Anton knew that if he remained in Ukraine, he would suffocate, and he was ready to do anything to escape the Socialist prison of mind and soul. However, short of tunneling under the Iron Curtain or swimming across the Black Sea, leaving the USSR without authorization was impossible, and the select few who got permission to travel had to have family members in the Soviet Union as hostages. The only way for Anton to leave was through marriage to a Western woman.

Anton befriended Nadine, a French-born mulatto student, and explained, "They seized my works and told me to paint in the social realist manner or stop painting altogether. I'm being followed and harassed by the KGB."

Without hesitation, Nadine agreed to marry him, and in 1979, Anton found himself in Paris, free of Soviet chains. He told me that when the KGB realized he was going to leave, they said, "OK, we'll let you go, but you have to sign a paper that you'll work for us."

He signed and then, once in Paris, refused all contacts with the KGB, even though they pestered and threatened him.

Anton studied at the Kyiv State Art Institute (Academy of Fine Arts), under the tutelage of Tatiana Yablonska, a professor and head of the Institute's Composition and Monumental Arts Department, and a great artist in her own right.[74]

"She made us draw eight hours a day," he told me, "day in, day out for two years before we were allowed to put a drop of paint on canvas. First, you had to prove that you could draw."

Anton could hold his own in a discussion on ancient history, mythology, biblical stories, the nature of man, migration of nations, and other subjects, but like many artists, he tended to embellish and exaggerate the facts. And

---

[74]   After Ukraine declared independence in 1991, Anton often traveled to Ukraine to work and exhibit. Eventually, he was nominated as a foreign member of the Ukrainian Academy of Arts.

embellish he did. Nor was he always logical. His command of Ukrainian was excellent, in any case, better than our tainted diaspora dialect, but he also spoke Russian and, eventually mastered French.

In addition to being a fascinating and prodigious artist, Anton was a travel partner and one of my closest friends. He was also ambitious. He intentionally created art that would be noticed by the Parisian art establishment. His method was to break the rules, to shock the public with unconventional and irreverent work, and to be politically incorrect.

Anton loved women, and they loved him. He dazzled them with his conversation and made them laugh, and they found his charm irresistible. One of his favorite tactics to capture their attention was to demonstrate his skill at palm reading. First, he asked a woman to extend her hand. He held it for a while and said how warm (or cold) it was. It didn't matter if the hand was warm or cold; it was his way of getting her to relax. Next, he opened her palm to identify the major lines for the heart, head, life, and destiny and proceeded to spin a story to fit practically any situation he encountered.

"You are sensitive to others, but you also tend to change your mind often," was a standard line. If he aimed to seduce a woman, he playfully continued, "I see you are a thinker, and I also see that you are creative, especially in your sex life. I can only imagine the ways you like to experiment when you are in that situation." All this was done in a lighthearted manner. Still, most women were eager to hear more.

Like Casanova, he was not a particularly masculine man, yet women found him charming. Since professional models were out of the question, he devised an approach where he would persuade attractive women to go to his apartment for the express purpose of being sketched or photographed. Contrary to what one might imagine about such sittings, Anton's behavior was always professional.

Anton painted on paper and canvas, and much of his work in the early 1980s was inspired by Ukrainian folklore and themes from traditional songs. I acquired these works by the dozen because I found them humorous, refreshing, and mildly erotic. With time, his art became increasingly provocative and capricious and took on surrealistic qualities.

Then, in the search for new means of expression, Solomukha turned to photography. The transition from canvas to photo was gradual. His first attempts were unimpressive, but he kept at it and eventually developed a new art form he called photo painting. On a large canvas, he fused paintings with photographic images, work that required special equipment, a large canvas printer, and a multitude of models. Personally, I was not thrilled to see him switch to photography because it did not make use of his superb drawing skills, but Anton was obsessed with experimentation, and his technique was constantly evolving.

I will not analyze or justify Solomukha's work. I leave that to critics and art historians. Numerous catalogs and monographs have examined his art with a critical eye, and there is a reasonably good write-up of Solomukha's career on *Wikipedia*. Here I will add only what you will not find elsewhere. Anton had a knack for naming his pieces. In my apartment in Georgetown, I have a large diptych he baptized *Jesus Christ and Catherine Deneuve*, a work that always raised questions and begged an explanation. Another work in my collection that evoked a hilarious reaction was *Czar Peter I Urinating*.

At the 1982 Salon d'Automne, an annual exhibition held in Paris since 1903, Anton displayed a number of very large format pieces. One of the works, *Femme en Extase,* hung prominently under a central arch of the giant glass dome of the massive Grand Palais exhibition hall. I bought Anton's stridently politically incorrect work and donated it to the Ukrainian Institute of Modern Art. It is one of the largest pieces in the institute's archives.

Some criticized Anton's work for excessive nudity and strong sexual connotations. Anton would agree, but he would also add that nudity has been part of art since the Greeks and Romans and that eroticism in painting has existed from the beginning of time.

"It does not matter what people say about my art," Anton said. "Some will like it; others will not. What's important is that they talk about it. The worst fate for an artist is to be ignored."

IN THE EARLY 1980S, Anton set up a studio in an eighteenth-century building in the 11th arrondissement in the up-and-coming Bastille district, a lively area popular with artists and galleries.[75] Rents were cheap and spaces large. He turned a *rez-de-chaussée* courtyard space, formerly a furniture

---

[75]   On the evening of Friday November 13, 2015, at the precise moment I was putting the finishing touches to this chapter, one of the oddest coincidences of my life took place. While I was describing Anton's atelier near the Bastille, my son Darian called to tell me that an attack by the Islamic terrorists had taken place in the 11th arrondissement. The attack killed 130 Parisians. Commentators agreed that it signaled the beginning of an existential conflict between Western values and the tenets of the Islamic Caliphate.

workshop, into a large studio. There was little direct sunlight, but the place had a very tall ceiling and enormous wall space on which Anton would spread his huge canvases and paint. His friend, the art dealer Jorge Alyshkewych, rented the storefront, which he converted into a small gallery. Jorge, trying to establish himself as an art dealer, had been working with Anton for some time. During the popular artists' open-door week in the Bastille neighborhood, Jorge and Anton made a fine duo. Jorge believed in Anton's talent as much as I did, and helped him to become an important presence on the Parisian art scene.

Surviving as an artist in Paris required a gargantuan effort. In one of the most competitive arenas in the world, only the most talented and aggressive survived. Anton distinguished himself from the multitude of Soviet artists in Paris because he was not only fluent in French but also quite articulate. Some Parisian galleries wanted to present him as a Russian artist because Russian art sold better, but Anton always insisted he was a Ukrainian artist. In time, his work was recognized, and his career took off.

Through my connections at the OECD, I was often invited to parties given by the diplomats in Paris. On occasion, I invited Anton to join me, and he invariably was a hit. At these gatherings, Anton began by being inconspicuous, but at some opportune moment, he would say something provocative or entertaining. On one occasion, he charmed the wife of the ambassador of New Zealand, an art connoisseur herself. She was instrumental in introducing Anton to her circle of acquaintances, who, in turn, opened doors to other invitations and other contacts.

During the day, Anton was hard at work on his canvases. In the evening and at night, he socialized, circulating in the art scene, establishing contacts, and doing PR. I often witnessed his attempts to sell himself cold to strangers. He was aware of the adage that if an artist could sell himself, he would sell his art, and Anton was able to sell himself.

In the '90s, Anton invited me to a birthday dinner party for a wealthy benefactor. Among the guests were Allan Lawson, an actor, and his wife Twiggy, the former British model. The host reserved a table for ten at the celebrated La Coupole. Most of the guests spoke only French, but Twiggy did not. The host solved the problem by seating me next to Twiggy for the simple reason that I would be able to carry on a conversation with her in English. I was honored. In the '80s, she was no longer the skinny Twiggy of the '60s but still a gorgeous face.

I told her in a general way about my work in Paris, and she explained how she had become a mother and an actress, and related her work for philanthropic causes. When she learned that I was of Ukrainian origin, she expressed concern about the children in Ukraine and Belarus suffering from the Chernobyl disaster and asked if there was a way she could help them.

I was at a loss to name specific organizations, but I told her that there were NGOs and foundations that focused on helping children of Chernobyl, and I would be happy to find out. I sent her the information but never heard from her again.

In May 1983, I persuaded Anton to accompany me to the Cannes Film Festival, something I had fancied doing since I arrived in France. Cannes, with its extravagant seafront hotels, glamorous people, exclusive beachfront concessions, topless female sun worshipers, and yachts was the quintessential Riviera resort and a place where appearances counted, especially during the film festival in May.

The festival lasted twelve days in mid-May 1983, but we intended to stay for only a few days to soak up the atmosphere and get some sun. For the majority of festival visitors, the event was more about people-watching and getting a glimpse of the stars. Tickets to screenings were hard to come by, but I managed to get two from a scalper for a viewing of Carlos Saura's *Carmen*, a work that got the Palme d'Or for the Best Artistic Contribution and the Technical Grand Prize. The Spanish filmmaker teamed with legendary choreographer-dancer Antonio Gades to explore the glamour, poetry, and fire of flamenco dancing. As a passionate aficionado of flamenco, this was a high point of my week, a treat comparable to a night of flamenco guitar and dancing in Seville or Granada.

AT THE BEGINNING OF 1985, my future in France seemed uncertain. The contract with the OECD would come to an end in the fall, and after six years in Europe, I had barely begun to discover the cultural wealth of the continent. This situation prompted me to cram in as much of Europe as possible during the next eight months. The year started with a business trip to The Hague in January, followed by a journey to Venice in February, skiing in the Swiss and the French Alps in March, home leave in the United States in April, and an excursion to Greece in May. In July, I traveled to Poland, and in the fall, I embarked on a weeklong tour of churches in Kosovo and Macedonia with friends Srjan Rascovic and Ivan Myhul.

The best time to visit Venice was in the spring and the fall. February, the month when the carnival usually took place, was the worst. Even if it didn't rain, the cold, dank air penetrated to the marrow, yet every year the carnival attracted thousands of visitors. I had set aside five days for this 1,100-kilometer trip, which meant a tiring two-day drive there and two back, leaving only one day to participate in the carnival. It seemed hardly worth the effort, but then I discovered a better alternative: a five-day excursion package on an overnight sleeper bus from Paris to Venice. I knew that Anton would not be able to resist this adventure, so I asked him to join me. We boarded a special tour bus on a Friday afternoon, crossed the Alps into Italy during the night, and arrived in Venice early Saturday morning.

Every year, hundreds of thousands descended on the Serenissima Repubblica to experience a few days of uninhibited fun and frolic. All hotels and *pensiones* in and around Venice were booked. Our travel agent, however, reserved rooms a year in advance in Cavallino, a peninsula connected to Venice by a *vaporetto*, water bus. Our hotel was no Ritz, but Anton and I were used to Spartan accommodations. What was paramount was the event we were about to experience.

As we boarded the *vaporetto*, I noticed that most passengers were already masked or wearing a costume. The spectacle had begun, and we were unprepared. At Piazza San Marco, we entered a sea of humanity, many dressed in the most elaborate costumes. Anton and I, dressed in our plain Parisian winter clothes, felt completely out of place. We did not even have simple masks, a catalyst central to the carnival, a ticket to freedom, and a way to abandon inhibitions.

It was too late to buy a costume: the situation called for improvisation, and Anton came up with an idea. During his youth in Kyiv, he had been a makeup artist experienced in painting masks on the faces of theater actors. "All I need are face paints," he said. Finding a shop that sold masks and face paints, therefore, became a priority. While he was looking for the face crayons, I purchased a black broad-brimmed tricorn hat.

Anton worked quickly, painting my face half white and half red, reflecting the dual personality of my astrological sign—Gemini. The combination of the mask and the tricornered hat produced a reasonable facsimile of an eighteenth-century bauta-like disguise. Anton painted his own face white in the image of the buffoonish clown Pierrot.

The face paints were not permanent, and Anton had to reapply them daily. In one café, Anton took out the face paints to retouch my mask, which attracted a few passersby who asked if he would do a mask for them. Soon, a crowd gathered to observe Anton work, and after every mask, he got a round of applause.

The peculiar thing about the carnival was that there was no single central event to bring it all together. It was a series of exclusive private parties in palaces and hotels like the exquisite Danieli. Crowds simply roamed along Venice's canals and landmarks in endless two-way currents. Needless to say, we were not invited to any of the palazzos and had to find other venues to socialize with the multitudes. After a day of wandering through the maze of Venice's interminable passageways, Anton and I entered one of the oldest and most prestigious cafés, the Florian. Opened in 1720, the ornate Rococo café was overflowing. There were no seats to be had. Anton, however, spotted two lavishly costumed young ladies sitting at a table that had room for four. We motioned if we could join them. They smiled and said in Italian, "*Prego* (Of course, please)." They did not speak a word of French or English, but that did not stop us from attempting a conversation. They had come from Napoli, and this was their first carnival. As best we could, we explained that we had come from Paris—that Anton was an artist from Ukraine and I was an American diplomat. They giggled, obviously thinking we were giving them a rehearsed Carnival line. To prove that we were not impostors, I took out my OECD diplomatic card, which they inspected, while Anton took out his crayon face paints and began sketching their portraits on a large napkin.

He was an excellent draftsman, and the sketches broke the ice. However, even though they understood the language of art, it was hard to carry on a conversation. The language barrier was intractable. Before we parted, I asked if we all could be photographed, and they agreed. The photograph bears witness to the charming encounter with two attractive Neapolitans.

As I began writing this chapter, in October 2015, I received the sad news from Paris that Anton had passed away. His sister from Kyiv, Tatiana, informed me that he became ill in July, gradually grew weaker, was hospitalized, and died on October 21. He died of an incurable brain tumor, only ten days short of his seventieth birthday, young for today's normal lifespan.

A friend in Paris who attended the funeral at the Père Lachaise told me that around fifty people were present. In addition to his young wife, Lena, whom I met several times, his daughter, Kristina, and a number of his former models, only a handful of Ukrainians were present.

21. A Covert Mission to Warsaw

AFTER SIX YEARS at the OECD, it was time to go back to the States. Texaco Oil offered me a position in their economics department, but that meant moving to Harrisonburg in New York State, a move I was not keen on. Fortunately, in the middle of that year, I was offered a position with Radio Liberty's Soviet Area Audience and Opinion Research (SAAOR), to begin in November.[76]

In the meantime, my future colleagues at SAAOR recommended that before going on Radio Liberty's payroll, I might consider visiting the USSR. Once at the Radio, access to the Soviet Union would be barred, probably forever. The advice was sound, and in the spring, I signed up for a package tour of the USSR. I was excited. After forty years, I would visit my homeland, Ukraine, and some big cities in Russia and Central Asia. Most importantly, I would get to see how people lived in the Communist paradise. I applied for a tourist visa and waited. As the departure date neared, I still did not have it. The tour coordinator said, "Don't worry, the Soviets are in the habit of granting visas at the last minute." So I waited . . . and waited. A week before departure, all the other members of the group had their visas, but I was still waiting for mine. Two days before the group was scheduled to board the flight for Moscow, I got word that my visa application had been rejected. No explanation or reason given, just "visa denied."

---

[76]   Soviet Area Audience and Opinion Research was the Paris-based audience research department and polling arm of Radio Liberty in Munich.

I was annoyed. Not only did the Soviets refuse to grant me a visa, they didn't even bother to tell me why. The Communist bureaucrats left it up to me to guess why they denied me entry to their "Socialist heaven." I began to speculate and came up with three plausible explanations: First, my passport indicated that I was born in Ukraine, a fact that automatically raised a red flag. Second, I had served in a US Army Intelligence unit, which had probably placed me on their blacklist. Finally, I was still with the OECD and had official diplomatic status. I had thought that this might expedite my visa processing, but then I recalled my encounter with the KGB agent Nikolai Kirilenko during Omelian Mazuryk's vernissage in 1980. Although any one of these facts was grounds for rejection, the meeting with Kirilenko was likely the prime reason for the denial. If the Soviets had a file on me, and I'm certain they did, there was enough information there to make me *persona non grata*.

A few days after the Soviet embassy rejected my visa application, I met with Omelian Mazuryk, the icon painter. As Omelian was telling me about his plan to visit family in Poland he hadn't seen for a dozen years, an idea popped into my head. Since I would not be going to the Soviet Union, perhaps I could do the next best thing—visit Eastern Europe. I figured that crossing the East German-Polish border would be easier, so I suggested to Omelian that we drive to Poland in my car, which still had the *corps diplomatique* license plates. He was thrilled; he would have the means to get around in Poland.

At about the same time, Roman Kupchinsky, president of Prolog, was passing through Paris. I had met Roman on several occasions in Paris, and also at Prolog's headquarters in New York when he was considering me for a position with Prolog. Kupchinsky was the driving force behind Prolog's book program, a CIA-funded operation to distribute miniature-format books and other material to dissidents in Ukraine and other Soviet republics. Anti-Communist literature was smuggled into the Soviet Union the same way Marxist texts were smuggled into Russia before the Revolution. Once inside, the books and pamphlets were clandestinely passed around from hand to hand and made their way into *samizdat*. Prolog and Radio Liberty had similar goals. Both organizations tried to penetrate the Iron Curtain with information—Radio Liberty through the airwaves and Prolog by sending forbidden literature through clandestine channels.

Roman Kupchinsky was a good example of why one should not judge a book by its cover. Underneath the rough exterior was a powerful intellect. His encyclopedic knowledge was buttressed by a witty and often irreverent sense of humor. His salty humor, unrestrained by political correctness, was relaxing and made him fun to be with. He was easygoing, generous, and kindhearted, and that's why most people loved and trusted him. Something Roman rarely talked about was his service in Vietnam, where he stared death in the eye. As a second lieutenant, he led men into combat, was wounded, and awarded the Purple Heart. After he died in January 2010, *The Economist* online featured a glowing obituary.[77]

The details of how the forbidden literature crossed the Iron Curtain into Ukraine and other Soviet republics were a closely guarded secret, in order to protect the network of couriers in Eastern Europe. Roman accomplished this by compartmentalizing Prolog's activities. Individual operatives were aware that they were only cogs in a bigger machine, but they did not know who the other cogs were. I only knew that fishing boats from Germany or Denmark smuggling contraband books met their Polish collaborators at prearranged locations somewhere along the Baltic coast to transfer the material.

The roots of Prolog's covert activities go back to the postwar period when the US government helped a variety of émigré groups to provide support for underground organizations behind the Iron Curtain after WWII. One of the organizations was Prolog Research and Publishing. Because of an influx of additional funding in 1978, the book program expanded its support to dissidents and opposition currents within the Communist Party of Ukraine. During its four decades of operations between 1952 and 1992, Prolog, along with the Ukrainian Service of Radio Liberty, played a key role in explaining Ukraine to Ukrainians behind the Iron Curtain. Such support demonstrated the success of US government assistance to émigré anti-Communist groups.

Taras Kuzio pointed out a 2011 article that the work of small organizations like Prolog helped bring about the collapse of the Soviet Union.[78] Kuzio first met Roman Kupchinsky in London in 1982 at the home of Bohdan Nahaylo, then working at Amnesty International and a freelance contributor to the *Spectator*. Kupchinsky offered to finance trips to Poland for Kuzio and others to transport Western books. After a few successful smuggling operations,

---

[77] *Say not the struggle naught availeth*, "Roman Kupchinsky, a scourge of Communists and post-Communist kleptocrats alike." *The Economist* online, January 28, 2010.

[78] Taras Kuzio, "U.S. support for Ukraine's liberation during the Cold War: A study of Prolog Research and Publishing Corporation" (2011).

Kupchinsky and Kuzio discussed the possibility of opening an office in London.

In 1984, while studying for his MA in Soviet Studies at the University of London, Kuzio set up the Ukrainian Press Agency (UPA). In the same year, the bimonthly *Soviet Nationality Survey* was launched by Prolog. It was edited by Alexander J. Motyl. In 1985, the Society for Soviet Nationality Studies (SSNS) was registered as a British company, with UPA as a sub-branch. Over the next few years, UPA opened small offices in Moscow, Warsaw, and Kyiv. The SSNS-UPA went on to publish the magazine *Soviet Ukrainian Affairs,* which was a kind of successor to the *Digest of Soviet Ukrainian Affairs,* published by Prolog in the 1960s–1970s.

In 1986, Kupchinsky received funding to send a group of Prolog and SSNS people to Copenhagen to disrupt the World Peace Congress, a Soviet front organization that was holding its first jamboree in a NATO country. That this was a CIA operation could be seen from the fact that NTS (a Russian émigré nationalist organization funded by the Americans) activists also disrupted the event. Their activities were so successful that the CIA provided funding for the launch of the Ukrainian Peace Council (UPC), which published a newspaper that focused on the Soviet occupation of Afghanistan, the Chernobyl nuclear disaster, and European peace movements. UPC also attracted followers among the British Left who were recruited as smugglers of books into the USSR. Later, Rutgers professor Alexander Motyl wrote that Prolog "was an excellent example of how, for little money, an organization was able to serve as a mouthpiece for the dissident movement and help keep it known and alive."

LATE ONE JUNE EVENING, I joined Roman and my old friend Ivan Myhul for dinner at the raucous La Brocherie on Rue Saint-Benoit. We had already downed a couple of drinks at Café Bonaparte and were in good spirits. Soon, Ivan mentioned that I was planning a trip to Poland.

When Roman heard this, his eyes lit up. "Slavko, I have a favor to ask of you. As you know, for years we've been smuggling literature into Ukraine through Poland. We get it across the border in small packages, and recently we began sending VHS cassettes. The problem, our people tell us, is that they have no VHS players on which to view the material. We need to get a few of them to Warsaw. How about if you take some VHS machines with you and deposit them with a contact in Warsaw? From there, it won't be of any concern to you—they have people who will smuggle them into Ukraine. And on your way back, I'd like you to drop off a box of literature and some cash with our contact in Budapest.

"Getting literature and VHS cassettes into Ukraine has been even more problematic than delivering such material to Russia and the Baltic states. Aside from couriers and humanitarian assistance organizations, the most common way is simply through the postal system. Much of it gets intercepted, but a significant amount gets past the censors. Once in the hands of the targeted recipients, it's passed around covertly from hand to hand or copied, although even copying literature is problematic. Reproduction technology like Xerox is unavailable in the Soviet Union. Only the KGB and trusted government authorities possess such equipment, and even that is under the strict control of the Party."

I was taken aback by Roman's bluntness. His proposal sounded exciting and tempting. It would be an opportunity to do something concrete to combat Communism. I asked about the logistics, the level of risk, and the consequences if I should get ensnared at a border crossing. He answered my questions and said Prolog would pay for some travel expenses. Other than that, there was no talk of compensation. I would be doing this out of patriotic feelings for my country of origin. After some reflection, I told Roman, "OK, I'll do it." We sealed the agreement with a double Remy Martin VSOP Cognac.

Roman purchased three VHS players at FNAC, the French electronic equipment megastore. I shaped a piece of plywood to fit over the spare wheel compartment of my BMW and placed the machines under it. If anyone searched the trunk thoroughly, they would find them, but the matching gray false bottom with suitcases stacked on it was good enough camouflage.

THUS BEGAN MY first foray into the world of covert operations. Off we went on a journey to Poland, where, over a twenty-day period, we would cover over five thousand kilometers (three thousand miles). Even though it was a relatively minor operation, the journey would not be without risk. It would require planning, steady nerves, and a measure of cunning.

The first stop was West Berlin. Seeing the Wall was a stark reminder that Europe was divided into "free" and "unfree" parts, and that West Berlin was an island in the middle of a tyrannical sea. After a brief visit to the Egyptian Museum to view the bust of Nefertiti, an icon of classical feminine beauty, we exited Berlin and crossed East Germany on the designated transit route to the German-Polish border. At Frankfurt-an-der-Oder, we crossed the Oder to Slubice, the Polish border control point. Tension rose to a feverish pitch. Although we had already crossed the Iron Curtain, we had seen so little of East Germany that it felt as though we were really crossing it here.

The moment of reckoning arrived. The border crossing had two lines, one for diplomats and the other for ordinary visitors and tourists. The regular line had about a dozen cars backed up waiting to be inspected. These people would spend many hours having their bags opened and probed and their documents scrutinized, passed around, and rescrutinized.

There were no cars in the diplomatic line, and I headed straight for it. This was one privilege CD plates conferred at border crossings. Still, I was anxious and hoping that my nervousness would not show. I had no idea if they would search my car or what they would do if they found the contraband in my trunk.

"Passports," the official said.

Omelian and I took out our passports—mine US and Omelian's French—and handed them to the customs agent. He glanced at me and then my passport photo and looked at me again and repeated the procedure with Omelian. Unceremoniously, he said they were taking a *pawza*, a thirty-minute break, and started to walk away. Since I had crossed Communist frontiers on other occasions, I realized that this was a subtle reminder that they expected some sort of a bribe.

Fortunately, I had brought two cartons of Marlboro cigarettes for such an occasion and slipped the agent a paper bag with four packs. Fifteen minutes later, the agent returned and asked if we spoke Polish.

"*Oczywiście* (Of course)," Omelian replied.

He turned to me. "*A pan?* (And you, sir?)"

I calmly responded, "*Tak, ale zle* (Yes, but badly)."

"*A czy pan jest diplomatą?* (Are you a diplomat?)"

"*Tak*," I said and presented my OECD credentials.

He looked at the documents, took our passports, and walked away again. I got a queasy feeling in my stomach. The next five minutes seemed like five hours.

When he came back, he handed us our passports and said, "I forgot to stamp them. Welcome to Poland." As we were about to pull away, he spoke one last time.

"Just a word of advice, with your car, be careful and don't drive too fast."

That was it. I was immensely relieved as we entered Poland. My French CD license plates and the orthography of my first name must have worked in my favor. With Jaroslaw spelled the Polish way, not in the typical Russian or Ukrainian manner, the border agent clearly assumed that I was an American of Polish descent as he waved us through.

My relief was short-lived. Crossing the frontier from the free world to the unfree produced a distressing sensation. In the West, barbed wire fences and walls were intended to keep people out. Here they were designed to keep them in, not much different from a high-security prison. The shock of the crossing was magnified by a change in the landscape. The tidy, colorful Western European landscape morphed into a dingy, gray Communist countryside of dilapidated villages and grimy buildings. The deeper we got into Poland, the more I felt that we were entering a vast open-air Marxist-Leninist penitentiary from which there was no escape.

Our itinerary in Poland called for stops in Warsaw, Krakow, Lemkivshchyna (Omelian's homeland in the mountainous region in the southeastern corner of the country), and, time permitting, Kholm, the land where I was born. The schedule was tight, but the roads were in decent condition, and I had a detailed road map of Poland.

I expected Warsaw to be an animated city like the capitals of other European countries. Instead, what I encountered was ugly modern Socialist architecture interspersed with a few old landmarks. The streets were relatively clean, but traffic was sparse. Omelian and I found a hotel near Warsaw's most prominent landmark, the Palace of Culture and Science. In the mid-'50s, this 230 meter (758 feet) Stalinesque Art Deco skyscraper had been conceived as a gift from the Soviet people to the Polish nation. I did not know whether to laugh or cry. Either would have been appropriate.

The first item on the agenda was to deliver the contraband to Prolog's collaborator in Poland. Roman had given me the names of two contacts, with instructions that the second was to be contacted only in an emergency. Things got off to a bad start. I was unsuccessful in getting in touch with the first contact, an individual by the code name of Chris Korchynski. After calling him several times, there was no response, and I was beginning to get exasperated. I found the second contact, Prof. Jerzy Turonek, at home, but he was surprised by my call. I explained that I had some books for him, and he tersely told me to come directly to his apartment on Ulica Tamka, which I did.

Parking my car on the street across from Turonek's apartment building, I noticed that my BMW stood out like a sore thumb among the Soviet Ladas, East German Trabants, and an occasional Czech Skoda. I had been warned to be careful because car thieves lurked around every corner. Fortunately, my car had an alarm, and the car thieves had not reached the level of sophistication of Western car burglars, who knew how to disarm them.

As soon as I stepped into Jerzy's apartment, he asked where the "goods" were.

"They are in my car," I said, "across the street."

He seemed nervous, as if someone might be watching. He called his son in the other room and instructed him to help me bring up the packages. When we returned with them, he called another collaborator to pick up some "new books." Within a short time, two men showed up, inspected and tested the contents in silence, and took away the boxes. I never saw the men or the boxes again.

I was immensely relieved and noticed that my host Jerzy breathed easier. He offered me some coffee, and we had a chance to get acquainted. I was not quite sure if the *Służba Bezpieczeństwa*, the SB, the Polish secret police, was keeping an eye on the professor, but from his nervous behavior, I suspected he might have been under surveillance. This perception was confirmed when he motioned for me to step out on the balcony, where we could talk more freely.

It turns out that Jerzy was a sixty-year-old former university professor turned journalist, with passable English. Employed as an editor by the trade magazine *Zagraniczne Rynki*—Foreign Markets—Turonek used the journal as a cover for his real passions, history, writing, and politics. He was working on a new book, *Belarus under the German Occupation 1941–1944*. Turonek was a Belarusian who had settled in Warsaw many years before, and was an active member of the Belarusian community. He told me he was also close to the Ukrainian community in Warsaw and a member of the Ukrainian Catholic Church, where his two daughters sang in the choir. He admired the Ukrainians because they were much better organized than the Belarusians. He also told me that the underground network between Poland and the Ukrainian SSR was well organized and assured me that the VHS players would reach their intended destination in Lviv.

Omelian and I did not stay in Warsaw long—there was not much to see. WWII had devastated the city during the 1939 German invasion, the month-long Jewish ghetto uprising in 1943, and the bloody Warsaw uprising of 1944.

NEXT, WE WERE OFF TO KRAKOW. On the road south, I witnessed the miserable state of the Polish countryside, a three-hundred-kilometer succession of poverty-stricken villages, shabby towns, unkempt farms, stray livestock, and destitute farmers. This was what forty years of Communist rule had inflicted on a once-prosperous rural landscape. Our ultimate destination was Bieszczady, a remote mountainous region in the extreme southeastern corner of Poland, known as *Lemkivshchyna*, Omelian Mazuryk's homeland.

Omelian was born in 1937 to a Ukrainian Lemko family (a specific ethnic sub-group) in a village called Brzeżawa. When he was ten, the family suffered the fate of most Ukrainians in the region—forced deportation and resettlement to the so-called "recovered lands" in western and northern Poland. The Mazuryk family was resettled near Żielona Gora (formerly the German city of Grünberg), not far from Wrocław. Except for an uncle, hardly any members of Omelian's family lived in the Bieszczady region.

In the early 1960s, Omelian studied at the Krakow Academy of Art.[79] His specialty was iconography and restoration. He still had some old friends in the city, and a few, like Omelian, were Ukrainian Lemkos. They welcomed us warmly, and soon we wound up at someone's apartment in the middle of a party where conversation and smooth Polish vodka flowed freely. It was not every day that these folks had a chance to welcome guests from the West—a successful Parisian painter and an American diplomat from France who had chauffeured him there.

The 1980s were times of great change and liberalization, but certain topics of history were still black holes. Eventually, the discussion turned to the details surrounding one of the most shameful episodes in postwar Poland, Operation Vistula.

Between the spring of 1945 and summer of 1946, most of the inhabitants of the eastern Lemko region of Poland were forcibly resettled in Soviet Ukraine, though many in the western part of Lemkoland remained in their native villages. They got caught up in the anti-Communist struggle led by the Ukrainian Insurgent Army (UPA), and for two years after the war, the ten-thousand-strong resistance movement operating in the Carpathian Mountains was engaged in a life-and-death struggle with Moscow-controlled Communist armed forces. The insurgents had the advantage of near unanimous support among the local population, and several divisions of Beria's NKVD were unable to subdue them.

---

[79]   Three years after graduating from the academy in 1964, Omelian left for Paris to study at the École des Beaux-Arts. In Paris, he met and married Odarka, a French-born woman of Ukrainian descent, and never returned home.

The Polish Communist troops were commanded by Gen. Karol Świerczewski. Although an ethnic Pole, he was a Communist and, during the war, a Soviet officer. He was a brutal but incompetent soldier, and an alcoholic. After the war, he reappeared as Poland's deputy defense minister, a Polish quisling carrying out Stalin's orders. He was given the dual task of persecuting the independence movement in Poland and suppressing the UPA. In March 1947, ambushed by a unit of Ukrainian insurgents, he was wounded, and died within hours. The Communist regime of Poland, under orders from Stalin, used Świerczewski's death as a pretext for launching Operation Vistula—the code name for the forced resettlement of the Lemkos and Boykos away from the Ukrainian border to western and northern Poland.

Numerous attempts to subdue the guerilla movement had failed, and it had become apparent that the only way to defeat the insurgency was by removing its base of support, the Ukrainian civilian population in the countryside. In today's parlance, this was a classic example of ethnic cleansing. From May to July 1947, Lemkos were rounded up at the behest of Moscow and forced to leave the homes their ancestors had inhabited for centuries.

Omelian vividly remembered this period, and on the long road from Paris to Krakow, he told me how, one peaceful spring day in 1947, when he was ten, he was awakened by the rumble of lorries moving into the village. Armed soldiers jumped off the trucks and began pounding on doors with their rifle butts, shouting orders for everyone to pack up what they could carry, and be ready to evacuate the village in an hour. The villagers had no idea what was happening, but they could see that resistance was futile. Young and old were loaded on wagons and lorries, and livestock was tied to the wagons. Omelian recounted that people looked back for one last glimpse about a kilometer outside the hamlet, but what they saw broke their hearts. Their village was on fire.

Deportation was carried out with brutal force, and many deportees died in transit. Those who lived were taken to concentration camps like Auschwitz, from where they were transported in crowded boxcars to staging cities in western Poland and the former East Prussia. From these cities, they were resettled among the local population, far away from their homeland. A consequence of Operation Vistula was the almost total depopulation of the strip of land bordering Ukraine from Hrubeshiv in the north to Sianok in the south, including the areas Nowy Targ and Nowy Sącz.

The ethnic cleansing deprived the UPA forces in Poland of human and logistical support, and the outnumbered Ukrainian partisans could not resist the Communist coalition forces. Nevertheless, the fight continued for a few more years. After the third and last population exchange of Ukrainians and Poles in 1951, UPA's activities on Polish territory died out. In the 1960s, this uninhabited area was turned into a national park, the *Bieszczadzki Park Narodowy*, populated by lynx, wild cats, wild boar, deer, brown bears, elks, wolves, European bison, and one hundred species of birds.

In 2002, Polish president Aleksander Kwaśniewski expressed regret over Operation Vistula, and in 2007, the presidents of Poland (Lech Kaczyński) and Ukraine (Viktor Yushchenko) condemned the operation as a violation of human rights. President Yushchenko also noted that the execution of the operation was the responsibility of a "totalitarian Communist regime."

22. Lemko Churches and Mission to Budapest

THE SOUTHWESTERN CORNER of Poland is referred to variously as Lemkivshchyna, Lemkovyna, Lemkoland, Pidkarpattia, and Podkarpacie in Polish, or simply Bieszczady (Bieshchady). The people who lived in this mountainous land called themselves Lemkos but were also known as Ruthenians, Rusnaks, or Rusyns. What's important to know is that the term *Rusyns* in English is often incorrectly rendered as "Russians." The Rusyns, in fact, are ethnic Ukrainians who speak a dialect of Ukrainian and more often than not are Greek Catholics, members of the Ukrainian Greco-Catholic Church. From 1947, the Ukrainian Church became illegal; however, in 1957, after a few thousand Lemko Ukrainians returned to their homeland, the Ukrainian Catholic Church revived.

Omelian and I began our tour of Lemkoland in Krynica, one of Poland's most famous spa towns.[80] In the middle of the nineteenth century, it was a fashionable watering hole of the Austro-Hungarian Empire. We, however, did not go there for the water cure. We wanted to visit a cluster of wooden churches in villages surrounding the city. Omelian knew the area intimately, and as an iconographer, he was familiar with the architecture of the wooden churches and was an ideal guide.

---

[80]   Krynica—Krynytsia, in Polish and Ukrainian, respectively, means "the well." For the sake of uniformity, I will render most place names in this chapter in Ukrainian.

Epifanyi Dvorniak, an artist who lived in one of these villages, suffered from a speech defect and gave his crayon drawings to people of Krynytsia for alms. Eventually, the art world knew him as Nikofor, a startlingly captivating naïve painter, and collectors in Poland and Ukraine paid thousands of dollars for these simple drawings. Many of them depicted churches that Omelian and I were about to visit.

Omelian's passion for Lemko churches matched my fervor for the Gothic and Romanesque cathedrals of Western Europe. We visited a dozen or so of the several hundred churches in the area. Omelian explained,

"The massive log structures were constructed without the use of nails or metal brackets or braces. Carefully matched logs, held together by complicated corner joints, oak pegs, and wedges, were amazing achievements of carpentry and reflected the creativity of the carpenter who worked on it. What you see in one village is not repeated in the next."

Omelian was especially fond of the *dzvinnytsias,* the bell towers, which often were as impressive as the churches. Every chance we got, we climbed to the top for a bird's-eye view of the surrounding landscape. Over the years, I have visited at least a hundred Romanesque, Gothic, and Byzantine churches, mostly constructed of stone or brick. Their massive edifices and vertiginous heights, however, could not match the warmth and spirituality of a Lemko church, whose pure beauty and human proportions blended in perfectly with the environment.

The Ulucz church, one of the oldest in Poland, was built in 1659 on a wooded hillside fifteen kilometers from Sianok. It was a Boyko church, and differed from the typical Lemko church because its central dome was in the shape of an octagon. The western section had a roof whose spreading eaves covered both the narthex and the exterior gallery. At the end of WWII, Ulucz's Ukrainian villagers were forcibly resettled, and Roman Catholic Poles were encouraged to settle in the region. As a result, the church was converted for use by Roman Catholics. The Ulucz church is now part of an open-air museum.

Most of the churches like Ulucz were parish churches until Operation Vistula got rid of the Ukrainian population in 1947. From then until 1957, hundreds of churches like these were destroyed or burned, and cemeteries plowed under. Many were confiscated and given to the Roman Catholic Church or simply abandoned to the elements.

Omelian continued his lecture. "In my youth, these icons, as well as the iconography I was exposed to in Bulgaria, Yugoslavia and Western Ukraine, influenced my style."

His unique, highly stylized, contemporary style of icon painting used earthy colors mixed with a broad spectrum of vivid greens. He respected the symbolism and proportions of the Byzantine icon, but instead of gold radiating over a saint's head, he employed intense red or sunny yellow hues to depict the halo. Omelian painted on canvas and wood panels using egg tempera, a tricky fast-drying but durable medium. Art critics said that he began with the traditional image and took it a step further, even incorporating elements of Cubism, as in his trademark treatment of the Holy Trinity, melding three faces into one, in the round *tondo* format.

We headed to the remote village of Brzezawa, where Omelian's uncle lived. It was raining, but as long as we stayed on the asphalt road, we were all right. Unfortunately, the paved road soon turned into a dirt country road and then a muddy cow path. The BMW swerved and slid, and halfway to the village, we had to negotiate a steep incline. As I made an attempt to thrust the vehicle forward, the rear wheels began to spin. We were stuck. It was one of those moments when you ask yourself, *What the hell am I doing here?* Fortunately, we were only a few kilometers away from the village. "I know this land well," Omelian said. "You stay with the car, and I'll walk to Brzezawa to get some help."

Two hours later, he was back with several men to help push the car out of the rut. The rain had let up, and in spurts and stops, we finally arrived at the house of Omelian's Uncle Mykola. Mykola was a wood sculptor, as was his son. The yard was full of wooden statues, large and small, of men, women, saints, angels, and animals. Evidently, woodworking was in the family's genes. Not only did his sculptures render a good likeness of the human form, but also each face had a unique expression. It was talented men like Omelian's uncle that had built the architectural wonders we had seen on the road to Brzezawa.

As an art collector, I thought I could pick up a piece or two at a decent price. After all, I figured, how many buyers come to this godforsaken village? Unfortunately, Mykola's price was more than all the cash I had on me. Lemkos are known to be shrewd businessmen, so we bargained, but still could not agree on a price. As we drank some tea, the son brought out "the saber," a prewar Polish officer's sword, oily but in excellent condition. The blade had a clear engraving *"Nie rzucim ziemi skąd nasz ród"* (I will not forsake the land of my ancestors). This whetted my appetite further. More tea and more bargaining, and, finally, they showed me something truly irresistible: two original Nikofor drawings, one of Jesus Christ and the other of the Blessed Virgin, small fourteen-by-eighteen-centimeter sketches, both with Nikofor's trademark rendering of penetrating eyes.

I asked him to name his price for the entire package in zloty. He set a price that was astronomical. Knowing that dollars spoke louder than zloty, I told him I didn't have that kind of money.

"Maestro, I will offer you $400 for everything you showed me: two sculptures, two Nikofor drawings, and the saber."

When he heard the word dollars, his eyes lit up, and he said, "In dollars? Hmmm. *Dobre, vizmu doliary* (Fine, I'll take the dollars)."

While we sealed the deal with homemade apple brandy, I wondered how I would transport the items to Paris. I could get the sculptures through Polish customs, but the Nikofors and the sword might pose a problem, since Nikofor was already an artist of prominence, and the sword was considered national patrimony. I convinced myself that I'd figure out a way to get these objects out of Poland later.

WE FOLLOWED THE MEANDERING course of the Sian River toward Peremyshl' (Przemyśl' in Polish), a city fifteen kilometers from the Ukrainian frontier, the northern limit of Lemko territory. The original plan was to visit Modrynec, the village where I was born, near the town of Hrubeshiv, two hundred kilometers to the north. We were, however, running short on time, and I realized I would never get to see it. We, therefore, put plan B into action and steered to the city of Jarosław, a city that had a special meaning for me and was worth a slight detour.

I photographed one of the town's historical monuments, the ancient tower purportedly built by Yaroslav (Jaroslaw) the Wise, who was Grand Prince of Kyiv in the eleventh century. After taking the city from the Poles in 1031, he renamed the stronghold Jaroslaw to demarcate the westernmost boundary of his kingdom. At the same time, he concluded an alliance with King Casimir I of Poland, sealed by the king's marriage to Yaroslav's sister, Maria.

We had been on the road for nearly two weeks; it was time to head back to Paris. I decided to return via Slovakia, to meet with another of Roman Kupchinsky's contacts in Budapest. We took the Great Bieszczady Loop Road, an incredibly scenic route, but oddly devoid of human beings. It felt as if I was driving through a vast cemetery.

In fact, the entire region had been converted into a national park and wildlife preserve called the *Bieszczdadzki Park Narodowy*. As a student, Omelian had hiked these mountains, and since both of us were avid hikers—we had done the Tour du Mont Blanc a few years previously—he suggested we climb the park's highest peak, the 1,300-meter Polonina Czarynska. The Bieszczady Mountains, covered mostly with beeches, were exceptionally beautiful. Firs, sycamores, and maples were plentiful, but I had never seen anything as remarkable as the twisted dwarf beeches that grow between 1,000 and 1,200 meters. The hike took up the entire day, but it was worth it. Far to the west in the Ukrainian part of the Carpathian Mountains was Turka, the border town where my family took refuge in June 1944. I was evoking a past I barely remembered.

ONE OF THE "RUSYN" emigrants from this region was called Andrej Warhola. He went to the United States in 1912. In 1928, he and his wife, Julia, had a son whom they also named Andrej or Andrij. The father was killed in an accident in 1942, but he had saved enough money to pay for his son's college education. In 1945, the young Warhola attended Carnegie Institute of Technology (now Carnegie Mellon University) from which he graduated in 1949. The abbreviated name of this young man was Andy Warhol, creator of the Pop art movement.[81]

Another factoid from more recent history relates to the Oscar-winning Vietnam film *The Deer Hunter*. One of the film's early scenes showed a Ukrainian Lemko wedding shot in the blue-collar steel town of Clairton, about ten miles south of Pittsburgh. The raucous reception was held in one of the city's landmarks, Lemko Hall. The wedding scene featured traditional wedding customs and Ukrainian music. These, of course, were the descendants of the Rusyns and Lemkos who came to the United States at the turn of the century to labor in the coal mines and steel mills of Pennsylvania.

THERE WAS ONE MORE formidable obstacle to overcome before we crossed the border into the Slovak part of Czechoslovakia: clearing Polish customs at the Dukla Pass, the lowest mountain pass in the Carpathian

---

[81]   Alexander Motyl's novel *Who Killed Andrei Warhol*, a satirical work in the absurdist vein, explores a friendship between pop artist Andy Warhol and an orthodox Ukrainian Communist who posed as a Soviet journalist in New York in early 1968 to cover the impending American Marxist Revolution.

Mountains main range. It was a hot July day, and I was sweating. Traffic at the border checkpoint was sparse, a bad sign. The agents would have all the time they needed to inspect my automobile thoroughly.

As I pulled up to the guardhouse, my BMW with diplomatic license plates evoked more than routine interest. I hoped the border guards would not detect my anxiety. The trunk contained articles which might be confiscated if the guards discovered them. I was not too concerned about the two wooden sculptures; I could claim they were souvenirs or gifts. I was more worried about the Polish officer's sword and the two Nikofors, since both items were considered part of the Polish patrimony that should not be taken out of the country. Before reaching the border control point, I wrapped the sword in a blanket and placed it in the secret compartment above the spare tire. Who would have anticipated that I would one day present it to my still-unborn grandsons, Joseph and Mathew, as a memento of my trip to Poland? To camouflage the Nikofors, I inserted both drawings in the large road atlas.

The border guard asked me to step out of the car. He looked at the large wooden carving of Saint Peter on the backseat and asked how I got it.

"It was a gift from pan Mazuryk's uncle," I responded.

Omelian intervened in Polish, "If you don't believe him, look at the signature at the bottom of the statuette."

He picked up the wooden sculpture and saw "Mykola Mazuryk" carved into the wood. Omelian displayed his French passport and pointed to his last name, which was also Mazuryk. The agent didn't say anything, but I could feel that he suspected that something was not kosher.

In the meantime, his partner brought out a flat contraption on tiny wheels with a large mirror, which he pushed under the vehicle to see if there was anything suspicious in the undercarriage. My nervousness increased. Would they ask to look in the trunk next?

"Open the trunk," he said.

I opened the trunk.

"What's in these suitcases? Open them."

He rummaged through the contents and, finding mostly dirty laundry, did not look any further. He did not even notice the atlas containing the two Nikofors, which I had placed conspicuously on the passenger's seat to avoid suspicion. We made it through the Polish checkpoint and entered

Czechoslovakia, where the guards checked our documents and waved us through.[82]

BEFORE I LEFT FOR WARSAW, Roman Kupchinsky had asked me to do one other favor: to deliver cash to one of his contacts in Budapest, a Ukrainian artist, Tereza Egressy, married to a Hungarian engineer. The task seemed relatively uncomplicated, so I agreed. Roman didn't tell me what the woman did, and I did not ask. He rarely discussed such things, and took it for granted that people helping him would infer such information through osmosis. I gathered that she was one of Roman's conduits for channeling contraband material to Ukraine.

Roman's operations to deliver books across the Iron Curtain included hiring fishing trawlers from Denmark and Germany to meet Polish boats at designated locations in the Baltic Sea. Prolog operatives on these trawlers would transfer boxes of contraband cargo intended for the Soviet Union. Except for the fact that they existed, I did not know the details of these operations.

My assignment in Budapest was to hand Tereza an envelope containing small bills, to purchase round trip Budapest-Paris airfare. When I called, Tereza was clearly surprised, but she invited us to come to her apartment on the Buda side of the city, across the river from the ornate gothic Hungarian Parliament Building. It was late in the day, too late to look for a hotel, so she kindly offered Omelian and me a small bed and a couch. At first opportunity, I took Tereza aside to tell her the reason for my visit.

"Roman would like to meet with you in Paris and, for that purpose, asked me to give you US$300 for airfare."

Tereza was startled. She said that she could not accept American dollars because such a sum would raise questions about where and how she obtained it. She insisted that I change the dollars into Hungarian forints, which would not raise suspicion at the travel office.

That meant I had to find a way to quickly convert $300 to forints. As a foreigner, I could change some of the money at the exchange kiosks, but they had a limit on the amount of dollars they could exchange in a single transaction, and going that route would be time consuming. There was only

---

[82] The split of the federal state of Czechoslovakia into the Czech Republic and Slovakia did not take effect until January 1, 1993. It was dubbed the Velvet Divorce.

one solution: the black-market money-changers that hung around the official currency kiosks. People had warned me that, even though the money changers promised better exchange rates, doing business with them was risky.

Maybe it was, maybe not. I began exchanging some twenty-dollar bills. It seemed to work, and as I became bolder, I asked one changer if he would exchange a fifty-dollar bill. He said, "Yes, of course," and directed me to a hallway of a nearby apartment building, ostensibly to avoid being seen. Inside the entrance of the building, he pulled out a thick wad of forints and started to count the amount I would get for the fifty dollars. Hungarian money had depreciated badly, so he was counting thousand forints bills so that I could see that he was not cheating me. As he was counting, he made a point of looking around to see if anyone was watching. I should have known better. It was a ploy to distract me.

After he had finished counting, he looked around again, rolled up the bills, handed them to me, and swiftly disappeared. As I stepped out of the hallway onto the street, I inspected the money. The top layer contained a thousand forint bill, but the rest were smaller denomination bills. Very deftly, the thief had switched rolls and handed me a similar-sized roll of forints worth about five dollars instead of the fifty I had given to the money changer. Fortunately, I had obtained the amount I needed for Tereza, but I was angry at myself for being so easily duped.

From Budapest, we drove to Munich, and ten hours later, we were in Paris. In twenty days, we had passed through six countries, covering roughly five thousand kilometers.

23. Shrines of Kosovo and Macedonia

TWO MONTHS AFTER I returned to Paris from Poland, I embarked on yet another tour of churches, this time the Serbian shrines in Kosovo and Metohija, followed by Macedonia. The excursion made me better understand the events that later took place in Yugoslavia, from the breakup of the country in the early '90s to the Kosovo conflict in 1998-1999. What I saw in Kosovo in the 1980s was remarkably reminiscent of events taking place in Western Europe today. The influx of Muslims is changing the demographic landscape of Europe, and in the long term, Kosovo serves as a viable lesson for Europeans.

Ivan Myhul, one of my oldest friends, was in Paris in 1983 on an extended leave from Bishop's University in Canada. He was helping out with the *Encyclopedia of Ukraine* at the Shevchenko Scientific Society in Sarcelles. One day, Srjan Rašković showed up. Ivan introduced me to Srjan, and we became friends.

Srjan had come to Paris ostensibly to gather material for a novel. He thought the city was the center of civilization, where many great artists and writers got their start. A polyglot with a photographic memory, he was able to communicate in practically all of the Slavic languages, including Ukrainian. Srjan was a professional translator of Slavic literature, but above all, he considered himself a writer. During all the years I've known him, he has been working on his "great novel," which would instantly elevate him to the ranks of Milan Kundera or Umberto Eco.

Srjan was one of the most interesting and colorful characters I encountered during my years in Paris. Born in Knin, he was a Krajina Serb whose ancestors originated in Metohija. His father was a Serb, and his mother Jewish, a fact that, for some reason, he kept concealed. Although well educated, he was secretive and extremely conspiratorial. He sported a long black beard and usually wore a black jacket or a trench coat with a black fedora. One could easily mistake him for an Orthodox rabbi or a modern-day Rasputin. Conversing with him was always a rousing experience. His gaze was penetrating, almost hypnotizing, while his eyes were warm and friendly.

The idea of touring Kosovo was born when Srjan offered to give me a tour of the Serb Orthodox churches and monasteries in Kosovo and Metohija. I took him up on the offer and persuaded Ivan to join us. Ivan had never been to Yugoslavia, and, for me, this was an opportunity to experience something out of the ordinary. The plan called for us to hire a car in Dubrovnik, cross Montenegro, tour the churches and monasteries of Kosovo and Macedonia, and return to Dubrovnik.

Ivan and I landed on a small airfield roughly ten kilometers south of the fortress city Dubrovnik, and we met Srjan at Hotel Argentina, just outside its walls. Dubrovnik is one of the jewels of the Adriatic. The old Venetian stronghold is protected on three sides by high ramparts facing the sea. On the landward side, there is a moat and a high wall. Over the centuries, these walls have withstood threats from Ottomans and other Muslim invaders.

October is a perfect month for touring in the Balkans. The weather is pleasant and the tourist season at an end. It took us three hours to cross Montenegro from west to east. It is a small country whose people are proud, tall, and fiercely independent. They do not like to be confused with Serbs. Montenegro's terrain is mountainous and devoid of any major sources of wealth. The country possesses a lovely coastline and impressive mountains. Unfortunately, it is located in a seismic zone. An earthquake in 1979 destroyed several of its picturesque old towns, Budva and Kotor among them.

Kosovo was the cradle of the Serbian civilization. Srjan explained that this is where the Serb Kingdom was founded. Numerous Serbian Orthodox churches and monasteries were built between the twelfth and fourteenth centuries, and for this reason the Serbs came to consider this as their Holy Land. Srjan was familiar with the land of his ancestors and could talk about it for hours.

From the moment we entered Kosovo, I felt tense. Its population consisted mostly of *shiptari,* a pejorative term Serbs use to refer to the Albanian Muslims. The roads were in poor condition and often blocked by flocks of sheep or crowds of people. Driving through the countryside was slow and tedious.

"Don't honk," Srjan warned. "Don't even look them in the eye, or we will have trouble."

This was in 1985, when Yugoslavia was still whole, but signs of hostility toward the Serbs were already evident.

THE FIRST TWO CHURCHES we visited were the thirteenth-century Studenica and Sopocani. Architecturally, they combined Byzantine design with an external Romanesque form. The church of Studenica was completed in 1195. In the same year, work on the Cathedral of Chartres, the superb Gothic masterpiece sixty miles west of Paris, was begun. Yet what a contrast between Studenica and Chartres! While the builders of Chartres were experimenting with new and innovative ways of enclosing vast spaces, Studenica's unique symbiosis blended a Byzantine internal structure with the outward Romanesque form and seemed stuck in the past.

Built seventy years later, the church of the Holy Trinity at Sopocani represents one of the high points not only of Serbian but also of Byzantine art in the second half of the thirteenth century. The mural depicting the Dormition of the Blessed Virgin, for example, is an excellent illustration of the gospels and, according to Srjan, represented the best of Byzantine culture at the time.

Srjan continued to guide us through Serb history. Ivan and I sometimes felt like students at a scholarly lecture. But his habit of embellishing his stories made me skeptical about some of his claims.

Only five kilometers south of Pristina, Gracanica ranked among the greatest treasures of fourteenth-century painting. It housed exquisitely preserved frescoes, which illustrated the lives of saints, along with the portraits of King Milutin and his wife, Simonida, and sixteen portraits of the Nemanjic family tree. It was comparable with France's Saint Denis Basilica, the necropolis of the French kings.

I found the iconographic repertoire of Gracanica captivating. The frescoes in the church represented the most complex artistic work of the time. However, what struck me immediately was that many of the saints and the royal family had been disfigured—their eyes had been gouged out. The Muslim Turks who occupied this land for five hundred years would not tolerate representations of the human figure and instructed the Turkish custodian of the monastery to remove them. The story, according to Srjan, was that the custodian did not have the heart to destroy these beautiful figures, so he did the next best thing: he gouged out their eyes, believing that by doing so they lost their power. What I had witnessed was only one example of how the Ottomans desecrated Christian iconography.

Twenty years after my first visit to Gracanica, I was in Kosovo on a research project, and I asked my hosts if it was possible to visit the Gracanica church. They were surprised by my request but, out of courtesy, went through the motions of finding a chauffeur willing to drive me the eight kilometers to the church. After a couple of days, the director of the institute admitted that it was simply too dangerous. Seven years after the Kosovo war had ended, most of the churches that I had visited in 1985 were under siege and protection by the NATO peace-support operation Kosovo Force (KFOR).

A few days later, while waiting for my flight at the Pristina airport, I ran into a detachment of Swedish KFORs in military uniforms. I struck up a conversation and, to my great surprise, learned that they were returning from guard duty of the Serb enclave around Gracanica. One of the officers told me about a recent incident at the Gracanica monastery.

"Not too long ago," he said, "an angry Albanian mob gathered around Gracanica and tried to storm the monastery. The crowd was violent, but since we were not issued live ammunition, there was nothing we could do except fire a volley of blanks. Fortunately, the mob did not know they were blanks and stopped charging." For a long time after I heard this story, I puzzled over the foolish UN policy of furnishing KFOR peacekeepers with weapons but not ammunition.

The final confrontation with the Turks came in 1389 in the Battle of Kosovo Polje in which the Serbs were decisively defeated, a turning point in Serbian history. "On June 28, 1389," Srjan said, "a date embedded in the psyche of every Serb, the Christian armies of the Serbian Prince Lazar met the Turkish forces of Ottoman Sultan Murad. The combined forces of the two armies numbered around one hundred thousand, but the Christian army was heavily outnumbered by the Ottomans. In the one-day battle, both Lazar and Murad were killed."

The clash ended in a Turkish victory, the collapse of Serbia, and the complete encirclement of the crumbling Byzantine Empire. The Serbs consider Kosovo Polje not only a defining moment in Serbian history but a pivotal point in the history of Europe as well.

What we saw in Dečani in 1985 prefigured the events that would unfold in the 1990s. Approaching the town, I sensed something was not right. Most of the people on the streets did not look like Serbs. The Visoki Dečani monastery in a river gorge about a kilometer from the town of Dečani was surrounded by mountains and forests. It was the largest and best preserved medieval monastery in Kosovo. It has also been a source of conflict between the remaining Serbs and local Albanians. The mid-fourteenth-century church represented the heyday of Serbian church building—a curious mix of Romanesque architecture, decorative patterns of the Byzantine world, and vibrant frescoes. Given that it was surrounded by a hostile Albanian Muslim population, I wondered how long this beautiful church would survive.

IN MACEDONIA, Srjan wanted us to see four special sites: the Greco-Roman ruins of Heraclea, Saint Sophia Church in Ohrid, and the monasteries of Sveti Naum and Sveti Jovan Bigorski. By this time, we had seen roughly half a dozen churches, and the information Srjan was feeding us was beginning to get muddled. Ivan and I were ready for something different.

After finding a hotel near Bitola, we had a tasty Macedonian meal beginning with a *shopska* salad consisting of chunks of tomato, peppers, cucumber and onion and *musaka*, a meat and potato gratin dish, and retired early. It was late October, and the days were getting shorter, so we had to make the most of the daylight.

Next day, we began our explorations at Heraclea. At first sight, it appeared to be a collection of nondescript ruins. Srjan explained that the city, founded by Philip II of Macedon in the middle of the fourth century BC, was named in honor of the mythological Greek hero Heracles. Over the centuries, Heraclea endured because of its strategic location on the main Roman road, the Via Egnatia, a road that linked a chain of Roman colonies stretching from the Adriatic to the Bosporus. After a quick look at the theater built by the Roman emperor Hadrian and a glimpse of the Great Basilica, we left for Ohrid.

Located on Lake Ohrid, the city has been called the Jerusalem of the Balkans, but today it is home to no more than a dozen churches. Among them is the *Sveta Sofiya* (Saint Sophia), Church of Holy Wisdom, built between 1036 and 1056. One of the most significant monuments of Macedonia, it houses some of the best preserved Byzantine frescoes from the eleventh, twelfth, and thirteenth centuries. When I discovered that construction of the Ohrid Saint Sophia began in 1036, it occurred to me that only one year later, in 1037, Yaroslav the Wise, prince of Kyiv, laid the foundation for his Church of Holy Wisdom, the thirteen-domed *Sviata Sofiya* in Kyiv. The Kyiv Sophia, however, was finished in 1044, twelve years before the Ohrid Sophia was completed.

The peculiarity of dates did not stop there. It appears that during the fourth and fifth decades of the eleventh century, it was common to name important churches after the sixth-century *Hagia Sophia* of Constantinople. Thus, just as the Kyiv Sophia was finished, work on the Cathedral of Holy Wisdom in Polotsk, Belarus, begun in 1044. Finally, one year after construction of the Polotsk Sophia began, the Cathedral of Saint Sophia at Novgorod Veliky in northern Russia was built between 1045 and 1050.

Since all four of the eleventh-century Sophias were named after Constantinople's *Hagia Sophia*, I wondered what had prompted such a movement. My hunch was that all of these Sophias attempted to elevate their status in the eyes of their faithful, and the simplest way to accomplish this was to name it after the great *Hagia Sophia* of Constantinople, one of the greatest feats of architecture of all time.

Before leaving Ohrid, we visited the monastery church of Saint Panteleimon, attributed to Clement of Ohrid, a disciple of Saint Cyril and Saint Methodius, where we got another lecture from Srjan. He said that the monastery was the site where the Glagolitic alphabet was first developed, but at the end of the ninth century, the Cyrillic replaced the Glagolitic. Intended for Slavic-speaking people of the Eastern Orthodox faith, the Cyrillic alphabet was an indirect result of the missionary work of the ninth-century "Apostles of the Slavs," Saint Cyril and Saint Methodius. One of the students of Methodius was Naum, a Bulgarian writer who settled in Macedonia. It was he who created the Cyrillic script that replaced the Glagolitic during the Middle Ages.

Our next stop was the monastery at the southern tip of Lake Ohrid dedicated to Saint Naum. Known as the Enlightener, he was one of the seven missionaries among the Slavs and is venerated as a saint in the Orthodox Church. He founded this monastery and is buried in the church of Saint Naum.

Our pilgrimage to the Serbian and Macedonian churches was nearing its end. It was time to return to Dubrovnik, but as we left sunny Lake Ohrid, Srjan sprang another surprise.

"Since we are in the vicinity," he said, "we cannot miss two other famous monasteries in the region. They are on the way to our last stop, the holiest of the Serb holy shrines—the Patriarchal Church of Peć."

Little did we suspect that the return leg of our journey would turn into the most dangerous part of our odyssey. From Struga, we followed the fast-flowing Black Drin, a river that runs along the western edge of Macedonia until it bends into Albania. I was behind the wheel of our VW Golf, and we were moving on the mountainous R1201 at a nice clip. Ivan and Srjan were talking, enjoying the scenery, and making inane remarks about my driving.

"Slavko, watch out for the sheep and don't hit any geese."

It sounded amusing coming from a nondriver Serb and a Canadian with a fear of heights. I was relaxed and thought that, at this rate, we would soon reach the Montenegrin border and, in another two or three hours, we would be back in our hotel in Dubrovnik. I was looking forward to a day in the jewel of the Adriatic to decompress from a rather stressful ten days on the road.

About forty kilometers north of Struga, the road narrowed, and soon we were wedged between the rugged Albanian border on the west and Lake Debar on the east. The road began to ascend and meander. This would not have been a problem in good visibility, but, unexpectedly, fog had rolled in, and the higher we climbed, the thicker it got. At some point, it became so thick "you could," as the saying goes, "cut it with a knife." I could barely see more than five meters ahead of the VW's hood. With no clearly visible road lines or markers or guardrails, our pace was reduced to a crawl, and I had to stop. In front of us was a sheet of white emptiness. Worse, it was getting dark, and our destination was still a dozen kilometers away.

We weighed the situation and devised a plan. With the windows open, Srjan would watch the edge of the road on the right side and holler, "*Na livo* (To the left)," when the VW got too close to the precipice. Ivan, who had a low tolerance for heights, would keep an eye on the left side of the road to make sure we did not blunder onto the rocks. If I got too close to the edge, he would shout, "*Na pravo* (Stay right)." With adrenalin elevated, the danger lasted about half an hour before the fog dissipated and I saw the sign for Debar. I took a deep breath and sighed with relief. It was a miracle that we did not go off the road, a miracle that I attributed to the religious fervor we exhibited during the pilgrimage and the dozens of the candles we lit in the shrines we visited.

We arrived at the monastery of Saint George the Victorious (*Pobedonosec*), a monastery for women, affiliated with the Sveti Jovan Bigorski monastery, late in the evening. The premises were completely dark, and I thought the monastery was closed, but Srjan went to the arched stone gate and knocked on the wooden door. When there was no answer, he knocked again, louder. After a few more tries, the door creaked opened slightly, and a woman holding a lantern appeared. Srjan approached and said something in Serbian, and from the expression on her face, I understood that the nun was delighted to learn that we were not Albanians. She opened the door and invited us to come in. Locking the door, she said, "We have to be very careful who we let in this late. The *shiptari* in the area sometimes harass us, but as soon as I heard Serbian, I knew I was among friends." Srjan explained that we were driving from Lake Ohrid and had been on the road all day and, pointing to Ivan, said we were his friends from America.

The nun was friendly. "I can show you the church, but I cannot put you up for the night. There is a hotel in Debar that will, though." It took her a while to light up the interior, but when she did, we realized what a magnificent little church this was. Its main attraction was a wood-carved iconostasis whose royal doors included a richly engraved cross of Christ's crucifixion that contained a fragment of the Holy Cross. From my travels, I was aware that such splinters were found in many places in Europe, and I wondered how many such fragments existed and how so substantial an object should have splintered into so many far-flung pieces.

Next day it took us almost five hours to cover the two hundred kilometers to Peć. Many of the churches and monasteries were located within a few kilometers of the Albanian border, and as we moved through the countryside, it was clear that the people living here, the *shiptari*, were not Serb-friendly. Moreover, the roads were in terrible shape, so we had to drive slowly. In every village, I sensed hostile looks from the locals. Srjan kept warning, "Don't stop, and, above all, don't look at them, or we will have trouble."

The Patriarchate of Peć, a group of churches situated at the entrance to the Rugova Gorge in the neighborhood of Peć, is the spiritual seat and mausoleum of the Serbian archbishops and patriarchs. Srjan told us it had been the center of the Serbian church for centuries and was one of the most important monuments of the Serbian past. Founded in the thirteenth century, the patriarchate attracted learned scholars, writers, and artists, and all of them had left traces of their work in it.

Bad roads and fog had set us back by a day, and we had to get back to Dubrovnik in time to catch our flight to Paris. Srjan suggested a shortcut via the Rugova Gap, a mountain road that skirted the north end of the Accursed Mountains, a range that extends from northern Albania to Kosovo and eastern Montenegro. With daylight coming to an end, we entered the dimness of the Accursed Mountains.

The shortcut soon turned into a nightmare. The road climbed and climbed with a series of seemingly endless switchbacks. Halfway to Titograd, we made a wrong turn and wandered off onto a military road that led to the entrance of an out-of-the-way border tunnel. Armed border guards stopped us. "What are you doing here? This road is not even on the map."

It was around midnight, and Srjan had a lot of fancy explaining to do. Exasperated, he came back to the car and said, "This road is closed, and there is no way through these mountains to Titograd." We would have to go back to Peć and take the highway to Ivangrad. I was utterly frustrated and exhausted, and when we got back down to Peć, Ivan took the wheel while I slept in the backseat. After about an hour, I woke up. My companions jokingly said I could go back to sleep; everything was under control. My internal compass, however, told me something was wrong. The hunch turned out to be right: instead of heading for Ivangrad, the next sign indicated that we were on our way to Beograd. The wrong road again! Fortunately, we had not gone too far out of our way and soon got back onto the M2, heading toward Ivangrad. After driving most of the night, we arrived in Dubrovnik at daybreak, washed up, and caught the 8:00 a.m. flight to Paris in the nick of time.

24. Undercover Interviewing

IN EARLY 1985, my return to the United States seemed imminent. My close friend Danylo Struk sensed my reluctance to return to the United States. "Slavko, I'm sure you'll find a way to stay in Paris," he said, and he was right. In November 1985, I joined Soviet Area Audience and Opinion Research (SAAOR), a unit of Radio Liberty (RL) in Munich.

The organization's mandate was to conduct audience research for Radio Liberty and other international broadcasters to the Soviet Union. During the Cold War, most of these stations attempted to explain the way of life and political positions of their sponsoring countries to Soviet listeners. Radio Liberty was different. It was a US Congress–funded station whose purpose was to act as a surrogate home service and provide Soviet listeners with news they could not obtain from their domestic media. In other words, Radio Liberty was complementing Soviet state radio, supplying its citizens with information ranging from Aeroflot crashes to the General Secretary's state of health to the latest casualty figures in Afghanistan. The Soviet press vilified RL's broadcasts, calling them "the voices of the enemy," and jammed them incessantly.

The story of how I joined SAAOR began in May 1981 when I met Charlie Allen, a young Russian-speaking American, during a four-week wine-tasting course at Steven Spurrier's *Academie du Vin*.[83] Perfect spring weather

---

[83]   Steven Spurrier was a British wine expert and merchant in Paris who championed French wines. He organized the famous Paris Wine Tasting of 1976 in which French judges carried out two blind-tasting comparisons: one of top-quality Chardonnays and another of red wines, Bordeaux wines from France and

combined with samplings of vintage wines put us in a relaxed mood, and we found many things in common. I recall telling Charlie about the decline Soviet oil production, a subject that seemed to interest him. Charlie was vague about what he did in Paris, but his Russian was unusually fluent for an American. In any event, we got off to a good start. It was only after I met Charlie at the SAAOR office a few years later that I realized how crucial this chance encounter had been. Charlie, who was in charge of SAAOR's field operations, told me later that because of my background, language skills, and travel experience, he had filed away my name for possible future collaboration.

As I was preparing to return to the United States, I learned from Kathy Mihalisko and other close acquaintances that SAAOR was searching for someone to help with their field operations. The individual had to be able to communicate in Russian and needed to be familiar with the area the organization studied. My name was put forward, and I was invited for an interview with Gene Parta, the director of SAAOR.

Through the American Episcopal Cathedral of Paris on Avenue George V, Gene was acquainted with the IEA's deputy director Wallace Hopkins, my former boss at that organization. Even though two years had elapsed since I left the IEA, Wally gave me a glowing endorsement. "He is dogged in his determination, and he can do anything you throw at him." That seemed to resolve any reservations Gene might have had about my qualifications. I was offered the job and was set to begin work on the first day of November.

Although I had studied Russian in college and passed the army's language aptitude tests with high marks, I knew that my Russian was not up to snuff. I did not reveal my apprehension, and almost everyone at SAAOR assumed that since I spoke Ukrainian, I was fluent in Russian, but understanding and fluency are not the same, and since I would be using Russian extensively, I had to upgrade my command of the language quickly. I engaged Victoria Makarenko, my artist friend's Estonian wife, to give me an intensive course in Russian conversation. We met every other evening at my favorite hangout, Café Bonaparte, and she methodically honed my Russian conversation skills. Soon, I began to think and dream in Russian. I read Russian newspapers and literature out loud, which helped with my enunciation. By September, I was ready. After thoroughly planning and practicing what I was going to

---

Cabernet Sauvignon wines from California. The Californian wine rated best in each category, causing a stir in France, the foremost producer of the world's finest wines.

say, I called Charlie and carried on a lengthy conversation in Russian. He complimented me on my fluency and pronunciation, and when I hung up, I knew I had passed the final hurdle.

When I applied for the position at SAAOR, I assumed I would have to be vetted by the appropriate agencies. With that in mind, I presented a document indicating I had been awarded a "top secret" clearance at the time I served in army intelligence. Many years later, I was surprised to discover that that did not matter. Apparently, what mattered more were my references and the people I knew. For a moment, I was concerned that even a cursory investigation might reveal that I had friends who were not only Leftists but actual card-carrying members of the Communist Party. Luckily, there were forces at work that cleared my way to join SAAOR.

IT WAS A PLEASANT fall morning when I entered the elegant six-story apartment building at 193 Saint-Germain, a boulevard lined with uniformly manicured plane trees. The address—just on the edge of the 6th arrondissement between the Latin Quarter and the prestigious 7th—was probably one of the most desirable in Paris. It was only a stone's throw away from Square Taras Shevchenko and the Ukrainian Greek Catholic Church of Saint Volodymyr. SAAOR's office was on the top floor of a mansard-crowned apartment building served by a small creaky lift. My window faced the boulevard and I could step out onto the balcony and absorb the charm and beauty of the neighborhood.

I plunged into my work with the zeal of an anti-Communist crusader. I saw myself as a foot soldier in the twentieth-century's titanic struggle between the forces of freedom and Communist tyranny. What better way to fulfill this aspiration than by being the eyes and ears of Radio Liberty, an organization on the front lines of the combat against the inhumane system? The "freedom radios" were by far the most effective tool to fight the Communist ideology that had enslaved one-third of humanity, including the country of my birth.

Until that point, my resistance to Communism had been mostly symbolic. In the '70s, I had participated in protests, demonstrations letter-writing campaigns and blood donation drives organized by Mata Farion to support dissidents and human rights in Ukraine and elsewhere, actions that were only marginally effective. No one expected such actions to lead to the collapse of the Soviet Union. Now, by an immense stroke of luck, I had discovered a way to engage Socialist tyranny directly and boldly, a challenge I found extremely gratifying. When I went to work in the morning, there was an eagerness in my step that hadn't been there before. Probably my colleagues at SAAOR did not share my passion for combating the Communist scourge to the same extent. They didn't have families on the other side of the Iron Curtain like I did.

Radio Free Europe (RFE) began broadcasting to Eastern Europe in 1950. Radio Liberty (RL) launched its broadcasts to the Soviet Union on March 1, 1953, the day Soviet leader Joseph Stalin suffered his fatal stroke. Headquartered in Munich, the Radios broadcast in over twenty languages. They would play a crucial role in Soviet Communism's ultimate demise.

Originally funded by the CIA, in 1974 the Radios came under the control of an organization called the Board for International Broadcasting (BIB). The BIB was designed to receive appropriations from the US Congress, give them to Radio management, and oversee the appropriation of funds. The CIA had taken a laissez-faire approach to RFE and RL, guaranteeing a distance from official government policies as well as journalistic independence, and the BIB also provided a firewall between the Radios and the State Department and other executive branch offices. RL's goal was straightforward—to provide truthful information that Soviet censors would never allow within the USSR.

The audience research operation came into being because Radio management understandably wanted to know the size and nature of audiences behind the Iron Curtain. It was not an easy task. In a hermetically sealed society like the Soviet Union, in-country research was out of the question. Initially, audience research tended to be unsophisticated and haphazard, and reliant on ad hoc anecdotal feedback—rather like fishing without a hook. Much of the early research relied on letters from listeners, which arrived in Munich by the thousands. There were two intrinsic problems with such letters: one, they were not representative of the population in the USSR, and, two, only about one-tenth of them got past the censors and reached Germany. Ad hoc interviewing increased in the 1960s, but it was not carried out in a systematic manner.

In the 1970s, the audience research office of Radio Liberty was moved from Munich to Paris to allow it to operate in a more objective manner. SAAOR developed two broadcaster-neutral questionnaires that posed questions about all the main Western broadcasters to the Soviet Union — Radio Liberty, VOA, BBC, Radio Sweden, Deutsche Welle, and Kol Israel. One questionnaire was designed for use with emigrants from the Soviet Union in Israel and Rome. The other was for use with Soviet citizens traveling for business or pleasure to Western Europe. The sample that concerned us most was the Soviet citizens, but the emigrant sample served as a way to check the consistency of the citizen data, and also provided additional background information on life in the Soviet Union.

The problem remaining was the fact that Soviet citizens traveling abroad were not representative of the Soviet population as a whole. They tended to be more highly educated, they came from urban rather than rural backgrounds, and they were more likely to be members of the Communist Party. Since sample deficiencies could not be corrected in the field, SAAOR developed a groundbreaking simulation methodology with the help of specialists at MIT to enable us to draw reliable estimates from uneven samples and project our interview data on to the Soviet population as a whole.[84]

The SAAOR office was headed by R. Eugene (Gene) Parta, who replaced Max Ralis as director of Audience Research in 1981.[85] Gene was the prime mover behind the MIT simulation methodology, initiating an approach that no one thought was possible. Parta had been in the business of interviewing Soviet visitors since 1969. After graduating from Saint Olaf College in Northfield, Minnesota, he studied at the School of Advanced International Studies of the John Hopkins University, where he obtained an MA in Soviet Studies before joining Radio Liberty in New York. In the mid-1970s, he was twice a visiting research fellow at MIT, and it was then that the simulation methodology was developed.

Gene was a low-key manager, always trying to hire the best talent he could find. He let the research analysts work independently, providing guidance and advice as needed. Gene was always fair, generous, and ready to discuss issues and problems in the field. His management style had the effect of encouraging new ideas and stimulating creativity. The office included a handful of analysts, an editor, an office manager, translators, and EDP personnel, roughly a dozen staffers in all. My role in this machine was to help Charlie Allen, the deputy director of SAAOR, oversee field operations in Europe.

When Gene hired me in 1985, it was a major career switch. In a short time, I shifted from oil economics to sociological work with Soviet visitors, which took my life in a dramatically new direction. The new job was a fulfillment of a subliminal desire to take part in the central struggle of the

[84] R. Eugene Parta, "Audience Research in Extremis: Cold War Broadcasting to the USSR," *Participations: Journal of Audience and Reception Studies*, volume 8, issue 1 (May 2011).

[85] Max and Gene appeared on Soviet radar early on, and the Soviet press dubbed Gene *Polkovnik* or Colonel Parta.

twentieth century. I will always be grateful for the opportunity to embark on this fascinating and exciting career.

SAAOR's primary mission was to estimate the size, characteristics, and media use habits of audiences to Western radio in the Soviet Union. We gathered information on times and frequency of listening to Radio Liberty and the other main broadcasters; on the shortwave frequencies used by respondents; and on the quality of reception and audibility (the stations were heavily jammed). We amassed feedback regarding programming content, announcers, and suggestions for topics to improve programming content. We gauged the attitudes and opinions of Soviet citizens on a range of topical issues such as the war in Afghanistan, questions related to nationality matters, the 1986 Chernobyl disaster, and *glasnost* and *perestroika*. We also collected data on the availability of food products, their quality, and their prices—indicators which reflected the quality of life in the Soviet Union, and the condition of the Soviet economy.

These findings allowed SAAOR analysts to construct a realistic picture of what was going on in the Soviet Union. We detected patterns and trends that no one else could, for the simple reason that apart from random anecdotal information, leaks, and rumors, no one possessed such data on such a scale. Using a data base that ultimately comprised thousands of respondents, we reported quarterly on trends in listening to Radio Liberty and the other main Western broadcasters. We provided reports analyzing attitudinal and opinion findings which enabled readers to piece together a picture of public opinion in the USSR, despite the lack of Western-style polling. Non-quantitative reports presented background information on life and conditions in the Soviet Union. In the early '70s, panel reviews evaluating recent programming were carried out by Soviet emigrants, and in due course these evolved into focus groups that studied programming according to the norms used in such research in the West.

Our work differed radically from the work of the conventional Sovietologists and Kremlin watchers who monitored Soviet politics at the highest levels. These experts, journalists and academics, spent an inordinate amount of time scrutinizing the printed press, analyzing speeches by the Soviet leadership, reading *Pravda* and *Izvestia* between the lines for hidden messages, or evaluating rumors of changes in the Kremlin hierarchy. Using such information, the experts speculated about conditions in the USSR and tried to infer trends. Meanwhile, SAAOR focused on what the average Soviet citizen was thinking, and was virtually the only provider of such information.

We gathered information from Soviet citizens on a scale unimaginable to the mainstream Sovietologists and Kremlin watchers.

The uniqueness of our work was widely acknowledged throughout the US government and academic communities. Our research was naturally geared to Radio management, and we did not accept assignments from outside entities, but it was also shared with various government and academic institutions in the US and Western Europe. (Apparently our reports were also monitored by the KGB and, according to reports from USIA officers, they even reached the Institute of Sociology of the USSR Academy of Sciences in Moscow.)

In 1985, Gene Parta presented the results of our research on Afghanistan to a panel of sociologists and Sovietologists at a Harvard University conference. Even though hardly anyone had thought that such polling was feasible, overall, the results were received favorably. Only a few questioned our findings—in particular, one Russian émigré scholar, Leah Greenberg. "There is no such thing as 'public opinion' in the USSR," she remarked. Others disagreed. Among those who thought our approach held promise was Andrew Marshall, director of the Office of Net Assessment, the Pentagon's internal think tank.[86] Marshall's office was particularly interested in our data on food availability and pricing in the USSR. Considering our findings valuable for his global assessments, Marshall requested that we provide him with a special computerized database and paid a nominal fee for the extra data processing involved. Because we were often ahead of the conventional wisdom in Washington and elsewhere, the quality and utility of SAAOR reporting gained widespread recognition.

One reason our research was credible was because it was based on a fairly representative geographic sample of the population of the Soviet Union, including Ukrainians, Belarusians, people from the Baltic States, and, less frequently, Trans-Caucasians and Central Asians. Consequently, our analysts were able to scrutinize data not just by demographic categories and Communist Party affiliation, but also by nationality. At the end of the 1970s, some US policymakers became increasingly interested in the Soviet nationality question when US national security adviser Zbigniew Brzezinski

---

[86]   The 2015 biography of Andrew Marshall, *The Last Warrior*, by Andrew Krepinevich and Barry Watts, is an excellent account of the work of Office of Net Assessment, a low-profile but vitally important Pentagon think tank. Marshall believed that assumptions about Soviet behavior were oversimplified, including a "model of the Soviet government as a single unified actor pursuing an easily stated strategy."

raised the issue under Pres. Jimmy Carter. The topic became more central as a growing number of Soviet visitors were permitted to travel to Western Europe and other destinations during the 1980s.

In the early days, our respondents tended to be Soviet businessmen, people in the entertainment world, athletes, sailors, and diplomats. In the '80s, the sample expanded to include a broader spectrum of Soviet visitors either visiting family in the West or tourists, students, trainees, and so on. In the mid-'80s, the pool of potential respondents expanded even further to include tourists arriving on cruise ships. Contrary to popular opinion, tourism from the Soviet Union during this period was not limited to the Communist elites and deserving workers.

The increase in traffic allowed SAAOR to expand its operations. By the time I came on board, the main interviewing points were in Athens, Copenhagen, Vienna, and Paris. Smaller ones, scattered among major European capitals and cities, included Antwerp, Brussels, and Helsinki. Outside of Europe, we had interviewing locations in New York and Japan. In time, we added Berlin and Hamburg in Germany, and India and Singapore in Southeast Asia. At the same time, a growing number of interviews were conducted with Jewish emigrants from the Soviet Union in Rome and Israel.

Around the globe, SAAOR engaged up to seventy interviewers, of which roughly fifty worked in Europe, eight in Israel, eight in Singapore and India, and four in New York. At its height, our network encompassed at least twelve locations, ten of which focused on Soviet visitors, while two, Rome and Israel, worked entirely with emigrants.

My part in this operation was to coordinate the work of roughly fifty interviewers on the European continent. During the early years, the mainstay of my job was reviewing questionnaires for completeness and internal consistency, and providing feedback to the institutes through which we worked. At times, my responsibilities included finding, recruiting, and training new interviewers.

SAAOR attempted to set up operations in other locations (Stockholm and London), but none materialized into full-fledged operationsm and were eventually abandoned. In any event, growing traffic through the ports of Copenhagen and Piraeus was more than sufficient to compensate for the loss of these marginal operations.

Various phrases come to mind in describing our field operations: indirect interviewing, surrogate surveys, undercover research, and covert human intelligence gathering. Some fit, some did not, and most of my colleagues eschewed such terminology. The generic term our office used to describe the interviewing we carried out was simply "unorthodox" or "unconventional" interviewing. Such benign terms, however, tell little about the real nature of how we carried out this sensitive task. Today there exists a legitimate term used by sociologists that comes close to describing the type of work our interviewers performed: undercover social science. We never used such a designation because the term was not invented until the '90s.

Western pollsters are trained to approach respondents openly and request an interview. It was not possible to adopt this approach with Soviet travelers visiting from a closed society. Instead, our interviewers were trained to engage potential respondents in a casual face-to-face conversation and steer it in the direction of media use. Interviews were carried out face-to-face, but without the questionnaire. Getting a respondent to cooperate was a skill bordering on art.

I quickly grasped the unstated rule that we should not talk about our work outside the office. Family and friends knew only that I was doing some sort of research for Radio Liberty and that I traveled a lot. Most of the interviewers working for us in the outlying locations were former Soviet citizens who still had family and friends in the USSR. If knowledge of their activities was to leak out, the KGB could use it to intimidate our interviewers or their families, with a detrimental impact on our work.

One of our interviewers, Valery, had special connections to Soviet circles in Paris, and even the Soviet Embassy. He was a valuable source because his contact—and it was never clear who his contacts were—was able to tell him what the Soviets knew about our operations in Paris and elsewhere in Europe. According to Valery, the Soviets were aware of our operation in Paris but did not consider us a priority. Most of their resources were allocated to military and strategic intelligence, which was not our brief. It did not mean, however, that they were not interested in our activities. They were very much interested and, according to Valery, would get around to looking at us in due time. For this reason, we took steps to strengthen our security measures.

OUR PARIS OFFICE hosted a constant flow of high-level distinguished visitors, including the chairman of the Board for International Broadcasting, Steve Forbes, and board members such as Lane Kirkland and author James Michener. Journalist-historian David Satter and others also came by, marveled at our success, and encouraged us to continue.

There were institutions and individuals who used our products that we were not aware of. One such individual was a diplomat I met years later who was the former ambassador to Kazakhstan and Georgia, William Courtney. He was an avid user of SAAOR's reports while stationed in Moscow in the '80s. Bill expressed amazement at how we were able to conduct opinion research with Soviet citizens—his attempts to duplicate or confirm our findings by random contacts with Soviet citizens had been fruitless.

In the USSR, there was no way to start a conversation. One of the pillars on which the system rested was the complete isolation of the average man from the outside world, and a foreigner, merely by existing, undermined that pillar. Even in the '80s, people remembered that for contact with a foreigner, Stalin would condemn a person to five to ten years in the Gulag, and often ordered them shot. Small wonder that Soviets avoided foreigners like the plague, especially those who were friendly and asked questions. Fear and suspicion were embedded in their subconscious.

On more than one occasion, Courtney sought to strike up conversations with Russians on trains or in shops. All his efforts came to naught. There was no way to speak with Russians while they were in the Soviet Union. However, the moment they left their prisonlike environment, a transformation took place. In a free and open society, the average citizen lost some of his fear and was ready to spill out his heart to anyone who would listen, and that is what made our operations possible, credible, and fruitful.

25. Modus Operandi

FIELD OPERATIONS were a pivotal aspect of SAAOR's work, and our interviewers used indirect means to engage Soviet tourists, and obtain the information the international broadcasters sought. The approach was the product of years of trial and error with opinion polling of Soviet citizens. During the 1980s, Soviet tourism grew steadily and, by the end of the decade, Soviets were visiting Western European cities by the tens of thousands. Over the years, SAAOR established a working relationship with marketing institutes across Europe and around the globe. The directors of these institutes were responsible for recruiting, vetting, and training interviewers, but SAAOR reserved the right to approve or turn down an interviewer. The educational level of the interviewers was not as important as command of Russian, a good memory, and "street smarts."

A good interviewer had to be outgoing and have the talent to strike up a casual conversation with Soviet visitors wherever he happened to find them—in ports, museums, or on the street. His goal was to elicit information from unsuspecting Soviet visitors without them realizing that they were being interviewed. To accomplish this delicate task, each interviewer had to commit to memory a standardized questionnaire and be sufficiently clever to guide the conversation in such a way as to extract the information required by the interview form. Crucial to this exercise was the interviewer's ability to locate a potential respondent and, using some invented pretext, start a conversation "cold." Once a rapport had been established, it was his or her job to steer the conversation toward radio listening, and extract relevant information. The steps were straightforward; executing them was an art.

235

MY ROLE IN THIS UNDERTAKING was monitoring and coordinating the work in several Western European cities where we had interviewing points. These included Copenhagen, Hamburg, Berlin, Paris, Vienna, Rome, and Athens. Smaller points included Brussels, London, New York, and a few exotic places like Barcelona and the Azores. My colleagues and I visited each of the major interviewing points once or twice a year to consult with the directors, get to know the interviewers, and oversee their work. Other places where we interviewed Soviet visitors were Helsinki, Israel, Singapore, Tokyo, and Bombay, but operations in these sites were small and not part of my brief.

Marketing research firms in each location acted as intermediaries between SAAOR and the interviewers. They were responsible for supervising the workflow, administering field controls, and providing a cursory review of questionnaires before sending them to our office in Paris. The institutes employed between fifty and sixty interviewers and checkers in over a dozen locations.

All interviews took the form of casual face-to-face conversations without the presence of a questionnaire. Accurate recall was essential, a skill that required a near-photographic memory. Every interviewer had to have the ability to record all relevant information the respondent provided, so we insisted that interviewers fill out the questionnaire immediately after each encounter. To help with recall, the interviewers employed memory techniques and mnemonic aids. To the uninitiated, this sounds like a daunting task, but with training and practice, the majority of interviewers managed to carry out these tasks quite satisfactorily.

Conventional wisdom during the '60s and '70s dictated that Soviet travelers were either too fearful or too loyal to the regime to enter into a conversation with a stranger. By the '80s, however, contacts with five out of six targeted respondents would result in an interview. Once a contact was made and rapport established, most interviewers were able to obtain information on a wide variety of subjects, including comments on foreign and domestic topics, the latest antiregime gossip, and even humorous anecdotes.

In early 1987, Gene Parta had the opportunity to meet with Vladimir Shlapentokh, a Soviet sociologist who emigrated to the United States in 1979.[87] Gene told him about our ability to interview Soviet citizens on a large

---

[87]   Vladimir Shlapentokh was a Ukrainian-born sociologist, historian, and political scientist, notable for his work on Soviet and Russian society and politics. He worked as a senior fellow in the Institute of Sociology in Moscow and is

scale without encountering serious problems. Shlapentokh was surprised at our ability to carry out such work, and deduced that there was a "sea change" taking place in the Soviet Union. Pervasive fear was starting to dissipate—one of the first indications of the impending collapse.

Despite the increase in the Soviet traveling population in the mid-'80s, the raw data sample was still not always representative of the Soviet population as a whole. As before, it was biased in favor of those strata of population most likely to travel abroad—namely, males, people with a secondary or higher education, urban residents, and individuals in the thirty-to-fifty age bracket, Communist Party members, and inhabitants of the European parts of the RSFSR, especially the Moscow and Leningrad areas. As outlined in the preceding chapter, to deal with distortions introduced by different sampling rates among various strata of the population, SAAOR employed a computer simulation procedure developed at the Massachusetts Institute of Technology. With time, the model evolved, and collaboration between SAAOR and MIT specialists allowed us to compute more reliable estimates of audience size. As the simulation methodology continued to be refined, SAAOR turned to Bayesian statistical methods to correct geographic discrepancies and issue fairly accurate estimates of listening levels in most of the republics of the Soviet Union.[88]

Our interviewing network was continually changing and evolving, a process that needed constant attention and maintenance. Ineffective or incompetent interviewers had to be let go and new ones found. Fortunately, with the network expanding, there were more hirings than firings. Dismissals had to be handled delicately and gradually by reducing an interviewer's quota. Either he improved or he dropped out of his own accord. A disgruntled interviewer could cause embarrassment. That is why we monitored the work of each interviewer, and if his or her work was not up to the required standard, we made sure that the interviewer understood the reason for his dismissal.[89]

---

considered a founding father (together with Vladimir Yadov, Boris Grushin, and Yuri Levada) of Soviet sociology.

[88] See "The Shortwave Audience in the USSR: Methods for Improving the Estimate," by R. E. Parta, J. Klensin, and I. de Sola Pool, *Communication Research*, vol. 9, no. 4, October 1982.

[89] Although our network of interviewers included a number of excellent female interviewers, the vast majority were male. For convenience, I will use the male pronoun "he" rather than the cumbersome "he or she."

Many of my trips to the field involved meeting new interviewers. Most of the time, they came via third-party referrals. Even though they were vouched for, it was still our responsibility to meet them and give our consent. Some of the following chapters describe my attempts to find interviewers and assess their competence and suitability for this kind of work. Since I was never sure if the individual was a legitimate candidate or a possible KGB plant, meetings with potential candidates often involved a touch of intrigue.

In the early years, before tourist traffic increased in the 1980s, the most challenging part of an interviewer's work was finding Soviet citizens. An interviewer had to know where Soviet visitors congregated in the city where he worked. In a metropolis such as Paris, interviewers might find Soviet trade delegations, exchange students, visitors to UNESCO, diplomats, and entertainers. Some visitors strayed to Russian bookstores in the 6th arrondissement or the office of *Russkaya Mysl* (Russian Thought), the Russian-language newspaper near the Place des Ternes, and others could be found visiting museums like the Louvre or famous monuments such as Notre-Dame and the Eiffel Tower.

Most interviewers developed a sixth sense about where to find visitors or tourists. In Paris, Soviet tourists flocked to a cheap clothing chain called Tati, which had one store in the Montmartre quarter and another in Montparnasse. With little currency to spend, they went to these shops to purchase inexpensive clothes, shoes, and other items. Soviets with more money patronized stores like FNAC and Darty to snap up shortwave radios, cameras, and video equipment. These shops were popular because they had a "de-tax" policy, which meant a 20 percent rebate on most electronic equipment that would be taken out of the country.

Spotting Soviet visitors in stores or on the street was relatively easy to the trained eye. The giveaway was their cheap apparel, clunky shoes, and a peculiarly tasteless way of matching clothes. Bad teeth and primitive dental work (steel- or gold-capped teeth) were other clues.

An interviewer might position himself in one of these stores pretending to be a customer. He kept his ears perked for Russian or Ukrainian speakers and, at the right moment, pounced on an unsuspecting visitor with a stock line: "Things are expensive here. I know of another shop where you can find better bargains," or some such time-tested approach that the target rarely turned down.

Soviet tourist traffic increased appreciably around the mid-'80s as more and more tourist ships began docking in the ports of Copenhagen and Piraeus near Athens. These two locations were veritable mother lodes of potential interviewees. It was also possible to talk to sailors in port cities like Hamburg and Bremen, but nothing matched the scale of Denmark and Greece where, during the warm months, tourists disembarked by the thousands.

OVER TIME, with the help of field directors, we developed informal guidelines summarizing the most effective ways to approach a candidate and initiate a discussion. They represented the essence of our *modus operandi*.

- The interviewing technique should never be heavy-handed. The approach must be simple and natural. Experience tells us that the best way for an interviewer to get results is to be cautious, patient, and modest.
- After a contact has been made, the interviewer is advised to change the topic several times before broaching the subject of radio listening. Talking about topics unrelated to Western radio relaxes people and allows the interviewer to control the conversation.
- Soviet tourists are among the poorest in the world. The ruble is practically worthless because it is not convertible, so many visitors have something of value to sell. The most common items are caviar and vodka. After initiating contact, an interviewer might suggest that he is interested in buying "something." Whether the respondent has something to sell is irrelevant. A basis for a friendly discussion has been established.
- It is imperative that the interviewer not turn the conversation into an interrogation. Experience tells us that such an approach will make visitors clam up.
- The tourists from higher Party circles are the most difficult to interview. Their response on most issues tends to be the standard Party line. In such cases, peasantlike simplicity and persistence are the interviewer's best tools.
- Easiest to approach are ordinary people from the countryside. Their numbers have been growing every year. It is useful to pretend to be a "dimwit" to loosen up a visitor's tongue.
- It is best to try to speak to a visitor when he is alone, away from other tourists. When they are in a group, they tend to be reticent, and their answers are not always useful or truthful.

- With the growth of listening to international radio, fewer people hide the fact that their most important non-Soviet source for information is Western radio. This makes it easier to broach the subject of foreign radio listening.

- There is a general anti-Russian bias among non-Russian nationals, particularly Ukrainians, that borders on detestation of all Russians. They openly refer to them as *katsapske bydlo* or *svoloch*, Moscow dirt bags or scum.

- The most sensitive question concerns Party membership. Some respondents will admit they are CP members, but many are not likely to answer frankly. An interviewer might ask, "Is it still true that only Party members are allowed to travel abroad?" or more directly, "How long have you been a Party member?"

- Soviet visitors are curious about such things as currency fluctuations, workers' living conditions in the West, wages, salaries, etc. Subjects like these offer opportunities to carry on a conversation.

- An interviewer should be ready with a token gift or money to purchase a trinket for a prospective respondent, or buy him coffee or a bite to eat.

- The interviewer must be a fluent Russian speaker, preferably well educated, cultured, and familiar with Soviet geography and territorial divisions. Approaching Soviets in a foreign language is a nonstarter and likely to scare them away.

- Male travelers outnumber females and, consequently, are overrepresented in the sample. An interviewer should strive to maintain the male/female ratio at approximately 70 percent male and 30 percent female.

- Female interviewers are less threatening and better at interviewing male respondents.

- There is no particular order to asking questions. Every interview situation is unique and requires a different approach, quick thinking, and improvisation, and each interviewer should devise an approach that works for him or her.

WHILE THE VAST MAJORITY of our interviewers carried out their work with integrity, the temptation to fabricate responses or invent interviews was ever present. Avoiding this was one of the central challenges of fieldwork. To prevent falsification, we adopted complex field controls and data checks to instill responsible habits, guarantee the integrity of the work, and maintain a reasonable balance between listeners and nonlisteners to Western radio. This is why we paid the same amount for all completed interviews whether the respondent listened or not. At the same time, each interviewer was made aware that the staff in Paris had a good idea of the ratio of listeners to nonlisteners, and that an examination of an interviewer's work would readily disclose significant deviations from these parameters. Too many interviews with nonlisteners would raise a red flag and be noted on the interviewer's record. A simple statistical analysis was sufficient to keep most interviewers honest.

When an interviewer was on the verge of taking an interview, he or she was expected to telephone either the institute or a controller and announce the likely location of the interview—usually some shop or coffee bar. A controller rushed to the place and observed the interview from a comfortable distance. Only about one in five interview situations was checked this way, but because the interviewer did not know when he or she would be checked, it was sufficient to keep most of them in line. It was also possible to distinguish actual interviews from invented ones by statistical analysis of an interviewer's work. If they revealed inconsistencies or signs of unusual or illogical patterns, the interviewer was reprimanded, and his quota decreased. It also sent a message to all interviewers that their work was closely scrutinized.

Still, the best method of preventing fraudulent interviewing was to have a personal rapport with an interviewer, to meet him face-to-face, to get to know his background, family, and so on. Such meetings constituted a good part of my job while I was on the road. Getting to know and keeping track of fifty interviewers was a colossal task and made my work challenging and exciting. Also, whenever I was in the field, I tried to convey a simple but effective message—*Doveryai, no proveryai* (Trust, but verify), drawing on a proverb President Reagan expressed during his talks with Mikhail Gorbachev in 1986. In Russian, the rhyme is catchy, and everyone understood its meaning.

Finally, the most effective means of keeping interviewers on their toes was a surprise visit to an interviewing location. In the next chapter, I describe one such visit, an incident that had a lasting impact on the work of the Copenhagen team.

26. Operations in Copenhagen

A FEW MONTHS AFTER I joined the research office on boulevard Saint-Germain, Charlie Allen and I flew to Copenhagen to observe field operations there. It was initiation by fire at one of our most important interviewing points. The objective was to meet Steen Sauerberg, director of Communication and Opinion Research, one of the leading marketing research firms in Copenhagen, to get to know his interviewers, and to monitor their work.

After our KLM flight had landed in Copenhagen, we took a cab directly to Steen's apartment in a restored eighteenth-century building on Købmagergade, a pedestrian street in the town center where he conducted business. Steen struck me as a personable, intelligent, and efficient individual, and I established a good rapport with him from the beginning. We shared an interest in art, history, and travel. Steen was also a Francophile, a wine connoisseur, and a gourmet cook who could whip up a delectable meal in minutes. He showed me how to prepare a *magret de canard* in under ten minutes, a recipe I use to this day.

Despite the risk, he believed in our mission and was instrumental in helping us collect information from Soviet citizens. In the 1980s, more and more Soviet cruise ships originating from Leningrad sailed the Baltic Sea. They stopped at some of the old Hanseatic ports, but Copenhagen was always the final and most anticipated destination.

Minutes after we entered Steen's residence, he informed us that a Soviet tourist ship had just docked at Nordhavn, the north end of the Copenhagen port. Steen had access to a register of Soviet ships arriving, and his interviewers were on standby.

Charlie and I checked in at Copenhagen's Admiral Hotel, next to the harbor's promenade where Soviet tourists would amble. As soon as they disembarked, they headed south along the harbor to get a glimpse of Copenhagen's famous bronze statue of the Little Mermaid, a magnet for tourists. Sauerberg's team of Russian-speaking interviewers knew this, and once they had assessed the volume of traffic, half a dozen of them picked their targets, waiting for the right moment to make a move.

After taking photos of the Mermaid, the tourists headed for the city center, crossing a diagonal street called the Esplanaden. It was full of shops peddling jeans, underwear, and other cheap merchandise scarce in their home country. They also knew via the grapevine that these outlets carried inexpensive electronic equipment, a highly prized commodity unavailable in the Soviet Union. We referred to them as the "Polish shops" because most of them were owned and managed by Polish immigrants. Soviet tourists swarmed around these shops like bees around a beehive. Many had been saving their hard currency just for this occasion; it was the high point of their cruise and the last chance to spend their few kroner on souvenirs.

From these shops, the visitors dispersed to other parts of town: the Russian Orthodox Church of Alexander Nevsky, the Nyhavn port area with its restaurants and bars, Christiansborg Royal Palace, the National Museum of Denmark, Ny Carlsberg Glyptotek, and the Tivoli Gardens. A few curious males not interested in art or history proceeded directly to Copenhagen's red-light district of Vesterbro.

Depending on the season and level of traffic, Steen employed between ten and twelve interviewers and controllers. All of them were Russian speakers who, for one reason or another, found themselves in Copenhagen. Most were recent Jewish immigrants from the Soviet Union who ended up there after the 1975 Helsinki Final Act gave them the right to emigrate from the USSR. Among the interviewers were also a few dissidents, former sailors who jumped ship, and a Russian-speaking Polish journalist. Information regarding the arrival of Soviet ships in Copenhagen's sprawling port was posted in shipping trade journals and newspapers, so most of the time, Steen did not even bother to warn his interviewers. Many of them kept track of the arrivals on their own, and once word got around they were ready to intercept the visitors.

The work was not dangerous in the physical sense. There was, however, the possibility of being detected by the KGB agents accompanying every group of visitors, and discovery could have unpleasant consequences. When passengers were leaving the ship, their escorts usually warned, "CIA agents are everywhere and will try to engage or recruit you for subversive work," and tourists were given strict instructions not to make contact with strangers. The passengers pretended to listen, but as soon as they were out of sight of the escorts, they did as they pleased. There were simply not enough KGB to monitor everyone's activities. Soviet visitors who had lived in a closed country all their lives were eager to make contact with Westerners, but the language was a barrier. Our people took advantage of this, and that's why it was relatively easy to engage a visitor in a conversation. Still, enticing them into an interview situation required a certain finesse, and getting them to talk freely and extracting needed information required considerable talent.

There was no magic formula for approaching an unsuspecting Russian or Ukrainian visitor. Each interviewer developed a personal approach depending on the circumstances. In the Polish shops, an interviewer would mingle with a group of visitors pretending he was one of the customers who just happened to speak Russian. When a Soviet tourist was examining a pair of jeans or contemplating buying a shortwave radio set, the interviewer would casually say something about the brand of the jeans or offer advice on electronic equipment. "Sony shortwave sets are very good, but they are expensive. Sharp is just as good but much cheaper."

A potential respondent might ignore such advice, but more often than not, it led to a conversation. In no time, an experienced interviewer would be talking about Western radio listening and eliciting opinions on a range of topics.

Another kind of situation might develop on the street where an interviewer following a group would pretend to overhear Russian and say something like "What a pleasure it is to hear my mother tongue. I don't get much of a chance to speak Russian, and I miss it. I lived in Moscow, and it was impossible to find an apartment there. By the way, where are you from?" and so on.

Rarely would an interviewer approach his or her target directly. The encounter always had to appear accidental, and begin by engaging a potential respondent in innocuous small talk about the weather and suchlike. The interviewer's success depended on his or her ability to spin a believable story. One favorite ploy was to offer a potential respondent a gift. For the Soviets, even simple trinkets—a ballpoint, a postcard, or a cup with the city's logo—would work. A good interviewer would carry a small supply of these items for just such an occasion. Soviet visitors were open to the gestures, but the best way to get them to talk was to invite them for a coffee or a beer. All of them were watching their pennies, so an invitation to a bar or restaurant would almost never be refused. If the respondent was too busy, the interviewer might propose to meet later at a designated place. Once behind a table in a café or an eatery, the interviewer would encourage the visitor to talk. All had stories to tell about their lives in the city or locality where they happened to be living. Such a conversation needed only slight nudging to keep the respondent on topic as required by the questionnaire.

An effective approach might be, "You know when I lived in Leningrad, I always listened to the BBC because the reception was good, but that was a long time ago. Can you still hear the BBC, or do they jam it like Radio Liberty?" Once the subject of radio had been broached, one question would lead to another.

Interviewer: When I lived in Odesa, I would listen to Liberty's Ukrainian service. Tell me, do they still broadcast the program *Pages from Ukrainian History*?

Respondent: Yes, the program is still on the air, but, recently, they changed the moderator. I don't like her voice.

Interviewer: Oh, really, who's moderating the program now?

Respondent: Kateryna Shcherbak. I don't like her arrogant manner, and she speaks Ukrainian with a Galician accent.

When a Soviet citizen was looking for a shortwave receiver in one of the electronics shops, an interviewer in the shop might casually comment, "I hear they are still jamming Radio Liberty in Moscow."

"Yeah, you can't get a signal in the center of the city, but if you go just outside Moscow at night, Liberty comes through loud and clear."

Or an interviewer might say, "In Minsk, I recall you could get Liberty on the 6860 waveband."

And the respondent would say, "I don't know about Minsk, but in Crimea where I live, the strongest signal on my German Grundig is 7010 kilohertz" . . . and so on.

OF COURSE, NOT EVERY interview was complete, and not every interviewee listened to international radio. Quite often, a respondent who got suspicious broke off an interview. Most of the time, however, interviewers elicited enough information about international radio listening to allow our analysts to construct a reasonably accurate profile of listeners to RL, BBC, and VOA, and other stations, with the wavelength used, quality of audibility, times of listening, and subjects and programs they liked or disliked. At times, a respondent might wittingly or unwittingly provide information about specific programming topics and personalities.

There was another immensely important part of the questionnaire that asked respondents' opinions on important issues of the day such as attitudes toward the ongoing war in Afghanistan, the Chernobyl tragedy, and Gorbachev's *glasnost* and *perestroika*. Raising such delicate issues with respondents was not easy. Sometimes they offered opinions on the state of affairs in the Soviet Union without coaxing, but most had to be gently encouraged to express their views. The following hypothetical interview situation illustrates how an interview might unfold after a contact with a possible respondent had been made.

"Here in the West, we hear that the war in Afghanistan is going well for the Soviet Union."

Most respondents would immediately react and say that that was not true and remark that "in fact, the war is going very badly. Every day our soldiers are coming home in coffins."

"Where did you hear that?" an interviewer would ask.

"We can't believe our media anymore. They lie. We get our news from Radio Liberty on the shortwave. Even the VOA, a propaganda station, informs us better than Soviet television."

From there it would be natural to segue to radio listening.

After the Chernobyl accident in Ukraine, all an interviewer needed to do was to breach the subject, and respondents spilled their hearts out about how the Communist Party lied about the tragedy. Ukrainians and Belarusians who experienced the brunt of the tragedy volunteered the most damning testimonials. A typical response might be, "The Communists deceived us into believing that the Chernobyl explosion was under control, and, five days later, they held the May 1 military parade, as the *nomenklatura* sent their children south to Crimea to escape the radiation. They lied to us about Chernobyl like they have been lying about everything for the past fifty years."

BEING IN THE CENTER of the Cold War struggle between the United States and the USSR was challenging but immensely rewarding. Unlike my previous job at the OECD, I believed that my work was critical, and I carried out my assignments with dedication and a strong sense of mission. On that first trip to Copenhagen, Charlie and I devised a clever plan to see how our interviewers contacted potential respondents and enticed them into an interview situation. I posed as a potential respondent, pretending I was a

Ukrainian tourist from Western Ukraine. My Ukrainian was native, so I was certain that language would not give me away, and if my Russian was colored with a Ukrainian accent, no one would be any the wiser. I was more concerned that the way I was dressed might give me away. To the trained eye, Soviet citizens stood out like hobos among a well-dressed crowd of theatergoers.

Steen thought our plan was original and made sure none of the interviewers were aware that we were in town to monitor their work. It was like a surprise bank audit. Charlie had already shown me the spots where Soviet tourists congregated—the Little Mermaid statue, the Russian Orthodox Church, and the Polish shops. At the shops, I split off on my own and mingled in the tourists, pretending I was one of them.

I was nervous about the experiment, but within ten minutes, someone approached me in Russian.

"This is a good shop for electronic equipment . . . What are you looking for?"

I said, "*Spasibo* (Thank you)," but did not engage in a conversation. The stranger was an interviewer by the name of Izya, whom I would meet later in an entirely different setting. Izya said that he was from Kyiv and asked where I was from. I told him,

"Lviv Oblast, from a town called Kamianka."

I was telling the truth. I just did not mention that I had left Ukraine forty years ago.

Izya tried to keep the conversation going by talking about Lviv, a city he had visited, but being slightly suspicious, he planted a trick question. "You know, my favorite place in Lviv is the Lychakiv Cemetery. Have you ever been there?"

"Sure, I've been there." I had never been there but was aware of its existence. Izya sensed I was uncomfortable and said he spoke Ukrainian, so we switched languages. Next, he offered to accompany me to the other shops on the Esplanaden, at which point I vacillated.

"Maybe we could have coffee," Izya suggested.

I said, "I don't have time now, but maybe later."

He seemed to be pleased with the response because it was much easier to talk to me in a café than on the street.

As we parted, I saw him talk to another person, a colleague also working the group of tourists that had arrived in Copenhagen that morning. I strolled to the other shops, and, sure enough, within minutes, I was approached by two other interviewers trying to steer me into an interview situation. That is when I discovered that there were several interviewers all trying to make contact with other unsuspecting targets. They were fishing in a swimming pool packed with fish and knew that if the lure was right, sooner or later, they would get a bite.

Later that afternoon, I met Izya for coffee. He was nervous. Nevertheless, we talked about the war in Afghanistan. I told him that no one who fought in that country had ever won. If the Soviet Union continued to fight, it would come to a bad end. During the conversation, he skillfully inserted questions about radio listening. Based on my knowledge of Liberty's broadcasts, I provided him with the generic answers of an occasional listener to foreign radio. Izya paid for the coffee and sandwich, and we parted. Although he seemed happy with what I told him, I sensed he was wary.

That evening, Steen called a routine meeting of all of the Copenhagen interviewers to discuss the work in the port and distribute questionnaires. Halfway through the meeting, he said that he had a surprise—two visitors from headquarters in Paris. That is when Charlie and I made our appearance.

When Charlie introduced me, I heard a gasp from a few of the interviewers who had spotted me at the shops, most of all from Izya. He was flabbergasted to see that the man he had tried to interview earlier in the day turned out to be the surprise guest from Paris. Visibly ruffled, he told the group that he had suspected something was not quite right but couldn't put his finger on it. He was more concerned that I might have been a KGB plant and was ready to report it to Steen. Relieved to learn that I was not, he invited me to dinner the next day and related the episode to his friends and family.

The experiment worked better than expected. Not only did I get to observe firsthand how our interviewers worked, but the exercise also sent a strong message that they were being watched even in the most unexpected times and places.

ROUGHLY A DOZEN interviewers worked for Steen Sauerberg, some full time, others part time. Their backgrounds and personalities varied, and this created factions and petty jealousies. For the Soviet immigrant community in the city, these jobs were highly desirable because we paid well for a relatively limited amount of effort. Added to the government stipend, subsidized housing, and medical care they received as refugees, their standard of living was somewhere between ten and twenty times that of a middle-ranking Communist apparatchik in the Soviet Union.

Copenhagen seemed like an ideal operation. In fact, irregularities in the quality of the work, or friction between personalities, were simply part of the game. On my next trip, I was confronted by an internal feud. Six angry interviewers presented Steen with a list of grievances against Slava, one of the more eccentric interviewers. They claimed that he participated in black market activities, had unauthorized contacts with Soviet embassy personnel, and was deliberately provocative. According to them, he took photos of interviewers without their permission. The plaintiff group presented Steen with an ultimatum: Slava must go.

Dismissing an interviewer was no simple matter. He could cause problems and jeopardize the Copenhagen operation. The risk was not that the Danish intelligence services would learn of our interviewing. They knew what we were doing, and looked the other way. The problem was that most of the interviewers, as refugees, were granted a housing allowance provided they had no other source of income. If the authorities discovered that they had undeclared income, they would lose their allowance, and the conflict might attract undesirable publicity, something Steen wanted to avoid at all costs.

I advised him not to take any action until I had spoken with Slava. He agreed, and I spent the next day and a half with this intelligent and complicated character, trying to understand what was driving him to behave in this strange way. I did not mention work and tried to show him that I was his friend. Knowing that he was a military buff, I told him about my experience in the US Army, which seemed to break the ice. He then brought up the subject of the French Foreign Legion, explaining that he had been considering joining the elite French fighting force but did not know what the qualifications were. "Can you find out what they are?"

"I'll be happy to," I said, "as soon as I return to Paris."

During our time together, I discovered that Slava was a lonely man hiding behind an aggressive facade, an insecure boy seeking attention, recognition, and approval. He claimed he didn't need the money from interviewing and was planning to open up an electronics shop. At the same time, he threatened that if he was punished, he'd see that other interviewers were, too—he claimed that he had compromising evidence on other interviewers. Seeing I was dealing with a disturbed personality, I told him there was no need for a confrontation and that I would intercede on his behalf with Steen.

As soon as I returned to Paris, I sent Slava the requirements for enlisting in the French Foreign Legion: anyone aged between seventeen and forty, who was in good physical condition, and in possession of an identity card, could report to one of the posts of the French Foreign Legion. Knowledge of French was not obligatory: it could be picked up during service with the legion. The service contract was for five years, with the stipulation that after four and a half a legionnaire could apply for French citizenship.

I suspect that if Slava were a little younger, he would have jumped at the opportunity to join the legion, but as he was pushing forty, he changed his mind. Over the next few months, after Steen reduced Slava's quota, things were quiet. Slava kept to himself and stopped bothering other interviewers. A potentially explosive situation had been neutralized for the time being.

In June 1988, I flew to Copenhagen to explain how to administer a new set of complicated questions regarding the Soviet pullout from Afghanistan, attitudes toward *perestroika,* and the rise of informal groups in the USSR. As usual, the team gathered in Steen's apartment. To my surprise, I discovered that there was still a problem between Slava and other interviewers, particularly his former friend Volodia. From what I could gather, Slava had decided against joining the French Foreign Legion and, instead, opened up a chocolate shop in the Sudhavn district. Other interviewers noted that all of a sudden, Slava was driving around in a Mercedes SUV. When I confronted him about this, he explained that he needed it for his business and was able to write it off as a business expense.

At the same time, I learned that, recently, two Soviet sailors had walked into the electronics shop Bazaar II and complained about one of our interviewers, Volodia. They showed the owner a photo of Volodia and said, "This man is extremely anti-Soviet. If we see him around your shop, you will lose our business and goodwill."

According to other interviewers, the act was instigated by Slava. Everyone knew that there was bad blood between Slava and Volodia, one an insecure eccentric and the other an alcoholic. At times, Volodia came to Steen's staff meetings drunk. Still, most of the interviewers believed that Slava was back to his old tricks and that he had persuaded the sailors to complain about Volodia. Jan, in particular, came to Volodia's defense, saying he might have an alcohol problem, but he was honest.

WHILE IN COPENHAGEN, I quite often visited with Izya and Ada Lubinski. They were from Kyiv and bilingual, so I was able to converse with them in Russian or Ukrainian. Ada always put out a delectable table of Ukrainian dishes all chased down with *horilka.* Alexander Specter and on occasion others joined us.

During one of our conversations, I discovered that we had a common friend: Yakov Suslensky, a teacher in the Soviet Union, who had been a dissident demanding the right to emigrate to Israel before the Helsinki Accords were signed. For this, he was sentenced to seven years in the Vladimir prison for "spreading anti-Soviet literature with intent to undermine the Soviet regime."

Eventually, Suslensky did emigrate to Israel where he set up a Ukrainian-Jewish friendship group and published a journal on Ukrainian-Jewish relations called *Dialogues*.

I met Yakov on one of his visits to Paris. Prof. Aristid Virsta, a conduit in Paris who attracted all sorts of interesting people, introduced us. Yakov was on a tight budget and was looking for a place to stay, so I offered him a bed in my apartment. During the week he stayed with me, I got to know him well, and I shared his passion for improving Ukrainian-Jewish relations. The topic of relations between Ukrainians and the Jewish people had always been sensitive. Yakov, however, was convinced that it was a contrived issue concocted by Moscow to stir up animosity between Ukrainians and Jews. "It was a typical example of NKVD/KGB's strategy to divide and rule," Suslensky said.

If any discord between the two peoples existed, Moscow exaggerated it tenfold by portraying a perception of widespread strife and anti-Semitism. Such disinformation campaigns worked up to a point and they had the desired effect in the West, where the conflict between Ukrainians and Jews was accepted as conventional wisdom, especially among academic circles. Many intellectuals and influential people in the United States also swallowed the KGB propaganda, hook, line and sinker.

But when Jews began to leave the Soviet Union in large numbers, Soviet propaganda was countered by the likes of Suslensky, the Lubinskis, Specter, and many others, including a friend of our office in Israel, Avraam Shifrin, and the well-known Soviet dissident Natan Sharansky. The last two witnessed firsthand how the KGB tried to set up Jews against Ukrainians, and vice versa, in the Gulag. Suslensky and his group in Israel exposed such misperceptions. My friend, the late Leonid Plyushch, who was incarcerated in a psychiatric hospital for criticizing the Communist Party, always talked about the widespread use of "divide and conquer" tactics by the KGB. Suslensky also noted that the harshest sentences were meted out to Ukrainian dissidents, who received sentences up to twelve years imprisonment plus exile, compared to three to four-year sentences for Baltic, Armenian, and Georgian dissidents.

The KGB adopted new methods of repression in Ukraine which they then applied to nationalist and dissident groups in other Soviet republics.[90]

Apart from the difficulties with Slava, who threatened to destabilize our Copenhagen operation, work in the port proceeded smoothly. Copenhagen was one of our most productive interviewing points accounting for a large portion of our interviews with Soviet visitors. To show our appreciation for the years of excellent work of the Copenhagen team, we organized a banquet. With *perestroika* and *glasnost,* we were beginning to anticipate that changes in the Soviet Unions would eventually impact our work. In the summer of 1988, Gene Parta and Charlie Allen flew to Copenhagen to express gratitude for the team's work and perseverance. It was a grand celebration, and our intuition proved to be correct—in November 1988, the Soviets stopped jamming RL. It was the first sign that they had lost the propaganda war.

---

[90] Taras Kuzio, *Ukraine: Democratization, Corruption, and the New Russian Imperialism*, Praeger Security International (2015), page 124.

27. The Front in Athens

GREEK CRUISES OFFERED a rare opportunity for sun-hungry Soviets to visit the warm waters of the Mediterranean. Leaving Odesa, cruise ships sailed south along the western coast of the Black Sea toward the Bosphorus. After a stop in Istanbul, the vessels entered the Aegean Sea, sailing to the port of Piraeus next to Athens, where half of Greece's ten million inhabitants lived. For many of the Soviet tourists, the sprawling metropolis was the first and often the only sizable Western city they would get to visit in their lifetime. In addition, Athens offered numerous attractions, museums, and unique historic monuments.

In Piraeus, our team of Russian-speaking Greeks patiently waited for the arrival of Soviet cruise ships, ready to intercept tourists by the thousand. Year-round traffic made Piraeus an ideal spot to interview Soviet visitors.

Our man in Athens was Christophor Geleklidis, a Crimean Greek in his sixties. For convenience and, in some cases, security concerns, we referred to people in the field by a moniker or initials. Christophor's code name was Zorba, taken from the film *Zorba the Greek*. He was, however, a far cry from the character Anthony Quinn played, who was a colorful eccentric verging on mad. Although our man in Greece was colorful, he was responsible, methodical, and thorough.

Handsome and strongly built, his full head of graying hair gave Geleklidis an air of gravitas. He spoke Russian with a slight Ukrainian accent, replacing the harsh "g" with the softer "h." For example, he pronounced the Russian *ya govaryu* (I speak) as *ya hovaryu*. Geleklidis understood Ukrainian and could speak some.

Christophor was a Crimean Greek. Like Tatars and Ukrainians, the Greeks in Crimea were not well disposed toward Communist ideology, so Stalin decided to deport them *en masse* to Uzbekistan. In 1944, when he deported all the Crimean Tatars to Central Asia, he threw in seventy thousand Crimean Greeks for good measure. In a further wave of deportation, about one hundred thousand Pontic Greeks left for Central Asia in 1949.

Christophor was one of the few who managed to escape this fate. He joined the Ukrainian nationalist underground led by Bandera in the life-and-death struggle to combat the Bolshevik beast by collecting intelligence for OUN. Contrary to conventional wisdom, OUN's operations were not limited to Western Ukraine but included Central and parts of Southern Ukraine. Christophor supplied the OUN with intelligence after WWII until they were brutally suppressed. By this time, the organization, heavily infiltrated by the NKVD, went underground. At some point, Geleklidis, to stay alive, fled to Greece.

When he learned of my Ukrainian roots, he recounted with enthusiasm the days when he collaborated with the Ukrainian nationalists. An uncompromising anti-Communist, he often told me that he was Stepan Bandera's eyes and ears in southern Ukraine during WWII and after. In addition to being Bandera's intelligence operative, his task was counterintelligence, a job that included weeding out Soviet infiltrators who might have penetrated the OUN organization. Christophor told me the Bandera story on several occasions, each time with slight variations and embellishments. However, one of the lines that were indelibly etched in my mind because he repeated it so many times was *"Bandera byl krepkiy chelovek* (Bandera was a strong man) . . . And if the Ukrainians had had a hundred men like him, Ukraine would have been free a long time ago."

Christophor's description of Bandera had a ring of truth. During my teenage years, I was exposed to Bandera's legendary exploits. He was a Ukrainian patriot who reputedly possessed a will of steel. His words *krepkiy chelovek* reminded me of my senior scoutmaster in Chicago, Jaroslaw Rak, one of Bandera's close collaborators in Ukraine during WWII. *Pan Rak*, Mr. Rak, was an inspiring figure during my formative years. An OUN member, he was tried for participating in the 1934 assassination of Bronisław Pieracki, the interwar Polish minister of Interior. Arrested again by Germans in 1941, he was incarcerated in Auschwitz. I recall vividly the six-digit number tattooed on his left forearm, which he wore like a badge of valor. As teenagers, only a few of us had ever heard of Auschwitz or knew what that number meant.

Rak's only mission on this earth was to raise a new cadre of young Ukrainian-American leaders who would be able to replace the ranks of OUN activists decimated by the NKVD. He was convinced that the Soviet Union would someday collapse, and that the Ukrainian diaspora should prepare itself for that moment.

As a scoutmaster, *Pan Rak* was a tough disciplinarian. He would not tolerate character flaws or weaknesses. We were trained to be the vanguard, the future leaders and, as such, had to adhere to a strict code of conduct, including abstinence from smoking and drinking. This was tough, but anyone who deviated from this rule was expelled from the scout group. "We might be few, but we were the best and toughest," he would say. Through such stern discipline, many promising young boys were eliminated from the ranks of this elite group.

Rak took seriously the Spartan motto, "*V zdorovomu tili, zdorova dusha*" (A sound spirit, in a sound body). On the intellectual front, it included a sound grasp of Ukrainian history, geography, and the like. Physical training included sports, especially track and field, long-distance marches, outdoor camping, survival training, and appreciation of nature. At the time, much of this seemed like harassment, but later in life, I realized that these habits built character and paid dividends in pursuit of my professional careers.

The parallels between Christophor Geleklidis and Jaroslaw Rak were striking. Although Rak was ten years older than Geleklidis, both were staunch anti-Communists and associates of Bandera, who, at the end of WWII, ended up as refugees in the diaspora.[91] Their stories about their relationship with Bandera were uncannily similar, and my association with the two was one of the most unusual coincidences in my life.[92]

WITH THE ADVENT of perestroika in the mid-1980s, Soviet travel to the West increased significantly. Soviets allowed more of its "deserving" citizens to travel to the West as tourists in supervised groups. Thousands were allowed to either leave on cruises from Odesa to points south, or tour Western European cities around the Baltic Sea from Leningrad. At the same time, increased

---

[91]   In 1959, Bogdan Stashinsky, a KGB assassin, murdered Stepan Bandera with a poison gun in Munich. The book to read is *The Man with the Poison Gun*, by Serhii Plokhy (2016).

[92]   Thanks to Stefan Welhasch, I was able to confirm the story of Christophor's activities independently from former Prolog associates and archives.

funding led to an increased volume of interviewing. During this period, approximately 1985–1990, SAAOR's network of subcontractors employed up to sixty interviewers and conducted about 4,500–5,000 interviews a year. By late 1990, when it became possible to conduct the first surveys inside the USSR, over fifty thousand systematic interviews with travelers had been conducted.

Growth in Soviet tourism permitted a more representative sample, and with more data, it was possible to simulate Western sampling methodology and provide improved audience analysis numbers to our clients. In the process, we obtained a more realistic picture of public opinion in the Soviet Union.

I reveled in monitoring the operation in Athens. Every flight on Olympic Airways transported me back two and a half thousand years in time to a different world. If I left Paris in overcast weather, three hours later, I'd be in sunny Greece. During the early years, the operation in Athens was modest, essentially a one-man operation, but with increased Soviet traffic and additional funding the team grew from a handful of interviewers to eight by the end of the decade. Piraeus was a delicate operation, and Christophor had to be careful whom he hired. He spent a lot of time vetting the candidates before offering them a job, selecting only the most promising and reliable. Happily, the Athens team did not have the personality issues of the Copenhagen operation.

Christophor's right-hand man was Vanya, a medium-built, personable, and thoughtful man. I got to know his family well, since his wife, Angela, and his mother, both Russian speakers, also worked as interviewers. Whenever I visited them, they prepared a Central Asian feast *(pelmeni, chebureki,* and *plov)* accompanied by vodka. Despite the warm family atmosphere of these gatherings, work was work, and they knew why I had come to Athens. Once or twice a year, I flew to Greece to observe them at work. I was familiar with every member of the team from the questionnaires they submitted, so my visits were largely pro forma: to send a message that their work was valued.

A typical visit would begin with a call from Athens informing me that a Soviet tourist ship was going to arrive in Piraeus on a particular date. Christophor had access to the schedules of vessels arriving at the busy port, including date and type of ship. I would then coordinate the date of my arrival with the arrival of a Soviet vessel. If I miscalculated, I risked wasting a lot of time. Most of my trips to Athens took place during the tourist season from early spring to late fall, not a bad time to be in Greece.

Christophor's office on the third floor of a six-story office building next to Agia Triada Church had a bird's-eye view of the port of Piraeus. The sign on the door announced *Metafrastico Grafion, Import–Export,* and his stationery logo indicated *Chris Geleklidis: Bureau of Russian Translation and Research.*

Whenever I came to Athens, Christophor summoned his team of interviewers for a briefing at his office, announcing that a representative from the *shtabkvartira* (headquarters) in Paris had come to verify their work. When the team showed up, he revealed the name of the vessel and its expected time of arrival and then gave a rousing pep talk.

"Our work in Greece is very important. The quality of information we collect is vital. I understand that working in the summer may be hard, but every quote you get helps our people in Paris to paint the big picture, and if you do a good job, you will be rewarded with more interviews."

The mention of Paris always evoked a certain respect among interviewers, not only in Athens but also at all of our interviewing points. Next, he picked up his high-powered binoculars and pointed to the wharf where a ship had docked and announced:

"*Vot, smotrite tam, priyekhal korabl k dok-stantsiyi. Pashli rabotat*" (Look over there, the ship has docked, off to work you go).

Off they went to the port to contact as many Soviets as they could, and I followed to observe them work. Zorba's pep talk was simple but motivating. They understood the importance of the mission as only individuals who had passed their youth in Communist Central Asia could.

The cruise ship from Odesa discharged three hundred wretchedly dressed tourists. Soon they began to dribble out past the gates next to the port police station. From experience, our interviewers knew the exact trajectory the visitors would take, so they positioned themselves along the quay at strategic locations. There was only one way to proceed: left along the busy Miaoulis Avenue with its cafes, restaurants, and souvenir and electronics shops. They seemed to know intuitively that this was where to buy cheap electronic equipment and other sundry paraphernalia. As usual, our people positioned themselves discreetly in the souvenir shops and listened. At the right moment, an interviewer would approach a potential respondent and say,

"How pleasant to hear Russian spoken. *Vy Ruski?* (Are you Russian?)"

"No, I'm Armenian," a tourist might reply.

"That's interesting. I was in Yerevan once to visit the Armenian churches. I was born in Uzbekistan, but now I live in Athens."

Once an interviewer got the tourist's attention, the conversation might go in one of several directions. To entice a potential respondent into a conversation, the interviewer would either offer help with a purchase of a souvenir or provide information on public transport to Athens. Since the vast majority of the tourists traveled this far mainly to see the Acropolis, this was an easy way to hook a respondent. An interviewer might also offer him or her a small token, a postcard of the Acropolis or an invitation to a bar for coffee. If coffee didn't work, an interviewer might say,

"How about a glass of Greek wine? There's a bar next door. Living here, I don't get to speak Russian, and it would give me pleasure to talk to you. How about it? *Ya vas priglashayu* (I invite you, it's on me)."

Such an inducement often disarmed even a reluctant target. To Soviets who had mere pennies to spend on trinkets, even a glass of wine seemed expensive.

There were, of course, refusals. In Athens, they numbered between one-fifth and one-quarter of the attempts to make contact, depending on luck, circumstances, and the skills of the interviewer. The female interviewers in Athens were especially successful at establishing contact with hesitant respondents simply because they were perceived as less threatening.

On several occasions, I tried my hand at interviewing. Walking along the touristy Plaka, I overheard two young women speaking Russian. I smiled and introduced myself as a Canadian tourist who studied Russian in college and uttered an apology for my rusty Russian.

"No, your Russian is very good. We understand you very well," they said.

I continued the conversation—where are you from, how long will you be in Athens, the usual small talk. As we were strolling, they stopped at a souvenir shop to inspect copies of ancient Greek vases. They picked up a few, examined them, and looked at the prices.

"Oni ochen' dorogo stoyut" (They are very expensive).

I looked at the price tag, which was the equivalent of $3.50 for each vase, and asked, "Do you like them?"

"Yes, they would make a very nice souvenir to take back home to Rostov," they replied.

I took the vases they had chosen, went to the cashier, and paid the equivalent of seven dollars in drachmas and handed them the vases, *"Eto vam podarek ot Kanadejtsa"* (Consider this a gift from a Canadian).

Next, I invited them for refreshments, and they were mine for the next hour, which was more than enough time to pick their brains for information about their listening habits and views about Chernobyl and the war in Afghanistan. In fact, when I mentioned the Chernobyl accident, which had taken place only a few months before, they did not stop talking.

"Since the accident, we haven't trusted what our television tells us anymore. We know more from foreign radio than from our media."

Not all of Metafrastico Grafion's interviewers worked in the port. Some operated near the city's numerous historical monuments and museums. The Acropolis was by far the most important site every Soviet tourist wanted to see. It's a huge site, built during the apogee of artistic development in the fifth century BC, during Golden Age of Pericles, and contains the remains of the Parthenon. The Acropolis was easy pickings. Soviet tourists stood out like a sore thumb. Our people would place themselves either near the Parthenon or the Erechtheion caryatids, both offering opportunities to strike up a conversation.

The most natural way to engage a tourist was to stand beside him and casually ask a question such as "Do you know when the Acropolis was built?" or "Did you know that the caryatids in the porch of the Erechtheion were copies? What you see are replicas."

"Oh, really," an unsuspecting Soviet might respond.

"Yes, the originals are kept in the Acropolis museum."

"And where is the museum?"

And so on. "Where are you from? How do you like Greece?"

It was also possible to find Soviet tourists at the Byzantine Museum, the National Archeological Museum of Athens, and the pedestrian Plaka restaurant area. Given the opportunities to encounter Soviet tourists of various nationalities, the Athens interviewers had no trouble finding respondents, especially during the tourist season. With time, Athens became one of the most prolific interviewing points and stayed that way until the last days of the Soviet Union in 1991. From then on, *in situ* survey work in the various republics of the Soviet Union became possible.

Over the years, I had grown fond of our dedicated Greek "Cold War warriors." They were the mainstay of our southern front, a unique information-gathering operation that no one had been able to duplicate anywhere.

Early in 1989, Geleklidis sent a message that he would come to Paris. Although he didn't state the reason, we suspected that he wished to formally announce his retirement. Our office, after all, had been associated with him for over twenty years.

I picked up Christophor at Charles-De-Gaulle airport at 5:00 p.m. and took him directly to his hotel. The next day, he showed up in our office with a one-kilo can of black Beluga. The caviar was the highlight of the reception we gave for him, along with French *hors d'oeuvres* and fine French wine.

Christophor also met with his old friend Max Ralis, the previous director of SAAOR, who lived in Orleans, 120 kilometers from Paris. Max had been ill, so I drove Geleklidis to Orleans. Both men were past seventy and gave me the impression that they preferred talking about their relationships with women rather than their information-gathering work. It probably made them feel young. Occasionally, they made a quick reference to work and then went back to reliving the good times in the cabarets and restaurants with Greek music.

Soon after Christophor retired, the management of the Athens operation was taken over by Madame Mouzaki of the marketing research firm Opinion Limited. The Athens team argued that they did not need an intermediary to supervise their work. The times, however, were changing. Eventually, the management of our operation passed almost entirely to Opinion Limited.

This was also a time of transition, and we began to explore the possibility of doing in-country polling, cautiously at first, and then full steam ahead. That was when I had to perform the difficult task of informing our institutes that we no longer needed their services. I was especially concerned about our team in Athens because their entire livelihood depended on interviewing. My last trip there was a sad affair. I tried to soften the blow by referring them to commercial marketing research outfits, but there was no way of avoiding the fact that we were entering a new era. A quarter of a century of unique media and opinion research had come to an end.

28. Interviewing Emigrants in Rome and Israel

SAAOR CONDUCTED two kinds of interviewing projects—the so-called "travelers' survey," and surveys of recent emigrants from the Soviet Union. Of the two, the travelers' survey was by far the bigger project, and the mainstay of audience and opinion research for our clients. Interviews with emigrants were done almost exclusively with Jews exiting the Soviet Union.

Emigrant surveys were less representative of the population of the USSR than the travelers' survey, and their opinions were deemed less objective than the views of visitors and travelers. Emigrant responses were often tainted by bitter memories of the Soviet Union. Still, they yielded valuable information and were used to corroborate the findings of visitors' surveys.

In 1975, the Soviet Union signed the Helsinki Accords on human rights, where, among other things, the Soviets agreed to grant Jews the right to leave the USSR. Over the years, hundreds of thousands of Soviet Jews and a few Soviet Germans became a new source of data for Western scholars. The number of Jewish emigrants peaked in 1979 when fifty thousand left the Soviet Union. Two-thirds of them opted for a destination other than Israel. During the next few years, when the US Congress failed to ratify the SALT II treaty, and refused to grant the USSR a most favored nation trade status, the Soviet authorities began to reduce the number of exit visas. They dropped precipitously from twenty-one thousand in 1980 to under a thousand in 1984. That figure remained stationary for two years. But a year after I joined SAAOR, in 1986, the volume of emigrant traffic started to increase noticeably.

Early on, Vienna was the first stop for all Jews exiting the USSR. There they were greeted by representatives of the Jewish Agency for Israel (JAFI) and the Hebrew Immigrant Aid Society (HIAS). Those going to Israel were assisted by JAFI and flown to Israel, and those destined for the United States and other locations were transferred to Rome, where they were processed by HIAS personnel.

In the 1970s and again in the late 1980s, more than 250,000 Soviet Jewish emigrants passed through Ladispoli, a resort town west of Rome, on their way to North America or to Israel. The town served as a visa-processing way-station for Jews streaming out of the Soviet Union by the planeload. Like many resort towns, Ladispoli was busy during the summer and largely empty the rest of the year. HIAS took advantage of this to house emigrants before they were sent to the United States or Israel. As the number of emigrants swelled, backlogs developed, and the time between their arrival in Rome and the HIAS interview grew to a month. By the summer of 1989, the overall processing time for some emigrants took up to three months. The backlog worked to our advantage because the longer the emigrants stayed in Ladispoli, the more time our people had to locate and interview respondents.

Although not representative of the general population of the USSR, Soviet emigrants provided a wealth of information for international broadcasters and other clients. As indicated in chapter 24, we were the only organization systematically collecting data on availability and prices of food and other products.[93]

In contrast to traveler surveys, most emigrant interviews were conducted openly. Still, there was some resistance to being interviewed. We believed it was best to interview them as soon as they "got off the boat," and this required considerable skill on the part of the interviewer. Years of life in the Soviet Union had conditioned these new arrivals to be suspicious and fearful, and many were reluctant to talk to strangers. With that in mind, we had established two interviewing points that dealt exclusively with emigrants: Rome and Israel.

---

[93]   SAAOR's interviewing project with emigrants is discussed in the book *The Last Warrior: Andrew Marshall and the Shaping of Modern American Defense Strategy*, by Andrew Krepinevich and Barry Watts. Basic Books (2015), pp 174–75.

ROME HAD BEEN AN ONGOING operation since the mid-1970s. In 1975, the Soviet Union signed the Helsinki Accords on human rights, where, among other things, they agreed to grant Jews the right to leave the USSR. With a mass exodus of hundreds of thousands of Soviet Jews and some Soviet Germans out of the Soviet Union, a new source of data became available to Western scholars. During this period, colleagues from the Paris office monitored the work in Rome. Later, as the number of emigrants began to increase, I became the principal liaison. I traveled to Rome as often as the situation required, sometimes several times a year.

Each landing at Leonardo da Vinci–Fiumicino Airport on the coast between Ladispoli and Ostia stirred my imagination. The moment I entered the boundaries of the Eternal City, I was transported to a different era of history. When the bus turned onto the Viale delle Terme di Caracalla, I got a glimpse of the colossal ruins of Caracalla Baths, a vast rectangular-shaped Roman thermal bath complex used during the last three centuries of the Roman Empire. After passing the Circo Massimo, the bus skirted the imposing elliptical-shaped Coliseum. In a matter of minutes, I got a glimpse of three of ancient Rome's most impressive historical sites.

Rome is one of those old cities where it's difficult to orient oneself. The city is a labyrinth of short narrow streets and random piazzas lacking obvious points of reference. Its great advantage, however, is that the center is compact, making walking easy, and I always carried a detailed map. From the Termini railway terminal, I would take a taxi to the Hotel Caprice near Via Veneto, where I usually stayed.

Our contact in Rome was Elena, who worked for HIAS, and helped us contact émigrés on a freelance basis. My meetings with her usually took place either at the hotel or the Café Greco on the Via Condotti, a stone's throw from Piazza di Spagna and the Spanish Steps. Elena acted as our liaison. Although the work was not as sensitive as in Copenhagen or Athens, Rome posed a number of challenges. It was difficult to persuade potential respondents to participate in an interview, and SAAOR had no formal standing or representation in Rome, which made it difficult to get around official structures without drawing attention to our operation.

Elena was a native Roman, and I usually met her after working hours in some restaurant or café only Romans patronized. She kept us abreast of the level of emigrant traffic in Rome and helped us find qualified Russian-speaking interviewers willing to interrogate arrivals in Ladispoli. Whenever she found suitable candidates, someone from Paris flew to Rome to check them out. Although there were some security concerns, our research in Rome was not as sensitive as our work with Soviet visitors, and it was no secret that emigrants in Ladispoli were being interviewed about their media use habits. The problem was that emigrant interviewers did not stay long, so we were always searching for new ones.

Fortunately, nearly all of the emigrants were located in Ladispoli, a resort that had been popular since Roman times. The triangle of Rome, Ladispoli, and Ostia/Fiumicino roughly defined the perimeter of operations where I worked during the dying years of the Soviet Union.

For a while, things seemed to be going smoothly—I flew to Rome, met with Elena, observed interviews in Ladispoli, and returned to Paris. Then in the spring of 1987, we ran into an unexpected obstacle. Our work had come to the attention of HIAS, who disapproved of our contacts with the emigrants. Interviewers in Ladispoli had been instructed not to interview emigrants. As soon as I learned of the problem, I rushed to Rome to meet with HIAS. If the problem was not fixed quickly, the Rome operation, an extremely rich source of information for radio-listening data and background reports, would be in jeopardy.

I met with a Ms. Heller, director of HIAS, on June 20, 1987, when she was transferring out of the organization. She introduced me to her successor designate, Merle Rosenberg. The meeting was tense. I tried to explain in general terms what our work entailed. They listened politely but replied that their superiors at the Joint American Distribution Committee in New York did not approve of our work. To complicate things, the rabbi of Rome was also negatively disposed to our activities in Ladispoli. I surmised that, because of the low profile our interviewers kept in Ladispoli, neither HIAS, Joint in New York, nor the rabbi in Rome had a complete picture of our activities. I put our interviewing operation on temporary hold and began working through back channels to try to get clearance from higher-ups in New York.

After I had reported the crisis to management in Paris, we developed a three-pronged strategy to overcome the setback. The tactic required time and diplomacy, and we needed to enlist the help of several players who could pull strings on our behalf. As a first step, I asked Sasha Avrasian, one of our interviewers in Rome who knew the rabbi, to intervene on our behalf, which he did. With a better understanding of the nature of our work, the rabbi tepidly gave his OK, while skeptically adding that he did not see much value in what we were doing.

We also contacted a man with ties to HIAS in Vienna, Leon Hendler. On my next trip to Vienna, I met with Leon at the venerable Cafe Central, a place with a fascinating history. In the late nineteenth century, it was a key meeting place of Viennese intellectuals and political personalities including Sigmund Freud, Adolf Hitler, Vladimir Lenin, and Leon Trotsky. When Victor Adler, an Austrian politician and founder of the Social Democratic Workers' Party told Count Berchtold, foreign minister of Austria-Hungary, that war would provoke a revolution in Russia, Berchtold replied, "And who will lead this revolution? Perhaps Mr. Bronstein (Leon Trotsky) sitting over there at the Café Central?"

Leon Hendler told me he would talk to a few people who might be able to help, but because politics at HIAS could be tricky, he did not promise results. At the same time, Gene Parta had the idea of contacting Ben Wattenberg, a member of the Board for International Broadcasting (BIB), the Radio oversight commission, and asking him to call Mr. Goldman of Joint in New York. For the next few months, we waited to see if the steps we had taken would lead to a resolution.

The uncertain situation with HIAS obliged us to suspend all interviewing in Ladispoli for six months. By the end of the year, Merle Rosenberg of HIAS informed me that we had permission to resume work in Ladispoli. By then, however, we did not have any reliable interviewers left. In the past, we had employed emigrants who stayed in Ladispoli for a few months, but, sooner or later, they all left for Israel and New York. We needed individuals who had a good command of Russian and lived permanently in the Rome area.

Between June 1987 and July 1988, I traveled to Rome five times to try to salvage the operation. I contacted Mauro and Luigi, Italians I had met while attending a Russian-language immersion course in Madonna di Campiglio, and interviewed several emigrant candidates. Most seemed excited, and a few did some interviewing, but for one reason or another—mainly inadequate work—none of them panned out. Even though we were offering 50,000 lire per interview, there were no serious long-term takers. Frustrated, I went to Rome in January 1988 and met with Elena in the hope of developing a plan to recruit new interviewers. Instead, Elena told me that she had decided to resign her position as director of the Rome operation.

"I do not see much point in continuing this work. It's not a question of money. I've been thinking about it for the past year. I no longer get satisfaction from this work, and, besides, after the close call last June, I do not wish to jeopardize my position at HIAS."

I told her I was sorry to see her go, "but I respect your decision. In the future, please let's stay in touch."

OVER THE YEARS, we had developed a network of friendly contacts including Carol Boren-Fellinzi at Radio Vatican and Don Sergio Mercanzin of the *Centro Russia Ecumencia* (Russian Ecumenical Center). Don Sergio referred me to another person open to our work, Monsignor Ivan Dacko, protopresbyter to the then Ukrainian cardinal Myroslav Liubachivsky. All were aware that we were looking for Russian-speaking candidates to help us with interviewing in Ladispoli.

After Elena resigned, I thought it a good idea to get in touch with Monsignor Ivan Dacko, whom I had gotten to know on earlier visits to Rome. We met in a lovely restaurant/café on the attractive Piazza della Madonna dei Monti, the square where the Cardinal resided, and over a delicious pasta amatriciana in a sauce of fresh tomatoes, chopped bacon, onion, and garlic, I had a great chat with the monsignor. A dedicated priest, personable and conscientious, it was evident that he enjoyed his assignment in Rome. We talked about art, history, and politics, and after a bottle of fine Barolo, he confessed that his relationship with the cardinal was exasperating. It seemed that the monsignor was more interested in unloading his frustrations with the Cardinal than helping me find interviewers for Ladispoli. He told me stories about the Cardinal's eccentric behavior that even today I hesitate to disclose, but in the interest of historical truth, I will mention one somewhat amusing incident.

Monsignor Dacko said that when he needed the cardinal's immediate decision, he entered the cardinal's quarters without knocking. To his astonishment, one day, he caught the cardinal watching *Bugs Bunny* and *Donald Duck* cartoons on Italian television and was told to come back later. Perhaps this was his way of unwinding. Later, Cardinal Liubachivsky was instrumental in the rebirth of the Catholic Church in Ukraine, and presided over the reestablishment of the church structure and regular eparchies.

In short, I learned a lot about the state of the Ukrainian Catholic Church and intrigues in the cardinal's office, but left without any leads. I was getting desperate. Rome/Ladispoli was crucial to our research efforts, and we needed to find someone quickly.

In March 1988, I got an urgent call from Don Sergio saying I must come to Rome as soon as possible—he had found the perfect candidate: Larissa, a

Moscow-born Russian, married to an Italian. Larissa was inquiring about a part-time job at the center. I flew to Rome at once.

Don Sergio introduced me to Larissa in his office, and we agreed to meet later that evening at Tucci's, a restaurant facing the Three Fountains on the Piazza Navona, a splendid ensemble of beautiful and fanciful sculptures by Bernini. It had to be one of the most charming settings for dinner in all of Italy. Larissa, an attractive buxom Russian in her midthirties, told me she was officially married to an Italian impresario, but they were living apart. She said that in Moscow, she was an actress, and to begin with, because of her gestures and manner of speech, I doubted her sincerity. "Slava, your Russian is wonderful, so melodious. It gives me such pleasure to talk to you. You have traveled so much and have a phenomenal grasp of history. It would be a pleasure working with you."

I spoke Russian with a softer Ukrainian accent, but my command of the language was far from perfect. Obviously, she wanted the job so badly she would say or do anything to get hired. I was not sure whether she needed the work to supplement her income, or if she was working as a KGB go-between trying to learn what we were up to in Rome. We knew the KGB was aware of our work in Paris, Rome, and Ladispoli, and this could have been an attempt to penetrate our network. As we were leaving the restaurant, she looked alluringly into my eyes and suggested a nightcap at her apartment.

Knowing that such a move would be risky, I said, "I very much enjoyed talking to you, Larissa, and think you could do the job, but I have to speak to my superiors in Paris. I will get back to you through Don Sergio." Then in one last attempt to seduce me, she tried to kiss me on the lips. I gave her a polite peck on both cheeks and bid her good night. An inner voice told me that in the long run, she would spell trouble. "Hell hath no fury like a woman scorned."

Larissa was insincere, a bit strident, and excessively flamboyant, but I had no evidence of her being a KGB plant until I met with Carol Boren-Fellinzi the following Monday. Carol informed me in confidence that one of her Czech colleges had learned from a trusted friend in Budapest that Larissa was suspected of working for the other side. The friend in Budapest was involved in the covert book program, and apparently anyone who had any dealings with Larissa was discovered and denounced. That was all I needed to know.

In the summer of 1988, there was a significant influx of emigrants from the Soviet Union. Even though most were going to Israel, HIAS in Rome was overwhelmed. All we had in Ladispoli was a skeleton crew of interviewers with no one to supervise their work on a permanent basis. By this time, Jews were not the only emigrants. The Soviets were releasing Armenians and persecuted religious minorities such as the *Piatydesyatnyki,* Ukrainian Pentecostal Christians. In early July, I made yet another trip to Rome to deal with the swell of new arrivals and got to know a group of Ukrainian Pentecostalists who had amazing stories to tell about their harassment and persecution by Communist authorities who saw them as a threat.

THE WEEKEND I ARRIVED in Rome, I experienced three of the strangest synchronistic moments of my life. First, masses of Ukrainians from all over the world converged on Rome to commemorate the one-thousandth anniversary of Christianity in Ukraine. In 988, Prince Volodymyr the Great accepted Christianity from Byzantium, one of the most important events in the history of Ukraine. On Saturday, Pope John Paul II, the first Slavic Pope, addressed nearly ten thousand Ukrainian pilgrims in the Vatican Square, condemning the continuing religious persecution in Ukraine. Then, on Sunday, July 10, when I attended the Pontifical Mass celebrating the millennium at Saint Peter's Basilica, I glanced at the back of the basilica to see if I recognized anyone, and by sheer luck, I spotted Dr. George Kuzycz and Dr. George Baranowski, two old colleagues and friends from my Chicago days. George Baranowski and I were *kumy*—I was his daughter Natalia's godfather, and he was godfather to my daughter Tamara. I hadn't seen the Baranowskis for ten years. We spent the entire afternoon and the next day catching up. More than a quarter of a century has elapsed since that meeting, and even though in the '70s we were the best of friends, we have never met or spoken since.

On Monday, I went to Ladispoli to meet with two interviewers, and while walking down the Via Regina Elena, I bumped into a group of French-Ukrainian friends from Paris who had come to Rome for the millennium celebrations. They were as surprised to see me as I was them. Zirka Vitushynska asked what I was doing in Ladispoli.

Telling them why I was there would have led to questions I was unwilling to respond to, so I improvised. "I came to see the ruins of Ostia and decided to make a detour to see Ladispoli, so here I am."

They were perplexed by my answer but let it pass. Subsequently, however, every time I came across them in Paris at the Café Bonaparte on Sundays, they brought up our accidental meeting in Ladispoli with a smile and a twinge of sarcasm. I never found out what they thought I was doing in Ladispoli.

Two months after this encounter, I was back in Rome. Carol Boren-Fellinzi of Radio Vatican telephoned to say that she had found the perfect candidate to supervise our work in Ladispoli. The lead looked promising, so I hopped on the first plane to Rome to meet with Yuri Stern.

Yuri struck me as an intelligent and charming man. He had a head of wavy blond hair and hazel eyes. He met Gabriella Barcucci in Leningrad when she was working on her advanced degree in Russian literature at Leningrad State University. Ironically, her scholarship was funded by the Italian Communist Party, but it did not take her long to realize what life in the Communist paradise was really like. Yuri, a dissident who detested Communists, courted Gabriella and persuaded her that the only way he would ever get to see Italy was if she married him, so she did.

In Italy, the couple settled in a sparsely-furnished modern apartment in Santa Marinella overlooking the Tyrrhenian Sea, some thirty kilometers north of Ladispoli. They lived a Spartan life on Yuri's modest income from the guided tours he organized for emigrants and Gabriella's small student stipend, but Gabriella was happy to be with Yuri, and he was ecstatic to breathe the free air of Italy.

My priority was to make sure Yuri was not a KGB informer. Russians who did not leave the USSR on an emigrant visa were suspect, and our policy was to vet them thoroughly. To that end, I spent a weekend getting to know him and Gabriella. Yuri knew the vagaries of the Russian/Soviet mentality well; he would know how to deal with the émigrés. Once I was convinced that he was not working for the KGB, I offered him an interviewing position in Ladispoli. If the couple was going to supervise the Ladispoli operation, they needed some sort of a front, and since Gabriella had Italian working papers, I recommended that they set up a translation bureau. Thus was born Barcucci Translations.

All was going well until Yakov, a strongheaded interviewer in Ladispoli, decided that Yuri was a threat, and began to complain directly to us that he did not need to be supervised and that Yuri was pocketing a large fee for doing nothing. It was a clash of personalities, and one of them had to go. I replaced Yakov with Igor, and the Rome operation got more or less back on track. Igor, a full-time HIAS employee, kept us informed about the level of emigrant traffic in Ladispoli, which facilitated our work considerably.

After a year in limbo, I had finally managed to rebuild a team that might work out on a permanent basis. Stern, because of his touring business, was a familiar personality in Ladispoli and had a good relationship with HIAS. He took over the supervision of the operation and stayed with us until we stopped interviewing emigrants in Rome and Ladispoli in 1991.

SAAOR INTERVIEWED emigrants in Israel too, though on a smaller scale. It was an operation handled by Gene Parta and Charlie Allen, so I was not directly involved with it. The interviewing was managed by Elenora Shifrin, the wife of Avraam Shifrin, a former Soviet dissident and political prisoner, with whom I had a lot in common. Eventually, the operation was taken over by Ariel Cohen, a young law student and journalist who arrived in Israel in 1976 with his parents from the Russian city of Saratov. Members of his family were Jewish activists and *refuseniks*.[94]

During the 1980s, the Shifrins and Ariel Cohen recruited, trained, and managed over a dozen interviewers in Israel. Although I reviewed the Israeli questionnaires on a regular basis, I never got the opportunity to travel to Israel. My hands were full with problems in Rome and other locations.

---

[94] Ariel Cohen eventually settled in the United States, obtained his PhD in Russian and Soviet studies from the Fletcher School of Law and Diplomacy at Tufts University, and became a senior fellow at the Heritage Foundation in Washington and later at the Atlantic Council. More recently, he became a commentator on Fox News.

29. Operations in Paris and Vienna

IN ADDITION TO COPENHAGEN, Athens, and Rome, I was responsible for liaising with institutes in Paris, Vienna, Brussels, Berlin, Hamburg, and New York. Paris and Vienna were medium-sized operations, while the others were relatively small. There were several interviewing points that were not part of my brief—Helsinki, Tokyo, and Singapore.

The modus operandi in all of these locations was identical. Mostly, though not exclusively, we worked through a marketing research organization that employed a handful of Russian-speaking interviewers tasked with finding and interviewing as many Soviet visitors as feasible. Although the research institutes supervised and checked the interviewers' work, they were essentially a go-between the interviewers and SAAOR. We paid the institutes for interviews completed, and the institutes, in turn, paid the interviewers. Although there were a few "lone wolves" in Paris, we discouraged direct contact with our office.

For some years before I came on board, the Paris operation was an assortment of one-interviewer institutes supervised by Charlie and others. I inherited the task of coordinating the work of these disparate individuals and finding new interviewers. Sondage Service was a one-woman operation run by Anne-Danièle, a mature Russian-speaking French lady. In July 1989, she mentioned in a letter she wrote me that she'd been with our office for twenty-five years, which meant that Max Ralis must have hired her in 1964. Over the years, she had developed valuable contacts that allowed her access to Soviet cultural and entertainment groups, dance ensembles, and musicians who came to Paris. In addition, she traveled to other parts of France and found

Soviet tourists in places like Nice, Marseilles, and Cannes. By the late '80s, despite suffering from diabetes, she was doing twenty interviews per month. Her contribution to our research was inestimable.

Anne-Danièle was expensive, probably our most expensive interviewer, and she was always demanding more, to cope with family problems and serious health issues. Because of her length of service, she reported directly to our office, and I met with her periodically to discuss her work. Like Charlie before me, I sometimes found my meetings with her long and frustrating.

Another small research operation employed a cryptic individual by the name of Valery, who had access to Soviet diplomatic and business circles in Paris. Although a good interviewer, he was difficult to control. For months, he would be unreachable, and then he stopped interviewing altogether. He was replaced by another interviewer, a former Soviet, Aline.

Quick and energetic, Aline tended to interview the same kinds of people, mostly Russians with higher education. Her interviews were acceptable, but I constantly had to remind her that we were interested in more mixed demographics. She told me once that she felt isolated in her work. I wasn't surprised—it was a lonely job.

We also engaged a German-Ukrainian journalist working in France, Kateryna Horbatch. Her brief was to coordinate the work of several interviewers who were obsessed with secrecy and insisted on remaining anonymous at all costs. They trusted Kateryna, who set up a bureau called Agence H to supervise their work. These paranoid interviewers—one of whom was my Serb friend Srjan Raščovic—were sure that SAAOR was on the KGB's radar. This was a time when we were beginning to do focus groups and panel reviews on a larger scale, and Agence H was instrumental in finding candidates and organizing them.

To enhance our Paris network, I was constantly on the lookout for new interviewers. Most of our candidates came to us through referrals, but, at times, I made forays to strange places to find them. There were plenty of Russian-speaking immigrants in Paris, the only question was where to find them and, more importantly, whom to trust.

MY ARTIST FRIEND Volodymyr Makarenko had picked up the *banya* habit in Estonia, where the Finnish sauna was popular, and I sometimes accompanied him. In Paris, he liked to attend the Turkish bathhouse, Hammam Saint Paul, on Rue des Rosiers in the Marais district, where male Soviet émigrés congregated. They liked this bathhouse because it resembled the ones in the Soviet Union. It was large, with at least one Finnish-style sauna, and another room where sauna-goers beat each other with leafy birch twigs. There was also a Turkish wet sauna, a massage room next to the cold-water pool, a shower, and a relaxation area.

Going to the *banya* took up at least half a day and provided opportunities to meet Russian-speaking men. Between rounds of dry and wet saunas, the Russians retired to a cafeteria/restaurant, where most of the socializing took place, and any weight lost from the hours of sweating was quickly put back on with rounds of vodka toasts to better health and *zakuski,* hors d'oeuvres.

Although I got to speak a lot of Russian, I was not there for the socializing. My aim was to find and recruit eligible interviewers who might be interested in working for us. One of the contacts I established at the *banya* was a writer/poet who went by the pen name Khvost. He introduced me to other contacts and the network grew, though I must confess that the results of my efforts were meager. I found more candidates by chance or through friends and acquaintances.

Working with such a diverse group of individuals was challenging, and meeting them individually was time consuming. They were always dissatisfied with the interview quota, the honorarium, the formulation of questions, and other issues. Often, I spent more time listening to their personal problems and health concerns than going over their work. At times, I felt more like a therapist than a researcher.

As I mentioned, the Paris interviewers were a suspicious lot. Some of them were convinced they were being monitored by the KGB, so we never met in the office. Usually, I chose cafes and restaurants in different parts of Paris, often in the Latin Quarter in the vicinity of Place Saint-André-des-Arts or the 9th arrondissement near the Opera. I also met contacts in the Marais district at La Tartine on Rue de Rivoli, a café that Lenin frequented when he moved to Paris in December 1908. (He disliked Paris immensely, lambasting it as "a foul hole.")

La Tartine was a working man's café that had been around for a hundred years. It was a far cry from voguish cafés such as Les Deux Magots or Le Select. La Tartine's food was simple and cheap. I loved their *jambon de Bayonne* on *pain de campagne* consumed with a *demi* of beer followed by an espresso. Purportedly, this is where Lenin used to meet Inessa Armand, a French Russian Bolshevik feminist with whom he had an affair. In 1911, she became secretary for the Committee established to coordinate all the Bolshevik groups in Western Europe.

On one occasion, one of our female interviewers remarked, "How strange that we are meeting at La Tartine to plot the demise of the Soviet Union in the same place where Lenin plotted to create it."

Although we were not what fiction writers would describe as a "cloak and dagger" operation, at times, it felt like it. More than once, an interviewer showed up for a meeting fearful that he or she was being followed. In those cases, we moved to another location to lose the tail, assuming there was one. These hide-and-seek games got exasperating, but because I could never be certain if what the interviewer felt was true or imaginary, I had to play along. Considering that we were working in a Cold War environment, it was plausible that we could have been a target of interest for the KGB.

It was not an efficient way to work, and corrective steps were needed. Toward the end of the decade, we consolidated our Paris operation under one umbrella organization, an established marketing research organization, Institut Français de Demoscopie. We paid them a little more than the going rate of 800 FF per interview, but it was worth it. I ended up dealing with a single competent professional, Anne Endress, an attractive young lady who saved me tons of time, and was a pleasure to work with. By September 1990, Demoscopie employed five interviewers. By that time, it was possible to do in-country interviewing, and we gradually began winding down our operations in Western Europe.

MY EFFORTS TO RECRUIT new interviewers brought me into contact with a variety of colorful characters whose stories demonstrated the extent to which Soviet citizens were willing to go to leave the "Socialist paradise." On one occasion, I met with George T., a young man who jumped ship at Le Havre. A champion swimmer who hated Communism, he decided to reach Western Europe any way he could. He told me his story when I met him in a café near the office of *Russkaya Mysl*, the Russian-language newspaper in Paris, which reported this episode in January 1986.

"I hid in a storage compartment near the ship's engine for ten days," he said, "with next to nothing to eat or drink. When I heard the engines stop, I knew the ship had arrived in a Western port, which turned out to be Le Havre. During the night I made my way to the deck and jumped into the cold water. I was utterly exhausted, and, for a while, I thought I would drown, but my desire for freedom was so strong that I reached the shore, where I asked to be taken to the nearest police station to request asylum."

George T.'s story was not unique. A few of those who jumped ship even became our interviewers. Still, other means of leaving the Soviet Union involved a *mariage blanc,* a marriage whose only purpose was to get to the West.

Anton Solomoukha, my artist friend, once introduced me to Lilya Ohienko-Olivier, a Ukrainian filmmaker from Kyiv. Tall, statuesque, and slightly dreamy, Lilya divorced her Russian husband to marry Thierry Olivier, a sympathetic and refined Frenchman she met in Moscow. I got to know Lilya quite well. Most of her life she spoke Russian, so her Ukrainian was halting, but she was very proud of her noble Ukrainian roots. Her linguist grandfather, Ivan Ohienko, was the church historian and Ukrainian Orthodox Metropolitan who translated the Bible into Ukrainian vernacular.

Although she was not interested in interviewing herself— she wanted to keep her Soviet passport for family reasons—Lilya was well connected in the Russian émigré community and introduced me to several of her trusted Russian-speaking friends who might be interested in interviewing, including Dimitri Vasilyevich and Andrey Volkonsky, a descendant of Prince Volkonsky.

Another interesting but sad case was Oksana. The librarian at the Symon Petlyura Library in the 19th arrondissement referred her as a potential candidate for a focus group or panel review. I met Oksana, a slim blonde around thirty, and heard her distressing story. She got out of the Soviet Union by marrying a midlevel Congolese diplomat in Kyiv. She did not love him, but, to leave Soviet Ukraine, she had a child with him. She ended up in the Congo, living in a primitive shack with no plumbing. Eventually, her husband was posted to Paris, where they lived in low-rent housing, sharing an apartment with other families who, in her words, "barely knew how to use a toilet."

One cold January day, Oksana recounted, the heating system in the housing project stopped working. To stay warm, the *dykuny* (the Ukrainian word for "savages") that she lived with gathered some scrap wood and built a bonfire in the middle of the living room, nearly setting the premises on fire. After this incident, she decided to seek help in the Ukrainian community. We had her participate in a focus group where she made a little money. Such was the price many Ukrainian women paid to obtain freedom.

ON MY FIRST TRIP TO VIENNA, in May 1987, I met Helmut Aigner, owner of Intora Absatz Marktforschung, a medium-sized marketing research firm that employed a relatively large number of interviewers, most of whom worked on audience research projects with Eastern Europeans for Radio Free

Europe. Visitors from the Soviet Union were less common in Vienna, but they were there. Aigner engaged six Russian-speaking interviewers to work on our projects, a mix of Bulgarians, Ukrainians, and Poles. Although the Vienna operation had been around for a while, the interviewers there required quite a bit of supervision.

I got to know a few of the Vienna interviewers quite well. A Russian-speaking Bulgarian couple, Brusov and Katja, were the best of the lot. Maria, a middle-aged Ukrainian soprano in the choir of the Ukrainian Catholic Church of Saint Barbara, was another. Maria interviewed primarily Western Ukrainians who showed up at the lovely church on Postgasse. They were a useful addition to our sample. On one Sunday, after High Mass at Saint Barbara's, Maria arranged a meeting with two male visitors from Western Ukraine and suggested that I join them in a nearby café. Over coffee and torte, she elicited feedback about their radio-listening habits. One of them said:

"Radio Liberty gives us facts about our history and information about the world that we never get from Soviet media. Thanks to them, we know about the Ukrainian genocide, which, by the way, was not limited to 1932 and 1933 but encompassed the 1930s and 1940s. We know about the executions, the starvation, and the mass deportations of Ukrainians after the war. The station gives us hope."

Both respondents volunteered anecdotal information about changes in Soviet Ukraine. I clearly recall the engineer's words: "Life in Ukraine has improved markedly. Today the villagers may slaughter pigs they have raised with no repercussions. In the past, killing a pig for personal consumption was a punishable offense." This implied a loosening of the State's iron grip over the agricultural sector, and indicated that important changes were taking place in Ukraine.

In Vienna, I spent much of my time meeting with interviewers and observing interviewing in such diverse places as cafés along the Kartnerstrasse, and on Mexikoplatz, with its numerous shops catering to tourists from Eastern Europe. Another area that teemed with Soviet tourists was the pedestrian streets between Stephansdom and the Opera, where contact was easy but finding a place to take an interview was not.

Between meetings with Aigner and the interviewers, I used my spare time to visit some of Vienna's famed landmarks and museums. Intora's office was on Hadikgasse, not far from Schloss Schönbrunn, the summer palace of the Hapsburg monarchs. Every chance I got, I strolled through the grounds gardens of the palace on my way to the Belvedere, the ornate baroque palace that housed the world's largest collection (twenty-four paintings) of Gustav Klimt's works.

Klimt had been one of my favorite artists since I was first exposed to his works in 1983, when the Centre George Pompidou hosted a magnificent exhibit of his paintings titled *La Décadence Joyeuse*. I spent hours deciphering the symbolism buried in his works. The theme of Klimt's work was prophetic: decadence in a lavish and joyful setting. Klimt documented the last great period of the Austro-Hungarian monarchy, from its opulent apex at the turn of the century to its decline and collapse in 1918. Klimt died the same year when he was fifty-six, and the monarchy expired at the ripe age of 392.

BACK IN PARIS, increased funding meant an increased volume of interviewing and the need to streamline operations. Until the end of 1987, all of our questionnaires were processed for computer data entry manually, a tedious and time-consuming operation. To speed up the procedure, we introduced a questionnaire that could be read by an optical reading machine. First, we field-tested the new questionnaire (Q47) in Copenhagen and Athens. The results were encouraging, and we decided to make the big switch in January 1988.

As with any big change, Murphy's Law kicked in. "If anything can go wrong, it will." Finding an outfit able to meet our exacting specifications was not easy. Optical reading technology in France was relatively new, and only a handful of printers could meet our demanding standards. Perfoguide Systems in Charenton helped us design the questionnaire, but their printing costs were exorbitant, almost 50 FF per questionnaire. I was delegated to find a cheaper alternative, and after an extensive search, I found Guy Gutman's printing shop, a mom-and-pop operation, willing to do the work at a reasonable price. It was located in a basement of a building on boulevard Magenta, around the corner from the Gare du Nord.

Working with Monsieur Gutman turned out to be an educational experience. As a small entrepreneur, he represented a microcosm of the business environment in France. When I first entered his shop, I was struck by the chaotic appearance of the place. Messy piles of printed matter lay everywhere. I almost walked out, but because I had made an appointment, I decided to stay and hear what he had to say.

Monsieur Gutman, originally from Alsace, showed me examples of his work, which ranged from multicolored opera programs to intricate sheet music, material that required a high degree of precision and attention to detail. If he could do such high-quality work, surely, I thought, he could print our questionnaires. For a brief moment, the image of the Gutenberg Bible flashed through my mind. The closeness of names Gutman and Gutenberg intrigued me. Was this an omen? I went with my hunch and entrusted the Gutmans with printing the first batch of Q47s and was not disappointed. He delivered high-quality work, and we never had any problems.

After I had picked up the first batch of questionnaires, I noticed Gutman looked tired, probably overworked. *"Je suis débordé* (I am overwhelmed)," he complained. "I cannot keep up with the orders I'm getting. My wife and I are working evenings, and I hardly have any weekends to myself. We even have our daughter helping us when she's free."

"But, Monsieur Gutman," I asked innocently, "why don't you hire someone to help you with the overload? Surely you have enough work to engage several individuals."

I got that glance one gets for asking a stupid question.

His answer provided fascinating insights into the French economy and how its labor laws contributed to the chronically high level of unemployment. "Monsieur Martyniuk, you don't understand. Yes, I could hire people, but my experience has been that as soon as I hire someone, I have nothing but problems. I have to train them and pay them the minimum wage even though they may not be productive. I also have to contribute to their social security, medical, and other benefits. Then I am saddled with a myriad of employment regulations always more favorable to the employee—rest breaks, a minimum of five weeks' paid holiday a year in addition to twelve public holidays. When an employee gets sick, I have to pay him sick pay for the first twenty-eight weeks. Worst of all, if an employee doesn't work out, I can't get rid of him even if he is stealing me blind. I have to go through a hundred hoops to prove that he is a thief."

Mr. Gutman's case illustrated why French unemployment had been stuck between 11 and 15 percent for a generation and why the Socialist policies regulating the labor market had failed. In reality, it was worse, especially among the young. Moreover, there seemed to be no light at the end of the tunnel. Every effort to reform the system was met with massive demonstrations by the unions and students indoctrinated by Marxist professors and the Socialist establishment. For small enterprises like Mr. Gutman's, the situation got even worse. Small businesses in France were dying at an alarming rate because all attempts to reform the system had been futile. *Plus ça change . . .*

Questionnaire 47 served us well for two years, but the situation in the Soviet Union was changing, and our instruments had to change with the times. In the summer of 1989, we began testing a new, shorter (fourteen-page) questionnaire, which we labeled Q48. The main difference between Q47 and Q48 was that beginning in January 1990, our interviewers would be asked to conduct interviews directly using answer cards. The days of undercover interviewing were over.

30. Peripheral Operations in Europe and Southeast Asia

THE PREVIOUS CHAPTERS focused on the largest and busiest interviewing points, Copenhagen, Piraeus, Paris, Rome, and Vienna. In addition to these cities, we had a presence in the Azores, Brussels, Berlin, Bremen, Hamburg, London, New York, Istanbul, Toronto, Tokyo, Seoul, Singapore, and the Indian subcontinent. These peripheral operations were small and did not differ methodologically from operations in Copenhagen and Athens.

One of my early assignments was to drive to Brussels to talk to members of a Soviet Ukrainian dance ensemble, *Veryovka*. I was prepared to take as many interviews as possible. Unfortunately, there was only a small window of opportunity after the performance, and before I was able to make contact, the troupe was rushed onto buses and whisked off to their hotel. I was hoping to run into them the next morning at their hotel during breakfast, but their "guardian angels" watched the flock like German shepherds, and every attempt to make contact failed. This made me realize how difficult it was to meet large organized groups. Still, it was not a total waste of time. I saw an excellent dance performance, a memory I prize to this day.

Eventually, we contracted an interviewing operation in Brussels with an outfit called Field Service. At its height, five interviewers were employed, but the volume of interviewing was never high. One of our Paris-based interviewers, Frano Donic, occasionally traveled to Brussels where he had some contacts. Paranoid in the extreme, Frano changed his identity like a chameleon. One day, he reported as FD, another as ALA, then SR. On some days, he presented himself as a Croat writer or a Serb translator, and on other days, a Georgian Jew. He was an excellent interviewer, but I could never figure out the rationale for such subterfuge. The office referred to him as "Beard" because he sported a long black beard.

We were aware that there were Soviets tourists in London, and in January 1987 Charlie went there to check out a few candidates and to see if we could set up an interviewing point. He met with Jaroslaw Szkadarek, a young Pole I had befriended at the Sakharov Free University the year before. Jaroslaw's Russian was good, and Charlie thought he had the makings of a crack interviewer. He did a dozen interviews for us and then resigned when he was accepted to do graduate work at the London School of Economics. Jaroslaw suggested Olga Gasparova to replace him. Olga lived in New York, although her aim was to be with her boyfriend in London. Our relationship did not last long. In the end, we abandoned London. The cost of interviewing there was simply too high. It was one of those locations where, after investing a lot of time and effort, the operation never met our expectations. Such was the nature of our business. Some places were gold mines, other deserts.

For some time, we suspected that northern Germany might be a good place to set up interviewing points. Like Copenhagen, Hamburg had a large port, as did Bremen with its Bremerhaven, but we had no interviewers in these cities. To take advantage of the Soviet traffic passing through, we needed an institute that could manage our project. Previously, Gene had met with the head of a leading German marketing research firm, Gesellschaft für Marktforschung (GfM), in Hamburg. They agreed to manage our project if we would help them recruit Russian-speaking interviewers. To that end, I flew to Hamburg to meet with Eberhard Wille, the individual responsible for our project at GfM, to see how I could help then find interviewers.

Through my friend Oleh Oleksyn, who had lived in Hamburg for many years, I learned that there was a Ukrainian Catholic church in the city. Its pastor, Monsignor Joseph Casanova Martorell, was a Spaniard who took a liking to the Greek-Catholic rite and decided to devote his calling to the Ukrainian Catholic Church, which, at that time, was short on priests. Monsignor Casanova was an amazing man and a polyglot. Besides Spanish, he spoke German and French, and had learned to speak Ukrainian, including the liturgy. He was a delightful man, curious about everything, and full of life. He offered to help me find Russian-speaking candidates in Hamburg. Soon, he introduced me to Pavlo Holovchuk, a political refugee with a special status in Germany, who expressed an interest in our work. Like so many others, after becoming familiar with the nature of our work, he declined our offer, explaining that he feared losing his special status, which included financial benefits.

Still, all was not lost. Mr. Wille contacted two other Russian speakers, Christophor Richter and his wife, Yolanda. I had met Richter in Lambrecht the year before. All this looked good in the beginning, but the respondents they encountered were mostly sailors and tradespeople, difficult to interview and not the kind of individuals we needed to enrich our sample. In July 1987, Mr. Wille informed us that Mr. Richter had quit, though Yolanda would continue working in Berlin.

I also met with Prof. Mikhail Goldstein, who lived in a studio at the back of the Petrikirche (Saint Peter's Church). Goldstein was an unforgettable character. Born in Odesa in 1917, this distinguished former Soviet violinist and composer was a steadfast anti-Communist and a good source of contacts and information. Professor Goldstein, however, was in no position to interview anyone. His health was failing, and he could barely walk, but he did lead us to other potential interviewers. One of them was Regina in nearby Bremen. Two years after I met him, Prof. Goldstein died at the age of seventy-one, and our office lost a valuable contact.

We had two interviewers in West Berlin but no one to supervise their work: Stanislaw Levitan, a Jewish émigré, and his wife, Valia, who helped out occasionally. Stasek owned a jewelry shop in Charlottenburg. Besides trading in antique jewelry, he bought gold in all forms—rings, broken jewelry, and old watches. He developed a reputation for integrity and good prices, and this made him popular with Soviet visitors who wanted to pawn their gold jewelry for cash to buy goods unavailable in the Soviet Union.

It was natural for him to start a conversation with Soviet visitors who came to his shop. He had an easy manner and the talent to steer the conversation to radio listening and switch it to life in the Soviet Union. What he was doing was not illegal, but he feared that if the KGB ever discovered what he was up to, it could hurt his business. Once, he confided that his main worry was that he would be identified as a CIA spy. As a result, Stanislaw was extremely careful about whom he interviewed.

On one visit to his shop, I stumbled on a Russian couple who had come to sell some gold jewelry. While Stanislaw was conversing with them in Russian, Valya engaged me in small talk in English. While I did not monitor the entire interview, I did hear how Stanislaw asked about the jamming of foreign radios and then adroitly shifted to a discussion about Afghanistan and the state of the Soviet economy. In his situation, he never had to seek out respondents. They came to him.

Levitan, the nominal head of the Berlin operation, kept an eye open for potential new interviewers. He found Vadim, a Ukrainian artist from Moscow, and four other interviewers, Galina, Ira, Warwara, and Zbigniew: a Russian, a Jew, a Ukrainian, and a Pole. To meet them, I timed my trips to Berlin to coincide with Wille's visits. Together we checked the new interviewers, and I observed their fieldwork and offered suggestions. Unfortunately, with a few exceptions, the quality of Berlin interviewers was not very high, and we wasted a lot of time correcting shortcomings.

One of the most colorful characters I met in Berlin was Dr. Bohdan A. Osadchuk, journalist, historian, and a professor emeritus at the Berlin Free University. The professor taught Eastern European history and, in 1978, became the director of East European Studies at the university. The Free University of Berlin was one of the most prominent universities in Germany. He also taught at the UVU (the Ukrainian Free University) in Munich, where he was a prorector. An erudite scholar, Osadchuk loved life to the fullest, liked to tell amusing stories, and appreciated good wines and spirits.

As a journalist, Dr. Osadchuk commented widely in the German press on developments in Eastern Europe under the pseudonym O. Korab. Born in Kolomyya in Western Ukraine, he came to Berlin in 1941 to study. I had the honor of meeting him before he retired. Osadchuk was the conduit who arranged clandestine contacts between intellectuals in the East and their counterparts in the West. What is less known is that he helped Roman Kupchinsky of Prolog to move "forbidden" literature to dissident intellectuals in Ukraine. At that time, Soviet Ukraine was extremely isolated, a kind of Albania the size of France. Osadchuk was instrumental in penetrating the Iron Curtain to keep the spark alive. While Berlin was not a major interviewing point, Korab helped us find Soviets passing through the city.

IGOR PANICH, A PART-TIME ACTOR, had been coordinating our work in New York since the early '80s. For most of the time, he was a one-man operation interviewing Soviet visitors. When SAAOR's budget increased in the mid-'80s, we gave Igor the go-ahead to find additional interviewers. New York was an expensive city—it was difficult to survive on fifty-five dollars an interview, which is what we were paying, so this was not an easy task. Igor considered getting a more permanent job, but the irregular nature of our work suited his acting career.

New York was never a big operation, but by 1988, the number of Soviet visitors increased, and the mix made it desirable to have a presence. On one of my visits to New York, I accompanied two of the interviewers to places frequented by Soviet tourists—cheap electronics shops, museums, and Brighton Beach—and found these places crawling with Soviet visitors. Igor expanded his team to six part-time interviewers that included a mysterious "couple" whom I never met but whose work was top notch. Three others, Anton, Zhenya, and Lyonya, also produced some useful feedback regarding VOA and RL programming. Some of the New York interviewers even wrote their comments in English, and that was a big plus because it saved us translation costs and speeded up processing time.

In New York, however, it was easy to confuse émigrés with visitors. In 1989, I began to notice anomalies in questionnaires submitted by the New York team. Twenty-seven percent of the interviews were with Jews, 7 percent with Central Asians, and only 5 percent with Ukrainians. Furthermore, they interviewed too many respondents with higher education who tended to work in the arts and cultural sectors.

I told Igor that I suspected that they were actually interviewing emigrants, respondents of lesser interest to us, and I warned that "if that doesn't change quickly, we will have to stop interviewing." Igor admitted that he had no reliable way of controlling their work and had to trust his interviewers. Within a month of my visit, the profile of respondents improved somewhat, but Jewish respondents, at 15 percent, were still overrepresented, compared to less than 1 percent of the population of the USSR. Luckily, the New York operation was not large. Eventually, Igor got a permanent job, and by the end of the decade, the operation terminated. I never discovered the extent of cheating taking place in the Big Apple.

During a September 1988 tour of Turkey, I came across a polyglot tour guide who spoke Russian. Turkey seemed like one of those countries that would attract Soviet travelers. During a twenty-day tour (see chapter 37, "Mediterranean Odysseys"), I got to know Hussein quite well, and at the end of the excursion, I proposed that he interview Soviet visitors, of whom there seemed to be plenty in Istanbul. He expressed great interest in the idea, and when I returned to Paris, I sent him some questionnaires. Having an interviewer in Istanbul would have been a coup, but it never materialized.

While Hussein's conversational Russian was acceptable, he lacked the necessary writing skills.

Through contacts in Canada, I learned that there were quite a few recent Ukrainian émigrés in Toronto. When I told my colleague Susan Roehm about this, she suggested a special research project.

"Do you know anyone in Toronto who would be willing to organize a panel review?"

"Yes, I know just the man. Jurij Darewych, professor of physics at the University of York."

An activist in the Ukrainian community, Jurij gladly organized candidates for a panel and interviewed ten recent émigrés. At fifty dollars per interview, the project was very cost effective, and the respondents provided us with valuable feedback about the general situation in Ukraine, the state of the economy, and the status of the Ukrainian language and church. This panel took place in early 1988 when RL ceased to be jammed, and the rigidly controlled environment in Ukraine was slowly beginning to thaw.

IN THE MID-'80S, we learned that Soviet ships were docking in Singapore. This was not a surprise. Singapore sits on the eastern end of the Strait of Malacca, one of the busiest shipping lanes linking the Indian Ocean to the South China Sea. A preliminary scouting report indicated that there were some Soviets in Singapore, but we also learned that there were many more in India. Based on this information, we set up an interviewing point in Singapore from where we could also control Soviet traffic on the Indian subcontinent.

SAAOR contacted Research Pacific, a marketing research outfit run by Irwin Hawking, to carry out research in the region. We also engaged my old friend Dr. Ivan Myhul, who was temporarily in Singapore, to help Pacific Research find potential local interviewers, train them, and eventually help supervise fieldwork there. From the late 1960s until the early 2000s, Ivan was a professor at a Canadian university and a friend of Roman Kupchinsky. Currently on study leave from his university, Ivan had secured a position as visiting fellow at the Singapore Institute of Southeast Asian Studies (ISEAS). He was a good fit because he was familiar with the psychological and ideological tactics used in dealing with Soviet citizens outside of their country.

In 1988, I had my hands full with the crisis in Rome, so Gene and Charlie took over the coordination of this tricky operation. Ivan arrived in Singapore in September 1988. It did not take him long to discover that, apart from some sailors and scientists, few Soviet visitors came to Singapore. Attempts to check out Malaysia and Thailand for possible Soviet visitors also failed to produce results, but India proved to be a much bigger hunting ground, especially New Delhi and Bombay.

In the course of three trips to the subcontinent, Ivan managed to find roughly ten Russian-speaking candidates. Unfortunately, only half of them turned out to be suitable for interviewing work. The problem was cultural. The Indian interviewers always assured us that they understood the instructions. Their questionnaires, however, revealed that they did not. Overall, their work was careless—their comments lacked depth, and their handwriting was often illegible.

While my involvement with the Singapore operation was tangential, I became aware of friction between Ivan and the owner of Pacific Research. Ivan considered Hawking to be incompetent in the area of interviewing Soviet citizens. Bad blood threatened the viability of the Singapore operation, and six months after Ivan arrived in Singapore, he returned to his university in Quebec, Canada.

31. *Pilgrimage to Galicia*

ONE OF THE MOST EXCITING and intriguing assignments during my years with SAAOR was a mission to Galicia in Spain in the summer of 1987. The aim of the mission was to meet with an Argentine-Ukrainian evangelist and prepare him for interviewing Soviet visitors and sailors on the Azores. The trip began with a long automobile journey from Paris to Santiago de Compostela in Galicia along a trajectory that approximated the pilgrimage route known as *El Camino de Santiago* and ended on a family farm near Lugo in the extreme northwestern corner of Galicia, thirty kilometers east of La Coruña.

By the mid-'80s, SAAOR had nearly sixty Russian-speaking interviewers in a dozen locations. Our busiest interviewing points, Copenhagen, Athens, and Vienna, had reached their saturation points. Adding more interviewers in these locations would not have appreciably augmented our sample, so we began to look for new places to establish interviewing points, especially outside of continental Europe.

For some time, we had been aware that Soviet tourists were showing up in the Azores. The islands in the mid-Atlantic were a refueling and pit stop for commercial airlines, cruise ships, and international shipping. Placing an interviewer on the islands would be a coup. The Azores, fifteen hundred kilometers west of Lisbon, were so remote that it would be next to impossible to find interviewers willing to work there. Still, we decided to give it a try. We floated the idea to our people in Copenhagen and elsewhere to see if anyone might be interested in such an assignment.

To my great surprise, one of our interviewers in Copenhagen, Jan, the Polish journalist, knew an individual who regularly traveled to the Azores: a Baptist evangelist and Bible distributor, Yaroslav Yaruchyk, an Argentine of Ukrainian descent. The Baptist community in Argentina dispatched Yaroslav to Spain to spread God's gospel among Soviet visitors on the Iberian Peninsula and to those who passed through the islands of the Azores. Since missionary work in the USSR was impossible, they did the next best thing: evangelize visitors from the Soviet Union anywhere they could find them.

Yaruchyk's work involved finding Soviets, engaging them in a conversation, and offering them a copy of a small-format Bible as a gift. In a way, Yaruchyk's evangelizing resembled the work of our interviewers in other locations. In fact, every time he engaged a Soviet in a conversation, he had already completed the most difficult part of the task. From that point on, it would be a cinch for him to follow up with questions about Western radios. In the process, Yaroslav would earn a nice sum simply for filling out a questionnaire after every meeting with a Soviet visitor.

Yaruchyk felt that our agendas overlapped, and he was receptive to working with us. In his case, the goal was to infiltrate the Soviet Union by distributing Bibles; for the radios, it was to penetrate the Soviet Union with news and information. It was relatively easy for him to meet visitors. As a man of God, he was perceived as nonthreatening. Even if visitors were not interested in Yaruchyk's message, they willingly took a Bible or two. Bibles were hard to come by in the atheistic Soviet Union and could be sold to those wanting one.

The Yaruchyk connection appeared promising. The next step was to meet him, tell him about our work, and familiarize him with the questionnaire. The only problem was deciding where and when, and that's when things got complicated. The French and Spanish take their vacations in July and August, and I expected my son, Darian, to visit me in Paris as he had done every summer since 1980. Yaruchyk informed me that in July, he, too, planned to spend some time with his family and that, in August, he would be on his way to the Azores to distribute bibles. Logistics seemed complicated, but I was determined to find a way.

Yaruchyk was married to Katarina, who lived in Gerona, near Barcelona. Every July, the family traveled one thousand kilometers to Galicia in northwestern Spain to spend a few weeks on Katarina's parents' farm. The plans, Yaruchyk told me, could not be changed. The sole option was for me to go to Galicia. Yaruchyk agreed to this, and we planned to meet in mid-July.

EARLIER THAT SPRING, I had read Edwin Mullins's classic account of *The Pilgrimage to Santiago*. The book planted an idea that had been fermenting in the back of my mind for some time: track the path of the pilgrimage, not on foot as thousands of pilgrims have done through the centuries, but in an automobile.

Darian arrived in Paris at the beginning of July. He was almost twenty, and I knew he liked to travel. "Darku," I addressed my son in Ukrainian, "next week we are going to Galicia. I have some business to take care of there, but the trip will be fun, and you'll get to discover parts of France and Spain that you have not yet seen. We will follow the pilgrimage route through France, cross the Pyrenees into Spain, and head for Santiago de Compostela." Darian was thrilled, and on Wednesday, July 8, 1987, we packed our suitcases and set off for Spain in my BMW.

In France, the four main pilgrimage routes lead to passes in the Western Pyrenees, the most important extending from Paris to Poitiers, Bordeaux, and the Pyrenees into Spain. Another from Vézelay takes a similar direction southwest by way of Limoges and Périgueux, joining the Paris route just before the Pyrenees. The third begins at Le Puy in Auvergne, and the last originates in Arles in Provence and heads for Toulouse. The routes converge at Puente la Reina, southwest of Pamplona. From there, the way continues as one to Burgos, Leon, and, finally, Galicia. The Spanish leg of the pilgrimage route is known as *El Camino de Santiago*. On foot, this pilgrimage would take two or three months; in an automobile, it takes about a week there, and a week back. I selected an itinerary that would cover some of the most important pilgrimage sites from among the four routes dissecting France, right up to Puente la Reina in Spain.

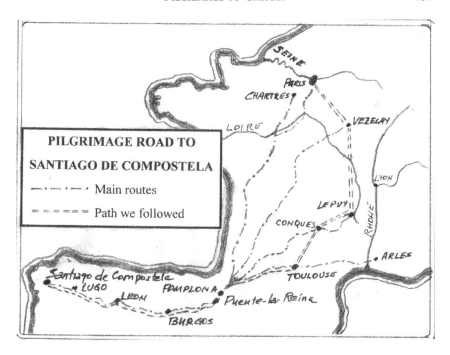

Thousands of churches and monasteries exist in every corner of France, and hundreds of them are remarkable. The vast majority were built after AD 1000, when the Big Bang, the expected end of the world, did not materialize. In thanksgiving that the world was still intact, a spirit of new optimism and church construction commenced, first, in the Romanesque style, and later the Gothic. There is no better way to discover France and its history than by touring its endless assortment of cathedrals, monasteries, and castles.

We started our pilgrimage from the flamboyant tower of Saint Jacques in central Paris on Rue de Rivoli near Châtelet. For a thousand years, this was the starting point for pilgrims embarking on the "way" to Compostela. Beginning here, I thought, would heighten the meaning of our modest attempt to duplicate the celebrated journey. We headed south to Vézélay in Burgundy, the second most important starting point for the Santiago pilgrimage. The twelfth-century Basilica of Sainte-Marie-Madeleine in Vézelay, purportedly housing the body of the Magdalene, is one of the outstanding masterpieces of Burgundian Romanesque art and architecture, as well as one of the most successful blends of the Romanesque and Gothic styles ever conceived. This is also where, in 1146, thousands flocked to hear Saint Bernard of Clairvaux preach in favor of the second crusade before King Louis VII and Eleanor of Aquitaine. Later, Eleanor's son Richard Coeur-de-Lion (Lionheart) came here as a pilgrim in 1190 along with King Philippe Auguste of France to launch the third crusade.

In the 1980s, travelers flocked to Vézelay for another reason. It had to do with the other French religion: gastronomy. French chefs had a habit of establishing great restaurants in out-of-the-way places. Darian and I feasted in L'Espérance, a Michelin three-star restaurant in the village of Saint-Père that offered the best cuisine of Burgundy at the most reasonable prices in France.

Next, we dashed four hundred kilometers south to Le Puy in southern Auvergne, a province rich in Romanesque churches. Le Puy was a center of worship from earliest times. Charlemagne was here in 772 and 800, and no French pilgrimage route was more frequented in the Middle Ages than the road from Le Puy. From far away, we could spot Saint-Michel d'Aiguillhe, a chapel perched on an eighty-five-meter-high needle rock jutting out of the plain. The chapel seemed inaccessible until we learned that there was a stairway cut out of the basalt rock that led to the summit. Without hesitation, Darian and I climbed the three hundred steps to reach the pinnacle. The tiny chapel with a Moorish façade was not particularly impressive, but the sweeping view of Le Puy, its cathedral, and the surrounding countryside was stunning.

From Le Puy, Darian and I crossed the bleak tablelands of the Cévennes and Southern Auvergne to the next church along this traditional pilgrimage route, Conques. The village of Conques occupied a spectacular site high on the steep wooded gorge of the River Dourdou, a small tributary of the Lot. This peaceful spot is both a natural and man-made wonder and probably one of the most outstanding religious sites in France, if not Europe. Conques (meaning "shell") is home to the magnificent Romanesque church of Saint Foy and was an important stop on the medieval pilgrimage route to Santiago de Compostela. Today, it survives exquisitely intact. Charlemagne founded this Benedictine abbey to provide isolation for prayer and meditation when the forested area was uninhabited. At the time the abbey was founded, the relics of Saint James were discovered at Compostela in Spain.

The massive twelfth-century Abbey Church of Saint Foy, in the center of the village, seemed more suited for a medium-sized city than for a hamlet of immaculately preserved medieval half-timbered houses. The tympanum over the church doors is a large Romanesque carving of the Last Judgment where Christ in Majesty presides over the scene in the center and includes a procession of saints and historical figures including Emperor Charlemagne. Conques was one of the few places in France where I had the impression that neither the picturesque village nor the magnificent church had changed since the Middle Ages.

After Conques, we slipped onto the fourth pilgrimage route known as *Via Tolosana,* which starts at Arles in Provence. Toulouse was always the major city along this important southern route to Santiago. Pilgrims from Italy and Eastern Europe who crossed the Alps passed through Toulouse and invariably stopped to pray at the vast Basilica of Saint-Sernin, the largest construction of its kind in Europe. The best way to describe this textbook Romanesque edifice is that it is big, dull, and disappointing. It's hard to say why, perhaps because it was constructed of bricks rather than the customary cut stone.

We crossed the Pyrenees in two places, the Col d'Aubisque and Col du Pourtalet, both over 1,700 meters in elevation, and then descended toward Jaca, the first big town in Spain. Our goal was to reach Pamplona in time to catch the last stage of the San Fermin festival celebrated every year from July 6 to 14. The main event was the *Encierro,* the Running of the Bulls, a spectacle that would be unimaginable in any other place in the world. Pamplona is among the most rumbustious and exuberant cities in Europe, in contrast to Burgos, the city we would visit next, where the people were more reserved, a description that characterizes the difference between the Basques and Castilians.

The first running of the bulls on July 7th was followed by one on each of the following mornings of the festival. The one-kilometer run lasts five minutes and concludes at the Plaza de Toros. Every year, between two hundred and three hundred people are injured during the run, although most injuries are not serious. Since 1910, fifteen people have been gored to death.

We arrived in Pamplona at noon of the last day on the festival, missing the last running of the bulls by three hours. Still, the atmosphere in the city center was festive and lively. The streets and bars were full of happy people from Europe and the United States, and it was easy to make contact. Over some tapas and Rioja wine, we befriended a few locals, and one pretty young Basque woman, eager to practice her English, told us about a follow-up festival near Puente la Reina, twenty kilometers southwest of Pamplona. Puente la Reina is also the point where all four pilgrimage routes from France join and become a single road all the way to Santiago. Halfway to Puente la Reina, along the N111, we spotted what looked like a bull-breeding farm where visitors gathered around a stockade to view the bulls. A walkway made of planks suspended over the stockade made it possible for clients to inspect them up close. I gathered that these bulls were destined for the corrida in nearby towns and cities like Pamplona.

Darian and I mounted one of these walkways and mingled with the visitors and professional buyers carrying long poles, poking the bulls to provoke them. Some bulls became more agitated than others, and these, I deduced, were destined for the bullring. To goad the bulls, some of the onlookers were unusually brutal with their poles, striking the poor beasts viciously and indiscriminately. I could see that Darian was uncomfortable with this spectacle.

Some distance from the stalls, we came across a market square that the locals had converted into a small makeshift bullring consisting of blue-colored barricades. Crowds surrounded these barricades, expecting a spectacle. A few of the less aggressive bulls were let loose to run around inside the improvised bullring, while young men and boys teased and taunted them. This unrestrained play went on for a while until it stopped as spontaneously as it began. The bulls were rounded up and driven back into the stockades, and the crowds dispersed to the local bars to talk about the show. Darian and I got into our car and headed for Burgos.

There are numerous accounts of the second stage of the pilgrimage between Saint Jean-Pied-de-Port and Santiago de Compostela. Although this part of the seven-hundred-kilometer route is lined with hundreds of abbeys, monasteries, and churches, there was not enough time to see even a fraction of these treasures. On Friday 17th, in two days, I had to be in Galicia to meet with Yaroslav Yaruchyk. I could not afford to be late for our meeting, and from this point, the sights along the *Camino* became secondary.

The next two days, we stopped in only in two places, Burgos and Leon, both notable for their role in Spanish history and splendid Gothic cathedrals. Gothic architecture is not native to Spain; it was a twelfth-century northern French creation that was imported first by the English, and later by the Germans, Spaniards, and Italians.

The Santa María de Burgos cornerstone was laid in 1221, but the cathedral was not completed until the sixteenth century. Modeled on the French cathedral at Bourges, it incorporated all the major phases of the Gothic, which explains the array of florid spires that can be seen from a distance. After inspecting the church, we continued west and entered the *sierra*, a high plain of rock and scrub devoid of trees. It had once been a fertile land, but centuries of erosion and despoliation of the topsoil had left the land barren, barely suitable for raising sheep.

León, on the main pilgrim route to Compostela, attracted travelers from all over Europe. It was an ancient city whose name was a corruption of the Latin "legion," referring to the Roman Seventh Legion. In 910, it became the capital of the Kingdom of León, which took an active part in the Reconquista against the Moors. The city subsequently grew into the capital of Christian Spain during the height of the Moorish invasion. The dreaded warlord Al-Mansur sacked it in 966 before he pressed on to take Santiago.

The inhabitants of Leon boasted that they had the loveliest Gothic cathedral in Spain, but I had found other Spanish cathedrals equally impressive, notably the Cathedral at Seville, which was the third largest church in Europe and the largest Gothic building in Europe; and the high Gothic cathedral of Toledo which is considered a *magnum opus*. Finally, La Seu, the cathedral in Palma on the island of Mallorca, is one of the most imposing Gothic buildings in Europe and the most magnificent buildings ever built.

The Leon Cathedral, completed in the late *rayonnant* (radiant) Gothic style and consecrated in 1303, struck me as gloomy. Its interior, however, held the best stained-glass windows in Spain, a feature that can only be appreciated when the sun comes out, as it did when we were there. After Darian had taken photos, we walked down to the cathedral's crypt, built between 1060 and 1063, that served as the Royal Pantheon for twenty-three monarchs of Leon. Highly decorated in blue, terra-cotta, and white, the crypt has been described as the Spanish Sistine Chapel.

From Leon, the plain edges toward the mountains of the north and west. At this point, we left the *Camino* and headed west along the A-52 toward Orense, where we spent the night. The next morning, we dipped down to the Portuguese frontier. Darian wanted proof that he was in Portugal, so we made a detour to get our passports stamped by Portuguese customs.

After that we got on the *Autopista* for Santiago. Motorways open up a country, but they also shrink and isolate it. We made it to Santiago in no time. Parking was a problem, so I left the car some distance from the cathedral, and we made our way down narrow alleys and streets on foot toward the vast Plaza del Obradorio, west of the legendary Cathedral of Santiago. Every year, hundreds of thousands of tourists come to visit this place where the alleged relics of Saint James rest in a crypt behind the High Altar of the Cathedral.

It was hard to imagine that, in 997, less than a hundred years before the cathedral was built, Santiago was the object of a damaging raid by the Moors. In spite of such dangers from the south, pilgrimages grew, and thus was anchored a powerful legend for the next thousand years. The stirring 2011 film *The Way*, starring Martin Sheen, is evidence of the durability of the Camino de Santiago mythos.

The Cathedral of Santiago was not a Spanish creation. Begun in 1078, it was finally consecrated in 1211. Architecturally, it was French and followed the pattern of pilgrim churches in Conques, Tours, and Toulouse. For many pilgrims, the final destination was not the Cathedral of Santiago but *Cabo Finisterra,* or Cape Finisterre, the farthest point west in Spain, a ninety-kilometer walk from Santiago. Our pilgrimage ended along the rugged shore and wooded bays where the earth ends and the emptiness of a vast ocean begins. I was about to embark on the second stage of our journey, whose nature and character would be utterly different.

YARUCHYK'S IN-LAWS lived in the tiny commune of Las Nieves in the extreme northwestern corner of Galicia. The commune was so small, it was not even on the map. Yaroslav gave me explicit instructions on how to find the farm. It was situated in a lush landscape where plentiful rain produces intensely green grass perfect for grazing premium cattle. This view of Spain's climate patterns puts a new twist on the rhyme, "The rain in Spain falls mainly on the plain"; it fell mainly on Galicia.

I have always been intrigued by the fact that there were two Galicias in Europe: one a province in Western Ukraine; the other a province in the northwestern corner of Spain. The two provinces were roughly two and a half thousand kilometers apart, but, historically, they were related, or at least the place names were. The Spanish Galicia was inhabited by the Artabrians, the Celtic tribe of the area. The term "Galicia" had its origins in the Roman name for Celtic lands—Gallia or Gaul. Ancient Celtic settlements once extended across a broad swath of territory from the Atlantic to the lands east of the Carpathian Mountains. Both the Ukrainian Galicia and the Spanish Galicia, I'm convinced, derived their names from the Roman Gallia. This, of course, is only my hypothesis, but one that I have investigated thoroughly, and which other historian friends find plausible.

The actual term "Gaul" or "Gallia" comes from the Greek root for "salt," *hal*. Etymologically, the roots *hal* and *gal* are interchangeable and often linked to Celtic settlements located near salt mines. That is why names of places throughout Europe are associated with the Gauls–Celts. In addition to Gaul, Rome's name for present-day France, and Galicia in Spain, we also had Portugal, which derived from Portogalia (the port of the Gauls), Halle in Germany and Hallstatt in Austria, and, of course, the Irish Gaelic tongue. The Ukrainian Galicia derived from Halych, an ancient Celtic settlement on the river Dnister, also founded around old salt mines that to this day yield salt.

We arrived at the farmstead on Friday afternoon. After nearly ten days on the road, I would finally meet Yaroslav Yaruchyk. It didn't take me long to see that he was a decent, modest, and intelligent man, dedicated to fighting godless Communism by distributing Bibles free of charge to visitors from the Soviet Union. Yaruchyk introduced us to Katarina's family in a mixture of Ukrainian and Spanish. Her parents welcomed us and said that supper would be served in three hours, but, first, some chores had to be done, work that even guests from France would not delay.

One of the chores was to cut some fresh grass and feed it to the cows. Katarina's father, a strong, wiry man in his fifties, pointed to the field. "Our cows love freshly cut grass. If we feed it to them before they retire, they will give better milk the next day." He looked at Darian, who was already six feet tall. "How would you like to cut some grass?" and, without waiting for an answer, handed Darian a scythe.

Darian, of course, had never used a scythe in his life, and the grass was tall, so the first few strokes were clumsy, but, eventually, he got the hang of it and quickly became a proficient grass cutter. Our hosts appreciated this gesture and said this was one way to earn an evening meal.

Galicians love good food. It is a way to get the family together and share a meal with wine, all part of the region's culture. The dish served that evening was the fan-shaped sea scallops that the French call *coquilles Saint Jacques*, harvested off the coast of Galicia. Galicians claimed the scallops off their coast were tastier and plumper than those found in the rest of Spain or France, and they may have been right. Katarina's mother served them in a creamy wine sauce, topped with breadcrumbs. The scrumptious meal was followed by cheese made from the milk of the cows we had fed.

After more wine and some socializing, the family made it known that they were ready to retire. That is when Yaruchyk and I stepped outside and walked to the barn, where we could have some privacy. Clean Galician air mixed with the odors of the barn made for an unusual environment in which to conduct business. As we sat on cow milking stools, Yaroslav told me about his routine on the Azores, how he located Soviet sailors and visitors and established a rapport with the port officials who knew and trusted him from previous visits. Since the most challenging aspect of our work was to locate and approach respondents, this was good news. The bibles Yaroslav was distributing free of charge would be a perfect entrée from which he could easily segue into the subject of Western radio listening. As I was explaining the questionnaire, he was already formulating the questions:

"Do the radio stations you listen to offer religious programming?"

". . . and what foreign stations do you listen to for news about religious matters?"

I took the time to review the questionnaire section by section, familiarizing Yaroslav with the terminology and technical aspects of shortwave radio broadcasting. We also conducted a mock interview with me posing as a respondent, but when I told him that all interviews were to be conducted without the questionnaire, he was slightly bemused.

"Are you serious, no questionnaire?"

The reaction was not unusual. Memorizing the entire questionnaire seemed daunting, but I assured him that it was not that hard and offered a few tips on developing some mnemonics. At the same time, I suggested ways to introduce the sensitive attitudinal questions. Over the next two days, we practiced, and by the time I left, he had mastered the questionnaire.

That Saturday, we were up early. The grass was fresh with morning dew, and everyone was asked to chip in with a few minor farm chores. At breakfast, the conversation got on to the subject of the *Camino*. Yaroslav picked up on my interest in old churches and monasteries and suggested a visit to the ruins of an abandoned Romanesque monastery a dozen kilometers south of the farm.

The only way to reach the monastery was on foot, so we left the car on the side of the road and hiked several kilometers along a path covered with shrubbery and loose rocks. The hike gave Darian and me a taste of what it would have been like to walk the *Camino* in the Middle Ages. The hike to the Caaveiro Monastery church was worth every strenuous step of the detour. It was not large, but it was splendid, set in a mountainous, forested landscape. The walls of the tenth-century monastery, despite being abandoned for centuries, stood solidly; the church's apse was frozen in time. Yaruchyk explained that the pilgrimage route in the region had many examples of Romanesque ruins. Caaveiro, he thought, was special. Very few visitors ever came here.

On our last day in Galicia, we took a scenic drive to La Coruña, a busy port city with a quarter of a million inhabitants, near an estuary on the Atlantic Ocean. It was the location of an ancient Celtic city. The Romans had come here in the second century BC, and Julius Caesar arrived in pursuit of the metal trade. Two thousand years later, a ten-year-old prodigy named Pablo Picasso began his art instruction at La Coruña's School of Fine Arts. I suspect that because of its wet and windy climate, neither Caesar nor Picasso stayed in La Coruña for long. Caesar returned to Rome to pursue his *cursus honorum,* and Picasso moved to Barcelona and then Paris to become the preeminent painter of the twentieth century and, in 1944, a committed Communist. When it was time to leave Galicia, I was satisfied that I had accomplished what I set out to do: recruit a valuable addition to our global network of operatives and share a few memorable experiences with Darian.

On Monday morning, after a hearty breakfast of fresh eggs and spicy Galician sausage, we left the farm. I had three days to get back to Paris, so there was not much time for sightseeing. Darian and I took the coast road to Santander and then picked up the *Autopista* to Bilbao and San Sebastian, where we stopped to rest and get the flavor of the city. In one afternoon and evening, I discovered that San Sebastian was a fabulous city, particularly its panoramic setting around the Playa de la Concha—a seashell-shaped city beach, probably the finest in Europe, and one of the most famous tourist destinations in Spain. I made a mental note to return to this lively city at the earliest opportunity.

Before leaving the land of the Basques, Darian persuaded me to make a detour to the *Sanctuario de San Ignacio de Loyola*, some twenty-five kilometers southwest of San Sebastian. He was a graduate of Loyola Academy, the Jesuit High School in Chicago, and the shrine, inaugurated in 1738, was constructed around the birthplace of Saint Ignatius of Loyola, founder of the Society of Jesus. The church's sixty-five-meter dome was impressive, but its heavy Baroque interior, marked by extreme, expressive, and florid decorative detailing, in our humble opinion, was over the top.

We crossed the French border at Hendaye, and, soon, we were skirting Bordeaux, where we had to forego the temptation to taste some of the world's great wines. From Bordeaux, the *autoroute* to Paris paralleled the westernmost pilgrimage route that included such famous sites as Saintes, Poitiers, Tours, and Orleans. Precisely two weeks and three thousand kilometers later, we arrived where we started, at the Tour de Saint Jacques in the center of Paris.

View of Eifel Tower from our salon window on rue Gaston St. Paul.

Ivan Myhul and Zoe in front of building on rue Gaston St. Paul. We lived in the apartment on the third floor just above the balcony.

In front of Papal Nuncio in Paris during Pope John-Paul's II visit to Paris in May 1980. From left to right, Omelian Mazuryk, Odarka Mazuryk, Elmira Floyd, Natalka Horodecka and me.

Wine tasting in a Burgundy cave: me, Jurij Darewych
and Danylo Struk in light jacket.

Anton and me at the entrance to metro St. Germain des Pres. Photo taken c. 2005

A portrait with Mazuryk icon and Zenon Holubec
sculpture in background.

Soiree in my apartment on rue Pelouze. Front rank, left to right: Omelian
Mazuryk, Danylo Struk, Volodymyr Makarenko, Anton Solomukha.
Standing, left to right: unidentified, Danylo Sztul, Lisa Centkiewicz, Danylo
Perehinec, Odarka Mazuryk, me, Olga Gomola and Sasha Haniak.

Luba Markewycz and Danylo Struk, Bastille Day, 1989.

Ivan Myhul and me at Christo's happening, the wrapping of Pont Neuf, 1985.

Ivan Myhul, Roman Serbyn, me and Iryna Popovych.

Darian Martyniuk on Place St Germain des Pres against the backdrop
of Café Le Bonaparte. During the 1980s, my group of friends met
here regularly on Sunday afternoons. Sartre lived in this building
on the third floor with his mother until his death in 1980.

Chateau D'Alleuze, a medieval castle south of Saint Flour.

Traversing extinct volcanos in Auvergne.

Darian during a stop on the high pass Col Galibier (2645 meters) with the Meije peak in the background.

Me, Ivan and Srjan in front of St Naum Monastery
Church on Lake Ohrid in Macedonia

Bircza, one of the numerous Lemko and Boyko
wooden churches in southeastern Poland.

Stopping at Conques on way to Galicia

A lesson in cutting fresh grass in Galicia. Darian with the rake on the right

Abandoned church of S. Gregorio near Lugo. Darian and
Yaroslav Yaruchyk standing in arched doorway.

Rocamadour, the extraordinary pilgrimage site near the
border of the Dordogne and Lot departments.

View of valley from fortress of Queribus, the last Cathar citadel
to fall to northern invaders in 1255. The outcroppings of Château
Peyrepertuse are visible in center right and Puilaurens center left.

Yaro Markewycz and me at the foot of Chateau Puilaurens,
a fine example of dozens of the vertiginous Cathar castles
scattered along the northern foothills of the Pyrenees.

Me, Oleh Oleksyn and Srjan Rašković inspecting Sancerre vineyards.

The SAAOR team during Christophor Geleklidis' visit to Paris. Standing, from left to right, Konstantin Golskoy, Gene Parta, Sallie Wise, me, Nina Geleklidis, Nicole Kostomarov, Christophor Geleklidis and Charlie Allen.

Christophor Geleklidis, me, Nina, Christophor's wife and Charlie Allen in Athens.

Eva Bauer, my wife, somewhere on the Côte d'Azure

Tamara, my daughter, and me in a poppy field in central France.

Roman Kupchinsky in Paris, unknown female and me.

32. Unique Revelations and Insights

DURING MY TWELVE YEARS in Paris—six with the IEA/OECD and six with SAAOR—I garnered insights that made me realize just how fragile the Soviet Union was. Like Russia today, the USSR was a one-resource economy, and any disruption in its oil or gas revenue would have grim consequences for the system. My research on behalf of Radio Liberty reinforced my gut feeling that the Soviet Union's days were numbered.

Among the reasons the Soviet Union collapsed were the rising tide of nationalism, alternative information disseminated by Western broadcasters such as Radio Liberty and Voice of America, infiltration by Prolog and other organizations, the war in Afghanistan, the Chernobyl catastrophe, and, last but not least, the collapse in the price of oil. Other factors played a role: the election of John Paul II as Pope, the Solidarity movement in Poland, and President Reagan's tough stand toward the "evil empire." At the root, however, was the fact that the Socialist/Communist model, as practiced by Moscow, was fundamentally unworkable.[95]

SAAOR's massive information-gathering operation allowed us to assess the size of audiences to international broadcasters in the Soviet Union, provide qualitative audience feedback to the Radio in Munich, report on the audibility and jamming level of international radio broadcasts, and gather public opinion data on topical issues of the day, matters of enormous importance to a wide variety of clients.

---

[95] Chapter 2 of this memoir *What Killed the Soviet Empire* elaborated these factors in some detail.

In an essay about her novel *The Angels of Russia*, Patricia le Roy, SAAOR's editor, notes that, "Our unconventional research methods, combined with privileged access to highly-placed sources, enabled us to accumulate a vast amount of information about what Soviet people really thought, and what their lives were really like behind the bland, shameless prose of official propaganda. We learned how they struggled to find food in the shops, what they thought of the war in Afghanistan, and how they viewed their leadership.

"Although the KGB knew of our research," she goes on, "they kept their distance. There was a bomb attack on Radio Liberty's Munich headquarters in 1981, but our office on Boulevard Saint-Germain remained unscathed. The truth was that we were probably useful to them. We published the kind of insights into Soviet attitudes and opinions that were not obtainable anywhere else. Concrete incidents were relatively few, although one of our interviewers was once beaten up in the street, and the KGB were a constant, lurking presence . . . Certain people were kept away from the office; others refused flatly to set foot there."[96]

Our principal client, the management of Radio Liberty in Munich, wanted to know how many people were listening to each of the language services, along with times and frequency of listening, and audience profiles (nationality, sex, age, profession, place of residence, and Communist Party affiliation). We also provided feedback on the programs' objectivity, moderation, timeliness, and relevance—information that was used to enhance the broadcasts' appeal.

Our findings showed that during the period 1980 to 1990, on average, 25 percent of the adult population of the Soviet Union listened to Western radio weekly. By 1989, the radios were reaching about twenty-five million people on an average day and over fifty million in the course of the week. Voice of America (VOA) was the dominant Western broadcaster, reaching around 15 percent of the adult population weekly. Weekly audiences to BBC and Radio Liberty fluctuated between 5 and 10 percent, and Deutsche Welle's were in the 2–5 percent range. Much of what follows comes from R. Eugene Parta's

---

[96] After several years as a research editor at SAAOR, Patricia began to write novels. At the last count, she had written nine. Her books include historical fiction and political thrillers set in Russia, Eastern Europe, and Burma, and draw on her writing and editing experience with SAAOR. See "KGB In The Mirror" on www.patricialeroy.com/timeline

short book *Discovering the Hidden Listener*, a comprehensive and in-depth analysis of audience trends during the Cold War.[97]

Audience feedback indicated that listeners perceived Radio Liberty as a surrogate radio that covered issues close to their hearts and relevant to their lives. VOA, on the other hand, was seen as an American information station. A general profile of listeners to Western radio stations showed that they were urban males in the thirty-to-fifty-year age range with at least a secondary education. Listening rates were highest in Moscow, Leningrad, and the Baltic states. They were lowest in Central Asia, Moldova, and the rural RSFSR. Interestingly, Communist Party members listened to Western radio at about the same rate as nonmembers. Radio Liberty, given its focus on internal Soviet developments, was most popular with people who were classified as "Liberals" in the Soviet context, while those considered as "Conservatives" and "Hard-liners" listened considerably less.

The Soviet authorities feared the truth and used the only weapon they had to prevent their citizens from hearing it—jamming the airwaves. In general, this was a good barometer of East/West relations. The Soviets first jammed the Western voices when the Berlin airlift crisis unfolded in 1948, and continued to do so throughout the 1950s. Jamming was temporarily lifted on VOA and BBC in 1963 and resumed in 1968 during the invasion of Czechoslovakia. It stopped in 1973, only to resume in 1981, when martial law was declared in Poland. Jamming of BBC and VOA ended definitively in 1987, during the period of *perestroika*, but Radio Liberty was blocked without interruption from its first day on the air in May 1953 until November 22, 1988. When jamming ended, Radio Liberty's audience spiked, reaching nearly 17 percent weekly or roughly one in six Soviet citizens, the highest of all the Western broadcasters to the USSR.

Throughout this period, the Soviet authorities considered Radio Liberty more dangerous and subversive than other stations like the BBC and VOA. They did everything possible to discredit it, accusing RL of spewing out poison into the airwaves and disseminating the CIA's "black propaganda." The Soviet media referred to this station as *vrazhiye golosa,* the enemy voices. Some estimate that it cost the Soviet Union up to four times as much to jam RL's programming as it cost Radio Liberty to broadcast. Still, listeners found

---

[97]   R. Eugene Parta, *Discovering the Hidden Listener: An Empirical Assessment of Radio Liberty and Western Broadcasting to the USSR during the Cold War* (Hoover Press, 2007).

ingenious ways to circumvent jamming. SAAOR collected information on audibility in the Soviet Union and forwarded it to RFE-RL engineers who tried to deal with these issues. It was common for people to record programs in places where audibility was better and distribute the recordings in the fashion of *samizdat*.

The Radios played a crucial role in providing an alternative version of events, and contributed to shaping attitudes that differed from those expressed by official Soviet media. Simply broadcasting objective information to Soviet citizens for decades had the effect over time of forming a critical mass of opinion that challenged the monopoly of Soviet media and eventually led to the demise of the empire.[98]

After the disintegration of the Soviet Union, it was possible to compare studies carried out using SAAOR's unorthodox methodology with studies that were carried out either officially or unofficially in the USSR. Eugene Parta's subsequent analyses found a close correlation between these studies and SAAOR survey data. Considering the unusual circumstances under which SAAOR carried out its surveys, the correlation was striking.

WHILE THE THRUST of research at SAAOR was audience estimation, one of the most edifying and well-regarded aspects of our work was bringing to light what Soviet visitors thought about pressing issues of the day. Over the years, we posed a variety of topical attitudinal questions that allowed us to gauge Soviet public opinion, a feat no other academic institution or government agency attempted to duplicate. Our interviewers elicited opinions on a range of topics that included the nationalities question in the USSR, the Solidarity movement in Poland, the 1983 Korean Airline incident, attitudes toward religion, and opinions of Andrei Sakharov. Soon after I joined the organization, the focus shifted to the war in Afghanistan, the Chernobyl accident, and the impact of *glasnost* and *perestroika*.

Reviewing these findings thirty years later, I am struck by how much SAAOR accomplished. The information we collected pointed to a profoundly troubled society that suggested that the days of the Soviet Union were limited. As the great economist Herbert Stein once put it: "If something cannot go on forever, it will stop." Indeed, it did stop in 1991—sooner than anyone anticipated.

---

[98] Parta, *Discovering the Hidden Listener*, pp. 90–93.

As early as 1983, SAAOR began to study the nationalities question, a topic that had been neglected by mainstream Sovietologists simply because they did not know what the Soviet public was thinking. Our research showed that the Soviet Union was not "a happy family of nations" as some academics sympathetic to the Soviet Union believed. History proved them wrong, and it was only a matter of time before the unnatural creation disintegrated.

Russian chauvinism aggravated the nationality problem in the Soviet Union. On this issue, feedback from Soviet visitors was remarkably consistent whether it came from Copenhagen, Vienna or Piraeus. Since the time of Lenin, the Communist Party's traditional goal had been "the merging of nations," or *sliyaniye* in Russian. This concept had been played down during the Brezhnev era and then resurrected under Andropov, though he soon backtracked when he realized that to non-Russians *sliyaniye* was tantamount to assimilation by Russians, a policy non-Russian nationalities would vigorously resist.

Many, if not most, scholars in the West had bought into the idea of *sliyaniye,* believing that the Soviet government had, at last, solved the nationalities problem. Others preferred to label it as *sblizheniye*, a kind of convergence of nations. They were convinced that the march toward Socialism would one day render nations obsolete. There were exceptions, most notably Robert Conquest, but he was seen as an outlier and persistently denigrated by mainstream academics, especially by prominent Leftist scholars such as Jerry Hough and Stephen Cohen.

These Sovietologists, Kremlin watchers, and other Russia specialists often swallowed Moscow's line that the Soviet Union had solved the nationality problem. To Marxist-oriented experts, in particular, the merging of nations, symbolized by the lofty and mellifluous Russian word *sliyaniye,* had already been achieved. Differences between nationalities had been replaced by a new identity: *Homo Soveticus*, "Soviet Man."

SAAOR investigated this question by asking ordinary Soviet people what they thought. What we discovered upended the conventional wisdom that the USSR was a blissful family of nations, and showed that *Homo Soveticus* was a phantom.

SAAOR made a great effort to incorporate non-Russians in the survey sample, in order to get a reading on what the various ethnic groups were listening to and, more importantly, what they were thinking. Quantitative findings were supplemented by respondent comments that revealed additional insights. For example, many Russians not only insisted on their right to govern but also believed that the nationalities were incapable of governing themselves, revealing a distinctly chauvinistic attitude and arrogance with anti-Semitic overtones. The following medley of comments by a cross section of Russian respondents illustrated this point.[99]

> The Russians are the most cultivated and progressive of all Soviet people . . . their culture is superior . . . A Russian is more just, more loyal and more responsible than the other ethnic groups who hate each other and the onus on keeping then together falls on the Russians. Never will we let ourselves be ordered by undeveloped national minorities who have only been able to evolve and progress thanks to the Russians . . . As creators of the Soviet state, the Russians are entitled to rule it.

> Giving non-Russians more power would increase corruption and speculation. Look at the Georgians and Armenians . . . The best positions have been taken by Jews, Georgians, and Armenians . . . They're everywhere, at the market, in the shops and restaurants. The directors of this or that are all Jews . . . while the Russian peasant is breaking his back for them.

Such attitudes exacerbated relations between the dominant and domineering Russians and non-Russians. Since there was no way to measure public opinion in the Soviet Union, the "experts" in the West misjudged the level of resentment and hostility that existed in the Soviet Union. Some may have suspected it, but only SAAOR polling was able to disclose such insights in a methodical way.

The process of breaking down national identities and integrating and mixing ethnicities began in the army. Imposing the Russian language and exalting Russian culture and achievements was another. By the mid-'80s, Russian had become the language of instruction down to elementary school level. A Kyiv friend once confided that only in the kindergartens were children still taught their native language. Decades of such policies nearly destroyed national identities. Survey data also revealed discontent with the status quo. A small number of respondents did not exclude the possibility—indeed,

---

[99] All respondent citations in SAAOR's analytical reports were identified by a unique five-digit questionnaire number and included a profile of the respondent noting his or her nationality, sex, occupation, approximate age, place of residence, and,when possible, Communist Party (CP) membership. For the sake of brevity, I've omitted most of these identifiers.

the desirability—of a struggle for independence. Quotes by Ukrainian respondents referring to Russians as *Moskali*, the pejorative Ukrainian term for Russians, began to appear more frequently.

> The *Moskali* are the gods and tsars in all of the national republics . . . They are the decision makers who control all of the higher positions . . . The national groups are completely under their thumb. The Russians think they are better than we are and that makes people extremely angry. (Ukrainian journalist in his 40s from Ternopil)

At the same time, non-Russian travelers displayed hostility to the policy of *sliyaniye,* but for certain respondents, the goal of *sliyaniye* was well on the way to being accomplished with the emergence of a "new Soviet man."

> Andropov will try to do away with national differences in the U.S.S.R. His aim is not to make Georgians into Russians but to make everybody Soviet. (Georgian dancer in her 30s from Tbilisi)

> The greatest danger to Ukraine, Russia, and other Soviet peoples comes from Andropov. He is the first genuine cosmopolitan leader in the history of the U.S.S.R. He is without a nationality and likely to enforce "de-Ukrainization" and subject the country to imperial interests. (Ukrainian engineer in his 40s from Kyiv, CP member)

> The majority of non-Russian nationalities look upon themselves as Russian already. I don't mean just the Ukrainian and Belarusians, but the Tatars, Kalmyks, and other Caucasian peoples. We are witnessing the appearance of the "New Soviet Man."

Non-Russian respondents loathed Russian chauvinism and had an aversion to Moscow's arrogant ways. This was the situation in the Soviet Union just before two events that would eventually change the course of world history and lead to the breakup of the Soviet Union: failing fortunes in the war in Afghanistan, and the Chernobyl catastrophe.

DURING THE SOVIET WAR in Afghanistan from 1979 to 1989, SAAOR conducted a total of 5,600 interviews that dealt with attitudes toward the war.

The results were published and distributed to management in Munich and US government agencies in three reports between 1985 and 1988.

Afghanistan was a sensitive issue that our interviewers found tricky to breach with respondents, but, gradually, they developed creative ways to elicit information on the subject. Interviewers were expected to weave in the following series of questions into the conversation with them:

I have a very confused picture of what is happening in Afghanistan. The few reports that we in the West have received are not very informative and sometimes even contradictory.

a. What do you think is happening there?
b. How will the situation develop in Afghanistan in the future?
c. What do you think about the situation in Afghanistan?
d. Where did you get the information on Afghanistan?

During the period under investigation, disapproval of the war rose from one-quarter of the population in 1984 to almost one half in 1987. These first rumblings of discontent would eventually become an earthquake. R. Eugene Parta's book *Discovering the Hidden Listener* points out that Soviets who received information from Western radio were considerably more critical of Soviet policy.[100] By the time General Secretary Gorbachev announced that the Soviet military would pull out its forces from Afghanistan (February 1988), SAAOR data indicated a high degree of disillusionment with the Afghan adventure. SAAOR analyst Sallie Wise wrote in one of her reports that 90 percent of respondents approved of Gorbachev's decision to pull out of Afghanistan.[101]

Parta correctly pointed out that this demonstrated "a loss of trust in the government and its institutions." The Afghan war stretched the Soviet military to the limit and made it nearly impossible to redeploy them to Eastern Europe, where unrest was threatening to break up the Soviet bloc. The disastrous military campaign in Afghanistan made the Soviets reluctant to send troops into battle anywhere else. The retreat from Afghanistan unleashed a chain of events with unintended consequences. Losing the war in Afghanistan forced

---

[100] Parta, *Hidden Listener*, section 5.1, "The War in Afghanistan," pp 47–51.

[101] "The Soviet Public and the War in Afghanistan: Perceptions and Prognoses," AR 4-85 (1985) and 4-88 (1988), Soviet Area Audience and Opinion Research, Sallie Wise, RFE/RL, Inc.

the Soviets to abandon their "outer empire." Without the implied threat of force, they were unable to hold on to their Eastern European satellites. The degree of discontent with the war was reflected in the collage of respondent reactions below.

> There is a shameful war going on in Afghanistan. People on both sides are suffering and dying. Why do Russians and Ukrainian soldiers have to die? The Soviet military actions amount to cold-blooded murder. No one can predict how this all will end.

> Soviet propaganda was trying to convince us that the partisans are savages, but I've heard from those who have returned that it is the Russians who are savage . . . the Afghans value their freedom more than their lives and property. It is obvious that our troops have been using this poor nation to test new types of weapons.

The anti-Russian sentiment was especially strong among Ukrainians, the Balts, and the Tajiks.

> The Russian invasion of Afghanistan has but a single purpose—to secure access to the Persian Gulf and the Indian Ocean, the goal Russian tsars always dreamed of having . . . But the Russian swine are indifferent to the suffering they are causing . . . They have no right to inflict such atrocities on those people. The subjugation of the Afghan state is unforgivable. What we hear about Afghanistan is plunder, ruin, and killing and our media call it "liberation." Liberation from whom?

Soviet involvement in Afghanistan caused considerable damage to the USSR's prestige worldwide. A large segment of the Soviet population rejected the official justification for the Soviet presence in Afghanistan: defending Socialism, establishing a people's democracy, providing humanitarian assistance, or, as the KGB officer Kirilenko once told me in Paris, "to prevent a CIA coup."

Many non-Russian respondents derided the Soviet coverage of the war in Afghanistan as completely false and cynical, while others held the view that Afghanistan was a veritable quagmire.

> The Soviet incursion into Afghanistan was a grave miscalculation our country will regret for years. Whatever you read in the Soviet

press, it's the other way around. It's one of Soviet Union's greatest postwar mistakes, a most egregious error in judgment. After five years of fighting, nothing seems to have changed. Soldiers returning from Afghanistan say there will never be peace there . . . We don't need Afghanistan; our territory is sufficient.

A few respondents expressed a disdainful attitude toward the Afghans, and a small minority of those interviewed, nearly all Russians, justified Soviet intervention.

> The Afghans are primitive savages. One must not forget that they are ignorant Asians who don't recognize any authority but their God. We went there to fulfill our "international duty" to help the Afghan people. We are teaching them to build and defend their country from its enemies . . . To protect Soviet interests in the region against threats from "foreign imperialists," such as NATO and the United States.

As the war in Afghanistan entered its seventh year, the Kremlin, under pressure of public opinion, began talking about a token pullout of Soviet troops, though there were no signs of diminishing its massive military presence. Then, in mid-1986, the CIA began covertly supplying the rebels with Stinger missiles capable of hitting a flying target five kilometers away. In 1987, two hundred Soviet aircraft fell victim to Mujahideen's new weapon. The Soviets were defeated and began to pull out their forces in earnest. That year, public disapproval of the war reached a critical mass, spreading to virtually all segments of the population—a level of dissatisfaction that played an important part in the decision by Gorbachev to pull out of Afghanistan.

IF THE WAR IN AFGHANISTAN was an earthquake, the catastrophic nuclear accident at Chernobyl on April 26, 1986, was the Vesuvius erupting. The explosion that released large quantities of radioactive particles that spread over much of the western USSR and Europe was a defining moment in the history of the Soviet Union. The event divided the history of the country into BC and AC: before Chernobyl and after Chernobyl. Information that trickled out from official sources was incomplete and often contradictory, and people relied on Western broadcasts to keep them informed. This was a pivotal moment for Western radio and a disgraceful one for the Soviet media, and one of the early nails in the Soviet coffin. Others would follow in quick succession.

Two months after the disaster, SAAOR queried five hundred citizens on the subject. The study aimed to find out how they learned of the accident and who they thought was to blame for it. The survey result showed that the primary source of information for respondents about the tragedy was Western radio (36 percent), followed by Soviet TV (28 percent), and word of mouth (15 percent). If we take into account additional sources about the catastrophe, half of the respondents got their information from Western sources. Survey respondents commented that Western media coverage of the accident was more reliable than their own Soviet media.

> I was startled to hear from Western radio about the event in Chernobyl because our media had not mentioned it. When they finally did, the information was limited to heroic efforts to contain it, as if nothing significant had occurred. To me, this showed that our radio is not competent to deal with serious issues. (Ukrainian engineer in his 40s)

> As information trickled into our office in Moscow, we got all sorts of alarming reports, but all we were allowed to print was the official TASS report. (Russian journalist in his 30s)

> I first heard about Chernobyl in a conversation with a friend. When television finally reported it, they played it down so much I immediately realized they were not giving us the full story. (Armenian blue collar worker in his 50s)

> Realizing it was impossible to hide the incident, our media began to mention it, but they didn't broadcast all the facts the foreign stations did. (Ukrainian mechanic in his 30s)

A Jewish blue-collar worker from Odesa in his fifties who emigrated from the Soviet Union in June 1986 gave the following account:

> On 4 May, the Soviet television nightly news *Vremia* gave a small amount of information about the incident in Chernobyl and claimed that Western radio was blowing the incident out of all proportion . . . On 14 May Gorbachev came on television to tell us that there was nothing to fear. Neither the papers nor television indicated that children in the Kyiv region were going to be evacuated.

As for why Soviet media suppressed coverage of the accident, some interviewees said the Moscow ministry responsible for nuclear energy was too panic-stricken to tell the truth. Others said that the Ukrainian party leadership did not wish to disrupt the upcoming May 1 celebrations. The May 1 parade was indeed held as scheduled.

Respondents blamed the accident on negligence at the plant level, shoddy Soviet construction standards, the centralized nature of the Soviet system, and the inability of managers at the local level to address even minor technical problems without permission from a higher authority.

> Radiation leaks at the Chernobyl station began a day before the accident, but no one had the authority to repair the reactor. Middle management, unaccustomed to making decisions and taking the initiative, simply froze. (Russian engineer in his 40s)

EXPERTS IN THE WEST had only sketchy information about food shortages in the Soviet Union. The closed nature of Soviet society prevented any systematic study of the situation until SAAOR began to collect data on the availability and quality of food in the Soviet Union, including prices. The project, originally conceived by Gene Parta, provided a relatively reliable indicator of the quality of life in the USSR, and served as a barometer of discontent. We developed a computerized database that tracked changes in the availability of certain basic foodstuffs, notably sugar, margarine, and, most importantly, bread. At times, the studies included availability and prices on a whole array of products from apples to vodka.[102] The effort was time consuming, but it enabled us to piece together a mosaic that captured the quality of life in the Soviet Union. SAAOR analyst Mark Rhodes collated and analyzed this data and produced a series of reports on the condition of the food supply in the country.

Many attempts were made over the years to improve the dismal food situation; however, instead of restructuring and privatizing agriculture along Western lines, Andropov began introducing even more bureaucratic directives calling for "increased labor discipline" and "vigilance against parasites." As part of an operation to reduce lines at food shops, the regime conducted spot checks of people standing in line to buy food during working hours, to

---

[102]   Apples, beef, beets, bread, cabbage, cheese, chicken, eggs, tinned fish, flour, margarine, milk, mutton, oranges, pork, rice, sausage, sugar, tomatoes, and vodka.

ensure that they had not taken an unauthorized leave of absence from their workplace. This had the effect of eliminating the so-called *meshochniki,* or "bag people," provincial residents who had been in the habit of making trips to larger cities to stock up on food.

Soon after Moscow took these steps, there appeared to have been a slight improvement, and the lines became somewhat shorter. The Soviet press began to write about an amelioration in the food supply, and the Western press cheerfully repeated this news. The improvement, however, turned out to be temporary. SAAOR survey data for 1983 showed little change from the previous years. We found that while there was increased availability of food products in the cities, it came at the expense of quality.

More and more survey respondents complained about the deteriorating quality of bread, sausage, milk, and butter. In contrast to the average citizen, the ruling elite continued to enjoy preferential treatment in the matter of food supply. Feedback, mostly from emigrants, demonstrated that there was a high level of disaffection with a system utterly incapable of meeting the people's basic nutritional needs. It was an issue more graphically conveyed by respondents' comments than by statistics alone.

> Bread is poorly baked and contains unpleasant tasting additives. Boiled sausage is inedible and smells nothing like fresh meat. If you try to cook it, it sticks to the pan and oozes out some gluey substance. A worker in the Leningrad meat *kombinat* told me that one ton of meat was made into 15 tons of sausage. (Pensioner from Leningrad)

> Dairy products delivered by the factory often reach our store in poor condition or contain additives. We put aside some of the milk for ourselves and dilute the rest with water, though we do not boil the water first. We also add water to vodka and wine. The meat is often so badly frozen that it's black. The rule is to cut off the bad parts and sell the rest. Other times, the meat is green and moldy. We rinse off the mold and sell it. The choice items are set aside for the privileged customers, such as the management of the city and high party officials. We have a list of the names of these people and five workers dedicated to packing up special parcels for them, like smoked fillet of sturgeon, smoked sausage, crab, cod liver, cognac, whiskey, high-quality chocolate, and coffee. Somewhat less exotic parcels—meat, butter, buckwheat, and eggs—are made

up for war invalids and a little trickled down to the sales staff. (Sales clerk from Leningrad)

I knew of several cafeterias and stores in Bukhara which sold meat dishes, or meat products, made from donkeys, cats, and dogs. Usually, it was turned into mincemeat, kebabs, cutlets and so forth. From what I heard, the same thing happened in Tashkent, and there were rumors about animal hunters, underground slaughter houses, and "meat processing" plants which supplied meat to the stores. (Sales clerk from Bukhara)

I visited *sovkhozy* (state farms) where they grew fruit and vegetables for Moscow and the ruling circles in Kazakhstan—everything from avocados to citrus fruits. Transport was always available so that the goods didn't spoil and everything was carefully packed with special shipping label. The only things that were sent to the stores are the reject items. (Agronomist from Alma-Ata)

They have been adding various fatty substances to imported butter that takes all its flavor away. Although the butter came from Finland, it tasted like bad margarine. Sausages contained so much spoiled meat they were practically inedible. Milk was mixed with powdered milk and water, and sour cream was diluted with sour milk. There were special closed shops in milk factories where Party bosses could get high-quality products. (Engineer from Leningrad)

Respondents pointed out that the rotten food people ate often led to dietary deficiencies and severe medical problems, and the food crisis was compounded by mismanagement of the *kolkhozy*, collective farms.

In early 1984, there was such a severe shortage of fodder the majority of *kolkhozy* in Rivne oblast lost more than half of their cattle. A directive was issued to slaughter the remaining cows and bring the meat to the cooperative stores. In February and March there was suddenly meat in the stores and meat dishes in restaurants, but since there were no cattle left, milk disappeared, and dairy factories had to produce milk from powder taken from old stock and military supplies. (Agronomist from Rivne, Ukraine)

In 1988 and 1989, SAAOR data showed that the overall food supply situation was continuing to deteriorate. For the first time, the Soviet press began to address the problem of food shortages and the low quality of foodstuffs. They pointed out deficient and defective food production, inefficient distribution, poor storage facilities, and the usual culprit, "climatic conditions," even though there was no evidence of it.

Respondents pointed to more specific causes: bureaucratic ineptitude, lack of fodder, poor animal husbandry, and unrealistic procurement prices. Centralized management of prices created a two-tiered pricing system. The kolkhoz markets, with availability and choice vastly better than in the state stores, commanded substantially higher prices. In fact, potatoes in the markets cost five times as much as in state stores, onions four times as much, and tomatoes double the price.

In state stores, the fruit and vegetable shelves remained empty, and the small amount of produce available was of third-rate quality. Meat and dairy products practically disappeared from the state stores but were plentiful in the market, though at substantially higher prices. Soviet citizens instinctively picked up the benefits of the free market without ever studying the principles of free market capitalism.

DURING THE SEVENTY-FOUR-YEAR life of the system, many entrepreneurial individuals found clever ways to improve their lot. Such undertakings usually provided a product or service from which the entrepreneur and consumer both profited. The problem was that such ventures clashed with Communist orthodoxy. If the activity was discovered, the individual was subject to arrest for "profiteering" or "parasitism," followed by a stint in the Gulag.

My friend, the artist Volodymyr Makarenko, once told me a story that poignantly illustrated one such undertaking when he lived in Ukraine.

> In the village outside of Dnipropetrovsk where I lived with my grandmother, there were always shortages of basic foodstuffs. The people who grew vegetables on their private plots were usually better off because they could supplement their diet with a few fresh vegetables. I remember days when I got up in the morning and there was nothing to eat, so I went to school hungry. On the way, I passed by some private vegetable plots, and when no one was around I picked a cucumber or tomato, and that would carry me for the day. Needless to say, there were no fat kids around. Two

enterprising young men in the village looking for a way to improve their lot decided to breed fish in a shallow pond outside the village. They enlarged the banks of the pond, diverted some water from the brook and began to breed carp. They fed them scraps no one would eat, and before long the carps grew big, and provided the village with fish, something that significantly improved their diet since there was no meat to be had. The villagers were happy, and in the process, the two young men made a few extra rubles pocket money. Then someone reported the operation to the village Communist Party official. The boys were called in, accused of profiteering, and severely reprimanded. Worse, a few days later, a bulldozer covered the entire pond with dirt, and that was the end of fish in the village.

33. Exploring Greece

CHRISTOPHOR GELEKLIDIS did well working with us. Over the years, he saved enough to purchase a country villa near the town of Marathon, some forty kilometers (twenty-five miles) northeast of Athens. He was proud of his *dacha*, a two-story stone and masonry house, surrounded by a lemon orchard so productive that he let his neighbors pick their fill. Every time I visited, I returned with two large sacks of fresh lemons that I gave away to friends in Paris.

"Lemons have therapeutic qualities," Christophor insisted. "Their oil provides health and aromatherapy benefits."

We spent hours discussing topics ranging from Ancient Greece's wars with the Persians, the Byzantine struggles with the Saracens, and the Ottoman Empire, to relations between Russia and Ukraine. On one of my visits to the dacha, Christophor told me, "Today, Slava, I will take you to the site of the most famous battle in ancient history."

"You mean Thermopylae?" I asked.

"No, I will take you to the plain of Marathon, where the outnumbered Athenian army defeated the Persians. Thermopylae came ten years later, and it's far to the north on the coast."

We drove to a place called Agia Panteleimon, on the Bay of Marathon, five kilometers south of modern Marathon. "This is where in September of 490 BC, ten thousand Athenian hoplite warriors faced twenty thousand of King Darius's Persian infantry," Christophor explained. "The two armies met on this flat battlefield surrounded by hills and sea, and the Greeks defeated the Persians." Christophor pointed to the ten-meter-high mound covering the bones of two hundred Athenians who fell here, and continued, "The Greeks had chosen a location surrounded by marshes and mountains to prevent Darius's cavalry from joining the main Persian army. Miltiades, the Greek general, lured the Persians' best fighters into his center, enveloped, and routed them. The Persian army broke in panic towards their ships." The defeat at Marathon marked the end of the first Persian invasion of Greece. For Greeks, it was sacred land where Athenians fought the might of Asia alone. This decisive victory preserved the experiment of Athenian democracy, which was the foundation of Western civilization. Today, however, the battle is perhaps more famous as the inspiration for the marathon race, the forty-two-kilometer distance between Marathon and Athens.

Ten years after Marathon, Darius's son Xerxes opened a second campaign to subjugate Greece. Everyone knows, of course, that in 480 BC, a small force of Spartans and Thebans led by King Leonidas made a legendary last stand against the massive Persian army at Thermopylae. Far fewer are aware of the more significant naval clash off the island of Salamis, which marked the high-point of the second Persian invasion of Greece.

It took us nearly an hour to drive back to Athens. A Soviet ship had docked in Piraeus, and there was work to do. Four of the Greek interviewers were standing by to pick the brains of unsuspecting Soviet tourists who marched past the dock gate by the hundreds and dispersed to the souvenir and gift shops. Some headed directly to the Acropolis, where a couple of more interviewers were waiting.

A Soviet cruise ship typically stayed two or three days in the port, and in between ships, there was some downtime. On one occasion, I went to Salamis, a mountainous, barren island with a few dockyards that repaired ships and oil tankers, three-kilometer ferry ride from Piraeus. Except for a monument to the Battle of Salamis, there was no sign of the existential clash that took place in these straits between the Persian and Greek naval forces. This is where the outnumbered Athenians and their allies withdrew their ships, to bring the Persian fleet to battle. The subterfuge worked. In these cramped conditions, Persia's superior numbers became disorganized, and the Greek fleet, forming a firm defensive line, scored a decisive victory. A Persian victory would have thwarted the development of Ancient Greece and, ultimately of Western civilization.

The three battles—Marathon, Thermopylae, and Salamis—represented crucial turning points in a decisive war between the despotic East and nascent democratic West. The struggle continues to this day in the form of the conflict between the Muslim East and the West.

I DISCOVERED GREEK history in small and often unrelated pieces: the Temple of Poseidon at Cape Sounion south of Athens, the oracle of Delphi to the northeast, Corinth on the Isthmus, Mycenae, the second millennium BC archeological site, and Epidaurus with its acoustically perfect amphitheater. Later in Paris, I relived the history of these places from books as I fit the pieces into a more coherent historical perspective.

One weekend, when there were no Soviet ships in Piraeus, Vanya and I headed for Patras on the Gulf of Corinth on a scouting trip to see if any Soviet vessels had docked in that port. The busy town was a nodal point for trade and communication with Italy and the rest of Western Europe. Dubbed Greece's Gate to the West, it was the country's third-largest urban area. Strolling through Patras, I noticed a few cafes with middle-aged men, some sipping coffee, others playing dominoes, and still others talking and smoking. Vanya and I sat down in one to grab a quick espresso, and I struck up a conversation with the waiter, who was also the owner and spoke English. After some small talk, he began to complain that he was overwhelmed with work.

I asked, "Why don't you hire someone to help you with the business? Unemployment in Greece is high, so it shouldn't be hard to find waiters."

He smiled. "It's not that simple. The young people don't like to work, and many of them are at the university and study until the age of thirty. And most of those men playing dominoes are getting unemployment compensation or some kind of pension or disability benefits. If they work, they'll lose the benefits. So why should they work?"

I found this strange. In the United States and most other countries, we are not eligible for a retirement pension until we're sixty-five, and most of these men were clearly in their fifties, some younger. The state seemed to be rewarding unemployment and encouraging parasitical behavior. I also learned that many of these pensioners were moonlighting on jobs where they did not declare income and pay taxes. Between the pension and a part-time job, they didn't fare too badly. I had witnessed similar scenes in other parts of Greece and realized that the majority of the populace was milking the system for all it was worth.

Fast-forwarding to the 2010s, it was clear that Greece's financial crisis had been long in the making. I realized that every other Greek was looking for the ideal setup, a low-paying government job to get early retirement and a pension while holding an "under the table" job where he didn't pay taxes. This had been a widespread practice since the 1980s, and the authorities tacitly ignored it. Today, nothing has changed except that the chickens have come home to roost. Indefensible became untenable, and the rest, as they say, is history.

In Patras, we learned that the only Soviets in the vicinity were occasional visitors to the island of Corfu, too far for our Athens team, but a visit to the castle of Patras was a rewarding experience. Built by the Byzantine emperor Justinian on top of the ruins of the ancient Acropolis, it sits on a hill eight hundred meters from the coast overlooking the Little Dardanelles, the narrows that close the Gulf of Corinth. With the help of binoculars, I could make out Lepanto (today Nafpaktos) across the channel where the Battle of Lepanto, probably the single most significant naval engagement in the history of modern Europe, took place. The victory at Lepanto—roughly two thousand years after the battle in the Straits of Salamis—saved the Christian West from defeat at the hands of the Ottoman Turks.[103]

For eight centuries, the Mediterranean was abandoned to the mercy of Saracen pirates who infested these waters and impeded trade and commerce. After the fall of Constantinople in 1453, the Turks turned the Mediterranean into a blind alley. To stop further expansion, a coalition of European Catholic maritime states arranged by Pope Pius V and led by Spanish admiral Don Juan of Austria (the Holy League) gathered at Messina, Sicily, and set sail for the Gulf of Lepanto to confront the Turkish fleet.

On October 7, 1571, the two fleets clashed in the Gulf of Lepanto. The Holy League forces defeated the fleet of the Ottoman Empire on the northern edge of the Gulf of Corinth, off western Greece, making the Christian victory complete. The victory of the Holy League prevented the Ottoman Empire from expanding further along the European side of the Mediterranean and delayed Muslim incursion into the heart of Europe to the gates of Vienna by 112 years. The victory of Lepanto is relevant to what is taking place in Europe in the twenty-first century—the Muslin invasion may not be a military one, but an invasion it is.

BETWEEN 1985 AND 1991, work took me to Athens once or twice a year. Much of this time I spent in Athens or the port of Piraeus, where Soviet tourists congregated. In Piraeus, I usually stayed at a hotel overlooking the

---

[103] The book to read is *Victory of the West: The Great Christian–Muslim Clash at the Battle of Lepanto* (2006), by Niccolo Capponi.

Mikrolimano lagoon, Athens's yacht harbor, surrounded by half a dozen waterside fish restaurants. This is where Athenians came to taste the freshest fish in the Athens area and enjoy Greek music. For me, it was a brisk fifteen-minute walk to the port where the action was.

The Mikrolimano hotel owner, Nikolaos, was one of Christophor's well-to-do friends, a retired real estate magnate and entrepreneur who ran the hotel and restaurant as a hobby. Christophor introduced me to Nikolaos as a special guest from Paris followed by what I sensed was the Greek equivalent of a wink-wink.

"Call me Nikos," he said, and from that point, I got the kid-glove treatment. Nikos was a personable English-speaking gentleman who liked to talk about himself. Quite often, he invited me to his table for a drink and chat. When he found out that I was of Ukrainian origin, he naturally assumed that I was a fellow Orthodox. For Greeks, the fact that I belonged to a church of the Byzantine rite was sufficient to form an unspoken bond. We exchanged life stories, and on one occasion, he told me how he had met his wife.

At age fifty, he was independently wealthy but still not married. All of the women he dated, he claimed, were gold diggers, interested in his wealth. Then on an Olympic Air flight to visit a cousin in Chicago, he was smitten by a beautiful Greek-American hostess.

"I tried to get her attention, but she insisted on treating me like the other passengers. The more she ignored me, the more I knew I had to meet her. When we landed in New York, I asked her if she would have a drink with me that evening, and to my astonishment, she said OK, but only a drink. I was in heaven. It was then and there that I decided that this was the woman I would marry."

Nikos recounted that after dinner that evening, he proposed, and she accepted. How much of this was true is hard to say; it was clear that he had told the story many times. "We've been married nearly twenty years, and we have three children," he said as he showed me their photos.

Nikos liked to dabble in ancient Greek history. "While in Greece," he said, "you must visit some of the Greek islands. The port of Piraeus is a hub for ferries to nearly all of the Greek islands. Visiting them is like taking a long bus ride to work. Pick up a ferry schedule, you'll see."

I began my exploration of the Greek Islands with the so-called home group, islands where many Athenians had their weekend homes. Beginning with Aegina, twenty-five kilometers from Piraeus, I eventually expanded my trips to the Cyclades, a group of two hundred islands in the Aegean Sea southeast of the mainland. Later, I made it all the way to Crete, the Big Island, halfway between Athens and Egypt.

On Nikos' advice, I hopped on a ferry to Mykonos. Daily departures from the port of Piraeus made the trip very convenient. Roughly one hundred kilometers by sea from Athens, the ferry called at two large islands, Poros and Naxos, two-thousand-meter humps in the pristine blue waters of the Aegean. These were the largest islands in the Cyclades group and stood like twin pillar gates to Mykonos and Delos.

MYKONOS WAS A CHARMING place. Its town, Chora, was a mosaic of white cube-shaped houses linked by a maze of alleys and arched pathways winding between white walls and flower-bedecked balconies and chapels with brightly painted domes.

When I got off the ferry and walked to the old harbor area, I noticed that the restaurants and bars had more than their share of men, all seemingly well-dressed, happy, chatty and gregarious. It was late in the day, so I began looking for a room. A lodging agency referred me to a private room, and I struck off through a maze of alleys and pathways. That's when I came across male couples strolling along, holding hands, some embracing, others kissing. I hadn't realized that Mykonos is one of the most gay-friendly islands in Europe, and its beaches a magnet for homosexuals.

Fortunately, I did not go there for the beaches. Even the famous nudist beaches such as Elia and Super Paradise that catered to the naturists were dominated by gays. What I found most shocking was that all of this was happening in the midst of a rampant AIDS epidemic, and yet it seemed to have little impact on the dangerously permissive lifestyle.

At the end of the '60s, the incidence of sexually transmitted disease increased fifty times in San Francisco because of promiscuous oral-anal sex among gays. In the '70s, in New York, liberal politicians loosened the legal restraints on sexual encounters between consenting adults and proceeded to license sexual gymnasia, "bathhouses," where hundreds of gay males per establishment indulged nightly in sexual free-for-alls with as many partners as possible.

By the eighties, "the increase in sexual infections was predictably, and astronomically, greater among gays than heterosexuals. By the early eighties, when AIDS was first identified, the prevalence of syphilis and gonorrhea among gays was *several hundred times* greater than among comparable groups of heterosexuals. Meanwhile, the diseases were being transformed as well.

The enteric diseases—amoebiasis, gay bowel syndrome, giardiasis, and shigellosis—were followed by hepatitis B, a disease that lowers the immune system of the host. The CDC said they didn't intervene because it would have been interfering with the alternative lifestyle of the gay community. Despite these realities, deference to political correctness led to tragic consequences."[104]

The radical counterculture's war against nature precipitated monsters like AIDS and resulted in an epidemic that killed nearly a million American men and spread to other parts of the world, most notably Africa, where it is still affecting tens of millions more.

NEXT DAY, I TOOK a ferry to Delos, the heart of the Aegean, only eight kilometers from Mykonos. The small island lies at the center of the ancient trading routes between the Dardanelles and Crete, a place that became a religious center for the Ionian League. One legend has it that Delos was the birthplace of Apollo, and it had an oracle associated with Delphi. It retained its reputation as a sanctuary throughout antiquity, until the emergence of Christianity. After viewing five of the remaining original twelve stone lions along the Sacred Way, I climbed Mount Cynthus, from where I could see the archipelago of the surrounding islands. No one lives on Delos, and that's why I could feel its past so vividly.

---

[104] See David Horowitz's *The Politics of Bad Faith: The Radical Assault on America's Future*, The Free Press, New York, 1998, chapter 5, "The Radical Holocaust."

34. *Touring with Darian*

THROUGHOUT THE 1980s, Darian and Tamara spent their summers in France. They were both in their teens, and old enough to appreciate the thrill of discovering new places. I used to take a few weeks' leave to introduce them to the cultural heritage of European civilization. I felt there was no better way to broaden their horizons than to have them see how people in different countries lived. On one occasion, Darian and I even made it as far east as Yugoslavia and Czechoslovakia, when these two countries were still whole.

From the summer of 1982, father and son had different priorities. Darian was fascinated by the Formula 1 Grand Prix circuit, while my interests focused on medieval cathedrals and abbeys. In July 1982, we drove eight hundred kilometers to see the Formula 1 race at the Paul Ricard Circuit in Southern France. In 1983, we went to the Hockenheimring near the Rhine in Germany.

In July 1984, the OECD sent me to Cambridge, England, to discuss issues related to chemical control with scientists at the university. At about the same time, Darian flew in from Chicago for his annual sojourn to France. Although he was almost seventeen, I did not want to leave him alone in Paris, so I did what I was accustomed to doing whenever business and personal life conflicted—I took him with me. We had been to England once before in the mid-'70s, when the children were small, but did not get to see much outside of London.

On this trip, Darian persuaded me to take him to the 1984 British Grand Prix (the XXXVII John Player British Grand Prix), a Formula 1 race held on July 22 at Brands Hatch in Kent. It was the tenth round of the 1984 Formula 1 season. That year, the race, contested over seventy-one laps, was won by Niki

Lauda for the McLaren team. What I took away from these experiences is that they were awfully noisy affairs—nonstop earsplitting vroom, vroom, vroom. Darian, with a deeper appreciation for car racing, was capable of discerning the finer points of the sport and could discuss nuances that escaped me. In any event, it was all great fun that brought father and son closer.

Next, we embarked on a tour of cathedrals: Ely and Peterborough north of London, and Winchester and Salisbury southwest of the capital. Most of the great cathedrals in England and Wales that were built during the Middle Ages still stand, testaments to the beauty and quality of their craftsmanship in stone, glass, and wood. The same is not true of the abbeys. Almost all, including the once austere but exquisite Cistercian abbeys of Fountains, Rievaulx, Tintern, and Jervaulx, lie in ruin in some of the most beautiful parts of the English countryside, as a result of Henry VIII's dissolution of the monasteries.

After visiting the cathedrals of Peterborough and Ely, I began to notice a pattern that distinguished them from the cathedrals of Picardie. While the French cathedrals amaze the visitor with the height of the nave, the cathedrals in southern England impress with their length and height of their spires. This was illustrated by the next two churches we visited, Winchester and Salisbury.

Winchester Cathedral, an amalgam of Norman and Gothic styles, was one of the largest cathedrals in England, with intricate ogilvied ceilings and massive columns. At 170 meters (558 feet), it had the longest nave of any Gothic cathedral in Europe. While it was only half as tall as Beauvais Cathedral in Picardie, its modest height accentuated the length.

It was easy to spot Salisbury Cathedral's immensely tall spire dominating the town and surrounding countryside. At 135 meters (404 feet), it is the loftiest in England. I got the impression that Salisbury had tried to accomplish with its spire what Winchester had with the length of its nave. Built between 1220 and 1258, its perfect proportions make it an outstanding example of English ecclesiastical architecture.

Sampling these four cathedrals gave me a new appreciation for English Norman and Gothic architecture. I found them to be neither superior nor inferior to the French Gothic cathedrals, just different. The experience whetted my appetite to one day visit some of the other prominent cathedrals in England such as Lincoln, York, Durham, and Exeter.

EARLIER THAT YEAR, my friend Srjan had invited me to visit him at his family's summer home on the Adriatic coast. Thus, a few days after returning to Paris from England, I told Darian to get ready for an even longer and more exciting trip. He was pleased. He knew Srjan; the two had developed a cordial relationship, and this was an opportunity to discover a different world. We packed our suitcases and set out on a two-thousand-kilometer journey to the Dalmatian coast.

We crossed the Alps at two of the highest passes—the Col du Galibier and the Col de l'Iseran, both around 2,700 meters. Once in Italy, we got onto the A-21 Autostrada at Torino, which took us to the heavily traveled west-east A-4 *Autostrada*, past Verona and Padua, and in no time, we were in Trieste. In Yugoslavia, however, our pace was reduced to a crawl, and it took us the better part of a day to reach our destination, the small town of Brodarica south of Sibenik where the Rašcovic clan had their summer house.

I had toured the lower Dalmatian coast around Dubrovnik and Montenegro a couple of years before, and in late December 1983, I had visited Sarajevo in Bosnia and driven from there to Jahorina, the site of the 1984 Winter Olympics. That was when I realized that the Socialist Federal Republic of Yugoslavia was an unstable artificial construct similar to the Soviet Union. The various ethnic groups simply did not like each other. By the mid-'80s, relations between the two major national groups, the Serbs and the Croats, were acutely strained. It was only a matter of time, I believed, before the country fragmented. In the '90s, Yugoslavia erupted into a civil war and broke up for good. Personally, I did not see it as a civil war but, rather, a series of wars of national liberation. The smaller nationalities were anxious to rid themselves of the yoke of Serb rule. The Croatians and Slovenes, in particular, resented being dominated by their larger Orthodox neighbor, Serbia.

Srjan and the Rašcovic family graciously welcomed us. The extended family included his parents, a sister with children, and cousins. They put us up in a tiny Spartan room on the second floor with a fabulous view of the azure sea. It had only one bed, so Darian and I took turns sleeping on the floor.

Like much of the Dalmatian coast, the shoreline around Brodarica lacked sandy beaches. Instead, rocks at the water's edge covered with poured concrete provided access to the water. The water was crystal clear and translucent, noticeably cleaner than the sea on the Côte d'Azur. The Dalmatian coast was lined with hundreds of elongated islands, large and small. One such island was Krapanj, half a kilometer across the channel from Brodarica. Srjan casually suggested that we swim there and back. I was never a distance swimmer, so I declined, but Darian took up the offer, and they soon vanished into the deep blue waters, while I lingered on the shore, waiting for them to return.

After about an hour, I saw them in the distance swimming back, but as Srjan stepped onto the shore, there was no sign of Darian.

"Where is Darian?" I asked.

"Oh, he's somewhere. He was swimming right behind me."

I looked out to the sea; Darian was nowhere to be seen. I started to worry as I scrutinized every meter of the coastline. I was on the verge of panic but continued to scan the shore as terrifying thoughts went through my mind. The water was deep, and he could have gotten a cramp. Suddenly, I glimpsed someone swimming between the moored boats and recognized Darian's bushy head. I was immensely relieved, but it took a while for me to calm down. Then I scolded him for putting me in a dreadful state of anxiety.

Every day ended with an outdoor evening meal of grilled fish, meat, and vegetables chased down with local Dalmatian white wine, not exactly Sancerre or Condrieu, but sufficiently drinkable to loosen up tongues. Srjan recounted the adventure of the day, telling us what a strong swimmer Darian was, and chiding me for not joining them.

The dinner party did not have a common tongue as neither Darian nor I spoke Serbo-Croat. Somehow, we still managed to carry on a conversation. With Srjan, we communicated in Ukrainian, and with his sister in English, while both acted as translators to and from Serbo-Croat. At times, I made an effort to mix Ukrainian, Russian, and Serbo-Croat, a kind of pigeon Slav that revealed the shared roots of these Slavic languages.

During one evening meal, two girls roughly Darian's age or slightly older showed up to practice their English. While I was discussing politics with the adults, Darian was chatting up the girls. They displayed a distinct interest in Darian, a tall, good-looking American of Ukrainian heritage, and quizzed him about America. I didn't know what they were talking about, but I could tell by Darian's smile that he was having a good time. Later Darian confided that both young ladies had made advances toward him, and that during the evening he had received two proposals of marriage.

The Raščovic *dacha* was in a predominantly Croat-populated area. Sometimes, the discussions included a few of the Croat neighbors, who were clearly resentful of Serb domination of their country and the corruption that came with it, a relationship similar to that between the Russians and Ukrainians. Like the Ukrainians, the Croats simply wanted to be left alone to rule themselves, without Belgrade telling them how to manage their affairs. Their attitude was encapsulated in the expression "*Khochu svoye, ne khochu tvoye"* (I want mine, and I don't want yours), a slogan that became popular during the conflict in the '90s.

Gradually, I learned about the long, complicated relationship between the Croats and Krajina Serbs. The Raščovics actually lived in Knin, the capital of the Serb enclave of Krajina, within the borders of Croatia. The Krajina Serbs had lived on a strip of territory north and west of Bosnia since the fifteenth century, when many Serbs fled from Ottoman-occupied territories in the south. Serbs fleeing their Kosovo and Metohija homeland were encouraged by the Austrian empire to settle the vacated area by giving them land in exchange for military service. This territory was called Krajina, a borderland military frontier that served as an Austrian-Ottoman buffer zone.

Apart from visiting with Srjan's family, there was time to discover the rich cultural heritage in the towns of Šibenik, Trogir, and Split. One morning, we walked a few kilometers to the Cathedral of Saint James in Šibenik, a fifteenth-century edifice built in the Renaissance style by masters from Tuscany. It was a modified Romanesque church with a triple-nave basilica, three apses, and a thirty-two-meter dome. The feature that impressed me the most, however, was the massive barrel vault roof made from huge stone slabs, a daring feat of construction, since this region is susceptible to earthquakes. The large fissures in the vaulting gave me the impression that the roof might come down any day. Belgrade did not provide the resources to repair the structure, probably because it was a Catholic cathedral. It was a miracle that the edifice still stood when we entered it. After Croatia broke away, extensive renovations took place, which made the cathedral safe again.

Trogir was a jewel on the Adriatic coast. Apart from its exquisitely preserved Romanesque-Gothic complex and attractive natural setting on the Adriatic Sea, the city had a fascinating history. As we walked along Trogir's palm-studded waterfront, Srjan recited the town's history.

Trogir was founded in the third century BC by Greek colonists, and the Romans developed it into a major port. An outpost of the Republic of Venice in the year 1000, it was completely demolished by Saracens in 1123. The Saracens and Moors were splendid at destroying cities and societies they considered as *Dar al-Kafr*, land of unbelievers. By the time they devastated Trogir, they had been doing it for almost five hundred years. Eventually, the town recovered to experience a strong economic prosperity in the twelfth and thirteenth centuries, with autonomy under Venetian leadership.

Split, a world-class tourist attraction, was twenty-seven kilometers east of Trogir. We left the car at the edge of the city and walked through the maze of ancient streets. Srjan led us directly to the city's centerpiece, Emperor Diocletian's Palace, a massive rectangular structure, much like a Roman military fortress. This was where, in AD 305, Diocletian retired. He was the first Roman emperor to voluntarily remove himself from office.

Our final stop in Yugoslavia was Knin. Srjan wanted us to meet his aging father, who was not at the *dacha*. We drove north through a hundred kilometers of nondescript Croatian countryside until we came upon a sight to behold: the ruins of the biggest defensive fortress in Europe. At least that's what Srjan told us. I learned later that the Knin stronghold was only the fifth largest castle in the area. Srjan was prone to exaggerate, and I took his superlatives with a grain of salt. In any event, the fort was big and impressive and represented an important bulwark against Turkish expansion. Its defensive walls, about two kilometers long and up to twenty meters thick in several places, enclosed the fortress from all sides. Its elongated shape reminded me of Peyrepertuse, a large Cathar castle in Roussillon, France.

ON THE RETURN LEG of our trip, we passed through Slovenia and entered Austria. It was late when we arrived in Vienna, and I found what looked like a decent hotel on Linzer Strasse in the 14th District, but as we stepped out to get something to eat, I realized that we were in one of Vienna's red-light districts. Scantily dressed ladies of the night seemed to occupy every corner. This was probably the first time Darian, almost seventeen, had been exposed to prostitutes on such a scale. It was awkward but too late to look for another hotel. Darian realized our predicament and joked, "*Tato* (Dad), is this why we came to Vienna?"

The next day we visited the Stephansdom and walked through the neighborhood where his mother's family lived when she was an infant in 1945 and 1946 after WWII ended. At that point, we had to make a decision: either press on to Munich in Bavaria, or detour to Prague in Czechoslovakia. I realized that this was an opportunity for us to see something out of the ordinary. It would be a unique experience for Darian: a sample of life in a Communist country that would hopefully inoculate him against the disease called Socialism. Without further ado, we headed for the Austro-Czechoslovak border.

We arrived at the border checkpoint at about seven in the morning, hoping to avoid a long wait at customs control. Luckily, there were no other cars, and with the CD tags on my auto, I expected to zip through without any problems. That was not to be. During the next two hours, in the no man's land between Austria and Czechoslovakia, Darian and I experienced the most bizarre search I had ever undergone.

"Reisepass bitte." The surly guard in a military uniform spoke in a brusque tone.

We gave him our passports, which he handed to a subordinate for checking at the customs booth. Next, he ordered us to get out of the car so they could search it. They slid a dolly with a large mirror under the car to check its undercarriage, ostensibly for drugs, weapons, or God knows what.

Since we had been on the road for over a week, the interior of the car was messy, which made them suspicious. The other agent came back and whispered something to the head honcho. I don't know if they found my name on some sort of blacklist or if they just wanted to intimidate us, but they started rummaging through our personal belongings.

He held up a box of cassette tapes. *"Was ist das?"* he asked.

"Das sind Musikkassetten (These are music cassettes)," I replied.

He flipped through some titles and found a few recordings of Ukrainian folk music. Next, he took one of the cassettes and inserted into the car's cassette player. It was the Ukrainian- American singer Kvitka. The guard turned up the volume and tried to make out the lyrics, skipping and fast-forwarding from song to song, as if he was searching for hidden messages. He inserted another cassette and sampled the content, and then another and another. I don't know what he was looking for, but the scene that was unfolding was beyond surreal. Early in the morning, the border control point was filled with music blaring from the car. Then they inspected the glove compartment, looked under the seats, and went through every item inside the car. Finding nothing particularly incriminating, they ordered me to open the trunk and take out the suitcases. Again, they found nothing, except dirty laundry. Between the suitcases, one of them noticed a few books in English and copies of the Ukrainian literary magazine *Suchasnist'* (*Contemporary Times*).

He started to leaf through one of the issues. *"Und was ist das?"*

"Literature," I said, trying to switch to English.

"Nein, nein, das ist keine Literatur. Das ist Propaganda. You cannot take this into our country."

There was no point in arguing, so I handed him the magazines. He had no excuse to keep us any longer. We repacked our suitcases, and the agent grudgingly returned our passports and waved us through.

As soon as we crossed the border, the landscape changed drastically from orderly and tidy on the Austrian side to dull and dreary on the Communist side. The countryside appeared deserted; the village buildings dingy and bleak. Soon, we were on the Brno-Prague divided highway, which, except for an occasional Skoda or Trabant, was largely free of traffic.

In spite of the unpleasant border incident, Darian and I were in good spirits, laughing and cruising between fifty and sixty kilometers an hour. (Someone had once warned me that one should not drive fast on the other side of the Iron Curtain. The police were aggressive and notoriously corrupt.) Since I did not see any speed limit signs, I thought I was driving at a reasonably safe speed, when suddenly a police car on the side of the road signaled us to stop.

A policeman with a stern look approached and said we were driving over the legal speed limit. I tried to explain that I had not seen any speed limit signs, but he cut me off and said the limit was forty-five kilometers, roughly thirty miles per hour, and I would have to pay a fine.

Obviously, this was a scam to fleece unsuspecting foreigners of a few extra koruna, but there was nothing I could do. I paid the fine and got a ticket labeled *za pokutu*, which translates roughly to "for penance." On the positive side, the penalty was laughably small, equivalent to about two dollars.

It took us almost four hours to cover the remaining 150 kilometers to Prague. Even after forty years of Communist neglect, Prague was a beautiful city. A friend in Paris once told me that if I should ever find myself in Prague, I should stay at the venerable one-hundred-year-old Grand Hotel Europa in the city's central plaza. It was one of Prague's most renowned architectural landmarks. Its unique Art Nouveau exterior was eye-catching, but the reception area and lobby were small and cramped. Darian and I walked to the front desk and asked if they had a room available.

"Yes, of course." The man behind the desk asked to see our passports. After he glanced at them and scrutinized us, he called his supervisor.

The supervisor looked at my passport. "Are you Ukrainian?"

"I am an American citizen of Ukrainian descent, and this is my son who was born in the United States," I replied. "What difference does it make?"

"If you are a Ukrainian-American, then you must be a *banderovets*." He had tagged me as a sympathizer of the nationalist movement Stepan Bandera founded before WWII.

"We do not like *banderovtsy* as guests at this hotel. Perhaps you should try somewhere else."[105]

I couldn't believe it. The manager must have been a Party member indoctrinated to detest and fear Ukrainian nationalists. This was evidence that, sixteen years after the 1968 Prague Spring, the Communist Party still had a firm hold on Czech society. All that would change in five years, but who was to know?

Angrily I took the passports and walked out of the hotel. We found another one in the old town where the receptionist did not know who the *banderovtsy* were. We stayed in Prague long enough to visit Prague Castle, one of the largest castles in the world, soak up the flavor of the city, and enjoy some Guláš and Czech beer.

On the third day, we were on the road again in the direction of Plzeň (Pilsen), about ninety kilometers west of Prague. Known worldwide for its Pilsner beer, it was also the home of the Škoda Works, armament and transport manufacturers. In 1984, Pilsen was a grimy and colorless city bathed in gray paint. On the outskirts of the city, we were welcomed by a flash and deafening thunderclap that sounded like a twenty-one-gun artillery salute. A ferocious downpour reduced visibility to a few meters, and I was forced to pull off the road into an empty parking lot to wait out the storm.

Eventually, the rain let up, and when we were getting ready to walk to the restaurant across the street, a police car pulled up. Two armed policemen stepped out and asked to see our passports. Thinking it was a routine check, I handed them our American passports.

One of them pointed to a No Parking sign. "Did you know you are not allowed to park here?"

I said I only stopped there because of the downpour and would move my car, but my response did not please them.

"The building behind you is the headquarters of the Communist Party. Parking is reserved for Party members only."

"I apologize. I didn't know this was the Communist Party headquarters. The heavy rain obscured the No Parking sign. I will move the car straight away."

"Before you leave, you will have to pay a fine." The policeman's tone was threatening.

---

[105] *Banderovtsy* is the Russian equivalent of the Ukrainian *banderivtsi*, a Banderite.

"But I don't have any more koruna. We are on our way to Germany and cannot pay a fine," I pleaded.

Then he said something that alarmed me. "In that case, you will not get your passports back." He started to walk away. Another damn scam. I asked how much the fine was, and he said, "Thirty koruna."

I had about fifty koruna in loose coins that I had saved for one final meal before entering Germany. Reluctantly, I gave the extortionist thirty koruna and got another ticket *za pokutu*. More importantly, we got out passports back. With the remaining koruna, we had just enough to purchase two small Pilsner drafts and one sausage on a bun, which we shared.

The German border was still seventy kilometers away, so I drove very slowly and carefully. As we entered Germany, I felt as if I had been released from an asylum. The series of unpleasant experiences in the Socialist Republic of Czechoslovakia had left me exhausted. I turned over the wheel to Darian and promptly fell asleep. When I awoke, we were near Strasburg. Darian had driven across the width of Germany, a distance of over four hundred kilometers, in about three hours. That was the kind of speed and freedom of movement only a German *Autobahn* offers.

EVER SINCE I PURCHASED my first guitar in Granada in 1976, I've been a flamenco enthusiast. In Chicago, I studied with Ted Rechine, a superb musician who played regularly at Geja's Café on Armitage Avenue near Lincoln Park in Chicago. He taught me to play flamenco guitar using the traditional method employing tablature notations. In the event, I brought my passion for flamenco to France, where there were many opportunities to appreciate the unique sound of that instrument. One of them was the *Concours International de la Guitare* in Tarbes.

As soon as Darian arrived in July 1986, I told him that we would drive to Tarbes in south-west France to attend the guitar festival, and return via a circuit that would take us to Lourdes, the tiny principality of Andorra, and the Cathar country along the eastern Pyrenees.

Compared to the guitarists I had heard in Granada and Seville, the mainly amateur guitarists at the Tarbes festival were disappointing. On the third day of the festival, we headed for Lourdes, ten kilometers south of Tarbes. Lourdes, of course, has been a pilgrimage destination for Catholics since the Virgin Mary appeared to Bernadette Soubirous (Saint Bernadette) in 1858. The place has developed a reputation for miraculous healings, and every year around five million pilgrims flock here in the hope of a cure or spiritual renewal.

From friends in Paris, I learned that it was possible to spend the night at a hostel run by the Ukrainian Catholic Sister Servants of Mary Immaculate. We arrived in the afternoon, and the nuns welcomed us with the news that we had come just in time to observe the procession of invalids at 5:00 p.m. I did not know how to react. I turned to Darian.

"Well, Darian, aren't we lucky? Shall we go to see the parade of invalids?"

"Of course," said Darian, grinning. "Isn't this why we came to Lourdes?"

For many years after this event, this episode became a private joke between father and son, a story we liked to relate to friends whenever we talked about our visit to Lourdes.

At 5:00 p.m., on the main street lined with kitschy souvenir shops and throngs of tourists, we watched a multitude of sick, blind, or terminally ill people, some walking, others pushed in wheelchairs, wind their way to the underground basilica for a blessing of the infirm. There are hundreds, if not thousands, of miraculous healings documented by families and doctors that the medical profession is still unable to explain, including spontaneous remission in cancer patients. I tend to agree with healers like Deepak Chopra, who say that we have not yet completely understood the relationship between the health of the body and the healing power of the mind and soul. Before leaving Lourdes, Darian purchased several plastic Blessed Virgin–shaped vials and filled them with holy water to present to grandparents in Chicago.

Driving along the picturesque Val d'Aran in the Pyrenees, we entered Andorra, a duty-free haven at two thousand meters that attracts up to ten million tourists a year. We did not go there to shop. Our goal was to observe and add another stamp to our passports. Those were the days when every crossing of a border was documented by an entry and exit visa stamp. While border controls may have inconvenienced some tourists, they served a purpose. The EU's elimination of border controls has turned out to have unintended consequences, which became fully apparent in 2015 when the migrant crisis hit Europe like a tsunami.

From Andorra, we drove through a corner of France known as Corbières, a large wine-producing region in the Languedoc-Roussillon responsible for half of the region's AOC wine production. It was also known as the *Pays Cathare*, Cathar country, a region studded with the ruins of scores of spectacularly-sited mountaintop fortresses.

Night had descended before we reached our destination, the Cistercian Abbey of Fontfroide. Rather than look for a hotel in this sparsely populated countryside, we pulled off the main highway onto a farm road, spread our sleeping bags on a grassy patch, and went to sleep with nothing but millions of stars for our roof. Perfect calm. No sign of people, no hum of distant traffic. Except for the crickets, it was silence, complete silence.

During the day, the hot Languedoc sun had warmed the ground sufficiently to permit us to sleep under the open sky, not unlike the Cro-Magnon man who dwelled in this region after the last Ice Age receded fifteen thousand years ago. The cloudless sky was perfect for star gazing. I pointed out the Milky Way to Darian and pondered the immensity of the cosmos made up of hundreds of billions of galaxies, each made up of hundreds of billions of stars like our sun, some of them billions of light years apart. I was overwhelmed by the sheer size of the universe, and the realization of how insignificant we were in comparison to the infinite cosmos.

In the 1980s, scientists estimated that around one hundred billion or two hundred billion galaxies swirled within the observable universe. In 2016, the same scientists determined that there might be two trillion galaxies, 90 percent of which were too faint for our most sensitive telescope to detect. The size of the universe is something impossible to behold. I read somewhere that this puzzle had created one of the greatest crises facing modern physics today. How could anything be infinite? Surely, the universe ended somewhere. And assuming there was a wall that enclosed the cosmos, how thick was it? And if the wall was finite, what about the space beyond the wall? And, finally, if the universe is finite, what did its edge look like?

These questions led me to ponder out loud the existence of God. Surely there must be a force or energy that started it all, a prime mover. If not a prime mover, then what? Agnostics say they don't know for sure, and that, at least, is an honest answer. Atheists say that the whole thing exists by chance, by accident, and dismiss the notion of God as ridiculous but proffer nothing in its place. As I was putting these thoughts into words, I realized Darian was fast asleep.

APPROACHING THE ABBEY of Fontfroide, I noticed silhouettes of two abandoned hilltop fortresses, Monséret and Saint Martin de Toques. Anywhere else in the world, these ruins would have been prize tourist attractions, but in Southern France, they were just two of the hundreds of unmarked and neglected vestiges of the violent Middle Age.

I parked a few hundred meters from Saint Martin, whose walls were still formidable and seemingly impenetrable. We were unable to find the entrance until I stumbled on a breach in the wall that was too high to climb but too tempting to resist. Darian planted himself firmly against the wall, and I climbed on his shoulders, trying to scale it. For a while, it was touch and go, but I finally got over the top and then extended my hand to Darian, and he, too, made it over the wall.

Most of this medium-sized castle was covered with vegetation, scattered stone, and fallen arches. We climbed on top of a rise in the center, wondering what the slightly curved mound of cut stone represented. It took me a few minutes to figure out that we were standing on top of a chapel groin vault that centuries of debris had covered. A small fissure in the wall provided enough light to confirm that the eastern end of the space terminated with a small semicircular apse.

By noon, we were in Fontfroide, a magnificent twelfth-century Cistercian abbey and a superb example of Romanesque construction. Fontfroide was a bastion of orthodox Catholicism, and its construction was temporarily interrupted by the Cathar wars. It was the murder of Pierre de Castelnau, a Fontfroide monk and legate to Pope Innocent III, that led to the Albigensian Crusade in 1208.

After touring the abbey's grounds, we got on the autoroute A-9 at Narbonne and drove straight north for eight hundred kilometers (five hundred miles). Eight hours later, we were back in Paris.

35. On the Road with Tamara

IN 1989, THREE YEARS after the trip to south-west France with Darian, I made plans for an even more ambitious circuit that would take us to Barcelona and back to Paris. A dear friend and guitar partner, Yaro Markewycz, came to Paris during the last week of May, and a few days later, Tamara arrived. June was the perfect month for touring—ideal weather, fewer tourists on the road, lower hotel prices, and greater availability. In Barcelona, we had an open invitation to stay with Isidre Compta-Carar and his wife, Melania. We set off on a ten-day jaunt that took us to the Loire, and through Périgord to the Dordogne, Quercy, and Roussillon regions, some of the most beautiful parts of rural France.

Our first stop was Chambord, probably one of the most recognizable châteaux in the world and the largest in the Loire Valley. We stopped to picnic on the lawn surrounding the château next to the Cosson, a river moat. The setting was out of a Charles Perrault fairy tale. The Renaissance structure constructed by King Francis I of France was never completed. Still, it remains one of the most impressive and popular castles on the Loire castle circuit. There are, of course, dozens of other famous châteaux in the region, but we had a lot of territory to cover before reaching our destination, Catalonia.

By late afternoon, we were in the Dordogne River Valley, one of France's most enchanting regions. Though less popular than the Loire, the region's culinary traditions, history, and castles are nearly as impressive. It is a part of France that has been inhabited since the prehistoric Cro-Magnon man drove out the Neanderthal. It was too late in the day to explore the nearby caves with their Paleolithic wall paintings, so I began looking for a place to spend the night. In the rural countryside between Les Eyzies and Saint-Cyprien, I spotted a sign pointing to a *Chambres/Table d'hôte,* two kilometers off the main road. Within minutes, we arrived at La Combe, a farmstead transformed into a guest house that offered rooms and meals. The proprietors, Françoise and Marc Wagon, welcomed us and said they had one room left that slept four. I took it without even seeing the room. Dinner would be served at seven.

The minute we stepped into the kitchen, an inviting bouquet from the pot on the stove got my digestive juices flowing. This would be no ordinary meal. It was no secret that in Périgord, one ate well. The region's two luxury ingredients, the truffle and goose liver, had enriched French cuisine for centuries.

Madame Wagon seated us at the long communal table. We began with *pâté de foie gras,* followed by chicken in a white wine and brandy sauce, washed down with a nice Côtes de Bergerac. The meal ended with the farm's own cheese. This was exquisite country cooking, an eating experience worlds apart from the bourgeois cuisine one finds in pricey restaurants.

Early the next morning, a rooster woke us up. I stepped out on the balcony to take a whiff of the pure country air and felt rejuvenated. At eight, we joined the communal table for a breakfast of hearty country bread and homemade preserves, served with an omelet made with truffles. For a day, La Combe returned us to the purity of the surrounding countryside, and that moment lingers in my mind to this day. I swore that one day I would come back to this enchanted spot for a longer stay.

We followed the great Dordogne, a river that flows between fifty-meter-high limestone cliffs, pausing at Beynac and La Roque Gageac, two picturesque villages on the river, and continued to Rocamadour. Strolling along Rocamadour's main pedestrian street, I explained to Tamara and Yaro that it was one of the most famous places in the Christian world. Built on the side of a cliff below the complex of monastic buildings and pilgrimage churches, the site was stunning. Hovering 120 meters above the entire complex was a medieval fortress built to protect the town's holy places. Kings, emperors, and saints all knelt at the foot of the miraculous statue of the Black Virgin Mary and the tomb of the ancient hermit named Zaccheus of Jericho, who allegedly conversed with Jesus himself. Every year, over a million visitors from all corners of the world come to see this unique monument to Christian civilization.

THE SHORTEST ROAD TO Cathar country in Roussillon was through the spectacular but narrow and perilous Gorges of Gelamus, one of France's most famous balcony roads that leaves no room for error. Cut into the sides of sheer cliffs, the road was so narrow it was impossible to turn around. It was not for the timid, nor for those with a fear of heights. Throughout the gorge's nine kilometers, my passengers, intimidated by the precipitous drop on their side, sat frozen like scared rabbits. When we emerged at Saint-Paul-de-Fenouillet, my shirt was damp with perspiration.

The Cathar saga had long fascinated me. I had read extensively about the Cathar phenomenon—a section of my library is devoted exclusively to the Cathars—and I offered Tamara and Yaro a primer on their history. It was not an easy task. The so-called Albigensian Crusade to eradicate them was one of the most shameful chapters in French history. I shared this story by taking them on a guided tour of three great Cathar castles—Peyrepertuse, Queribus, and Puilaurens.

"Catharism came from the Balkans," I explained. "A Bulgarian priest, Bogomil (Beloved of God) founded a movement that preached a Gnostic-Manichean dualist theology that believed in a constant struggle between good and evil. Mainstream Orthodox and Catholic churches considered Bogomilism a heretical doctrine that needed to be eradicated. To avoid persecution, the heretics migrated first to northern Italy and then to southern France."

In the 12th century the Cathar faith spread because its credo implied that you did not need an intermediary to mediate your relationship with God. In southern France, it was a reaction to the rituals and practices of the Catholic Church that many deemed corrupt and irrelevant. In that respect, the Cathars were the precursors of the Protestants. Instead of priests, they had "perfects," extreme ascetics who renounced meat and sex, who were curiously not too different from ascetic monks in the Catholic Church's monastic orders. At the same time, they were healers of the body as well as healers of the spirit, much sought after for their power to cure the sick and diseased.

I had been reflecting on the healing aspect of this faith and got to understand why the belief appealed to so many people. The perfects knew that much of the sickness in their world, as in the modern world, had psychosomatic origins, and that much illness was related to diet, overeating, and stress. The healers were aware of this and used common-sense fasting practices and herbs to cure the sick. I believe there is something we can learn from a religion that healed both the body and the soul. Some historians have compared the Cathars to Western Buddhists, considering that their view of the doctrine of resurrection taught by Jesus was similar to the Buddhist doctrine of reincarnation. The Cathar movement also proved to be extremely successful in gaining female followers because of its proto-feminist teachings at a time when women felt excluded from the Catholic Church.

While some aspects of the Cathar faith appealed to me, others did not. They believed, for example, that all visible matter, including the human body, was created by an evil god and therefore tainted with sin. They believed that the body, being material, was bad, false and objectionable. They preached that the goal was for the soul to leave the body and exist as spirit only. All this was contrary to the orthodox Christian view that Creation is good, that the body is good, that sex is good — not, as the Cathars believed, something to be shunned. The Cathars also viewed marriage and reproduction as a moral evil to be avoided, as it continued the chain of reincarnation and suffering in the material world.

The danger was that the triumph of these heretical principles would mean the extinction of the human race, given that all intercourse between the sexes ought to be avoided, and that suicide under certain circumstances, is not only lawful but commendable. From this perspective, the Orthodox cause was the cause of progress and civilization.

The Cathar heresy therefore presented a threat to the authority of the Catholic Church. By the twelfth century Catharism had become a dominant force in Languedoc, but when efforts to stop its spread proved futile, Pope Innocent III engaged the ferocious Frankish barons from the north to eradicate the heresy by force. The Pope declared that any man taking up the cross against the Cathars for a period of forty days or more was to receive the same Crusader's privileges as if he had undertaken the long and perilous journey to the Holy Land to wrest Jerusalem from the Muslims: remission of all past sins, the right to claim any booty captured in battle, and rights to the lands confiscated from those who sheltered the heretics. Thus, without delving into the theological intricacies, what started out as a matter of doctrine turned into a land grab of monumental proportions.

The brutal struggle began with the massacre of Béziers in 1209 and went on for twenty years. Still, the heresy persisted. To finish the job, the Church enlisted the help of the Dominicans. This led to the formation of the Inquisition in 1231. The Inquisition had some curiously modern aspects to it. It kept records. Virtually everything we know about the Cathars comes from these records. It means that our knowledge is inevitably one-sided.

The remaining Cathars were hounded down with stark cruelty that culminated in the burning of 400 Cathar perfects at Montségur in 1244. The Albigensian Crusade eradicated the last of the Cathars along with the secrets of their healers. [106]

DURING THE 1980S, there was a movement to revive the memory of the Cathars, and many of their hilltop castles became tourist attractions. The ruins of the so-called *châteaux vertigineux*, vertiginous castles, are strung out along the foothills of the Pyrenees from the Mediterranean coast to Toulouse, over some two hundred kilometers, many in view of each other. Rising from their mountaintops, the fortresses seem impregnable. The Cathars positioned their castles on mountaintops for strategic reasons. They were ideal for watching the movements of the Frankish armies in the river valleys below, and, more importantly, they served as signal posts for transmitting messages from the coast to the interior.

Queribus rests on a rocky outcropping seven hundred meters above sea level. It was the last refuge for numerous Cathar deacons who sought safety there after the fall of Montségur, but this seemingly unconquerable castle was finally forced to surrender in 1255. Looking east from its summit, we could see the blue Mediterranean, and to the northwest, the massive fortress of Peyrepertuse, stretched along a rocky outcrop of the Corbières. Unlike Queribus, Peyrepertuse hardly suffered from the Albigensian Crusaders. Built by the kings of Aragon in the eleventh century, the castle served as a Cathar refuge, and capitulated to French forces without a battle in 1240, a portentious year not only for the Cathars, but for the history of Ukraine. That was the year Kyiv succumbed to the Mongols.

The last castle we visited was Puilaurens, another of those indelible moments that I recall as if it were yesterday. After climbing the approaches to Peyrepertuse and Queribus, we paused for a snack at the foot of Puilaurens. Yaro decided he had had enough climbing and took out his guitar. While he played, Tamara and I trudged up the zigzagging path to the top of Puilaurens.

Today, the Cathars are gone, as is the Holy Inquisition. Still, the Cathar experience offers opportunities for reflection about current threats to free speech. It appears we have not learned from past mistakes. Eight hundred years after the first Inquisition was launched, speech and thought control

---

[106] Stephen O'Shea's *The Perfect Heresy*, is an excellent source of information about this chapter of French history.

at institutions of higher learning is arguably even more insidious than the thirteenth-century Inquisition.

ISIDRE AND MELANIA were an uncommon couple. He was a handsome polyglot (fluent in seven languages including Ukrainian), and his wife, Melania was an attractive German-Ukrainian from Munich. I had met them in Munich the year before, and they had stayed with me in Paris.

They welcomed us in their apartment on Carrer de Nàpols, around the corner from Barcelona's signature attraction, the Basílica Sagrada Família, where they lived with their two sons. Since we arrived in midafternoon—it took us only two hours to drive from Perpignan to Barcelona—Isidre proposed a stroll along Las Ramblas and tapas barhopping in the Barrio Gotico, the Gothic Quarter. Tapas are small portions of various delicacies, not quite a snack, not quite a meal. The experience was new to us, so we let the experts, Isidre and Melania, do the ordering. The tapas were consumed standing in a crowded, lively bar, shared over a glass of wine with friends. The experience was all about sociability, a ritual intended to stimulate conversation and camaraderie. [107]

The next morning, we got a quick tour of the city that ended with a visit to the Basílica Sagrada Família, an architectural wonder that has been under construction for over a hundred years. It is hard to find words to describe Gaudi's masterpiece. Construction of this unconventional edifice began in 1883. Interrupted by wars, progress was extremely slow and arduous. When Isidre took us on a tour of the basilica, it was less than half complete. On my visit to Barcelona in 2010, construction was 70 percent complete, and the goal is to finish the project by 2026, the hundredth anniversary of Gaudi's death.

We left Barcelona on Saturday morning and, by noon, were in Béziers. Rather than continue to Montpellier and on to Paris, we took the time for one last detour: the spectacular Gorges du Tarn, France's smaller version of Grand Canyon. The Gorges is a canyon formed by the Tarn River on the northeastern edge of the Parc National des Cévennes in northern Languedoc-Roussillon. The Tarn, a smaller version of the Colorado River, cuts through old rock formations for a distance of fifty kilometers. In places, it is five

---

[107] While reviewing this manuscript on Thursday August 17, 2017, I was shocked by the news that an Islamic terrorist mowed down pedestrians walking along Las Ramblas, a central thoroghfare popular with tourists and residents, killing at least fourteen people and injuring over a hundred.

hundred meters deep, the deepest river in Europe, but still only a fraction of the Grand Canyon, which, at 1,500 meters, dwarfs the Tarn Gorge. The Gorge offered fantastic vistas, perched villages, hiking, and white-water rafting and kayaking. This was the last stop on our 2,500-kilometer circle tour that took us through some of the most scenic parts of France to Catalonia in Spain and back to Paris.

YARO AND I shared a passion for the guitar. During the mid-'70s, we had the pleasure of hearing some of the greatest guitarists of the age in Chicago's Orchestra Hall, including Andrés Segovia, the Spanish classical guitar virtuoso, and Carlos Montoya, who helped make the flamenco guitar popular. Both of these artists lived to a ripe old age—ninety-five and ninety, respectively—and we were thrilled to have seen them in their prime. Their performances inspired us to work on our respective techniques, classical guitar for Yaro and flamenco for myself.

Days after we returned from Barcelona in 1989, I learned of yet another special event that would take place in Paris in a few days: the *Nuits de Flamenco*, flamenco night in a large theater off the boulevard des Italiens not too far from the Opera Garnier.

The first performers were relatively unknown, intended to warm up the audience for the big names on the program, two world-class flamenco guitarists, Sabicas and Paco de Lucia. At midnight, the theater was full. It seemed like every flamenco aficionado in France had come to hear the two dazzling flamenco guitarists.

Regrettably, Sabicas, one of flamenco's greatest-ever guitarists, did not arrive from New York. He was nearly eighty, and had been forced to cancel at the last minute for health reasons. I learned later that, in April 1990, he died of complications from pneumonia and multiple strokes. Sabicas was a mentor to Paco de Lucia, who was widely considered the world's premier flamenco guitarist. Paco's influence on flamenco guitar has been compared to that of Andrés Segovia's on classical guitar. The maestro finally appeared on the stage at around two in the morning. The invigorated audience received him with a resounding applause. For a decade, de Luca had been experimenting with Nuevo Flamenco, jazz fusion and rock, a genre I was not particularly keen on. However, with the release of his last album *Sirocco*, it was clear that he had returned to his pure flamenco roots. The performance that evening was brilliant, and the ecstatic audience expressed its admiration with endless *olés* and *bravos*.

Remarkably, at 4:00 a.m. the concert was still going strong, but as more performers came on stage, Yaro and I were getting tired. By 5:00 a.m. the pace slowed, and at six, the concert was over. When we stepped outside, it was daylight; the Grand Boulevards were empty of people. It was an odd sensation. Strolling in the direction of the Opera, we found a café that was open, ordered café-au-lait and croissants, and savored the surreal moment. Most of our lives are made up of things like concerts that last until 6:00 a.m. Everything in between such moments is mere existence.

36. Paris: The Later Years

BY 1989, IT LOOKED like I was going to stay in Paris for good. A secure job with Radio Liberty got me thinking about buying an apartment. I was not unhappy living on Rue Pelouze in the 17th, but the time for a permanent residence seemed ripe. Affordable apartments in the central arrondissements were in old buildings and lacked sunshine and street parking, so I purchased a four-room apartment on rue Francoeur on the northern slope of Montmartre in the 18th, not as bourgeois as the 17th but more representative of the French middle class. Unlike the central arrondissements on the Left Bank, the area was still mostly populated by French people rather than foreigners. Danylo Struk, who loved this location, said that it was one of the last areas in Paris that still preserved its authentic French character. The neighborhood contained a mix of small, inexpensive cafés and restaurants, shops with regional products, fromageries, boulangeries, and pâtisseries, all at reasonable prices. A few hundred meters up the steps, on Rue du Mont-Cenis, was the famous cabaret Au Lapin Agile, a place that offered traditional French entertainment and sing-alongs.

I got into the habit of jogging uphill along the Rue du Mont-Cenis to the summit of Montmartre where one of Paris's most iconic monuments stood: the Basilica of Sacre Coeur on Montmartre, the Hill of the Martyrs. Every time I reached the top of the hill, I experienced a high in the form of the most magnificent view of Paris, all gratis.

From two sides, Montmartre was accessible by a series of picturesque steps that ended at the place de Tertre, the square where artists had been peddling quick portraits and stock scenes of Paris for over a century. Descending the hill, just below the Place du Tertre on Rue Ravignan at Place Émile-Goudeau, I skirted the rebuilt Bateau-Lavoir where some of the twentieth century's greatest names in art—Georges Braque, Henri Matisse, Amadeo Modigliani, and Pablo Picasso—lived and created at the turn of the century. Later they began moving elsewhere, mainly to Montparnasse. Vincent Van Gogh's brother Theo lived down the sloping, curving Rue Lepic. He stored his brother's paintings in his apartment, waiting for the genius to be recognized. It took some time, but long after Van Gogh was gone, his paintings set record prices. His *Portrait of Dr. Gachet*, for example, sold at a Sotheby's auction in New York for US$153 million.

OF THE ARTISTS named above, Pablo Picasso is widely viewed as the foremost artist of the twentieth century. In the spring of 1980, curious to discover what all the fuss was about, I attended a massive retrospective of Picasso's works at the Grand Palais in Paris. Some thousand Picasso paintings, sculptures, prints, and ceramics made up the exhibition. The twentieth century's most famous artist was portrayed as a towering creative genius, the most extraordinary, the most original, and, indeed, the most idealized artist of the age.

My interest in art had always been eclectic. I appreciated everything from Greek classicism to early twentieth-century post-Impressionism and Expressionism. Modern art and abstractionism were not my cup of tea, but I was open to learning why art historians and experts considered Picasso to be the twentieth century's Michelangelo.

The exhibit was impressive, but I could not comprehend what generated so much adulation. To me, Picasso was an artist who lived a long time, produced a lot, and was marketed better than any other artist in history. I could not understand why his grotesquely distorted art was so revered.

My next encounter with Picasso was a few months after the opening of the Picasso Museum in 1985. The museum was located in the Hôtel Salé, a seventeenth-century Baroque mansion in the historic Marais district, and it housed the world's largest assembly of Picasso's works.[108] Much of the museum's collection dated from the late 1920s to the early 1930s when Picasso was emerging from his post-World War I Cubist phase and beginning

---

[108] In 2009, the museum was closed for expansion and finally reopened in 2014 at more than twice its former size, after a renovation that was plagued by controversy and intrigue.

to think of himself as a Surrealist. I was disturbed by the preponderance of teeth and genitals, penetrations, and impalings. Bodies, mostly female, were an assemblage of detached limbs. Picasso repeatedly appeared in the alter-ego of the Minotaur, the man with the head of a bull monster from Cretan mythology who ate people. As I later discovered, the image was appropriate.

Ten years after the Grand Palais exhibit and five after I visited the Picasso museum, I came across Arianna Huffington's brilliantly researched opus *Picasso: Creator and Destroyer*, an exposé of the artist's dark side as a man.[109] Arianna Huffington writes,

"Picasso was a wretchedly flawed genius, a misogynist who tormented a succession of wives and mistresses, a wife-beater unable to love the women he seduced. Tragic victims of his maniacal ego were the suicides of Jacqueline, his second wife, his grandson, and Marie-Thérèse Walter, his mistress of many years. His first wife, Olga Kokhlova (a Ukrainian ballerina from Kharkiv) went mad, and Dora Maar, once a proud and talented painter and photographer, had a nervous breakdown."

In the last ten years of his life, Picasso turned away three of his four children and a grandson. His son Paolo died of cirrhosis of the liver, and his grandson swallowed a pint of chlorine bleach. Jacqueline blew her brains out, and Marie-Thérèse hanged herself. The only one who survived Picasso's deadly embrace was Françoise Gilot, his young mistress who survived to write her memoir *Life with Picasso*, painting him as an evil and wicked man "who seared her cheek with a burning cigarette." Françoise noted what Dora Maar had told her about Picasso: "As an artist, he was extraordinary, but morally he was worthless."

In 1944, Picasso refused to exert his considerable prestige with the German Occupation authorities to free the poet Max Jacob, his longtime friend, from the Nazi transit camp at Drancy. To a mutual friend who was raising a petition on Jacob's behalf, Picasso is said to have explained, "It's not worth doing anything at all. Max is a little devil. He doesn't need our help to escape from prison." Max Jacob died in Drancy.

Huffington concludes that Picasso was a grotesquely evil human being whose nastiness of spirit infected his paintings, and whose evil ways disfigured and poisoned his work. Her portrait of the artist as a monster provoked outraged responses from establishment critics. (Paul Mellon, the great American philanthropist, collector, and benefactor/trustee of the National

---

[109] *Picasso: Creator and Destroyer* by Arianna Stassinopoulos Huffington (1988).

Gallery in Washington DC, once noted that one of the failings of collectors and art critics was lack of curiosity about the personal lives of the artists, their social backgrounds, and their political leanings.) *Picasso: Creator and Destroyer* has been scorned as soap opera, and derided as factually inaccurate. Huffington, said the critics, was unqualified as a Picasso scholar, did not know how to read a painting, and was incapable of separating the man from his work.

So how has this evil modernist deity managed to inveigle thousands of collectors into paying exorbitant prices to hang one of his pictures in their living room? There are several reasons. Picasso, first of all, was the product of contemporary critical acclaim, and he benefited from clever marketing by his dealers. Rhapsodic hagiographies were penned by his friends and early biographers Pierre Daix and Ronald Penrose, the photographer Brassai, and Alfred Barr, the founding director of the Museum of Modern Art. I wonder how these art illuminati would have perceived Picasso if it became know that he was a member of the Nazi Party.

Instead, adulation for the artist was further reinforced by the praise and approval of left-wing intellectuals who considered his support of Communism courageous and commendable. "I am a Communist, and my painting is Communist painting," Picasso declared, when he joined the Party. In an article in *L'Humanité*, the chief Communist Party organ in France, entitled "Why I joined the Communist Party," he explained: ". . . it was the logical conclusion of my life, my whole work."

In August 1948, Picasso attended the Communist-sponsored Congress of Intellectuals for Peace in Warsaw. The Soviet delegation deplored his decadent painting and his style. Picasso chose to ignore the attack. He let his work be used for posters for Party organs, and provided drawings and lithographs for *L'Humanité*. He seemed to be untroubled by the paradox of aligning himself with Stalin's ruthlessly oppressive regime.

Among Picasso memorabilia displayed on the lower level of the Hôtel Salé, I noticed a small drawing in a glass-enclosed case that struck me with the force of a branding iron. It was a simple drawing of a hand holding a fluted glass of champagne with a handwritten salutation: *À votre santé, camarade Staline* (To your health, comrade Stalin). A friendly greeting for Stalin's seventieth birthday! Even when the Soviet regime brutally put down the 1956 Hungarian revolt and many CP members tore up their membership cards, Picasso did not disown the Party.

Despite his predilection for personal and political evil, collectors continue to buy Picasso's paintings, and the price of his works has reached astronomical levels. On May 11, 2015, his painting *Women of Algiers* sold for US$179 million at Christie's in New York. It was the highest price ever paid for a painting.

ON *QUATORZE JUILLET* every year during the 1980s, I, along with millions of Frenchmen, celebrated Bastille Day. It was a joyous event that began with an impressive parade of the French military, armored vehicles, and cavalry on the Champs-Élysées. The finale was a spectacular flyover by military jets emitting a tricolored vapor trail. In the afternoon, it was customary to attend one of the "balls" at a fireman's station in every arrondissement. After dark, celebrations concluded with a mighty fireworks display at the Eiffel Tower.

The Bastille Day of 1989 was unique. France was celebrating the Bicentennial of the French Revolution, a defining moment in the history of France and Europe. That year, a few of my friends from the United States and Canada attended one of these balls held at the fire station in the 2nd arrondissement. They were Liuba Markewycz from Chicago, and Danylo Struk from Toronto, and joining the group were local artists Makarenko and Solomoukha, my close friend Danylo Sztul, and the journalist Kateryna Horbatch.

The square in front of the fire station was decorated with tricolors and Japanese lanterns hanging from the trees. There was a small stage with an orchestra that played French songs and dance music. The atmosphere was gay and couples danced wherever they could find a place. A thousand people were crammed into a constricted space like sardines in a can, but the mood was festive and friendly.

Before we realized it, our group had broken up, and it was impossible to regroup. Only Danylo Struk and Kateryna Horbatch stayed together, and eventually made their way to her apartment on the nearby Île Saint-Louis. Liuba wound up in Anton's studio near place Bastille, and everyone else made their way home on foot because métros were few and far between. The next time we all met in my apartment, we told stories about how we survived the "crush of 1989." There was something unforgettable about this episode. Two of my dear friends, Liuba and Danylo (both departed), recounted this experience to friends on numerous occasions.

This event contrasts sharply with the massacre that took place twenty-seven years later on July 14, 2016. As the fireworks display marking the French

National Day in Nice ended, a truck driven by a Tunisian Islamist terrorist entered the Promenade des Anglais near the airport. He broke through a police barrier and entered the pedestrian zone, zigzagging along the city's crowded seafront, and mowing down those who had gathered to watch the fireworks, trying to kill as many as he could. The truck careened into families and friends listening to an orchestra or strolling above the Mediterranean beach toward the century-old Grand Hotel Negresco. Within five minutes of entering the promenade, the driver, thirty-one-year-old Mohamed Lahouaiej Bouhlel, was shot dead by officers next to the Palais de la Méditerranée. In all, eighty-four lay dead and scores injured. All this was just eighteen months after the Charlie Hebdo massacre, and eight months after the Bataclan theater slaughter where gunmen killed 130 people.

The news of this attack disturbed me profoundly because I had a personal connection to the place where it happened. Only a few years before, my wife Eva and I had spent a few days in Antibes on the Riviera some twenty kilometers west of Nice. One day, we drove to Nice and walked along the Promenade des Anglais and relaxed on the beach near Hotel Negresco at exactly the spot where the tragedy took place.

The Nice assault fundamentally transformed France as a country, a land I appreciated more than any other place in the world. I fear it is not the last attack by Islamists. It will take decades, if ever, for the French to celebrate Bastille Day in the same carefree manner my friends and I had in 1989.

37. Mediterranean Odysseys

EVERY ISLAND I VISITED in the Mediterranean was a lesson in history. Over and over again it was brought home to me how Western civilization has been threatened by another religion since the middle of the seventh century. This lesson is especially relevant to the world of today.

My Mediterranean odyssey began in the beautiful Western Mediterranean island of Mallorca. With time, I would travel to Corsica, Sardinia, Sicily, Crete, and the western coast of Asia Minor, ending up in Troy, where the real Odysseus started his journey. Just as he wandered in the Middle Sea for ten years, my journeys were also spread out over a period of ten years during the 1980s, but that's where the similarity ends.

Mallorca

Eva and I flew to Palma in late September when the crowds thinned, the prices reduced and the weather still warm. Mallorca, "the Paradise Island," is one of the three Balearic Islands—the other two are Minorca and Ibiza. Compact, roughly forty by fifty kilometers, and spectacularly beautiful, the island is a Spanish jewel in the middle of the Western Mediterranean.

The first thing that caught my eye from the air was La Seu, Palma's massive late Gothic cathedral towering over the old port. My interest in Gothic architecture bordered on obsession, so when I discovered that La Seu's forty-four-meter nave matched the most impressive Gothic edifices of northern France in height, I was truly awestruck. It was only four meters shorter than the chancel of Saint Pierre at Beauvais and two meters higher than Amiens's forty-two-meter nave.

Mallorca's capital, Palma, is a populous cosmopolitan city with a lively historical center. We stayed at a beachside hotel at the Cala Major, just east of Palma, where Joan Miró lived from 1956 until his death in 1983. The island's rocky northwestern coast consists of steep cliffs plunging into the sea, hiding numerous coves, caverns, and caves. The southwestern coast offers fine beaches and crystalline turquoise waters. I was surprised to find that the island possessed five-thousand-year-old megaliths, Greek and Roman settlements, and vestiges of Vandal and Byzantine rule, all of which came to an end with the first Arab raids in 707. During the eighth century, attacks by Moorish pirates disrupted all trade and commerce in the Mediterranean. The conquest of Menorca and Mallorca was completed by the Emir of Cordoba, later the Caliph of Cordoba, at the beginning of the tenth century. The Moorish occupation lasted for more than three centuries.

There is no agreement as to what happened during this period. Scholars and historians favorably predisposed to Islam claim that, like in Andalusia, the Muslim rule was a model multicultural society that introduced new irrigation techniques and planted crops like rice and cotton and, on terraced hillsides, oranges, limes, and olives. More recently, evidence suggests that Muslim rule was anything but tolerant and benevolent, and the opposite appears to have been more likely. Andalusia was a two-tiered society composed of the believers and the *dhimmi*. The latter were tolerated only if they paid the *jizya*, a capitation tax levied on non-Muslims that went into the caliph's treasury and made his lavish lifestyle possible.

In 1229, the Catalan King Jaume expelled the Moors and encouraged Catalans to settle the reconquered islands. All citizens were promised exemption from taxes and guaranteed equality before the law. To stimulate trade, the Catalan king also granted special privileges to the Jews.

Today, it is hard to imagine that the island was once ruled by emirs and caliphs who occupied two-thirds of the Iberian Peninsula, including Mallorca. In Palma, there's hardly a trace of Moorish occupation—only the small tenth-century *Baños Arabes* (Arab baths), whose dome rested on twelve columns, was a reminder of the oppressive three-hundred-year Moorish presence on the island.

We took the narrow-gauge electric train that connects Palma with Soller, a small town across the rugged mountain chain paralleling the northwestern coast of Mallorca. The train wound its way to a pass at one thousand meters where it stopped long enough for us to get a glimpse of Soller and the dramatic coastline. In Soller, we switched to a tram that descended to Port de Soller on the coast, and within an hour, I found a delightful waterfront hotel.

To get the feel of the terrain, we hiked a rugged coastal trail that offered breathtaking views. The silence was broken only by a gentle wind, chirping birds, and the braying of a few mountain goats. Somewhere on the horizon, three hundred kilometers to the northwest, lay Catalonia.

From Port de Soller, we set out to discover the mountainous spine of northwestern Mallorca. A rented SEAT Ibiza took us south to Deia, a coastal town where Robert Graves wrote his classic *I, Claudius*. Alas, the house where he lived was not open, so we meandered around Deia's picturesque narrow streets before continuing down the coastal road toward Valldemossa.

I remembered viewing the BBC's series *I, Claudius* in the late '70s and making a mental note to read the book as soon as possible. When I did, I found it a fascinating piece of history and a must read for anyone interested in the early years of the Roman Empire under Emperor Augustus and his successor, Tiberius. Most riveting was the picture Graves painted of the evil Livia, wife of Augustus and mother of Tiberius.

Ten kilometers south of Deia is Valldemossa, a colorful town surrounded by steep mountains, with a fabulous view of the sea. Above the town sits La Cartuja, the fourteenth-century Carthusian monastery where Frédéric Chopin spent the winter of 1838–39 with Aurora Dupin, better known as George Sand. The couple went there because Chopin suffered from tuberculosis. Unfortunately, Valldemossa's high altitude, chilly winds, and damp air made him worse. What came out of the couple's four-month sojourn was a short book by Sand, *A Winter in Mallorca*, in which she derided the locals as savages. Nevertheless, the book made Valldemossa a magnet for future tourists. After rounding the northern tip of the island, I discovered yet another delicious morsel of history. According to Pliny, Hannibal was born on the tiny island of Cabrera, today a nature reserve visible off the eastern coast of Mallorca.

Corsica and Sardinia

During the 1980s, I covered nearly every part of Southern France except Corsica, the gem in the Mediterranean 170 kilometers south of Nice. The ancient Greeks called it "the Island of Beauty," a place where mountains met the sea. The terrain of Corsica is mostly mountainous, covered with *maquis*, dense scrubby underbrush of aromatic evergreen shrubs, and small trees, together with cork oak and chestnut forests in the south, and pine trees at higher elevations. The flowers of the maquis produced a fragrance that earned Corsica the name Scented Isle.

I learned about Corsica from Volodymyr "Vova" Mykolenko, a Paris friend who had done the 170-kilometer GR 20 trail, one of Western Europe's toughest hiking routes. Wild and rugged, it traverses the island diagonally, roughly from Porto-Vecchio on the eastern coast to the rugged coastline near Calvi in the west. His description convinced me that I must visit this ancient granite massif containing a cluster of twenty peaks exceeding two thousand meters.

The most direct route from the mainland was by ferry from Nice. Eva and I landed at the northern tip of the island at L'Île Rousse, a ferry port, from where a narrow-gauge railway wound its way along the scenic coast to Calvi. In Calvi I rented a Fiat Panda, a nimble car that seemed to be tailor-made for the narrow Mediterranean island roads.

We drove south at a leisurely pace along Corsica's jagged west coast toward Piana. To the east, I made out Corsica's highest peak, the 2,700-meter snow-capped Monte Cinto. The road led to Les Calanches, the giant red granite cliffs between Porto and Piana. The landscape of spiky outcrops, carved into bizarre shapes by wind and water, was Corsica's most spectacular attraction. As we entered the Calanches zone, the road narrowed, leaving barely enough room for two cars to pass. There was no median, no road signs; only a meter-high wall separated the road from a precipice that plunged several hundred meters into the sea. Every breathtaking turn had to be negotiated with vigilance. The experience was comparable to going through the Gorges of Galamus in the Ardèche, or the tortuous road up to the Plateau of Lasithi on Crete.

Ajaccio, the town where Napoleon Bonaparte came from, continues to revere the man's extraordinary career. The house where he was born is a museum, and the nearby town hall displays his birth certificate and family pictures. The certificate, by the way, was written in the Genoese dialect, in case anyone had doubts about Bonaparte's origins.

Our destination in Corsica was Bonifacio, a magnificently sited town perched on a seventy-meter outcrop of chalk-white limestone at the southern tip of the island. We arrived too late to find a hotel and resigned ourselves to sleeping in our rented Panda, but that did not prevent us from exploring the town's special ambiance and unique music. Bonifacio's old town was compact and easy to explore, and residents from all over the isle came to hear Corsican traditional polyphonic singing. A few café restaurants offered capellas of three to five voices accompanied by an array of instruments such as the *cetera*, a lute-like instrument, the *mandulina*, a variation of the mandolin, and the Spanish guitar. These capellas sang into the night, producing a sound that was a cross between Portuguese fado and Spanish flamenco with Neapolitan and Sicilian overtones, so full of emotion and pathos that it moved me to tears. The tradition of Corsican polyphonic singing had become nearly extinct until its revival in the 1970s. In the 1980s, it was in full swing, and we were lucky to hear its rebirth, which was a central part of Corsican national identity.

I was puzzled by Corsica's symbol as depicted on its flag: a Moor's black head wearing a white bandana. It all became clear when I discovered that the origins of this symbol go back to the beginning of the ninth century when the Saracens attempted to take control of Corsica.

The next morning, we walked to the lower part of town, the port quarter, and took a ferry to Sardinia, some ten kilometers across the Strait of Bonifacio. Once we were out to sea, I looked back and saw Bonifacio perched atop its white cliffs like Dover on the cliffs of the English Channel. Less than an hour later, we landed at Santa Teresa at the northern tip of Sardinia, where the forest-covered mountain ridges and deep bays had become a favorite of holidaymakers. After touring the pink granite headlands of the coast, we returned to Bonifacio just before sundown.

Sicily

The road from Munich to Sicily included stops in Ravenna, Naples, Ischia, and Capri. Eva and I entered Italy at the Brenner Pass in the north, and a week later, we boarded the ferry at the boot's toe, Reggio di Calabria, to cross the Strait of Messina to Sicily, a distance of only three kilometers.

The triangular-shaped island is the largest in the Mediterranean and, with five million inhabitants, the most populous. In six days, we did a circular tour of the island taking a route that included such three-star attractions as Taormina, Siracusa, Agrigento, Selinunte, Segesta, Monreale, Palermo, and Cefalù. To sum up Sicily, I would say the island has some of the most dazzling Byzantine mosaics on the European continent, and a concentration of ancient Greek temples unequalled in the Mediterranean.

After a weeklong descent of the Italian boot, we were looking forward to a few days of relaxation on the beach. Regrettably, it was raining, so we decided to take the funicular cable car to the upper part of Taormina to see some of the sights the town is known for—its third-century BC Greek theater with magnificent views of Mount Etna, the coast, and the Mediterranean Sea. When we learned that the cable car was not working, we walked to the upper city. What happened next was one of those synchronous moments that I remember as if it had happened yesterday, a dreadful episode that took place in Sicily on May 23, 1992, two days before my birthday.

The main street of Taormina, the Via Umberto, was practically deserted. I thought that was strange because the season had only begun. On approaching the vestiges of the Greek theater, we stopped at a few souvenir shops; but instead of being greeted with typical Italian charm and smiles, I saw sad faces and sensed a somber mood reminiscent of a funeral. Since all the newspapers were in Italian, I asked one shop owner why so many places were closed and why there were so few tourists.

"Have you not heard?" he said. "The Mafia assassinated Giovanni Falcone, the Italian judge and magistrate prosecuting the Corleonesi Mafia. Yesterday, he and his wife and three bodyguards were killed by a massive explosion, a bomb planted under the motorway leading from the airport to Palermo."

The people of Taormina and all of Sicily were stunned, traumatized into a visible display of mourning for a brave hero. Falcone spent most of his professional life trying to overthrow the power of the Sicilian Mafia. His long and distinguished career culminated in the famous Maxi Trial in 1986–1987. For that remarkable success, he paid with his life. Less than two months later, Falcone's close friend and fellow anti-mafia magistrate Paolo Borsellino was killed by a car bomb near his mother's house in Palermo. The bomb attack also claimed the lives of five policemen protecting the magistrate. Giovanni Falcone and Paolo Borsellino became iconic symbols of the struggle against Cosa Nostra.

Alexander Stille, the author of *Excellent Cadavers*, which is probably the best book on this chapter of Italian history, concluded that "the killings shocked the Italian state into its most vigorous anti-mafia campaign in decades. The Italian parliament quickly passed many of the tough anti-mafia measures Falcone and Borsellino had been pushing for years: greater incentives and protection for mafia witnesses, tougher prison conditions for mafia defendants, and streamlined procedures in mafia trials. In addition, 7,000 army troops were sent to Sicily to set up road blocks, guard judges and politicians, and free up the police for investigative work. The results over the next two years were nothing short of extraordinary: several hundred mafiosi turned against the Cosa Nostra and offered to cooperate with police. Italian police dismantled entire organizations overnight and tracked down more than three hundred longtime mafia fugitives, including several of the most powerful bosses, and in particular, the 'capo di tutti capi' Salvatore (Totò) Riina, who had eluded arrest for twenty-three years."

In the next few years, more than 1,200 members of the criminal organizations, mostly in southern Italy, turned against the mafia and "repented." The *pentini* (informers) were given new identities, escorts, protection, money, and shelter, although the lavish treatment produced complaints from taxpayers who thought the ex-villains were treated too leniently. Still, it was true that over the next three years, the *pentini* helped net some of Italy's worst criminals. Perhaps more importantly, the *pentini* broke the cohesiveness of the mafia. The myth of *omertà* had been cracked, the age of impunity that had lasted forty-five years had ended.

My dear and now deceased friend Roman Kupchinsky, an expert on corruption and graft in Ukraine, once told me after reading Stille's book, "Until Ukraine adopts similar measures to clean house, the problem of dishonest oligarchs and corruption will never be solved."

At the time of this writing, such steps have yet to be taken.

ANOTHER PLAGUE had visited Sicily thirteen hundred years earlier: Islamic piracy. The first attacks by Arab ships occurred in 652, only twenty years after the death of the Prophet Muhammed. The Arabs remained on the island for several years, plundered it and, after collecting a large amount of booty, returned to Syria. By the middle of the seventh century, Muslim piracy had begun to disrupt trade between East and West, with attacks coming in fits and starts for the next 150 years.

A second Arab expedition to Sicily in 669 consisting of two hundred ships from Alexandria attacked Syracuse and returned to Egypt after a month of pillaging. After the Umayyad conquest of Africa, completed around 700, attacks by Muslim fleets became incessant. Assaults were met with substantial Byzantine resistance, but in 805, Muslim fleets from other parts of Africa and Spain launched attacks on Sardinia and Corsica, both of which fell in 826 and stayed under Muslim rule for 130 years.

In June 827, when Taormina, the last major Byzantine stronghold on Sicily fell, the island succumbed to the Muslim onslaught. By 846, the Saracen fleet had sailed up the Tiber, sacked the Borgo district of Rome, and plundered Saint Peter's. Next, the corsairs sailed west, raided Saint-Tropez and Marseilles, and navigated up the Rhône to Vienne.

The Muslim Conquest of Sicily lasted until 902. Under Muslim rule, Sicilian culture became Arabicized, but the Christian communities in the central and eastern parts of the island resisted Islamization. It was the Normans who finally defeated the last of the Muslims in the 1160s and achieved the kind of *convivencia* usually attributed to the "peaceful" coexistence of Muslim, Jewish, and Christian communities during the Caliphate of Cordoba. The two *convivencias* were vastly different for one overriding reason: the Caliphate of Cordoba tolerated Jews and Christians and allowed them to practice their religion as long as they paid *jizya*, the head tax. In Norman Sicily, there was no head tax, and peaceful coexistence was achieved by treating all of Sicily's residents equally.

WE LEFT THE SPRAWLING Greek ruins of Agrigento on the southern coast of Sicily, passed through the Mafia town of Corleone, strangely ominous-looking and deserted, and arrived at the Greek temples at Segesta. Apart from the Acropolis, there is nothing in all of Greece or Italy as spectacular as these ruins.

By the time I arrived in Sicily, I had seen hundreds of churches in Europe, so I was not easily impressed. When I entered the Cathedral of Monreale, however, I was overcome by this singularly beautiful achievement of Norman rule in Sicily. The cathedral's pointed doorway arches were enriched with carvings and colored inlays that represented a combination of Norman-French, Byzantine, and Arab influences. The cathedral's interior dazzled with multicolored marbles and twelfth-century mosaics by Byzantine artisans representing the complete cycle of the Old and New Testament, culminating with its giant Christ Pantocrator, the Greek equivalent of "Almighty" or "All-powerful." The only church that comes close to this "Norman-Arab-Byzantine" structure is the sixth-century Saint Vitale in Ravenna.

Palermo, on the northern coast, was a fifteen-kilometer downhill drive from Monreale. We arrived at the Cappella Palatina, Palermo's outstanding attraction, literally five minutes before the chapel closed for the day. The guard opened the doors for those going out, but was not letting people in. I was disappointed and pleaded with him to let us in, if only for a few minutes.

"We came from America to see this chapel, and we leave tomorrow morning."

He let us in and even lit up the interior so we could appreciate the most impressive mosaics to be found anywhere in the world. The relatively small Palatine Chapel is adjacent to the Norman Palace. It incorporates Norman elements, Saracen arches, a Byzantine dome, and a roof adorned with Arabic scripts. It is perhaps the most striking product of the brilliant and mixed civilization over which the Norman kings ruled. Built between 1130 and 1140 by King Roger II, the mosaics of the Palatine Chapel are of unparalleled elegance with their subtle modulations of color and luminance, particularly the oldest which cover the ceiling, the drum, and the dome.

The next day, instead of relaxing and exploring Palermo, I decided on a detour to Cefalù, some sixty kilometers east of Palermo. This small fishing town boasts a splendid Romanesque cathedral, also erected by Roger II at about the same time as Monreale. The church, marked by Norman features, is home to probably the most famous intact Christ Pantocrator in all of Christendom.

In the afternoon of the same day, we boarded the ferry for Naples, which saved us hours of driving on the mainland, a distance of over seven hundred kilometers. The voyage provided an opportunity to recover from the intensive schedule and enjoy some fresh Mediterranean air and sun.

Crete

On one of my last business trips to Greece, I flew from Athens to Crete during a break when Soviet ships were not docked in the port of Piraeus. Crete felt more like a small continent than an island. As the commuter twin-engine plane approached Iraklion (also known as Heraklion), I saw that the island was a chain of mountains in the middle of the Mediterranean. Unlike other islands, Crete had verdant valleys with no lack of water or greenery. In history, it was a stepping-stone between Egypt and Athens. The Cretans had seen it all, from the collapse of the Minoan Empire and the rise of Venice, to Turkish occupation and German parachutists during WWII. To do the island properly would have taken a week at a minimum. I had only three days.

According to legend, Zeus was born here, and King Minos, after whom the Minoan culture was named, was the son of Zeus and Europa. From his capital in Knossos, Minos developed the island's sea power that bestowed security on this part of the Mediterranean. The Minotaur was part of the mythology, a creature with the head of a bull and the body of a man that dwelt at the center of the Labyrinth, which was an elaborate mazelike construction built at the command of King Minos. Archeologists have sifted through ten levels of remains from the Neolithic period (3000 to 4000 BC) through late

Minoan periods (1200 to 1000 BC), but have failed to date precisely the Minoan Civilization.

The morning after I arrived in Iraklion, the capital, I rented another nimble Panda and took off on a whirlwind tour of the island—not the best way to become familiar with the terrain and people but a great way to cover a lot of territory in a limited time. The first stop was Knossos, only five kilometers from Iraklion. The ruins of Knossos exude a poise that comes from beautifully proportioned architecture, even though the frescos were over-restored and in effect falsified by Sir Arthur Evans. The fact is, the Minoans did not produce any sculpture that rivaled that of Greece and Egypt, while the jewelry displayed in the museum does not compare with that at Mycenae.

The other worthwhile destination was near the southern coast of the island, Phaistos, from where many of the richest and most elaborate finds came. The most famous one is the mysterious and beautiful Phaistos disc from about 1600 BC, seven inches in diameter and imprinted on both sides with pictograms which spiral inward to the center. It is displayed at the Archeological Museum of Iraklion and, to this day, remains undeciphered. The museum gift shop was selling reproductions of the disc in various sizes as gold jewelry. I was mesmerized by the two-inch copy of the disc—it looked like some enigmatic ancient charm or coin, so I bought one as a gift for Eva, a piece she enjoys wearing as a necklace pendant.

High up on the great massif of Crete sits the Lasithi Plateau. Twelve kilometers long and six wide, the plateau is known as the roof of the Mediterranean world. Winters are harsh, and snow on the plain surrounding mountains can persist until mid-spring. It was also a place with a long history. Zeus was born in a cave here.

The road to the plateau was steep and rose through a pass full of hairpin turns along a daunting gorge. My Fiat Panda handled every turn deftly, but stopping to admire the panorama, which grew more impressive with every turn, was out of the question. Driving alone on such a road was intimidating. If I had swerved off at one of the turns, no one would have missed me for days.

People have lived on the plateau since Neolithic times. Its soil is fertile thanks to alluvial runoff from melting snow, and this has attracted inhabitants and invaders throughout the ages. I recall that the landscape was dotted with colorful windmills, but like the ones in Holland, they served mostly as tourist attractions.

Coming down from the plateau, I took a different road thinking it would be less perilous, but the descent turned out to be even more treacherous. I spent the night at the picturesque Agios Nikolaos, a resort town on Mirabello Bay and continued to Malia on the northern coast, another holiday resort with a fine sandy beach and one of the most popular tourist locations in Europe. In November, the strip was quiet, so I visited the archaeological site of Malia three kilometers east of the town.

The Palace of Malia is the third largest of the Minoan palaces, built at about the same time as Phaistos and Knossos, around 1900 BC. Destroyed by an earthquake, it was rebuilt in 1700 BC, only to be leveled by another tremor at around 1450 BC. The palace foundations and outcrops of walls allowed me to visualize what it must have looked like during ancient times. From a scale model of the complex, I got the impression of a thoroughly modern structure, not unlike a building designed by Frank Lloyd Wright in the twentieth century.

THE POST-MINOAN HISTORY of Crete includes rule by Greeks, Romans, and Byzantines, and in the early ninth century, the island was overrun by Muslims. The conquest of the island in 826 transformed the naval balance of power in the Eastern Mediterranean and opened the Aegean coast to frequent and devastating raids.

By the early 870s, the Muslim raids out of bases in Crete had reached a new intensity. The impact was felt across the Aegean. Athens was attacked in 896, and Thessalonica, the Byzantine Empire's second city, was sacked in 904. Over twenty thousand Thessalonian captives were sold as slaves in Crete. Cretan piracy reached another high in the 930s and 940s, devastating southern Greece, Athos, and the western coasts of Asia Minor. Non-Muslim inhabitants everywhere were forced to pay the *jizya,* poll tax.

Nearly all Byzantine efforts to recapture Crete failed until Emperor Romanos II entrusted the capable general Nikephoros Phokas to head a massive fleet and army. Phokas landed on the island in 960 and, after a yearlong struggle, defeated all Muslim resistance, which ended a devastating 130 years of Muslim rule.

Asia Minor

The next phase of my Mediterranean odysseys took me to western Turkey. I was getting closer and closer to Troy. As a history buff, I wanted to see what remained of the Greco-Roman cities that once were the economic core of the Roman Empire and its successor, Byzantium. In the late '80s, I joined a group tour for a three-week circuit that included seven illustrious Greco-Roman sites, along with Cappadocia, Ankara, and Istanbul. The journey concluded with Troy, the ancient city where the real Odysseus began his ten-year wandering through the Mediterranean.

There was not much to see in Troy, if it was indeed the Troy of Homer. The site consisted of a thirty-meter-high (one hundred feet) mound of debris made up of nine distinct layers representing the remains of nine periods. After one city was destroyed, a new city was built on top of it, creating a man-made mound, a "tell."

There was much more to see among the ruins in the great urban centers of antiquity: Ephesus, Pergamon, Aphrodisias, Hierapolis, Aspendos, Perge, and Side. Each of these cosmopolitan centers of learning and culture, trade, and medicine, philosophy and art left a mark on history. Unlike the Greek ruins and temples of Sicily, the cities of Asia Minor were essentially Roman in architecture and character. At their height, they were centers of urban culture, vastly richer than cities in the West. During Byzantine times, they were important centers of Christianity. Each of these cities possessed beautiful colonnaded streets, lined with colossal architecture in the form of thermal baths, libraries, theaters, forums and temples, and later Christian churches and basilicas.

Among the sites I visited was Ephesus, a city whose population during the reign of Augustus was 225,000. To the north, Pergamon also reached the height of its greatness under Roman imperial rule and was home to about 200,000 inhabitants. The city possessed a Greek theater that could seat fourteen thousand spectators; a library second only to the library of Alexandria; and the Asclepeion, a center for healing specializing in psychosomatic diseases.

Aphrodisias, named after the goddess Aphrodite, became known as a center of medicine and philosophy, but above all, of sculpture and art. Its stadium could hold thirty thousand and was one of the finest Greco-Roman structures in the world. Aspendos featured a Roman theater, one of the largest and best-preserved buildings in Asia Minor; Perge had a theater with forty-eight rows of seats; while Side's theater, with fifty tiers, was one of the largest on the southern coast. Side, on the southern coast, increasingly became the target and then a naval base for pirates. Under Seljuk occupation, it was a large and internationally renowned slave market where pirates auctioned off their prisoners,.

The point I wish to emphasize is that all of these cities thrived until the Seljuk Turks arrived. In AD 1071, a Byzantine army of 150,000, mostly

Armenian mercenaries, was routed by a force of 15,000 Seljuk horsemen at the Battle of Manzikert. From that point, the whole of Anatolia lay open to invasion, and the Turks replaced the Arabs as the main threat. The second nail in the Byzantine sarcophagus came in 1204 when the Fourth Crusade sacked Constantinople. The once-mighty empire had been reduced to a rump state. Two hundred and fifty years later, on May 29, 1453, Byzantium disappeared forever and with it the last of the Roman culture and its cities.

ARAB PIRACY AND BANDITRY in the Mediterranean began in the middle of the seventh century with the first raids on Sicily and lasted for no less than 1,200 years. By 674, the Arabs launched their first siege of Constantinople. A second siege came in 717–18. Fortunately, both attacks were repulsed by Greek technology. The Arabs were helpless against the "Greek fire," but the Muslim raids continued and reached their climax during the ninth century in Crete.

The historian John Julius Norwich, in his magisterial *The Middle Sea*, wrote that "when Crete fell to the Muslims in 826, the conquest radically transformed the strategic situation in the entire Mediterranean. During 130 years, the Emirate of Crete had become a base for Muslim pirates, a quintessential 'corsair's nest,' surviving on brigandage and the slave trade. Muslim piracy in the Mediterranean not only disrupted trade and commerce between the East and West but brought it to an abrupt halt. The consequences of that disruption brought on the so-called 'Dark Ages.'"

38. An Existential Threat to Western Civilization

THIS IS NOT A CHAPTER I intended to write. However, given my Mediterranean experiences, and the obvious threat of Islamic expansionism into Europe, I feel compelled to address this crucial issue from a historical perspective. I fear Samuel Huntington's "clash of civilizations" is a reality. With a catastrophic decline in Europe's indigenous population, along with out-of-control immigration, the Western world is facing an existential threat.[110]

I was intrigued by the parallels between the fall of the Roman Empire and the events of the early decades of the twenty-first century. As an amateur historian, I found the conventional view that the Roman world expired in the fifth century woefully lacking and searched for an alternative explanation. I discovered one in the work of the Belgian historian Henri Pirenne. His thesis clashed with the view elucidated by Edward Gibbon, the eighteenth-century English historian, and his followers, who attributed the fall of Rome to Germanic invasions and Christianity. Pirenne questioned this interpretation of history.[111]

---

[110] Samuel P. Huntington presented the clash of civilizations hypothesis in his prophetic book *The Clash of Civilizations and the Remaking of World Order* (1996) which suggested that people's cultural and religious identities will be the primary source of conflict in the post-Cold War world.

[111] *Mohammed and Charlemagne,* Henry Pirenne, posthumously published in 1937 from Pirenne's draft after his death in 1935, re-edited in 2001.

Henri Pirenne concluded that the real destroyers of classical civilization were not the "barbarians" of the north—Franks, Goths, Vandals, and others—but the Muslims. The dissolution of the Western empire in AD 476 was not the catastrophic event portrayed by historians such as Edward Gibbon. Barbarian Goths came to Rome not to destroy it, but to benefit from its advantages, and they tried to preserve the Roman way of life. Roman civilization survived until the eighth century, when Islamic piracy and banditry finished off first the Western Roman Empire and, eventually, the Eastern Roman Empire (Byzantium) as well.

After reading Pirenne's opus *Mohammed and Charlemagne*, I realized that everything I thought I knew about the last days of Rome was wrong. Having traveled around the Mediterranean, I grasped how Saracen piracy had devastated trade and commerce in the Mediterranean Sea, causing the abandonment of Greco-Roman cities in the Levant and on the western coast of Asia Minor which had once been centers of commerce and learning.[112]

It should be noted that Gibbon did not have access to certain documents and archeological findings available to later scholars, and that *The History of the Decline and Fall of the Roman Empire* ended with the fifth century AD. Gibbon was also wrong in claiming that Christianity contributed to the fall of the Roman Empire, a notion many scholars continued to perpetuate well into the twentieth century. Later archeological findings revealed that civilization did not come to an end, but saw a revival in the sixth century in places like Gaul and Spain. The dissolution of the Western Roman Empire in 476 was actually a nonevent because, for some time, power had already passed to the new seat of the Roman Empire in the East.

Whatever the causes, Greco-Roman civilization died out, first in the West, and then in the East. The mostly urban, learned, and literate Roman world was replaced by a society and civilization we now call medieval, a society overwhelmingly rural and largely illiterate with a barter economy. The *coup de grâce*, Pirenne concluded, came suddenly in the middle of the seventh century and was caused by the severe disruption of trade and commerce in the Mediterranean by Arab pirates.

---

[112]   *Saracen* derives from the Greek word for Arabs. I use Saracen, Arab, and Muslim interchangeably, even though not all Muslims were Arab: the Persians, Berbers, and Seljuk/Ottoman Turks being the significant exceptions. Moors is the name given to North African Muslims.

Pirenne's thesis went against the grain of contemporary academic thought, and for decades, an anti-Pirenne cabal tried to discredit it. For half a century, he was ignored and disparaged. However, recent studies in archeology and Islamology show that Pirenne was correct. He argued that if we wish to chart the decline and fall of classical civilization, we must not confine ourselves to the West but must pay close attention to what happened in the East because for centuries the eastern half was the economic core and cultural heart of the Roman Empire. Gibbon has often been criticized for underestimating the cultural and political importance of the Eastern Empire. He downplayed the fact that for nearly eleven centuries, Constantinople was the greatest city in the world, and Europe's bulwark against Persia and Islam. John Julius Norwich considered Gibbon's views of the Byzantine world flawed, and blamed him for the lack of interest in the subject throughout the nineteenth and early twentieth centuries.

The historiography of Islam dates back to the Enlightenment, when most scholars accepted Edward Gibbon's thesis that the barbarians and Christianity between them had destroyed Roman civilization. At that time, there was an active pro-secular undercurrent, sparked and reinforced by the French Revolution that disparaged Christianity. Scholars from this movement began to look for a substitute to replace Christianity as a force of progress and enlightenment. They came up with the hypothesis that a great debt was owed by medieval Europe to the Islamic world. They noticed that many scientific and scholarly terms in the languages of Europe were of Arab origin, including algebra and alcohol, and Europeans began using the Arabic numbers system, which gave us the concept of zero. (In reality, neither algebra nor the Arabic numeral system was of Arab origin. Algebra and the concept of zero derived mostly from China and India.)

By the early nineteenth century, even though Muslim pirates continued to be a problem in the Mediterranean, the age of Islamophilia had arrived. Scholarly opinions of Islamic civilization became ever more enthusiastic. Historians began to view European civilization through a negative prism. A certain class of politicized intellectuals adopted an increasingly hostile approach to all things Christian and European. After the cataclysm of WWI, the age of disillusionment dawned. Criticism of medieval Europe and Christendom increased. The medieval world was seen more and more as the "Dark Ages." Although the *philosophes* and *illuminati* of the eighteenth century had used this pejorative term to englobe medieval European civilization right up to the Renaissance, many historians had since demonstrated that the label was unjustified. For one thing, the Europeans never lost contact with the Byzantine Greeks, who continued their classical studies until the fall of Constantinople in 1453. For another, knowledge of the classical period had gone on filtering into Western Europe for centuries, and monks at the Mont Saint Michel, Canterbury, and the Irish monasteries had assiduously preserved the ancient philosophers and classics.

Today, historians are split into two camps. One is the conventional Islamophile view that the Arabs were a civilizing force that rekindled the light of classical learning in Europe after it had been extinguished by the Goths, Vandals, and Huns in the fifth century. They maintain, for example, that in Spain, the Moors created a rich and vibrant civilization that saved the remnants of classical culture.[113]

On the other side are those who, with Pirenne, maintain that Islam was not a civilizing influence, and that Muslims destroyed the very culture of learning. The notion that al-Andalus was "a tolerant and progressive culture" was a myth without any grounding in history. Dario Fernandez-Morera effectively demolished that myth in a brilliant work published in 2015.[114] His research was conducted in a scientific manner and relies extensively on primary sources backed up with 120 pages of dense footnotes,.

The division is stark. How can such radically divergent interpretations of history exist among learned authors, scholars, and the media? And why does this debate continue to elicit such passionate and radically opposing interpretations?

I began reading voraciously. After a dozen books representing both sides of the argument, I came down on the side of Pirenne. When he came out with his controversial thesis in the 1930s, Islamic radicalism was not an issue. By the end of the century, however, Islamist terrorism and conflicts in the Middle East had made Islam a central concern.

---

[113] Fairly recent examples of this view are David Levering Lewis's *God's Crucible: Islam and the Making of Europe, 570–1215* (2008), and Maria Rosa Menocal's *The Ornament of the World: How Muslims, Jews, and Christians Created a Culture of Tolerance in Medieval Spain* (2002).

[114] Darío Fernández-Morera's *The Myth of the Andalusian Paradise: Muslims, Christians, and Jews under Islamic Rule in Medieval Spain* (2015) and Emmet Scott's *Mohamed and Charlemagne Revisited, The History of a Controversy* (2012) and *Impact of Islam* (2014), to name a few.

More and more of the public began to doubt the notion that Islam was a "religion of peace and tolerance," as the elites would have us believe. In fact, Islam is not a religion; it is a political movement masquerading as a religion. It is a totalitarian political ideology with ambitions to remake and rule the world, by force if necessary.[115] It is no longer possible to pull the wool over people's eyes: in every country where Muslims are the dominant majority, there is nothing but endless conflict, wars, and terror of the ugliest kind.

Emmet Scott, in his book *Mohamed and Charlemagne Revisited,* puts forth some convincing arguments that question the conventional Islamophile explanations. Scott maintains that four factors were responsible for the decline of Roman civilization in the West and East: Saracen piracy in the Mediterranean, destruction of agriculture and deforestation, depopulation of Levantine cities, and the fundamental nature of Islam.

Saracen piracy

As I discovered from my travels, Muslim piracy in the Mediterranean came into being in the seventh century. It was a constant threat to merchants who traded by sea. By the twelfth century, Berber piracy became a formidable menace to shipping for European Christian nations. It reached its peak during the first half of the seventeenth century. Corsairs from Algiers and armed troops of the Ottoman Empire stormed harbor villages as far afield as Ireland, and took away their captives to a life of slavery in North Africa. Even the United States, as late as the nineteenth century, was not immune to Barbary piracy and was obliged to pay tribute for protection from attack. The point I wish to underscore is that Muslim piracy in the Mediterranean has been a menace for over 1,200 years. During this period, millions of Europeans have been captured and taken as slaves to North Africa, Asia Minor, and Istanbul.

According to Emmet Scott, these facts were widely known, but it was Pirenne who concluded that Islamic piracy dealt a lethal blow to Mediterranean trade and commerce and caused the onset of the Dark Ages in Europe. Throughout its existence, the Roman Empire was essentially Mediterranean. While Italy, Spain, and North Africa were important in many respects, the later Empire's cultural, economic, and population centers were the great cities of the East: Alexandria, Antioch, Ephesus, Pergamon, Aspendos, and, until 1453, Constantinople. The West boasted only one true city, Rome, but by

---

[115] *Christianity, Islam and Atheism: The Struggle for the Soul of the West,* William Kilpatrick (2012).

the fourth century, intellectually and culturally, Rome had grown more and more out of touch with the new progressive thinking of the Hellenistic world. The Roman academies and libraries were no longer any match for those of Alexandria, Pergamon, and Antioch.

Saracen pirates and raiders, Pirenne claimed, had blocked the Mediterranean from the 640s onward, terminating nearly all trade between the Levant and Europe. The cities of Gaul and Spain, which depended on that trade, began to die, and the German kings who controlled those regions, deprived of taxable wealth, lost much of their authority and power. All this happened abruptly in the seventh century. Arab piracy and invasions broke up the unity of the Mediterranean world and turned the middle sea, previously one of the most important trading highways, into a battleground.

The most essential product from the East was papyrus. Until the first quarter of the seventh century, Egyptian papyrus was ubiquitous in the documents of Western Europe, but by the 640s and 650s, it had disappeared more or less completely, and been replaced by parchment. Parchment was immensely expensive, and the loss of the papyrus supply had a devastating effect on the state of literacy and literature in Europe. The Dark Ages had begun.

Pirenne saw the disappearance of papyrus in the West as a seminal event. The vast majority of classical authors were written and copied on papyrus, but since papyrus is vulnerable to damp and mold, works had to be recopied regularly. This meant that most of the classical works were doomed to disappear. Pirenne estimated that 90 percent of them did. The unavailability of papyrus in the West, Pirenne concluded, caused the Dark Ages in Europe.

The trade in foodstuffs and papyrus was replaced by the slave trade, consisting almost entirely of slaves acquired by raiding, piracy, and general banditry. The raids became a perpetual feature of life along the borderlines of the Arab-controlled world, an impact felt even into the early years of the seventeenth century.

Destruction of agriculture and deforestation

The long-term consequences of Arab lawlessness had another immediate impact. The Romans were an agricultural people who extended their way of life into their African provinces. The climate in the Middle East and North Africa was arid, and agriculture needed enormous systems of cultivation and terracing. It was what made great expanses of the Middle East and North Africa fertile and productive. It was the existence of this agricultural infrastructure that made it possible for the late classical cities to thrive. Conversely, it was the destruction of this infrastructure that led to their abandonment.

The Arabs were a nomadic people. Nurtured in the desert of Arabia, they were unused to an agricultural economy and incapable of managing the highly-developed irrigation systems of North Africa bequeathed to them by the Romans. As quintessential goat herders, after conquering a territory, they allowed their flocks to graze on lands that had previously been under cultivation. This destroyed the agricultural viability of these territories and reduced them to arid semidesert within a very short time.

By the end of the eighth century AD, there were over one million Arabs in North Africa, and each Arab family kept a flock of sheep. Some families owned flocks of fifty sheep. The added presence of several million goats, notoriously close croppers, destroyed vast areas of grass, scrub, and trees, increasing runoff and decreasing precious supplies of groundwater. The result was the collapse of agriculture and the abandonment of cities whose populations depended on productive farming communities to survive.

Oddly, the Arabs did not value trees, except as lumber or firewood. In both Arabia and North Africa, their failure to understand the long-term value of tree cover had a further deleterious effect on the economy. According to Emmet Scott, the primary cause of the economic decline was deforestation, responsibility for which he lays at the door of the Arabs.

Depopulation of cities

One immediate consequence of agricultural decline and deforestation was a dramatic drop in population in Anatolia, Syria, and Egypt. By the Middle Ages, large parts of the Middle East and North Africa had become a sparsely populated wasteland of largely impoverished populations. Landscapes extensively cultivated in Roman and Byzantine times had turned into semi-arid territories.

It was only after the appearance of Islam, Pirenne claimed, that the cities of the West and East, which depended on the Mediterranean trade for their survival, began to die, and with them went the entire structure of classical culture. Emmet Scott's investigation, based on recent archeological excavations, concluded that from the seventh to the tenth century, virtually nothing was built in the Middle East.

The same archeological investigations revealed that, from the mid-seventh century, Arab destruction throughout the Near East was so great that many cities and towns which had thrived under the Byzantines and remained prosperous until the first quarter of the seventh century were abandoned, never to be reoccupied. Curiously, the anti-Pirenne historians claimed that during this period, the Islamist regions enjoyed a "Golden Age."

Citing from Emmet Scott's 2012 essay "The Fate of the Roman Cities of the Near East and North Africa:"

> The great Roman cities of the Middle East and North Africa were abandoned and now stand in semi-arid territories. Landscapes that have been cultivated for many centuries in Roman and Byzantine times were deserted, and agriculture in the surrounding countryside collapsed. The settlements, with their large populations, needed productive farming communities to survive. The desertification of the territories in which they stood would have been a death sentence for them.

In 2016, I read in the newspaper that ISIS had demolished what was left of the archeological jewel and fabulous tourist attraction of Palmyra in Syria. It seems that what Muslim fanatics did not destroy during the Middle Ages they were determined to level in the twenty-first century.

The nature of Islam

What is it about Islam that can lead to such universal and complete destruction? Even a cursory examination of the tenets of Islam is enough to convince us that it is not a faith like any other. On the contrary, it is a religious-political ideology whose fundamental principle is aggressive expansionism through the doctrine of a perpetual holy war or jihad, plus the notion of entitlement central to Sharia law.

Islamic law divides the world into two parts: the Dar-al-Islam (House of Islam) and Dar-al-Harb (House of War), and dictates that there can never be genuine peace between them. In the 1,300 years since the death of Mohammed, almost all contacts between Muslims and the outside world have been warlike. Islamic generals launched attack after attack against the southern shores of Europe during the seventh and eighth centuries, while minor Muslim commanders and private individuals carried out lesser raids. It was considered legitimate for the Muslim faithful to live off the infidel world. Whatever spoils could be taken were divinely sanctioned.

In the words of the historian Emmet Scott:

> The coming of Islam signaled a wave of banditry and piracy in the Mediterranean such as had not been seen before the second century BC, when such activities were severely curtailed by Roman naval power. Ordinary pirates might be deterred by powerful navies which threatened them with an early death, but Muslim pirates would not be put off by such dangers since, in their minds, they were executing a divine order, and to die in such activity was considered a sure way to paradise.

Constant Muslim raids throughout southern Europe led to the abandonment of the scattered settlements of classical times, and set off the retreat to hilltop fortifications—the first medieval castles. The raids also led to the abandonment of old agricultural systems, irrigation dikes, and ditches, and caused a layer of silt to form along the Mediterranean coast lands, covering the port areas of classical settlements. But the destructiveness of the Arabs and their misuse of agricultural land was not enough to explain the rapid and complete degradation of the cultivated territories of the Middle East and North Africa.

The Arab invasion differed from previous invasions, however destructive, because of the unique nature of Islam and its method of political and social control through Sharia law. After the conquest of a territory and the submission of its inhabitants, the application of Islamic law meant that non-Muslims living there would never again enjoy lasting peace and security. In theory, the religions of the Book (i.e., Christianity and Judaism) enjoyed a special protected status (*dhimmi*) under the new regime. In practice, the position of the Christian and Jewish populations was anything but protected. As Dario Fernandez-Morera succinctly puts it: "They were the victims of an extortion system that gave them the choice gangsters give their victims: pay up to be protected, or else."

Even tolerant Muslim rulers viewed non-Muslims with contempt. The *dhimmi* were inferior citizens with hardly any right to due process. Under Islamic law, Muslims had the right to subsist off the labors and property of the infidel. It was enshrined in the concept of *jizya*, the tax that all infidels living in the Dar al-Islam had to pay to their Muslim masters, and it was not just the Caliph and his emirs who were entitled to live off the infidels.

All Muslims, irrespective of position, had this right, and Islamic law thus sanctified the exploitation of the local Christian and Jewish populations by individual Muslims.

Among the immediate consequences was a dramatic decline in the population, and the abandonment of their cities. The medieval populations of Anatolia, Syria, Egypt, and North Africa were perhaps only a fifth of what they had been under the last Byzantine administration. The result was that by the later Middle Ages, large parts of the Middle East and North Africa became a sparsely populated wasteland, housing economically oppressed and largely impoverished populations.

CURRENTLY, EUROPE IS witnessing a massive invasion by Muslims. The main causes are wars and conflicts in the Middle East. The ingress of people from different, often inimical cultures, does not bode well for European and Western civilization, and it appears that the Europeans are not willing to address the problem in a serious way. On the contrary, their generous treatment of refugees is an invitation to more to come.[116]

Where will all this lead, and when will it end? As Mark Twain once said, "History never repeats itself in the same way, but it certainly rhymes." I hesitate to venture into the realm of prophecy, and so I leave these thoughts to my grandchildren, their grandchildren, and future generations to judge if my fears were justified.

---

[116] In October 2017, while preparing to send this volume to the publisher, I began reading Douglas Murray's *The Strange Death of Europe: Immigration, Identity, Islam*. Released earlier that year, the seminal book paints a dire future for Europe, a continent caught in the act of suicide through declining birth rates, mass immigration and cultivated self-distrust and self-hatred rendering Europeans incapable of resisting threats to its culture and society.

39. Skiing in the Alps: The Ultimate Freedom

IT WAS ON THE SKI SLOPES that I experienced ultimate freedom—the freedom that comes from solitude and isolation from worldly concerns— a zone of silence, away from media, TV, telephones, and *Big Brother*. Free to slide down a mountain at any speed I chose, letting gravity take me anywhere I wanted to go.

The winter months in northern France were mostly bleak and dreary. Rarely did the sun penetrate the ever-present cloud cover, drizzle, and occasional fog. Life in Paris moved indoors. Cafes and restaurants relocated their clients indoors. The theater, cinema, and live music scene thrived. Another way to get away from the damp and dreary weather was to head for the Alps. Every year, I took time out to pursue my favorite winter sport, downhill skiing. It was my way of decompressing from my intense travel schedule and getting in touch with nature.

When I arrived in Paris in 1979, I was already an avid skier, if not an accomplished one. I had skied the Rockies from Taos in New Mexico to Vail in central Colorado, including resorts such as Aspen, Steamboat Springs, Breckenridge, Telluride, Keystone, and Arapahoe Basin. Even though I caught the ski bug in Colorado, I never got past the level of a mediocre intermediate skier because I never took the time to get proper ski instruction.

Still, I was smitten by the skiing virus perfectly described by William F. Buckley in his memoir *Miles Gone By:*

The pleasure of skiing is not a function of speed or performance. I know of no sport, no hobby, and no avocation as indulgent as skiing in giving you exactly the combination you wish of challenge, relaxation, thrill, and exhilaration. Lifting your spirit with every turn and reminding you day after day, year after year, the singular pleasure that issues from a mountain's height. Skiing is always doing that kind of thing for you.

ON ITS EASTERN END, the Alps chain begins with the Dinaric Alps in Slovenia and ends abruptly in Haute-Savoie in France, where it curves south and sinks into the Mediterranean at the Cote d'Azur. The chain passes through the magnificent Dolomites in Northern Italy, getting gradually higher in Austria. In Switzerland, the mountains become more massive with dozens of summits over four thousand meters, reaching their apex at Mont Blanc, a peak nearly five thousand meters high.

During the 1980s and into the early '90s, I had the good fortune to ski, hike, climb, scale, or trek the most interesting sections of the Alpine chain. The Alps I know best are the French Alps. I skied mostly in the northern part, which included Haute-Savoie, La Tarentaise, L'Oisans, and Les Écrins. Each of these areas contained dozens of first-rate ski stations. The variety of terrain and resorts was superabundant. For five months of the year, they offered fantastic skiing conditions, modern infrastructure, spectacular scenery, and a lively ambiance, a choice seemingly endless.

The event that aroused my fascination with the Alps began with my first trip to Chamonix. A ski club I belonged to in Chicago offered an excursion to this renowned ski resort in the French Alps. The station boasted the world's highest and longest off-piste ski route, the unique Vallée Blanche—a three-kilometer vertical descent over a twenty-kilometer long glacier called the Mer de Glace. The Colorado Rockies provided a lot of fine skiing, but nothing close to the nine thousand feet vertical in Chamonix. That was in 1978.

Over the years, my interest in mountains grew. I found the open skies, the magnificent vistas, and the pristine air liberating and energizing. When Leonid Vereshaka, an Australian friend from Chicago, visited me in Paris in March 1980, we took in a weekend of spring skiing at Chamonix. I was anxious to show him the Vallée Blanche, but inclement weather and limited visibility made the world's longest ski run inaccessible.

The Vallée Blanche expedition is more appropriately called ski mountaineering. Apart from the crevasses, a skier has to be prepared for changes in weather and terrain. The winds at the top of the Aiguille du Midi

(3,842 meters) are unpredictable, and visibility can change in a split second. We began by climbing down a long, steep, one-meter-wide windy ridge with our skis over our shoulders. One misstep in either direction, and our skiing days would be over forever.

Once we reached the glacier, we fixed our skis and continued over shallow powder, sidestepping occasional rock outcroppings or balancing on a snow bridge spanning a deep crevice. The descent over the moonlike landscape of Vallée Blanche was not particularly challenging, but one had to be on constant lookout for rocks and crevasses. What made the descent tricky was the constant distraction of the surrounding landscape of spectacular jagged peaks and mountains, all famous in the annals of mountain climbing. The temptation to gape at them made it hard to concentrate on control. The Grandes Jorasses were the most strikingly complex and impressive structures of the entire Mont Blanc massif. They exuded, most spectacularly on the famous north face, an air of mystery and power that had no rivals in the entire Alps. If Mont Blanc was the king of the Alps, the Grandes Jorasses complex was the queen. Then there was the needlelike Aiguille du Dru, which towered above the glacier, Europe's longest climbing vertical.

The most dangerous part of the descent came where the Vallée Blanche transformed into the Mer de Glace, a region of ice falls called the *seracs*. The ice got suddenly steeper, the crevasses wider and deeper, treacherously camouflaged by snow. Four guides, barking at us to stay in line like sheep, guided our group between the crevasses and seracs. We navigated these obstacles slowly and carefully. More than one solo skier had disappeared in this sea of ice, never to be heard from again. "Mountaineering on skis" would become my passion for the next fifteen years.

When I came to France, I was not a great skier. During my years of unsupervised skiing in the United States, I had picked up a lot of bad habits I needed to break. They say it's easier to teach someone to ski from scratch than to break long-established bad habits. However, with a regular diet of instructions and practice, I developed a passable technique that enabled me to tackle the most challenging slopes.

DANYLO STRUK HAD FRIENDS in Geneva. One of them was Bohdan Hawrylyshyn, a Canadian-Ukrainian business educator who headed the International Management Institute in Geneva. Another was Oleh Nyzhankivsky, an opera and concert baritone, and his wife, Zoya. Both had chalets in the region of Valais, east of Geneva. Through them, I met a

Ukrainian-Swiss couple, Mykhailo and Chrystyna Katchaluba, he a doctor and she an artist-sculptor.

The Katchalubas lived in Montreux, a town on the northeast corner of Lake Geneva at the foot of the Alps. Whenever I drove through this region on the way to the ski areas to the east, I stopped for a visit. The Ukrainian diaspora in Switzerland was small, so the Katchalubas were always glad to welcome visiting Ukrainians. Their home sat on a slope overlooking Lake Geneva, and what stuck in my mind from these stopovers was the view from their drawing room, a magnificent panorama of the snowy French Alps whose peaks erupted from the tranquil waters of the lake like mighty pyramids of nature.

Just south of Montreux, the Hawrylyshyns had a chalet in Villars, and further on, past Martigny in the Val de Bagnes, the Nyzhankivskys owned a vintage chalet next to the commune of Le Châble in the village of Bruson. They split their time between Geneva and Bruson, and after Oleh had retired, they spent a lot of time in their chalet. Oleh and Zoya were gracious hosts. Bruson, located on a northern slope, provided excellent spring skiing through April, and across the valley from Bruson stretched the exclusive ski area of Verbier.

Oleh worshiped his chalet and always had interesting stories to tell about this region.

"Most people don't realize that this part of Switzerland, the Valais, was not always as prosperous as it is today. The region was always rich in scenery but poor in arable land, and as late as the nineteenth century, the mountain people here barely eked out a living. At times, they found themselves on the verge of starvation. Privation forced them to conserve and make the most of limited resources. Quite often, households found it hard to feed their large families, and many migrated to cities like Lausanne and Geneva, bringing with them their work ethic and frugal habits. That is how the Swiss got their reputation for saving, making the most of sparse resources and hard work. It was not an accident that industries like clock making and banking evolved from such a work ethic."

The chalet was built of aged logs, which, according to Oleh, were highly prized and, when available, sold at a premium. Old dry logs apparently kept the cabin insulated and, in combination with an ingeniously designed heating system, comfortably warm night and day.

Oleh explained, "Instead of a fire chamber, the stove contains a huge stone, heated by electricity. We heat the stone during the night when hydroelectric current is inexpensive. It stores the heat, and by morning, when the current is switched off, the stone is hot enough to keep the chalet warm for the rest of the day. By repeating this process on a daily basis, we hardly need to rely on firewood or other fossil fuels."

OVER THE YEARS, I SKIED at no less than twenty ski stations, large and small, in France, Switzerland, Italy, and Austria. Among them were a few places and experiences that left a lasting impression. By 1985, I had been skiing the Alps for five years and was searching for an out-of-the-ordinary experience that I could one day tell my grandchildren about. The tour of the region called La Tarentaise, organized by Club Méditerranée (Club Med), sounded like that event. The preconditions were straightforward: you had to be a good skier and in excellent physical condition.

The group met at the Club Med in Tignes, where more people came to party than to ski. Still, there was a cluster of hardened skiers who came to do the so-called Nine Valleys Ski Safari. As was often the case with such events, a large number of skiers signed up, but not all qualified. The instructors put us through a rigorous trial for several days, and those who consistently lagged behind were not accepted. In this respect, the guides were merciless, pushing us through an exhausting routine of traverses, climbs, and descents, and more climbs. Obviously, the groups could move only as fast as the slowest skier, so after two days, the original group of twenty had been whittled down to ten.

It was the first week of March, and skiing conditions in this part of the French Alps were superb—bright sunny days, a deep snow base, and new snow practically every other day. The Tarentaise, one of the Savoyard valleys created by glaciers many millennia ago, led to the high passes used by travelers for centuries to cross into Italy. This pastoral habitat was one of the most extensive ski areas in the world, integrating a dozen world-class resorts. Its upper reaches consisted of barren mountains that provided excellent skiing conditions from October to May.

The trials took place on the slopes of Val-d'Isère, but the actual starting point for the hundred-kilometer trek was the 3,450-meter Grande Motte, high above Tignes, where the cobalt-blue sky and the absolute silence created an eerie atmosphere. Only a gentle wind whistled across the crusty early morning snow. We went off-piste down a three-kilometer stretch of ungroomed powder snow that eventually wound its way through trees and brush.

Backcountry valley-to-valley skiing was once the exclusive province of the expert deep powder skier. In the 1980s, with expert guides, it began to change. An advanced intermediate skier could savor the thrill of off-piste skiing, an endless series of short climbs and traverses across virgin patches of the raw, the natural, and the untamed world of backcountry skiing. We moved nonstop down ravines and through forests of pine and brush. We traversed barren patches and climbed or lifted above the tree line where the trees became smaller and fewer.

Every day during the ten-day trek, we slept in a different *gîte* (mountain refuge) or hotel. Our baggage followed from station to station along a path from Tignes to Les Arcs, Nancroix, La Plagne, and, finally, the resorts at Courchevel, Méribel, Les Menuires, and Val Thorens, a giant ski domain known as Les Trois Vallées. The schedule was tight, and the guides pushed us relentlessly. The distance from Tignes, the starting point, to Val Thorens was roughly one hundred kilometers as the crow flies, and with constant detours and transport connections, the trek was easily double, if not triple, that distance. No one tried to keep mileage.

We concluded the safari with a run from the 3,400-meter summit of the Trois Vallées, Pointe du Bouchet above Val Thorens (at 2,300 meters, the highest of any European ski resort), to Saint-Martin-de-Belleville at 1,400 meters. I was exhausted, completely drained of energy, and went to sleep without eating the evening meal. After a long sleep the next day, I felt stronger than ever. This experience prepared me for my mountaineering exploits, which were to follow a few years later.

I lived on the memory of this experience for a long time. It was memorable not only for the adventure, but also for the camaraderie I found on this expedition. One of my skiing partners was a young Italian radiologist from Avellino, Italy. Domenico was a personable and easygoing individual, and we stayed in touch for many years after the Tarentaise expedition. In 1992, I visited him in Avellino, a town some fifty kilometers northeast of Naples in the heart of Campania. He shared a radiology practice with his father, and by Italian standards, the family was well-to-do. Besides an apartment in Naples, they owned a villa on the island of Ischia. He gave me keys to both properties, and Eva and I spent a few days discovering Naples, the ruins of Pompeii, the Amalfi Coast, and the Island of Capri. It was easy to see what made this region so attractive to Emperor Tiberius as well as to nineteenth- and twentieth-century artists and writers such as Maxim Gorky and Gore Vidal. Over a period of thirty-three years, Vidal spent many months of the year in the Villa La Rondinaia near Ravello, where he wrote many of his books. One never knows whom one will meet on the slopes, and my chance encounter with Domenico gave me the opportunity to discover this part of Italy.

OVER THE YEARS, I became intimately familiar with the region of the Swiss Valais, the valley of the Rhône River from Martigny to the town of Brig. The map depicts the extent of the region, whose spine of "four-thousanders" ran along the border with Italy connecting the highest peaks of the Alps from Chamonix in the west to Monte Rosa in the east.

Through the Ukrainian grapevine, I learned that a group of Ukrainian skiers was organizing excursions to the Swiss Alps. The group, the KLK, *Karpatsko Leshchetarskiy Klub,* the Carpathian Ski Club, was led by Orest "Gogo" Slupchynsky from New York and consisted of a dozen or more ardent skiers, mainly from the New York area, but also from Toronto and Chicago.

In March 1986, my artist friend Volodymyr Makarenko (Makar) and I joined the KLK group in Crans-Montana, the first of many excursions that were to follow—Zermatt (1987), Grindelwald-Jungfrau (1988), and Verbier (1989). Crans-Montana consisted of two villages on a high plateau above the Rhône River. The KLK group chose this station for its 150 kilometers of intermediate slopes, relaxed atmosphere, and short ski lift lines—perfect for our group of skiers who ranged in age from forty to sixty-five. Clearly, they did not come to Montana to train for its famous Kandahar race. They went to enjoy majestic Alpine scenery, Swiss hospitality, and the company of interesting people. There are few greater pleasures in the world than to be on the slopes with like-minded friends.

Makar was thrilled to go on his first ski trip. I had given him my old set of K2 "short magic" skis, and I thought a few lessons were advisable, but he insisted he didn't need them. He claimed that he had skied in Ukraine, and because he was athletically inclined, he persuaded us that he would be fine.

On the second day, the group decided to tackle Plaine Morte (Dead Plain), a gently descending glacier run. As Makar looked down the vista to Montana, his face turned ash white.

"You mean we have to go down that slope?" He was ready to get on the ski-lift and go back down.

Slowly he overcame his initial fear and started to move. It is then that we realized that Makar was a total beginner, but there was no choice. It was too late to turn back. A couple of us stayed behind and taught him some basic snowplow turns, which he mastered quickly, and then escorted him down the mountain one measured turn at a time. When we reached Montana, Makar had developed a unique snowplow technique and was ready for another run.

That evening at dinner, the group recalled the day's adventures. Makar, a natural storyteller, turned his experience on Plaine Morte into a skit, mimicking the movements and gestures, and parodying our instructions in a hilarious manner.

"I saved a lot of money today. Slavko and Taras showed me all I needed, the snowplow. If I want to turn right, I'm supposed to place all my weight on the left foot, and if I want to turn left, I place my weight on the right foot. I just couldn't figure out why I needed the ski sticks."

Makar kept us in stitches late into the evening. A talented entertainer, he transformed even the simplest experience into a funny story. He and Ihor Chuma from Toronto kept us entertained every day for the rest of the week.

OREST SLUPCHYNSKY, known to us affably as "Gogo," was the driving force behind the KLK ski expeditions to the Alps. Although in his sixties, he was full of drive and energy. Gogo was one of those exceptional individuals who hardly aged and whom one never forgot. Born in Poland, raised in Ukraine, he was first and foremost an outstanding Ukrainian patriot. As a young man, he joined the Galicia Division and fought in the Battle of Brody in July 1944. The stories Gogo told, and he loved to talk, would require a separate volume. Gogo and his cohorts were the heroes that stemmed the onslaught of the Bolshevik horde long enough to give my family and thousands of others the time to escape west. Even though it was clear that the Germans had lost the war, the men who joined the Galicia division did so to obtain German military training to continue the fight for a free and independent Ukraine when the war was over.[117] After internment at Rimini, Orest eventually wound up in the United States, where he was an active member of the Ukrainian community in New York. He resurrected the KLK, the patriotic sports organization. During the '80s, ski excursions to the Alps were the highlight of their program. Gogo had been organizing ski expeditions for many years, but he once told me that the pinnacle of his efforts was Zermatt in 1987 and Jungfrau in 1988.

In its fairy-tale setting, Zermatt remains the world's quintessential ski and mountaineering resort. It sits at the end of a long valley and is bounded

---

[117] The best book on this subject is *Galicia Division,* by Michel Logusz, Schiffer Publishing, 1997.

by three major ski areas. It differs from every other resort in the Alps in that it can only be reached via a mountain cog railway. Except for a few electrified taxis and ambulances, the town does not allow automobiles. The resort's outstanding feature is the indomitable Matterhorn, whose triangular shape rises three thousand meters above the village. The four-and-a-half-thousand-meter pyramid protrudes like a sentinel demarcating the boundary between Switzerland and Italy. The Italians call the Matterhorn Monte Cervino.

The station was not for beginners. Most slopes required considerable control and stamina. It was easy to stray onto a demanding "black" slope, so our group was cautioned to stay off those runs. A few of us, however, itched to do something more adventurous. On a clear day, an opportunity presented itself: a one-day cross-border excursion to Breuil-Cervinia, a resort on the Italian side of the immense glacier separating Switzerland and Italy.

I persuaded Makar and a couple of other skiers to take the cable car up to the Klein Matterhorn. The cable car itself is an engineering feat matched only by the aerial tramway to the Aiguille du Midi in Chamonix. The "Little Matterhorn" was a solid rock with a shape that mimicked its bigger brother. At 3,883 meters, it was the highest point in the Alps that could be reached by cable car, about fifty meters higher than the cable car station at the Aiguille du Midi on the way to Mont Blanc. A T-bar tow pulled us across the vast and windy Theodul Glacier/Pass, a flat plateau at 3,800 meters, into Italy. Covered year-round by a blanket of snow, the pass was permanently whipped by crosswinds, so I held on to the T-bar for dear life. Suddenly, at the end of the towline, we were in Italy and gently descended to Breuil-Cervinia. The change was abrupt and the contrast striking. The fog hanging over the pass cleared, and as the cold wind dissipated, the Italian sun welcomed us. Suddenly, we were on a different planet. As we skied down at a leisurely pace, I understood the full meaning of the expression "the sunny side of the Alps."

Cervinia, at an impressive two thousand meters, boasts an exceptional Alpine snow record. Its sunny, well-groomed runs are heaven for intermediate skiers not interested in difficult terrain or fearsome challenges. We managed only a few runs. The crossing from Zermatt took up the entire morning, and soon it was time for lunch. We found a restaurant at the foot of the slopes, Casse-Croûte, ordered pasta, and relaxed with a liter carafe of Chianti. Even the people there seemed friendlier. Makar flirted with some pretty Italian ladies sitting near us. Despite the lack of a common language, his sign language and gestures made them laugh. But time was short. We did not have the luxury of dawdling. At midafternoon, we had to catch the last lift that would take us back to Zermatt.

IT'S HARD TO BEAT Zermatt, but the Jungfrau comes close. It's a spectacular region only an hour's drive from Bern. Its ski areas, set against the stunning backdrop of three impressive mountains, the Jungfrau, the Mönch, and the Eiger, are on posters the world over. Even though the north face of the Eiger enjoyed legendary status before WWII, it was Clint Eastwood's 1975 movie, *The Eiger Sanction*, that raised it to iconic distinction. Orest and his friend Svat told me they had dreamt of skiing this region since being released from the Rimini internment camp after the war.

We met in the village of Grindelwald where comfortable accommodation, lots of good food, drink, and lively company created a convivial and relaxed atmosphere. From our hotel, we were within walking distance of the rail station that connected to Kleine Scheidegg, the starting point for the Jungfraubahn, a cog railway that burrows its way through the mountain to the Jungfraujoch rail station. No skiing here, just spectacular views of the eternal snowy peaks and the Aletsch Glacier, Switzerland's longest glacier.

THE MOST BEAUTIFUL MOUNTAIN chain in the Alps is the Dolomites, also known as South Tyrol. Strangely, few Americans know of this sunny side of Europe's mountain spine, although it is only a few hours by rail or car from Venice, Milan, or Munich. On several occasions, I skied the area around the spectacular Sellagruppe, north of the Marmolada massif.

I was first exposed to the Dolomites in the summer of 1986, when I attended a Russian- language immersion course in Madonna di Campiglio, one of the jewels of the Brenta Dolomites. The Brenta massif consisted of a series of wild limestone formations—multicolored rocks that were as stark and beautiful in winter as they were in the summer. These "castles built by God" had to be seen to be believed.

On one of my ski excursions to the Dolomites, I uncovered a fascinating piece of history. Even though the South Tyrol today is part of Italy, historically, it was part of Austria for a millennium. Here they spoke a Germanic dialect called Ladin, which a friend told me resembles the vernacular spoken in Vienna. South Tyrol was Austrian until the end of WWI, when the German-speaking region was transferred to Italy.

Almost immediately, the Italians embarked on a broad program to Italianize this German-speaking territory by changing place names. First, they outlawed the name South Tyrol and renamed it Alto Adige, and replaced traditional German place names with Italianized or invented versions. Thus, just south of the Brenner Pass, Sterzing became Vipiteno; Bruneck, Brunico; Tobiach, Dobbiacco; Bozen, Bolzano; Meran, Merano; Brixen, Bressanone; Clausen, Chiusa; Saint Ulrich, Ortisei; and the Jaufenjoch Pass became Passo di Giovo; Stilferjoch, Passo dello Stelvio; and so on.

A particularly rankling aspect of the forced rechristening urged people to accept Italianized versions of their Germanic names. Incredibly, Italianization extended to the removal of German names on cemetery tombstones, changing them into Italian-sounding ones, a process that was stupid, costly, and demeaning to the Tyrolean population. Thus, a long defunct Joseph Collman posthumously became Giuseppe Colma. The renaming was intensified under Mussolini's fascist regime, striving to eradicate any lingering reminiscences and loyalties to Austria.

The Great Dolomite Alps Panoramic Road, connecting Bolzano with the winter sports arena in Cortina d'Ampezzo, passes through stunningly beautiful landscapes. Simply driving through the Dolomite mountain range is an uplifting experience. When combined with skiing in one of the largest interconnected lift systems in the world, the pleasure doubled, maybe tripled. The panorama found in the Dolomites around virtually every turn in the road is incomparable.

Another reason I found this part of Italy interesting was because it had been the scene of furious fighting between Austria-Hungary and Italy during WWI. Mountain troops faced each other from 1915 through 1917, and the war in the Dolomites was indeed a bloody affair. It was described vividly by Ernest Hemingway in what many consider his best novel, *A Farewell to Arms*.

As an amateur historian, I found great pleasure in connecting these historical dots. I visited the sites where the most ferocious fighting took place: the massif of Marmolada, the Col di Lana, and the mountain of Lagazuoi above the Falzarego Pass on the final section of the Great Dolomite Road to Cortina d'Ampezzo. All had witnessed furious fighting at terrible cost to human life on both sides. Opposing armies faced each other from mountaintops and fired at each other with howitzers and mortars. They tunneled through ice and rock, dug grottoes and trenches on the flanks of the mountains, descended by rope on enemy positions in daring surprise assaults, and blew up each other's strongholds by burrowing underneath them and planting enormous mines.

I saw the remains of a high-altitude front line on the Lagazuoi Mountain overlooking Falzarego Pass where I stopped to ski for a few hours. A single cable car whisked me to the summit of Mount Lagazuoi, one of the highest points in the Dolomite Alps. The view from Lagazuoi (2,779 meters) offered an unobstructed 360-degree panorama from the majestic Tofane Dolomites to the Sella Group and the Marmolada massif in the distance. As inconceivable as it seems, those high mountains served as the front lines where the Italian and Austrian armies slugged it out during WWI, not only against each other but also against the elements.

As I skied down the seven-hundred-meter run from Lagazuoi to the pass, I noticed that the surrounding mountains were pockmarked by caves, grottoes, and bunkers. The old military roads and tracks had become ski paths. In summer, one could still find war shell casings, military accessories, and bunkers. The whole top of the mountain was a giant open-air war museum. Tens of thousands of soldiers lost their lives in these mountains, many to avalanches and the elements as well as to fighting. I could sense the ghosts of the bloodletting that took place there. It was not unlike Verdun, but on a smaller scale. That was when I understood why so many Italians considered this heart of the Grand Dolomites sacred ground. Unfortunately, so did the Austrians.

The ultimate fate of the border between Austria and Italy was never decided on the battlefield, as the two countries pretty much fought to a draw. With the Great War winding down in other parts of Europe, the region's destiny was decided (unfairly, I might add) at the negotiation table in Paris in 1919. Italy had been promised the Dolomites when it switched allegiance at the start of the war, and so it was granted this beautiful region, and a new border with Austria was formed.

Artificial redrawing of borders that does not follow ethnic lines not only fails but also causes resentments. (One such example that lasted for centuries was when King Louis XIV appropriated German-speaking Alsace in the seventeenth century, because he thought the Rhine was France's natural eastern boundary.) South Tyrol was another clear example of such inequity. In 2016, nearly a hundred years after WWI ended, Austria's Freedom Party candidate Norbert Hofer denounced the Tyrol division. He told a Tyrolean rally that the border "was unjust, is unjust and will remain so," as long as it stands.

MY MOST DARING exploit on skis took place on the slopes of Courchevel. On one of my trips to this chic resort, I found the courage to try my hand at delta wing hang gliding on skis. Delta wing gliding was the precursor of the currently popular paragliding. The difference between the two was that the delta wing hang glider had a rigid aluminum primary structure, while the paraglider did not. By the 1980s, delta wing gliding technology had improved significantly, and taking advantage of thermal updrafts allowed one to soar for hours. In France, hang gliding was controlled by the Fédération Aéronautique Internationale, and at Courchevel, one could enjoy this sport with the help of an experienced pilot. It was a challenge I could not resist.

For a fee, one could descend two vertical kilometers from a perch at three thousand meters to a landing site at approximately one thousand meters. I will never forget the moment when the pilot buckled me into a harness and brought me to the edge of an abyss overlooking a thousand meters of emptiness. Even though he was harnessed next to me and would control the descent, my feet became wobbly, and I lost my nerve. The pilot, François, realizing my tenseness, unharnessed me, led me to the nearby cabin, and suggested I drink some wine. After fifteen minutes, I was sufficiently relaxed to approach the abyss again. We were on skis, and he asked his partner to push us off the cliff, and in no time, we were airborne, gliding into a gentle breeze that took us up and up. François had an instrument that measured the thermal updraft, and we rose in a circle, soaring like eagles between Alpine peaks. Being suspended in the air was the ultimate sensation of freedom and one of my most memorable experiences on skis. After half an hour, we gradually descended toward a treeless snow-covered patch and landed on a rising slope, gently coming to a full stop.

Author racing downhill in Tignes.

Descending on Deltaplan, a fixed-wing hand glider, in Courchevel.

The KLK group in Verbier. Left to right, Marichka Slupchynskyj,
me, Gogo (Marichka's husband), Eva Bauer and Makar.

Makar and I preparing to descent to Cervinia, Italy

Gogo, me and Ihor Chuma in Zermatt against the
backdrop of the mighty Matterhorn pyramid.

Makar, Eva, Darian and me near the Pointe du Montet (3400
meters), the highest skiable part of Val d 'Isere.

Marichka, Eva, me and Gogo in Kleine Scheidegg waiting
for the Jungfrau Railway narrow gauge rack railway to take
us to Grindenwald, 9 kilometers (5.6 mi) away.

40. Scaling Mont Blanc du Tacul

FOUR MONTHS AFTER I turned fifty, I made my first serious climb. I scaled Mont Blanc du Tacul, one of the peaks of the Mont Blanc massif. My passion for mountain climbing began with a weeklong trek called Tour du Mont Blanc with my artist friend Omelian Mazuryk. This was not "real" mountain climbing—*escalade*, as the French would say—but it was challenging enough to get me hooked on mountaineering. This was when I first contemplated climbing Mont Blanc.

The Massif du Mont Blanc was daunting. There is no exact English equivalent for the French word *massif*, the closest being "a mountain mass." The *massif* straddled France, Italy, and Switzerland, and consisted of stunning needlelike peaks surrounding the nearly five-kilometer-high Mont Blanc. Mont Blanc itself is unspectacular. A rounded bald mountain covered by snow year-round, it is famous mainly because at 4,810 meters, it is Western Europe's highest peak.[118]

The Tour du Mont Blanc trail consisted of a chain of strenuous ascents and descents around the *massif*, and passed through France, Italy, and Switzerland. The allure of hiking in the Alps was enhanced by the ubiquitous alpine refuges, where one could rest and get a decent hot meal. They were small islands of civilization in otherwise inhospitable terrain. After crossing several high passes west of Mont Blanc and negotiating tongues of glaciers, we ended up at Courmayeur, a charming resort town on the Italian side of the *massif*.

---

[118] Europe's highest peak is the 5,621-meter (18,442 feet) Elbrus on the Russian side of the Caucasus Mountains.

In Courmayeur, roughly the halfway mark of the tour, I realized that we would be unable to complete the entire circuit. I had to get back to Paris for an important meeting. The easy way to return to Chamonix was to take a bus connecting Courmayeur and Chamonix via the fifteen-kilometer Mont Blanc tunnel. Omelian and I, however, opted for the more adventurous route: take the cable car to Pointe Helbronner (3,500 meters), cross the Glacier du Géant, one of Europe's largest glaciers, to the Aiguille du Midi (3,850 meters), and descend via the cable car to Chamonix. The trek across the glacier offered perhaps some of the most spectacular scenery in the Alps, but to cross it, we needed a mountain guide. Because Courmayeur was the Italian equivalent of Chamonix, a Mecca for mountain climbers, this was not a problem. Our guide, Massimo, provided us with the necessary equipment, crampons and ropes, and the three of us crossed the crevasse-pocked moonscape of the Glacier du Géant. That was my first serious foray into the high Alps. I was smitten by the mountain climbing virus.

After ten years of hiking and skiing in the Alps, I gathered enough nerve to take on more adventurous climbing. A Parisian friend, Danylo Perehinec, who had climbed Mont Blanc, told me that it was not a particularly difficult feat. Although he was twenty years younger than me, his account encouraged me to join the *Club Alpin Français,* where I signed up with a group preparing to climb Mont Blanc. For several weeks before the climb, our group of aspiring climbers met with Laurent, a fifty-five-year-old professional mountain guide who taught us some basic rock-climbing techniques and told us what equipment we needed—sturdy climbing boots, crampons, a *baudrier* harness, ropes, and, of course, a fifty-liter backpack for all the equipment.

In mid-September, our group of eight hopeful climbers met in an alpine cabin at La Tour, a few kilometers east of Chamonix. There, Laurent trained us in the use of ropes, knots, ice ax techniques, crampons, and harnessing, and got us acclimatized to the high altitude. Except for the guide, I was the oldest member of the group. At the outset, Laurent said that he would take only five of us on the climb and he would tell us who was fit enough to go after a five-day trial of endurance. At first, I thought that my chances of overcoming the younger members were slim. However, as we began our trial, my years of hiking and jogging paid off.

One of the members of the group dropped out quickly because he was overweight. After strenuous hikes up the Glacier du Tour, he quickly ran out of breath. Another climber could not take the heights when rock climbing. On one occasion while practicing *escalade* halfway up a 150-meter vertical slab of schist, she lost her grip and plunged five meters before my rope broke her fall. The jolt nearly snapped my harness, but I had my feet firmly planted on a meter-wide perch, which kept both of us from going down a hundred meters to meet our creator. A third member of the group fell out when she sprained her ankle by stepping into a small crevasse. These mishaps reduced the group to five—two men in their twenties and a couple from Nantes in their thirties; he an engineer and she a physician.

Still, I faced the prospect of the climb with some trepidation. My desire to climb my first "four-thousander" was great, but fear of the unknown was intimidating. Alpinism, after all, was a hazardous sport. A day before the big climb, Laurent learned that the west ridge of Mont Blanc was swamped with amateur climbers. Mont Blanc was attracting an unusually large number of climbers, so he proposed the Mont Blanc du Tacul, one of Mont Blanc's neighbors.

The massif consists of three main summits: Mont Blanc (4810 meters), Mont Maudit (4465 meters), and Mont Blanc du Tacul (4248 meters). Together they make up the well-known 3M *(Trois-Monts)*, the eastern route, or the Mont Blanc Traverse, which begins with the Tacul.

A peak with steep granite walls seared by ribbons of ice, Mont Blanc du Tacul drew climbers from all over the world. Its north face was one of the most taxing peaks in the Chamonix Valley. The crevasse-scarred north face of the Tacul, according to Laurent, was more challenging than the smooth western approach to Mont Blanc, and the ascent was *"plus interessante."* By "more interesting," he meant, of course, more difficult. The south face of Tacul is a three-thousand-meter vertical wall that is practically unclimbable even by most professionals. Only a few Alpinists like Walter Bonatti and Reinhold Messner have scaled this rugged "back side" of Tacul.

From the French side, Tacul was doable in a day. We set out at 4:00 a.m. to catch a cable car to the Aiguille du Midi, where we would begin to traverse the glacier. That was when Laurent announced that we must summit before 11:00 a.m. He explained that around noon, the ice began to soften and the crampons did not hold firmly. At extremely high altitudes such as the Pamirs or Himalayas, where the ice rarely melted, soft ice was not an issue, but in mountains between four thousand and five thousand meters, daily thawing and freezing meant that one had to summit early and descend before the frozen snow got soft and mushy. Moreover, there were no *gîtes* (shelters) on the Tacul, so the choice was between bivouacking at four thousand meters and being rescued by a helicopter. Every minute counted.

The normal route to the summit of Tacul began with a steep one-hundred-meter descent along a meter-wide snow-covered ridge. This short descent with the precipitous drop on both sides of the path was enough to panic climbers suffering from vertigo. Many simply turned back. I had descended this narrow ridge on several occasions before, when I skied the Vallée Blanche, so I knew what to expect. The crossing of the Col du Midi was uneventful until I was face-to-face with a six-hundred-meter wall of snow and ice.

This was when the dangers of Tacul's north face suddenly multiplied. At first, the gradient increased to thirty degrees and then to forty, and fractures in the sloping ice field created crevasses and seracs. Laurent reminded us that the weather could change quickly: the temperature might drop, and fresh snow could camouflage crevasses and increase the chances of an avalanche. A change in wind direction could unexpectedly roll in clouds, reducing visibility to a few meters.

Soon, I realized that climbing above four thousand meters was exhausting, even for those in good physical condition. The nonstop stabbing and hacking with the ice ax and vigorous plunging of crampons sapped my energy. After every twenty or thirty vertical steps, I was gasping for breath, my heart pumping like a scared rabbit. Our pace was reduced to a crawl. Laurent insisted we never climb vertically; always traverse in a zigzag fashion, which added steps but saved energy.

Walking on pitched ice was hazardous; the climber had to remain focused and vigilant. A misstep could result in an uncontrolled slide and end badly. Being tethered by a rope made it safer, but it also restricted movement. We all had to move in unison. When I stopped to take a photo, Laurent yelled, *"Ne vous arrêtez pas!"* (Do not stop). Roughly halfway up the Tacul, we paused to cross a two-meter wide crevasse with no discernible bottom. "Don't look down," he warned. "Just do as I say." I admit I was frightened, and for a few moments, my heart stopped. Before I realized it, Laurent somehow swung across the crevasse (to this day, I don't know how he did it) and screwed in two special ice pitons into the hard ice a few meters above where we were standing. These pitons, he told us, could hold for about five minutes before they got loose. It meant that five climbers had five minutes to jump and pull themselves up to the overhanging ice above. When my turn came, I jumped, plunged my crampons into the ice wall with full force, and pulled myself up like a gymnast. Soon, we crossed two more similar crevasses. With each crossing, the task got easier.

Near the summit, we encountered several sizable seracs that we bypassed. Seracs and avalanches are extremely dangerous and had killed many climbers in the vicinity. In 1998, eight climbers, attacking Mont Blanc via the less challenging western route from the Dôme du Goûter, were caught in a freak summer snowstorm and died. Years later in 2008, Mont Blanc du Tacul took the lives of experienced British climbers Rob Gauntlett and James Atkinson.

The last stretch was relatively easy, and we knew we were at the summit when we encountered partially exposed rocks overlooking the abyss on the Italian side of the mountain. As we reached the rounded summit, a stinging wind lashed my face, while a thick cloud attached itself to the mountaintop like a magnet. It was the ultimate irony. After a strenuous five-hour climb, I was unable to see either the adjacent Mont Blanc or the Vallée Blanche below. We barely spent fifteen minutes at the summit—just time for a quick snack and a couple of photos of rocks. Still, after summiting, I felt the joy and freedom of an eagle flying in the low troposphere. That's when it occurred to me: the higher the climb, the greater the joy.

Laurent broke the spell with a stern warning. "Most accidents happen on the way down because, in the afternoon, frozen snow turns soft and mushy."

Now I understood why we had to summit early. On the way down, the obstacles were the same three crevasses we had encountered on the way up. The only way to get across those gaps in ice was to jump down and across and land in a squatting position to absorb the shock. All of us managed to clear the widest crevasse except Nathalie, the thirty-five-year-old physician. She jumped but did not land in a squat and twisted her knee. Because she was unable to step on her right foot, the men took turns helping her down to the base camp.

Many people regard mountain climbing as an escape from the reality of modern times. This is unfair and should never overshadow its real essence: victory over human frailty. Climbing is an obsession with the addictive power of heroin. After my experience on Mont Blanc du Tacul, I was smitten by this urge. Those who have never climbed may find this incomprehensible. To paraphrase the famous Alpinist Walter Bonatti, "When I climb, I feel alive. The more challenging the climb, the more alive I feel. Everything in between climbs is mere existence."

The Soviet singer-songwriter and poet Vladimir Vysotsky made this point succinctly in one of his songs: *luchshe gor mozhut byt tolka gory na kotorykh ya yeshcho ne byval.* A rough translation would be, "The only thing better than mountains are mountains I have not yet climbed."

I understood the obsessive nature of the *escalade* when I shared a cable car to the Aiguille du Midi with three hardened climbers on their way to do the 3M route in the winter. The Alpinists' bodies seemed made of wire, and their faces were rugged and weathered. Each was weighted down with mountain-climbing paraphernalia—crampons, pitons, ice axes, ropes, and provisions. I struck up a conversation, and one of them began recounting his mountaineering exploits. "In summer, the 3M route is challenging, but in winter, it's twice as difficult." When he noticed that I was staring at his hand, with stubs instead of fingers, he casually said, "Oh, I lost my fingers to frost on the Grandes Jorasses."

You'd think a sensible man would say enough is enough, stop climbing in the winter, and yet this climber seemed thrilled at the prospect of another tough climb. Men like these lived only to climb the next mountain, and that is why one year later, some inexplicable force drove me to scale Monte Rosa.

Training for the Mont Blanc du Tacul climb.

Rock scaling in preparation for the climb; I'm in the blue shirt with raised arm.

Team resting on a perch next to a waterfall.

Acclimatizing to higher altitude and training on glacier.

Ascending Mer de Glace toward the Grande Jorasses.

The glacier gets steeper.

Training on ice.

Inspecting a small crevasse and rescue training.

Crossing the Valle Blânche glacier toward the Tacul

Taking a break near the summit of Tacul with the rounded
summit of Mont Blanc in the background.

Epilogue

MONTE ROSA covers the first fifty-one years of my life, from my birth in 1940 to the fall of the Soviet Union in 1991, with major emphasis on my professional activities following my move to Paris in 1979.

In 1991, with the disintegration of the USSR, open polling in most of the former Soviet republics became possible. The same year SAAOR merged with its Eastern European counterpart into a unit called Media and Opinion Research, which was part of the Munich-based RFE/RL Research Institute. I was responsible for conducting media and opinion research, first in Ukraine, and later in Russia.

I remained in Munich until 1995, when RFE/RL relocated its broadcasting operations to Prague, and Audience Research moved to Washington DC. The new group became the Open Media and Research Institute (OMRI). Since OMRI considered me to be one of its more experienced analysts, I began to travel to all the formerly Communist countries of Eastern Europe. Eventually, OMRI became InterMedia. The organization was the sole provider of audience and opinion research to international broadcasters.

Soon my brief expanded to include research in all of the republics of the former Soviet Union (FSU). During the twenty-year period from 1991 until I retired in 2011, I travelled to some twenty-five countries in Eastern Europe and the FSU, including the Baltic States, the Caucasus region, and Central Asia. I began documenting my trips in annual letters which, in addition to travel, included observations and reflections on a variety of subjects. Friends found these letters interesting and encouraged me to edit and publish them in a book, a project I expect to complete as a sequel to Monte Rosa in the near future.

Appendix: Travel Log 1980–1991

Below I list places I visited when I lived in France. I exclude towns near Paris such as Versailles, Saint Denis, and other suburbs, but include visits to the United States and Canada. The log reflects travel for business and pleasure to places where I stayed long enough to get a lasting impression.

1980

March	London, Chamonix, Val D'Isere
April	The Netherlands: Ghent, Zierikzee, Delft, Leiden
May	Loire Valley: Amboise, Blois, Chaumont, Loches
	Switzerland: Baden, Valle di Blenio (Ticino), Biasca
July	Amiens, Beauvais, Chantilly
August	Switzerland: Brig, Simplon Pass, Domodossola, Locarno, Lago Maggiore, Mondada, Interlaken, Meiringen, Grindelwald, Jungfraujoch glacier, Baden, Zurich, and Freiburg in Germany
	Normandy: Rouen, Bayeux, Arromanches, Omaha Beach, Coutances, Mont Saint-Michel
September	The Netherlands: Den Haag, Delft, Amsterdam

1981

January	Washington DC; Langley, Virginia; Harrisonburg, New York; Chicago, Illinois
February	Rouen, Les Arcs

March	The Netherlands: Den Haag, Amsterdam, Rotterdam (Groot Works)
April	Bavaria: Munich, Berchtesgaden, Neuschwanstein, Schwangau, Lindenhof, Wies, Regensburg; Austria: Salzburg, Obertauern Mountains
May	Reims, Sully, Blois, Chambord, Germigny-des-Prés, Saint-Benoît-sur-Loire, Chenonceau, Loches, Azay-le-Rideau, Orleans, Tours
July	Mantes, Uzès, Pont du Gard, Orange, Aix-en-Province, Arles, Saint Tropez, Saint Raphael, Sainte-Maxime, Les Issambres, Cannes, Frejus, Grasse, Mougins, Antibes, Nice, Monte Carlo, Grand Canyon du Verdon, Digne, Sisteron, Gap; Winterthur, Rhine River castles, Tournai, Belgium
September	Tour du Mont Blanc: Chamonix, Les Contamines, Entreves, Courmayeur, Pointe Helbronner, Aiguille du Midi, Chamonix
December	Cannes, Nice, Les Corniches, Monte Carlo, Arles, Nice, Aix-en-Province

1982

February	Amsterdam, Valbella, Saint-Gervais
April	Chicago, New York, Toronto, Washington
June	Tours, Poitiers, Biarritz, San Sebastian, Burgos, Madrid, Cordoba, Seville, Granada, Ronda, Malaga, Murcia, Alicante, Valencia, Barcelona, Perpignan, Orange
July	Toulon, Marseille, Arborn, Rothenburg, Munich, Konigsdorf, Mittenwald, Garmisch-Partenkirchen, Oberammergau, Neuschwanstein, Schwangau
August	Trouville, Honfleur, Deauville, Bec-Helloin, Jumieges, Florence, Venice
October	London, Metz (Ukrainian non-Conformists exhibit)
December	Geneva, Bruson, La Chable, Verbier

1983

April	Chicago, Toronto, New York, Boston, Washington.
July	Côte d'Azur: Les Issambres, Cannes, Frejus, Saint Paul-de-Vence

August	Leuven, Verdun, Hockenheim, Speyer, Munich, Konigsdorf, Bad Tolz, Koblenz, Bonn
October	Den Haag, Scheveningen, Amsterdam, Brugge, Brussels
December	Titograd, Cetinje, Budva, Sveti Stefan, Sutomore, Kotor, Herceg Novi, Cavtat, Dubrovnik, Korcula, Metkovic, Pocitelj, Mostar

1984

February	Zermatt, Courchevel
March	Washington, Boston
April	New York, Washington, Chicago
May	Dijon, Cote d'Or, Beaune, Vezelay
July	Brussels, Ghent, Brugge, Den Haag, Ostend
	London, Canterbury, Brands Hatch, Winchester, Salisbury, Oxford, Cambridge, Eli, Peterborough
August	Chambery, Alpe d'Huez, Susa, Torino, Milano, Padua, Venice, Trieste, Rijeka, Zadar, Sibenik, Brodarica, Krapanj, Split, Trogir, Knin, Zagreb, Maribor, Vienna, Prague, Pilsen Nürenberg, Strasbourg; Munich, Bad Tolz, Leuven
September	Geneva, Bruson
November	Abbey of Fontevrault, Abbey of Fontgombault, Saint-Savin, Bergerac, Perigueux, Montbazillac, Chateau de Bonaguil, Bourdelles, Brantôme, La Roque-Gageac, Souillac
December	Villars, Zagreb, Dubrovnik, Korcula, Petrovac, Mostar, Sarajevo, Jahorina

1985

January	Den Haag, Scheveningen
February	Carnival in Venice
March	Bruson, Verbier; Circuit de Ski de la Tarentaise: Tignes, Val d'Isere, Les Arcs, La Plagne, Courchevel, Meribel, Les Menuires, Val Thorens, Chambery
April	Chicago, Newark, New York, Washington
May	Athens, Aegina, Hydra, Poros, Corinth, Mycenae, Epidaurus, Cap Sounion

July	Berlin, Źielona Góra, Poznan, Warsaw, Krakow, Krynica, Brzezawa, Bircza, Sianok, Peremyshl, Jaroslaw, Bieszczady, Dukla Pass, Presov, Miskolc, Budapest, Vienna
September	Provins (Normandy)
October	Yugoslavia: Dubrovnik, Novi Pazar, Sopocani, Pristina, Gracanica, Skopje, Titov Veles, Bitola, Ohrid, Sveti Naum, Struga, Debar, Sveti Georgio, Sveti Jovan Bigorski, Tetovo, Popova Sapka, Prizren, Decani, Pec
December	Tours, Azay le Rideau, Chinon, Ussé, Saumur, Angers, Cunault, Le Mans, Chartres

1986

March	Brussels, Athens, Besancon, Crans-Montana, Zermatt
May	Chateau Sully, Saint-Benoit, Germigny-des-Prés, Bourges, Sancerre
June	Copenhagen, Rome
July	Arromanches, Omana Beach, Coutances, Saint-Malo, Cap Ferrat, Dinan
	Bourgogne: Barbizon, Fontainebleau, Abbey of Fontenay, Beaume, Saint-Romain, Chateau de la Rochepôt, Autun, Vezelay, Saint-Père-sous-Vezelay
	Cognac, Tarbes, Lourdes, Val d'Aran, Andorra, Foix, Carcassonne, Chateau Saint-Martin, Abbey of Fontfroide, Armagnac, Pau, Montpelier
August	Lambrecht, Deidesheim, Durkheim, Neustadt, Strasbourg
	Chamonix, Courmayeur, Val d'Aosta, Milano, Lago di Garda, Riva, Madonna de Campiglio,
	Brenta Dolomites, Verona, Sondrio, Chiavenna
September	Athens, Copenhagen
November	Rome
December	Edmonton, Chicago

1987

January	Megeve, Rome, Ladispoli
February	Hamburg

March	Geneva, Montreux, Zermatt, Germersheim, Baden-Baden
May	Vienna, Dürnstein, Germersheim, Riquewihr, Kaysersberg, Colmar, Heidelberg
June	Copenhagen, Rome, Chablis, Bourges, Sancerre, La Charité-sur-Loire
July	Germersheim, Basel, Lucerne, Meiringen
	On road to Galicia: Vezelay, Le Puy, Espalion, Estaing, Conques, Cordes, Albi, Toulouse, Saint-Bertrand-de-Comminges, Jaca, Puente de Reina, Burgos, Leon, Orense, San Gregorio, Vigo, Santiago de Compostela, Lugo, Caaveiro, La Coruña, Sanctuario de Ignacio Loyola, San Sebastian, Hendaye
October	Athens, Piraeus, Corinth, Delphi

1988

January	Rome
February	Courchevel
March	Rome, La Plagne
April	Chicago, Los Angeles, San Francisco, Squaw and Heavenly Valley–Lake Tahoe, Honolulu, New York
May	Copenhagen
June	Les Andelys, Chateau Gaillard
July	Saint-Flour, Chateau d'Alleuze, Puy Mary, Salers, Brioude, Chaise-Dieu, Aurillac, Mauriac, Puy Marie, Mont Dore, Orcival, Saint-Nectaire, Royat, Puy du Dome, Clermont-Ferrand, Anzy-le-Duc, Paray-le-Monial; Rome, Orvieto, Perugia, Assisi, Terni, L'Aquila
August	Evreaux, Bec-Hellouin, Arromanches, Barfleur, Cotentin Peninsula, Cherbourg, Lassay-les-Châteaux, Coutances, Mont Saint-Michel, Senlis, Chantilly
September	Rome, Santa Marinella, Orvieto, Montepulciano, Siena, Volterra, San Gimignano, Pisa, Lucca, Florence, Copenhagen
October	Reims, Germersheim, Arlberg, Lake Constance, Bergen, Landeck, Saint Anton, Lech

| November | Athens, Crete, Iraklion, Knossos, Phaistos, Lasithi, Agios Nikolaos, Malia |
| December | Chicago |

1989

January	Vienna, Berlin
March	Verbier
May	Germersheim, Basel, Splugen, Lugano, Locarno; Copenhagen, Stockholm
June	Itinerary to Barcelona: Chambord, Azay le Rideau, Brantôme, Perigueux, Saint-Cyprien, Rocamadour, Beynac, Cahors, Carcassonne, Quillan, Puylaurens, Peyrepertuse, Barcelona, Corbieres, Cevennes, Florac
July	North of Paris: Montagny, Sainte-Felicite, Morienval, Pierrefonds
August	Orange, Grenoble, Die, Serres, Roissans, Vaison-la-Romaine, Carpentras, Mont Ventoux, Fontaine-de-Vaucluse, Abbey of Senanque, Cavaillon, Aix-en-Province, Abbey of Thoronet, Saint-Tropez, Les Issambres, Nice; Corsica: Ile Rousse, Calvi, Porto, Ajaccio, Bonifacio, Bastia, Sardinia
	Arras, Saint-Omer, Calais, Wissant, Cap Gris Nez, Boulogne, Le Touquet, Crecy, Abbey of Saint-Riquier
September	Les Andelys, Chateau Gaillard, Chateau de Gisors, Compiègne
November	Athens, Patras, Olympia
December	Copenhagen

1990

March	Val d'Isere
April	Chicago, New York
May	Cancun (Mexico), Black Forest (Germany), Fôret de Retz (France)
June	Athens, Piraeus; Islands of Naxos, Mykonos, Delos
July	Mountaineering excursion to Chamonix: La Tour, Glacier des Bossons, Mer de Glace, Mont Blanc du Tacul

Italy: Verona, Ravenna, Rimini, San Marino, Urbino, Gubbio, Perugia, Lucca, Pisa, Rapallo, Portofino, San Fruttuoso, San Remo, Monaco, Nice, Var, Entrevaux, Digne, Sisteron

August	Chateaudun, Vendôme, Angers, Nantes, Noirmoutier, Saint-Nazaire, Chateaubriant, Chateauneuf (Bourgogne), Condrieu, Issoire, Saint-Nectaire, Mont-Doré, Bourboule, Orcival, Riom
September	Copenhagen, Athens, Marathon
October	Reims, Nancy
November	Amboise, Aulnay, Saintes, Royan, Medoc, Bordeaux, Saint-Emilion, Pomerol, Moissac, Carcassonne, Montpelier, Aigues-Mortes, Saint-Gilles, Arles, Nimes

1991

January	Fecamp, Abbey Saint-Wandrille de Fontenelle, Le Havre, Pont Leveque, Lisieux, Livarot
March	Annecy, Moutiers, Val Thorens, Megeve, Chamonix; Pavia, Bergamo, Brescia, Bolzano, Merano, Naturno, Saint-Ulrich, Val Gardena, San Cassiano, Cortina d'Ampezzo, Corvara, Arabba
June	Lindau, Solothurn, Annecy, Privas, Aubenas, Joyeuse, Ardeche, Nimes, Arles, Marseilles, Les Issambres, Saint-Raphael, Cannes, Nice, Menton, Sospel; Piacenza, Cremona, Monaco
August	Ronda, Zermatt, Schwarzsee at the foot of Matterhorn and ascent of Monte Rosa

Acknowledgements

I should like to start by thanking three individuals who have read the manuscript in its entirety and made valuable suggestions to improve it. First, I am very grateful to my memoir writing teacher Lynn Stearns for providing substantive suggestions and edits to improve the book. Second, I am grateful to the Xlibris editor Aileen Guinto whose copy-editing found many grammatical and technical mistakes that I would have overlooked. Last but not least, Patricia Leroy, a colleague from my days with the SAAOR in Paris who turned our reports into prized documents read by countless individuals at the highest level of various government agencies. As a writer and an editor with the eyes of an eagle, she asked hard questions and helped turn this rough rock into a gem. Many thanks also to Charlotte Don Vito whom I often used as a sounding board to test my ideas.

I am also grateful to Gere Parta, the Director of SAAOR in Paris and Charlie Allen my immediate supervisor for their contributions and suggestions that filled in many pieces missing in the original manuscript. I am also indebted to my sister Ivanka Richardson and other members of the Martyniuk family for their contributions to family history. Finally, my gratitude to my wife Eva Bauer for her moral support and patience in seeing this project to the end.